I TAUGHT MYSELF TO CROCHET AS A TWENTY-ONE-YEAR-OLD HIPPIE WHILE LIVING ON A HOUSEBOAT IN AMSTERDAM.

With no background at all in knitting or sewing, I began to make crocheted garments out of brightly colored weaving yarns a friend had given me. I brought my projects to a boutique, where they put them in the shop window and, much to my astonishment, they were sold within a day.

In 2003 I revisited crochet, having not held a hook in decades. The intervening years were filled with my training and subsequent career as a professional singer. By the early aughts, when my performing life was winding down, I felt the need for a creative outlet. Recalling my earlier success with crochet, I picked up the hook again.

I'm a first-generation American, and both of my parents came to the United States as World War II refugees. Crafts were not a part of their lives. Until I was on that houseboat I had no experience crafting anything. That turned out to be a good thing—I knew nothing about making garments and dived into it with no preconceived notions or fears. At a Crochet Guild of America conference, I met publishers in the yarn industry—the great Jean Leinhauser and Rita Weiss—who were interested in my designs, and who mentored me through the process of becoming a professional designer. I've been learning on the job ever since.

One thing that's always fascinated me about crochet is the limitless number of stitch patterns and the fabrics that they create. Depending on which stitch you pick, crochet fabric can be light and airy or heavy and dense, and the designs can range from simple and clean to intricately patterned laces and dazzling color work. Naturally, over the years I've purchased every stitch dictionary I could find, both old and new. A major part of my studies in designing has involved hours of swatching stitches to discover which yarns and fibers bring out their beauty.

My training also involved studying how to shape with stitch patterns. Information about this topic is, however, quite scarce. I found some excellent guidance in *Crochet Workshop*, a book published in 1979 by James Walters, a highly influential British yarn artist. Another source for my education has been Japanese knit/crochet magazines with full pages of charted garments showing exactly how a particular stitch pattern could be used to create the shape of an armhole or a neckline. The rest of my study was done on the hook with many experimental swatches. At this stage, after a dozen years of designing, I feel ready to share my ideas on shaping crochet stitch patterns by presenting them in this book.

So, what does it mean to shape in pattern? Crochet stitches can easily be manipulated to form surface designs, and the legibility of these designs is dependent on maintaining the stitches in the same order. If we need our fabric to grow or shrink, stitches must be added or subtracted. The challenge is to do that without distorting the surface design. James (now an email friend) and the Japanese design I studied taught me a lot about how to approach the task. Designing hundreds of patterns for magazines and my own books helped me gain further knowledge and confidence.

I resolved to create a stitch dictionary that included shaping—something that, to my knowledge, has not been done before—in the hope that it sheds light on crochet's possibilities and allows many more people to design with crochet. This book spells out the inherent shaping potential of each stitch, and can help you gain a deeper understanding of how crochet stitches can be maneuvered to make whatever you can imagine.

I've learned so much from working on this book, and the swatches have yielded countless design ideas right at my fingertips. I encourage you to make some of the swatches for the sheer pleasure of it, and because I firmly believe learning on the hook is the best way to study crochet.

My heartfelt thanks to the folks at Abrams who have given me the opportunity to write this book. Its contents are a record of my crochet studies that I hope will benefit all those who love working with the hook.

STITCH PATTERNS

WHAT ARE STITCH PATTERNS?

Because crochet stitches are so malleable—they can bend, cross, reach, stretch, puff up, and pull—they are amazing little design tools. Lines, angles, and curves can be formed with crochet stitches, and these can be combined to mimic more elaborate shapes and designs. It's no surprise that the craft has yielded a seemingly infinite number of stitch patterns exploiting this remarkable pictorial quality of crochet. Over the brief two-hundred-year history of crochet, via the simple medium of the crochet stitch, a vast collection of designs has emerged from hooks around the globe. Crochet stitch patterns can create fabrics resembling a floral garden, a facade of arched windows, tiled walls, or ancient line drawings.

Stitch patterns are arrangements of stitches that produce a distinct, repeating design on crochet fabric. The scale of these designs is determined by how many stitches and rows are needed to create them. They can range from only one or two stitches and rows to more than a dozen stitches and rows. As the designs become increasingly complex, they grow larger and more demanding to work.

HOW STITCHES CREATE DESIGNS

Many different techniques are used to create designs with stitches, including:

1. *making many stitches in one stitch*
2. *adding dimension to the fabric*
3. *creating holes in the fabric*
4. *gathering many stitches into one*

Often stitch patterns have two distinct elements that are alternated to create a visual pattern. I am using the term "element" for any easily recognized combination of stitches used as a repeating unit, such as a Bobble, a V-stitch, a group of chains, etc. In the stitch pattern called Vs and Blocks, for example, the two elements are V-stitches and a block of three double crochet stitches; V-stitches are used in one row of the pattern and blocks in the next, so we can say they alternate from one row to the next. But in the pattern called Staggered Vs and Blocks, both elements are used in every row, alternating within the row. You can see that this produces quite a different effect.

Elements can be combined and elaborated to create far more complex designs, like the pineapples and spiders you'll find in the last chapter.

HOW THE STITCH PATTERNS ARE ORGANIZED

All the stitch patterns in this book are beautiful—that was the number-one criteria for choosing them. Many of the stitches are small- and medium-size patterns suitable for beginning and intermediate crocheters. For those who thirst for a challenge, complex stitches are also well represented.

Certain stitches are so basic and sacred to the crochet vocabulary that they must be included. Beyond these old friends, I selected stitches from many sources with an eye to uniqueness and freshness. Another consideration was finding stitches that display clean lines and simple shapes, which are particularly appealing to the modern eye. Of course, there are some florid stitches, as these never go out of style and can always find a place at a cuff or a collar.

Chapters are organized to include stitches that share characteristics either in the way they are made or the design they create. At the start of each chapter is an explanation of what makes this group of stitches distinct and how they can be used in projects. In general, simpler stitches are at the beginning of the chapter and more difficult ones at the end. Stitches are grouped together if they look similar or behave in a similar way, or demonstrate a particular shaping technique.

We begin in Chapter One with "Closed Stitches," that is, stitches that make a solid fabric, as that's often desired for projects like afghans and throws, pillows, baby clothes, and warm sweaters. Most of these stitches are quite simple, and this chapter shows how basic crochet stitches can produce a pleasing profusion of surface textures. Almost all the stitches are shaped in two ways.

Chapter Two is "Mesh, Filet, and Easy Laces," a collection of simpler openwork stitches. These stitches are excellent stepping stones for building your skills, especially if you want to move into more elaborate lacework in crochet. Another plus is that simple laces have great potential for contemporary-looking design.

Crochet is fabulous for creating texture, explored in Chapter Three, "Popping Out: Textured Stitches," where posts, puffs, bobbles, popcorns, and many other textures are featured. Dig in here if you want to get creative with fabric, learn how texture can give it dimension, and discover how textured stitches can be delicate when combined with lace.

The lines and angles previously mentioned are very evident in the marvelous stitches in Chapter Four: "Exploding Shells." You will be amazed at how many stunning designs shells can create. Shells are perhaps the most versatile stitches in the crochet vocabulary. Shaping easily flows from their inherent angles, and they present excellent options for internal shaping.

OPPOSITE, CLOCKWISE FROM TOP LEFT: Pineapple Columns, page 218; Vs and Blocks, page 100; Staggered Blocks, page 90; Spider and Blocks, page 224

If you've made your way through some of the stitches in Chapters Two and Four, you should be ready for the "Classic Laces" in Chapter Five. These beautiful stitches can be tricky to shape, but we offer at least one way to do so for each stitch. I'm particularly pleased with the pattern enlargements, seeing many new design possibilities with this rarely used technique.

No crochet stitch book is worthy of its name unless ripples and waves are included. The "Undulating Stitches" of Chapter Six are sensual and chic, while also having age-old design roots. Ripples are especially resistant to shaping, however, since increasing and decreasing must occur in each row to create the ripple effect. By enlarging patterns, finding clever stitches that mimic ripples, and spelling out multiple rows of wave patterns, we show some nice options for shaping undulating stitches here.

WHAT IS A PATTERN REPEAT?

"Pattern repeat" is a convenient phrase to define the repeating elements that exist in all stitch patterns. Pattern repeats are also important tools for keeping track of our work, because with many patterns it's easier to count the pattern repeats than the individual stitches. Always take note of the pattern repeat of the stitch pattern you are working on, to ensure you've worked all the elements of the stitch in the right sequence for the right number of rows.

The term "pattern repeat" can be used in two ways: It can mean all the stitches and rows needed to complete a stitch pattern, and it can also mean the repeated stitches on any particular row of a stitch pattern. It is conventionally used in the second way in crochet instructions. In the instructions below, for example (from Puff Lace, see page 154), the pattern repeat consists of the stitches located between the single asterisk and the word "across." This pattern requires two rows, each worked differently, so the pattern repeat is different in row 2 and row 3. The double asterisks in the instructions are not relevant to the pattern repeat, except for the very last time it's done in the row.

ROW 2: Long ch, Puff in first sc, *ch 1, sk 3 dc, sc in next ch-3 sp, ch 3**, Puff in next sc, rep from * across, ending last rep at **, hdc in last sc, turn.

ROW 3: Ch 1, sk first hdc, *(sc, ch 3, 3 dc) in next ch-3 sp**, sk (sc, ch 1, Puff), rep from * ending last rep at **, sc in ch 1 above Puff, turn.

You will always find the pattern repeat between the asterisk and the word "across" in the Basic Pattern instructions. You can also see the pattern repeat in a shaded box on the stitch diagrams.

Small stitch patterns have smaller pattern repeats, perhaps just one or two stitches over one or two rows. As stitches become more complex, pattern repeats have more stitches and rows.

There are many possible start and end points for a pattern repeat, so you may find similar stitches spelled out in different ways in various publications. In this book, in addition to taking note of the stitches between the single asterisk and the word "across," you will find the pattern repeat outlined in a shaded box on all stitch charts.

ETCHED HALF DOUBLES

page 48

ZIGZAG MESH

page 86

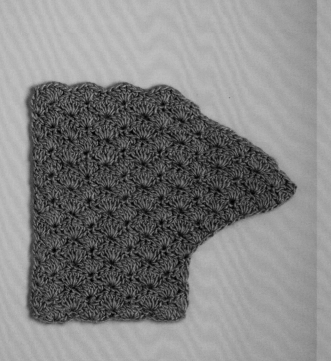

BASIC SHELL

page 166

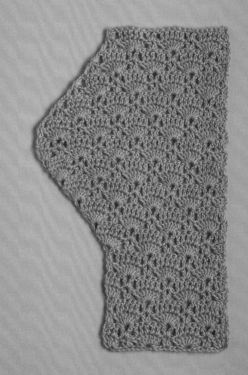

BOTANICAL SHELLS

page 192

ALL ABOUT SHAPING

WHAT IS SHAPING?

Shaping is how we achieve the dimensions needed to make a particular item. Working row after row of crochet stitches with the same number of stitches produces a rectangle, but other shapes require adding or subtracting stitches. Adding stitches is called "increasing," and subtracting them is called "decreasing." Working rows without adding or subtracting stitches is called "working even."

There are two commonly used methods of shaping: at the edge of your work, either at one edge or both, which we call edge shaping; or within the row, generally termed internal shaping. Some stitch patterns can be utilized with both techniques, and some are more suited to one or the other. There are numerous creative ways to use both types of shaping to create a huge variety of designs, and other shaping strategies besides these two, as well.

Edge Shaping

If we add one stitch at the edge of the work for several rows, the fabric will expand in a straight diagonal line along that edge. If we add several stitches at the edge on each row, the diagonal line will have a more acute angle, because the fabric is growing larger more quickly. The same is true for decreasing: The greater the number of stitches removed per row, the more acute will be the slant at the edge. The terms "rate of increase" and "rate of decrease" are used to express how quickly stitches are being added or removed, and to refer to both at once we say "rate of shaping."

Note the different rates of shaping for Etched Half Doubles versus Zigzag Mesh. Clearly, the more or less acute slants created by the rate of shaping have consequences for the kind of shape you can make.

Maintaining a steady rate of shaping is how one creates a straight line at the edge of the fabric. If one were to change the rate of shaping in a

random way, for example, adding one stitch on one row, three stitches on the next, and none on the one after, the edge of the fabric would be crooked.

Simple stitch patterns, where stitches align vertically over one another, are usually quite easy to shape at any given rate—one or two or more stitches per row. As stitch patterns become more complex and incorporate shells, clusters, chain spaces, and other elements, they become harder to shape, because adding or subtracting stitches will disrupt the pattern in an obvious way. Still, in many cases there are ways to shape complex stitches.

The strategy I used in this book was to examine the natural lines formed by the stitches in the pattern, seeking diagonal lines that could be exploited to create an angle at the edge.

For example, shell stitches are created by working multiple stitches into one, causing the groups of stitches to fan out from the bottom and thus forming diagonal lines in opposite directions. Most shell stitch patterns have a half shell at the edge on one of the rows of the pattern repeat to avoid this angle at the edge. But when we want to increase, we can turn the half shell at the edge into a whole shell, allowing the natural slant formed by the stitches to become the shaped edge. Note that in the case of the Basic Shell shown on page 14, this is a rather acute angle. In our stitch pattern called Botanical Shells (see page 14), the same strategy is applied over a multi-row lace pattern.

It's fascinating to explore how stitch patterns want to shape themselves if you follow the pattern's lead. I did not invent this technique, but once I began really exploring it, many shaping possibilities presented themselves. I designed all the shaping in this book with an eye to maintaining the natural lines of the pattern with minimal disruption and finding rates of shaping that could be put to practical use in projects.

Edge shaping can happen at one or both edges of the work. In this book we show the shaping on one edge only, so that the slant created is easily seen in comparison to a straight edge. The swatches in this book that demonstrate edge shaping begin with several rows worked even, followed by several rows of increasing and several rows of decreasing.

You'll see that with some stitch patterns, it's best to begin shaping on a particular row of the pattern. The shell pattern discussed above is a perfect example, as shaping starts most easily where the half shell is at the edge of the work. In many cases, both increasing and decreasing can begin on the same row of the pattern, but there are also instances when it's best to begin decreasing on a different row. This is all dependent on the individual stitches and the angles they present. These considerations affect the swatches you see presented in this book, where in some cases there are

rows worked even between the increase and decrease section and in other cases there are no even rows between them.

For almost all the shaping in this book, the sequence of shaping rows is repeatable; that is, the same shaping rows can be repeated row after row for as long as you wish, and you will always end up back in pattern after shaping, allowing you to resume working even in pattern. Where necessary, you will find specific instructions for the last row of shaping detailing how to end shaping and return to pattern.

To use edge shaping on the opposite edge than the one shown in the book, reverse the instructions so that what is indicated at the start of a row is done at the end of the row, and what is instructed at the end of the row is done at the beginning of the row. For example, let's look at the increases in the stitch called Zigzag Mesh (see page 86). The first increase row reads:

> **IncRow 1:** Ch 5 (counts as dc, ch 2), dc in first sc, ch 2, sc in next dc, continue in row 2 of patt across.

The increase here is made by placing a dc and ch 2 over the *first* stitch in the previous row. If you wanted to do the same increase at the opposite edge of that row, you would work (ch 2, dc) in the *last* stitch of the row.

The second increase row reads:

> **IncRow 2:** Work in row 3 of patt to tch, ch 2, dc in 3rd ch of tch, ch 2, sc in same st, turn.

Note that (dc, ch 2, sc) are worked into the turning chain, which is of course the *last* stitch in the row. To make the same increase at the beginning of that row, you would work (sc, ch 2, dc) in the **first** stitch of the row. You will find more information on reverse shaping for individual stitches on pages 22–25.

Shaping at the edges of the work has many applications for projects we want to make. For example, a sweater often has shaping at the sides of the body to accommodate the difference in circumference between bust and waist. Shaping is required to make well-fitting sleeves that grow smaller from upper arm to wrist. Skirts will also require shaping when moving from waist to hips, or creating a flared hem. To make a purse that's not just a rectangle, you can use shaping to make the bottom wider than the top, or make a triangular flap for closing the bag.

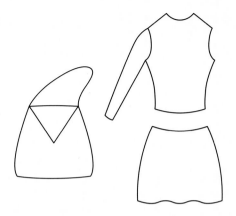

When designing projects, you will need to do some measuring and math in order to get the exact shapes you want. Different rates of shaping are required to achieve various dimensions, and many variables are involved, including the weight of the yarn, the size of the project, the size of the pattern repeat, etc. The informa-tion in this book is a jumping-off point from which you can develop other rates of increase and decrease needed for the projects you want to make.

Internal Shaping

Shaping at the edges of the work is one option, and another is shaping internally, meaning adding or subtracting stitches within the row. Internal shaping has the advantage of allowing us to make items with no seams. When a garment is made in several pieces with shaping at the edges, the separate pieces must be sewn together to complete the garment. But seamless garments can be made by working in the round and inserting shaping at specified points within each round.

In this book, we focus on internal increasing, as this is more commonly used than internal decreasing. The sample swatches begin with one or two rows worked evenly, then shaping begins along the pattern's natural lines. Internal shaping is usually done around a designated center point in the row. You'll notice on our internal shaping swatches that when several stitches are added in a single stitch, row after row, a bulge is created at the increase point. The greater the number of stitches added at one point, the point-ier the bulge. Simultaneously, the outer edges of the work expand. When the rate of increase is more rapid—that is, when more stitches are added in each row—the slant at the edge is also more acute.

Theoretically, one can make internal increases using the exact sequence of stitches used to shape at the edge, but doubling it by placing two increases around a center point. In this book I often stray from replicating the edge in the internal shaping, because I found other options that may have better practical use, especially for garment-making.

To execute internal shaping, a center point is designated with a stitch marker—which can be just a safety pin or short piece of yarn—and stitches are added on both sides of the marker. A commonly used strategy is to place a chain-one space at the center point, but the center point can also be a single stitch. The first of these alternatives will create a noticeable visual element—a small hole made by the chain-one space will appear all along the center point—while the second results in a more closed fabric where the shaping is less visible. See pages 23 and 24 to compare how these two techniques look when applied to simple stitches (and to compare half double crochet and double crochet internal shaping swatches).

In this book, the instructions for internal shaping will tell you to mark a stitch on each round. You work in pattern until you get to the marked stitch, then make the increase as instructed, moving the marker to one of the stitches just completed for the increase, then continue in pattern again. As the stitch patterns become longer, instructions may have you mark not the center stitch or chain but some other stitch in the row. This is purely to make the instructions easier to follow. There will still be a center point. Note that we use the term center to mean the center of the increase, not necessarily the center of the fabric. For the purposes of our internal shaping swatches, they are indeed at the center, but when working on projects the increase point can be wherever you need it to be.

A common use for internal shaping is the classic technique of seamless raglan sweaters, derived from knitting. The sweater begins at the neckline and shaping occurs at four points running from the neck to the underarm, allowing the garment to expand from neck dimensions to body dimensions. Many of the sample internal swatches in this book can be used as a basis to make seamless raglan garments. The "center" referred to in the pattern would be placed at one of four raglan shaping points and increases would occur at all four points as you make the yoke. Just as in all projects with shaping, however, measuring and math are needed to pinpoint the exact rate of increase needed to make a well-fitting garment.

Internal shaping can also be used to make shawls that are wider at the bottom than at the top. Depending on the amount of expansion desired, shaping can be done, for example, at four, six, or more points that are plotted at regular intervals. If you want to create a shawl with lots of extra fabric at the bottom, you would increase at more points, or increase more rapidly at each point, or both.

Circular Shaping

When we work in a circular manner in crochet, we are using internal shaping. Crochet hats worked in the round from the top rely on internal shaping, where typically stitches are added in each round till reaching head diameter. The sides of the hat are worked even, and a decrease is made at the bottom to tighten it on the head. If you turn this upside down, the same strategy can be used to make a bag, beginning at the bottom with a circle or oval till you reach the desired dimension for the bag's bottom. From that point, you can work the sides even or use internal shaping to make the bag widen as it reaches the top.

Note that circular shaping is different than internal increases made around a center point. In circular work with plain stitches, stitches can be added anywhere in the row, as there is no pattern to disrupt. The technique can be applied in other cases where the pattern repeat is only two or three stitches. We show this strategy in Chapter One in the stitch called Forked Clusters (see page 76). Keep in mind that even though we use circular shaping, there is no need to create a flat circle. The technique allows us to add stitches randomly as needed throughout the row or round, and it can be used with many smaller stitch patterns to achieve precise dimensions.

Shaping in Pattern

In order to preserve the legibility of the design created by any particular stitch pattern when shaping, we try to maintain the same stitches, be they sc, hdc, puffs, dc2tog, or whatever else, in their same order, as we add or subtract them. That is what is meant by "shaping in pattern."

When working with stitch patterns that have large pattern repeats, adding a full or half pattern repeat is often the best strategy for maintaining the design. Stitch patterns based on shells make for a good example.

While this strategy keeps the design intact, it presents limitations when we want to make a particular shape that doesn't mimic the angles you see at the edges. Those in the swatch at right are not very useful for the sides of garments, because the angle is too acute. The deep slant does work well, however, for necklines and armholes.

Earlier we discussed the importance of maintaining a regular rate of shaping when increasing or decreasing at the edge. With internal shaping, however, one can vary the rate of shaping and still have straight edges on your work. For this reason, when working with larger stitch patterns internal shaping can be a better option, allowing the pattern to be built up in smaller increments at a center point without creating crooked edges.

NECKLINE

ENLARGING THE STITCH PATTERN

Some crochet stitch patterns just don't want to be shaped. Due to a pattern's complexity, alignment of stitches, or other factors, both edge shaping and internal shaping are either too unwieldy or disruptive to the essential design. There is one strategy that can be applied to some of these stitches, and that is enlarging the stitch pattern itself.

This technique is particularly useful when working with ripple stitches that are nearly impossible to shape at the edge or around an internal center point. It is not useful past a certain point, however, as there's only so much growth a pattern can withstand before it becomes a gross overstatement of its original self. Certainly some can enlarge further than what we have shown here. Experiment by following the increase method till the stitch pattern is as large as possible and still attractive. Then, if you measure the difference between a repeat of the pattern at its smallest and a repeat at its largest, you can plot out whether the pattern can be adapted for a wrap, skirt, or other flared shape. Instead of increasing on every row, you can spread out the increases over more rows, inserting as many rows as necessary between increase rows to get to the length you need. If you want a flared edge at the bottom of your design, increase on successive rows close to the bottom at a more rapid rate.

PEEPHOLE RIPPLE
page 254

My aim has been to work with each stitch to show its inherent shaping capabilities, and explore what shapes that stitch can easily be made to form. In this book, simple stitches are shaped at the rate of one stitch per row. But one can readily see that with simpler stitches it's possible to increase or decrease two, three, or more stitches each row, should that be required. In other words, simpler stitches are more flexible when it comes to shaping, and if you need a very precise shape, they are a better choice.

As the stitch patterns become more complex, we often shape at the edge at the rate of one pattern repeat or half a pattern repeat. There are many variables that affect this rate of shaping—from the size of the stitch pattern itself, where any angled stitches might be, and much more—as you will see as you study the stitch patterns and shaping swatches.

Sometimes shaping in pattern will not allow you to achieve the dimensions you need for your project. In those cases, there are other strategies you can use, such as breaking from the stitch pattern and using plain stitches on shaping rows, or using several stitch patterns of different sizes to achieve your desired dimensions. The possibilities are really endless!

For those who are drawn to the topic of shaping, or who would like to create their own designs, I encourage you to make the swatches in this book, from which you can gain a deeper understanding of shaping strategies. From there, you will be able to experiment to vary the rate of shaping and develop your own ideas.

SHAPING BASIC STITCHES

Before tackling shaping with stitch patterns, let's examine how basic stitches are shaped at the edge at the rate of one stitch per row. Here are patterns and swatches for single crochet, half double crochet, double crochet, and treble stitches. If you have not done much shaping in crochet before, making these little swatches can teach you a lot.

We also explain how to shape each basic stitch at the beginning and end of a row. This information will come in very handy when you want to work the shaping on the opposite edge from what we show in this book.

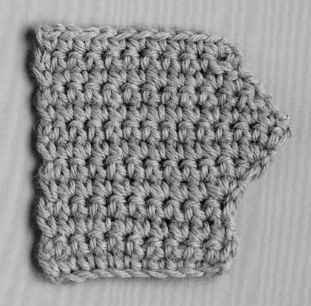

SINGLE CROCHET

(For swatch, ch 11.)

ROW 1: Sc in 2nd ch from hook and in each ch across, turn.

(Swatch has 10 sts.)

ROW 2: Ch 1, sc in each sc across.

Rep row 2 to continue.

(Swatch has 4 rows in patt.)

Edge Shaping

INCREASING

IncRow 1: Ch 1, 2 sc in first sc, continue in patt across. "Continue in patt across" means work as in row 2 from this point on.

IncRow 2: Work in patt to last sc, 2 sc in last sc, turn.

Rep IncRows 1 and 2 to continue increasing.

(Swatch has 4 increase rows, ending with 14 sts.) **This means work 2 more increase rows. Count your sts—there should be 14—to see if you've worked correctly thus far.**

DECREASING

DecRow 1: Ch 1, sk first sc, sc in next sc, continue in patt across.

DecRow 2: Work in patt to last 2 sc, sc2tog.

Rep DecRows 1 and 2 to continue decreasing.

(Swatch has 4 decrease rows, ending with 10 sts, followed by 1 row worked even.) **This means work 2 more decrease rows, then count your sts—there should be 10. Then work DecRow 2 once more.**

REVERSE SHAPING WITH SC

Increase at start of row: Ch 1, 2 sc in first sc.

Increase at end of row: 2 sc in tch.

Decrease at start of row: Ch 1, sk first sc, sc in next sc.

Decrease at end of row: Sc2tog over last 2 sts.

HALF DOUBLE CROCHET

Remember to skip the first stitch—the chain two at the start of the row is the first stitch. Make your next stitch in the second stitch of the row. When increasing, you do work into the first stitch.

I like to make a modification to the traditional half double crochet decrease, because it is less bulky. It avoids one yarnover in the second stitch of the decrease and is spelled out at the end of DecRow 2.

(For swatch, ch 11.)
ROW 1: Hdc in 3rd ch from hook (2 sk ch count as hdc) and in each ch across, turn.
(Swatch has 10 hdc.)
ROW 2: Ch 2 (counts as hdc throughout), hdc in each hdc across, hdc in tch, turn.
Rep row 2 to continue.
(Swatch has 4 rows in patt.)

Edge Shaping

INCREASING

IncRow 1: Ch 2, hdc in first hdc, continue in patt across.
IncRow 2: Work in patt to tch, 2 hdc in tch, turn.
Rep IncRows 1 and 2 to continue increasing.
(Swatch has 4 increase rows, ending with 14 hdc.)

DECREASING

DecRow 1: Ch 1, sk first hdc, continue in patt across.
DecRow 2: Work in patt to last 2 sts, (yo, [insert hook in next hdc and draw up loop) twice, yo, draw through 4 loops on hook]) (decrease made), turn.
Rep DecRows 1 and 2 to continue decreasing.
(Swatch has 4 decrease rows, ending with 10 hdc, followed by one row worked even.)

REVERSE SHAPING WITH HDC

Increase at the start of the row: Ch 2, hdc in first st.
Increase at end of row: 2 hdc in tch.
Decrease at start of row: Ch 1, sk first st, hdc in next st.
Decrease at end of row: Yo, insert hook in last hdc and draw up loop, insert hook in tch and draw up loop, yo, draw through 3 loops on hook.

Internal Shaping Around a Center Stitch

This sample shows internal increasing with hdc stitches on both sides of a center stitch, maintaining a solid fabric and adding two sts per row.
(For swatch, ch 10.)
ROW 1: Hdc in 3rd ch from hook and in each ch across.
(Swatch has 9 sts.)
Place marker in center st of row.
IncRow 1: Ch 2, hdc in each hdc to marked st, 3 hdc in marked hdc, move marker to center st of group just made, continue in patt across.
Rep IncRow 1 to continue increasing.
(Swatch has 6 rows total, 5 increase rows, ending with 19 hdc.)

DOUBLE CROCHET

(For swatch, ch 12.)
ROW 1: Dc in 4th ch from hook (3 sk ch count as dc), dc in each ch across, turn.
(Swatch has 10 dc.)
ROW 2: Ch 3 (counts as dc throughout), dc in each dc across, dc in tch, turn.
Rep row 2 to continue.
(Swatch has 4 rows in patt.)

Edge Shaping

INCREASING

IncRow 1: Ch 3, dc in first dc, continue in patt across.
IncRow 2: Work in patt to tch, 2 dc in tch, turn.
Rep IncRows 1 and 2 to continue increasing.
(Swatch has 4 increase rows, ending with 14 dc.)

DECREASING

DecRow 1: Ch 2 (does not count as st), sk first st, dc in next dc, continue in patt across.
DecRow 2: Work in patt to last 2 dc, dc2tog, turn.
Rep DecRows 1 and 2 to continue decreasing.
(Swatch has 4 decrease rows, ending with 10 dc.)

REVERSE SHAPING WITH DC

Increase at beginning of row: Ch 3, dc in first st.
Increase at end of row: 2 dc in tch.
Decrease at beginning of row: Ch 2 (does not count as st), sk first st, dc in next st.
Decrease at end of row: Dc2tog over last st and tch.

Internal Shaping Around a Chain-One Space

This sample shows internal increasing with dc stitches around a center ch-1 sp, again adding two sts per row.
(For swatch, ch 11.)
ROW 1: Dc in 4th ch from hook and in each ch across.
(Swatch has 9 sts.)
Place marker in center dc.
IncRow 1: Ch 3, dc in each dc to marked dc, (dc, ch 1, dc) in marked dc, move marker to ch-1 sp just made, continue in patt across.
IncRow 2: Ch 3, dc in each dc to marked ch-1 sp, (dc, ch 1, dc) in ch-1 sp, move marker to ch-1 sp just made, continue in patt across.
Rep IncRow 2 to continue increasing.
(Swatch has 6 rows total, 5 increase rows, ending with 18 dc and 1 ch-1 sp.)

TREBLE CROCHET

(For swatch, ch 13.)
ROW 1: Tr in 5th ch from hook (4 sk ch count as tr), tr in each ch across, turn.
(Swatch has 10 tr.)
ROW 2: Ch 4, tr in each tr across, turn.
Rep row 2 to continue.
(Swatch has 4 rows in patt.)

Edge Shaping

INCREASING

IncRow 1: Ch 4, tr in first tr, continue in patt across.
IncRow 2: Work in patt to tch, 2 tr in tch, turn.
Rep IncRows 1 and 2 to continue increasing.
(Swatch has 4 increase rows, ending with 14 tr.)

DECREASING

DecRow 1: Ch 3 (does not count as st), sk first st, tr in next st, continue in patt across.
DecRow 2: Work in patt to last 2 sts, tr2tog, turn.
Rep DecRows 1 and 2 to continue decreasing.
(Swatch has 4 decrease rows, ending with 10 tr, followed by 1 row worked even.)

REVERSE SHAPING WITH TR

Increase at beginning of row: Ch 4, tr in first st.
Increase at end of row: 2 tr in tch.
Decrease at beginning of row: Ch 3 (does not count as st), sk first st, tr in next st.
Decrease at end of row: Tr2tog over last st and tch.
Now let's look at internal shaping with two basic stitches.

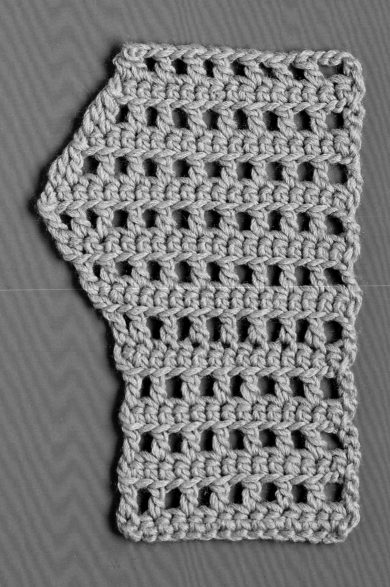

HOW TO USE THIS BOOK

As you browse through these pages, you'll find certain information provided for each stitch right at the top. Let's look closely at how that information can be useful to you.

Each stitch pattern begins with a short description of its main characteristics, which may include the stitches or techniques used and the nature of the resulting fabric. We then provide details about important features, such as the number of stitches and rows, the pattern multiple, and whether the pattern is reversible or not.

Number of stitches in pattern repeat: This number is given where possible. Many stitch patterns have a consistent number of stitches in a pattern repeat on all rows. As stitch patterns become more complex, the number of stitches may vary from one row to the next, in which case there is a letter "V" to stand for "Varied" in this spot.

Number of rows in pattern repeat: Knowing the number of rows in a stitch pattern is useful for determining when to end your work. Some stitches only look right if all the rows in the pattern are completed, but in other cases you can end on any row.

Multiple: This term refers to the number of chains you need in the foundation chain for each pattern repeat. The number may or may not correspond to the number of stitches in the pattern repeat. The multiple will be followed by a plus sign and another number. The second number tells you how many additional chains are needed in your foundation chain. Knowing the multiple

allows you to be creative with a stitch pattern. See Convert Any Stitch into a Scarf or Wrap (page 30) for more on this topic.

Reversible/Not reversible: Some stitch patterns look great on both sides, and those are reversible. Non-reversible stitch patterns are those that have a definite front and back. A few stitch patterns have two fine-looking sides that are quite different from each other, in which case we provide views of both.

Basic Pattern: Each row of the stitch pattern is spelled out in standard crochet terminology and with a symbol chart. All abbreviations used in written instructions can be found on page 32. All symbols used are explained on page 33.

Edge Shaping: Here is information about the rate of shaping and on what row it begins.

Increasing/Decreasing: Row-by-row instructions are given for how to increase and decrease at the rate specified.

Internal Shaping: We provide a separate swatch, instructions, and chart showing internal shaping.

Make sure you read any Notes given for the stitch pattern, as they include important information. Take note of the Special Stitches, too. If you come upon an abbreviation you're not familiar with in a pattern, you can look it up on page 32, where all abbreviations used in this book are spelled out.

MAKING THE SWATCHES

I heartily advocate working swatches from this book. The knowledge you can build includes:

1. Improved pattern and chart reading
2. Deeper understanding of how stitches behave and how to work with them
3. Insight on how to adapt patterns to your needs
4. Learning to choose the best yarns for various stitches

There are three types of swatches in this book. For stitch patterns that can be shaped at the edge, the swatch shows the stitch worked even for several rows, then increasing, and then decreasing, sometimes with an even row or two between them. A second type of swatch is used for stitches that aren't suitable for edge shaping: These are presented in a swatch that is worked even for multiple rows. The third type of swatch shows internal shaping, where the first one or two rows are worked even in pattern followed by several rows of increase and often ending with a row worked even to show how to return to pattern.

To make any of these swatches, follow the directions in parentheses that you see throughout the pattern. Note that the stitch diagram also spells out the swatches precisely. See page 22 for how to interpret all the instructions in parentheses related to swatches.

When you're done, your swatch should look similar to the swatch in the photo (but keep in mind that the swatches in the photos have been blocked). You should always end up in pattern, so you can pick up and use the basic pattern again from this point on.

HOW TO READ STITCH CHARTS

I have met quite a few crocheters who are intimidated by charts. Nevertheless, I've always managed to teach even the most wary how to read them in just a few minutes. That's because reading charts is super easy! Before we take a close look at chart-reading, check out the stitch key on page 33, where you can see what each symbol used in this book stands for. It's rather obvious that the little cross stands for sc, a taller line with a short line crossing it near the top is a double crochet, a little round blip is a chain, and so forth. In other words, this is not Greek but quite intuitive representations of what stitches look like.

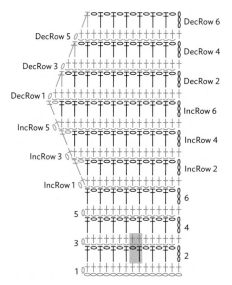

Always begin reading your chart from the bottom, where you will see a line of chains for the foundation chain. As you can see in this chart, there are 15 chains across the bottom, and one more chain along the side next to the number 1. That is the 16th chain, and it forms the turning chain that begins row 1. Continue reading row 1 from left to right: You can see that a sc is worked into each chain of the foundation chain. When you come to the right edge, you will see the number 2 along the side of the next row up, the second row of the pattern. You will now read from right to left, and it begins with 3 chains for the turning chain and one more chain, shown lying horizontally, before working a double crochet stitch. You can also see that the double crochet is worked into a single crochet in the previous row after skipping a single crochet stitch. As you continue reading row 2 from right to left, notice that after the first double crochet there is another chain 1, then another double crochet is worked after skipping a single crochet, then another chain 1, and so on to the end of the row. This brings us once again to the left edge and we are ready to begin row 3.

Now we have one more symbol to deal with in row 3, and that is the little curved line below the single crochet symbol. You can be sure it belongs to row 3 because we use alternating colors from row to row. This little symbol means work into the front loop of the stitch. So every single crochet in that row is worked in the front loop only. From this point on you will not encounter any additional symbols on this chart. Just keep reading the chart left to right on one row, and right to left on the next row. The row numbers are always placed at the beginning of the row. And that's it!

On the stitch charts throughout this book, note that the stitches involved in increasing and decreasing are always shown in red, and the pattern repeat is boxed in light gray.

If you've not worked much with stitch charts, I strongly encourage you to use this book to get more comfortable with them. When I teach a class on this topic we work three or four stitches with both charts and instructions, and then I present the class with several charts and no written instructions. After a moment or two, the students realize they know exactly what to do just from the chart! Just remember, you can look up any symbol you aren't familiar with, and very soon you will recognize them instantly. Of course, all the stitches have written instructions too.

You may notice that many of the swatches are made with single-ply yarns. I chose them because they provide such clean stitch definition—in other words, you can very clearly see each stitch and all the strands it's composed of. All of the yarns are either DK or fingering weight, except for a few done in lace-weight yarn.

Well now, why not gather some stray balls of yarn from your stash and start swatching? I recommend smooth yarns without fluff or texture, because that way you will see the stitch pattern most clearly. If you are a new crocheter, start with the first chapter, where you'll find plenty of easy stitches. If you are more experienced, perhaps explore stitches that you haven't ever seen before, or find a favorite stitch and study how it can be shaped. Whatever your level, I urge you to avoid working too quickly or allowing too many distractions. Find a comfortable rhythm so you are enjoying the process, not anxious about it.

A stitch dictionary is for stimulating the most creative side of your crochet. I guarantee that as soon as you have a lovely finished swatch in your hands, you will have numerous ideas for projects you can make with it. To inspire you further, here's a recipe you might want to try.

CONVERT ANY STITCH INTO A SCARF OR WRAP

Follow these steps to design your own scarf or rectangular wrap.

Make a swatch with the yarn you want to use with no shaping; in other words, a square or rectangular swatch.

Block your swatch so it's neat and has the same width across the top and bottom and along each side (within ¼ inch is fine).

Measure your swatch carefully, especially the width. Take the width measurement from the beginning edge to the end of the last pattern repeat. Measure the length of your swatch too. Record both numbers.

Now we need to determine how many pattern repeats are on your swatch, and find the width measurement for one pattern repeat. At the end of row 1 of each Basic Pattern we give the number of pattern repeats (or stitches) in the swatch. With a calculator, divide the total width of your swatch by the number of pattern repeats. This tells you the width of one pattern repeat. For example, if my swatch measures 5¾ inches and has 3 pattern repeats:

$$5¾ \div 3 = 1.916666$$

In other words, each pattern repeat is slightly under 2 inches in width.

Determine how wide—in inches—you would like your scarf or wrap to be. A good way to figure this out is by measuring garments you own.

Next we want to know how many pattern repeats are needed to achieve this width. To get that number, divide the desired width for your garment by the pattern repeat width. If I want m scarf to be 10 inches wide and my pattern repeat is 2 inches wide, I divide 10 by 2, resulting in the number 5. This tells me I need 5 pattern repeats for the width of my scarf. Remember, though, that's using the same yarn and stitch, worked at the same tension as your swatch and then blocked.

At this point you have figured out how many pattern repeats of the stitch pattern you will need to make your design. To begin your project, you need to determine how many foundation chains that will require. Look for the multiple for your chosen stitch. This multiple tells you how many chains you need in the foundation chain per pattern repeat. You've already determined the number of pattern repeats you need, so to figure out how many foundation chains are required, multiply that number by the stitch pattern's multiple. Then add the number after the plus sign, which is for any extra chains that are needed for the stitch pattern. For my 10-inch scarf, I require 5 pattern repeats, and the multiple for my stitch pattern is 14. My math would be

$$5 \times 14 = 70$$

The number after the plus sign for my hypothetical scarf is 5, so to determine the total number of chains needed for my foundation chain I add 5 to my previous total.

$$70 + 5 = 75$$

I need 75 foundation chains to start my scarf.

Once you have this number for your project, you are really ready to roll. Chain the number you came up with (if it's a very long chain, add several extra chains that you can pull out later—trust me). Now just follow the basic pattern and work till the scarf or wrap is as long as you like.

You can also determine how many rows you'll need using math, based on the length of your swatch and the length you want your garment to be. Simply divide the desired length by the length of your swatch, then take that number and multiply it by the number of rows in your swatch.

People often ask, "How do I know how much yarn I will need for a project?" It's not a simple question to address, because there are so many variables. Solid stitches require more yarn than do lacy ones. Thinner yarns require more yardage than thicker ones. You could start by researching similar projects that use the same weight yarn as yours, and see what the yardage requirements are. With experience, you'll get a feel for this.

But please don't let this stop you from getting creative and making a scarf. Just gather up some pretty yarns in a variety of colors and similar weights and make stripes or blocks of color!

ABBREVIATIONS

BL
back loop

BP
back post

ch
chain

dc
double
crochet

DecRow
decrease row

FL
front loop

FP
front post

hdc
half double
crochet

IncRow
increase row

patt
pattern

rep
repeat

RS
right side

sc
single crochet

sl st
slip stitch

sk
skip

sp
space

st(s)
stitch(es)

tch
turning chain

tr
treble crochet

WS
wrong side

yo
yarn over

WORKING STITCHES TOGETHER

sc#tog
(Insert hook in next designated st, yo and draw up loop) # times, yo, draw through all loops on hook.

hdc#tog
(Yo, insert hook in next designated st, yo and draw up loop) # times, yo, draw through all loops on hook.

dc#to
(Yo, insert hook in next designated st, yo and draw up loop, yo, draw through 2 loops) # times, yo, draw through all loops on hook.

tr#tog
[Yo twice, insert hook in next designated st, yo and draw up loop, (yo, draw through 2 loops) twice] # times, yo, draw through all loops on hook.

Note: You will find instances where worked-together stitches have other conditions, such as FL, BL, FP, and BP. In those cases insert the hook as indicated while following above instructions.

SYMBOL KEY

Standard Crochet Symbols

- • = slip st (sl st)
- ⌢ = back loop (BL)
- ⌣ = front loop (FL)
- ◠ = chain (ch)
- † = single crochet (sc)
- T = half double crochet (hdc)
- Ŧ = double crochet (dc)
- ₮ = treble crochet (tr)
- �??? = front post dc (FPdc)
- = back post dc (BPdc)
- = front post tr (FPtr)

- ▨ = pattern repeat

Decrease Crochet Symbols

- A = sc2tog
- A = sc3tog
- ↑ = hdc2tog
- A = dc/hdc/sc3tog
- or = dc2tog
- or = dc3tog
- or = cluster (cl)
- or = tr2tog
- or = tr3tog
- = tr5tog
- = tr7tog

Post Stitch Decrease Symbols

 = front post 2 dc tog (FPdc2tog)

 = front post 3dc tog (FPdc3tog)

 = front post 5 dc tog (FPdc5tog)

 = back post 2 dc tog (BPdc2tog)

 = back post 3 dc tog (BPdc3tog)

 = back post 5 dc tog (BPdc5tog)

= FPdc/BPdc2tog)

= BPdc/hdc2tog)

= FPdc/hdc2tog)

Additional Crochet Symbols

- = long ch
- ⬦ or = picot
- = extended sc (Esc)
- = Esc dec
- = sc in sp between 2 sts
- = sc spike
- = extended hdc (Ehdc)
- = Ehdc dec
- = 3 dc in sp between 2 sts

- = dc enclosing a st
- = crossed sc/dc
- = Crossed dc (Crdc)
- or = Loop stitch (LS)
- = Marguerite
- = Herringbone dc (HBdc)
- = Linked dtr (Ldtr)
- = Double Post (DP)
- = Splitt Puff (SP)

- = 4-dc popcorn
- = 5-dc popcorn
- = Bobble
- = 3-dc Bobble
- = 4-dc Bobble
- = 5-dc Bobble
- = 2-st Puff
- = 3-st Puff
- = 4-st Puff

CHAPTER ONE

CLOSED STITCHES

Closed Stitches are much sought after by crocheters for the simple reason that solid fabric is so practical. When we want to make a sweater, scarf, sock, bag, or table mat, a closed fabric with no open spaces is often desirable. In this chapter you'll find great-looking closed stitch patterns, using both short and tall stitches, most of them easy to work and shape.

We begin with several stitch patterns made with single crochet stitches, continue with patterns that combine basic stitches, then feature patterns with built-in angles, and stitches that use loops in unconventional ways. Loop stitches are represented not only by the well-known Marguerite Stitch (also known as Star Stitch) but also by two other loop variations that are easier. All of these stitches create fabric with intriguing surface designs, some subtle, others striking and bold, some lightly textured, and some smooth. These stitches will work with any yarn. Keep in mind that the heavier the weight of the yarn you use, the more dense and heavy will be your finished project. Where weight is desirable, say in a bag or rug, worsted or bulky yarns can be an asset. Where a more fluid fabric is sought, as in a garment, lighter yarns—sport or fingering weight—are better choices. There are many more closed stitches in this book beyond those in this chapter, especially in Chapter Four (Exploding Shells) and Chapter Six (Undulating Stitches: Ripples and Waves).

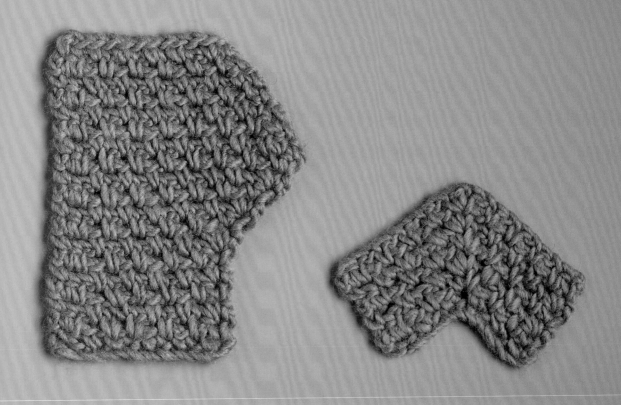

SEED STITCH

A well-loved and easy stitch that goes by many names, including Moss Stitch and Linen Stitch. It consists of single crochet stitches and chain-one spaces alternating across a row, with the next row having the single crochet stitches worked into the chain-one spaces. This creates a far suppler fabric than is possible with plain rows of single crochet stitches, and the fabric, while not completely solid, appears so.

NUMBER OF STITCHES IN PATTERN REPEAT	NUMBER OF ROWS IN PATTERN REPEAT
2	2
MULTIPLE	REVERSIBLE
2 + 2	

BASIC PATTERN

(For swatch, ch 12.)

ROW 1: Sc in 2nd ch from hook, *ch 1, sk next ch, sc in next ch, rep from * across, turn.

(Swatch has 11 sts.)

ROW 2: Ch 1, sc in first sc, sc in first ch-1 sp, *ch 1, sk next sc, sc in next ch-1 sp, rep from * across, sc in last sc, turn.

ROW 3: Ch 1, sc in first sc, *ch 1, sk next sc, sc in next ch-1 sp, rep from * across to last 2 sc, ch 1, sk next sc, sc in last sc, turn.

Rep rows 2 and 3 for patt.

(Swatch has 6 rows in patt.)

Edge Shaping

Shaping is at the rate of 1 st per row and can begin on any odd-numbered row.

INCREASING

IncRow 1: Ch 1, 2 sc in first sc, ch 1, sk next sc, sc in next ch-1 sp, continue in row 3 of patt across.

IncRow 2: Work in row 2 of patt to last sc, 2 sc in last sc, turn.

Rep IncRows 1 and 2 to continue increasing.

(Swatch has 6 increase rows, ending with 17 sts.)

DECREASING

DecRow 1: Ch 1, sk first sc, sc in next sc, sc in next ch-1 sp, ch 1, sk next sc, sc in next ch-1 sp, continue in row 3 of patt across.

DecRow 2: Work in row 2 of patt to last 2 sc, sc2tog, turn.

Rep rows 1 and 2 to continue decreasing.

(Swatch has 6 decrease rows, ending with 11 sts.)

Internal Shaping

The increase adds 2 stitches per row. Note that there is always a ch-1 in patt before and after the (sc, ch 1, sc) increase.

(For swatch, ch 12. Work row 1 of patt. 11 sts.)

Place marker in center ch.

IncRow 1: Work in row 2 of patt to marked ch-1 sp, (sc, ch 1, sc) in marked ch-1 sp, move marker to ch-1 sp just made, continue in patt across.

IncRow 2: Work in row 3 of patt to marked ch-1 sp, (sc, ch 1, sc) in marked ch-1 sp, move marker to ch-1 sp just made, continue in patt across.

Rep IncRows 1 and 2 to continue increasing.

(Swatch has 6 rows total, 5 increase rows, ending with 21 sts.)

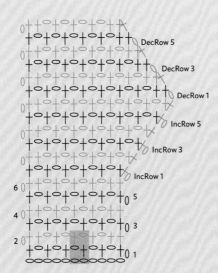

SINGLE CROCHET COLUMNS

This stitch resembles the Seed Stitch. In Seed Stitch the order of the two stitches varies in succeeding rows, but here they appear in the same order on every row, creating columns of single crochet stitches and chain-one spaces.

NUMBER OF STITCHES IN PATTERN REPEAT
2

NUMBER OF ROWS IN PATTERN REPEAT
1

MULTIPLE
2 + 2

REVERSIBLE

BASIC PATTERN

(For swatch, ch 12.)

ROW 1: Sc in 2nd ch from hook, *ch 1, sk next ch, sc in next ch, rep from * across, turn.

(Swatch has 11 sts.)

ROW 2: Ch 1, sc in first sc, ch 1, sk next ch-1 sp, *sc in next sc, ch 1, sk next ch-1 sp, rep from * across, sc in last sc, turn.

Rep row 2 for patt.

(Swatch has 6 rows in patt.)

Edge Shaping

The rate of shaping is 1 st per row and it can start on any row.

INCREASING

IncRow 1: Ch 1, 2 sc in first sc, ch 1, sk next ch-1 sp, sc in next sc, continue in patt across.

IncRow 2: Work in patt to last 2 sc, sc in next sc, ch 1, sc in last sc, turn.

Rep IncRows 1 and 2 to continue increasing.

(Swatch has 6 increase rows, ending with 17 sts.)

DECREASING

DecRow 1: Ch 1, sk first sc, sc in next ch-1 sp, sc in next sc, ch 1, continue in patt across.

DecRow 2: Work in patt to last 2 sc, sc2tog, turn.

Rep DecRows 1 and 2 to continue decreasing.

(Swatch has 6 decrease rows, ending with 11 sts.)

Internal Shaping

2 sts are added per row.

(For swatch, ch 12. Work row 1 of patt. 11 sts.)

Place marker in center ch-1 sp.

IncRow 1: Work in patt to marked ch-1 sp, (sc, ch 1, sc) in marked ch-1 sp, move marker to last sc just made, sc in next sc, continue in patt across.

IncRow 2: Work in patt to marked sc, ch 1, sc in marked sc, ch 1, sk next ch-1 sp, sc in next sc, move marker to ch-1 sp just made, ch 1, continue in patt across.

Rep IncRows 1 and 2 to continue increasing.

(Swatch has 9 rows total, 8 increase rows, ending with 27 sts.)

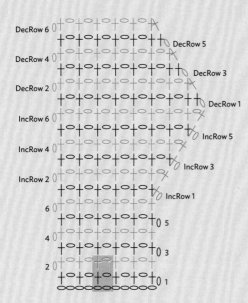

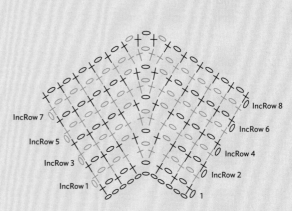

39

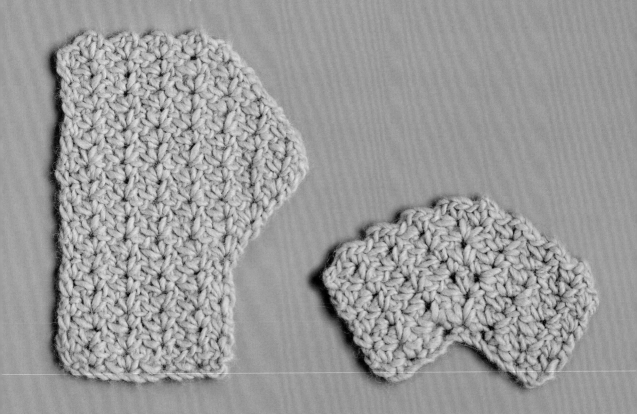

SINGLE CROCHET V-STITCH

This stitch is another great way to use single crochet stitches and achieve a supple fabric. The easy pattern repeat consists of two single crochet stitches separated by a chain-two space, a variation of the V-stitch, which is commonly made with double crochet stitches. In this version, using a shorter stitch, we get a more closed fabric.

NUMBER OF STITCHES IN PATTERN REPEAT	NUMBER OF ROWS IN PATTERN REPEAT
4	1
MULTIPLE	REVERSIBLE
3 + 3	

BASIC PATTERN

(For swatch, ch 15.)
ROW 1: Sc in 2nd ch from hook, sk next ch, *(sc, ch 2, sc) in next ch**, sk next 2 ch, rep from * across, ending last rep at **, sk next ch, sc in last ch, turn.
(Swatch has 4 patt reps, 2 sc.)
ROW 2: Ch 1, sc in first sc, *(sc, ch 2, sc) in next ch-2 sp, rep from * across, sc in last sc, turn.
Rep row 2 for patt.
(Swatch has 6 rows in patt.)

Edge Shaping

Shaping is at the rate of 1 patt rep every other row and can begin on any row.

INCREASING

IncRow 1: Ch 1, (sc, ch 2, sc) in first sc, (sc, ch 2, sc) in next ch-2 sp, continue in patt across.
IncRow 2: Work in patt across, sc in last sc, turn.
Rep IncRows 1 and 2 to continue increasing.
(Swatch has 6 increase rows, ending with 7 patt reps, 2 sc.)

DECREASING

DecRow 1: Ch 1, sk first sc, (sc, ch 2, sc) in next ch-2 sp, continue in patt across.
DecRow 2: Work in patt to last ch-2 sp, sc in last ch-2 sp, turn.

Rep DecRows 1 and 2 to continue decreasing.
(Swatch has 6 decrease rows, ending with 4 patt reps, 2 sc.)

Internal Shaping

This increase adds 2 patt reps every 3 rows. When instructions say to place marker between 2 pattern reps, place it between the sc at the end of a patt rep and the sc that begins the following patt rep. When working the increase of IncRow 1, insert hook in the space between these 2 sc.
(For swatch, ch 15. Work row 1 of patt. 4 patt reps, 2 sc.)
Place marker in sp between center 2 patt reps.
IncRow 1: Work in patt to marker, work next (sc, ch 2, sc) in marked sp, move marker to ch-2 sp just made, (sc, ch 2, sc) in next ch-2 sp, continue in patt across.
IncRow 2: Work in patt to marked ch-2 sp, (sc, ch 2, sc, ch 2, sc) in marked ch-2 sp, move marker to last ch-2 just made, (sc, ch 2, sc) in next ch-2 sp, continue in patt across.
IncRow 3: Work in patt to marked ch-2 sp, (sc, ch 2, sc) in marked ch-2 sp, (sc, ch 2, sc) in next ch-2 sp, move marker to sp between 2 patt reps just made, continue in patt across.
Rep IncRows 1–3 to continue increasing 2 patt rep every 3 rows.
(Swatch has 6 rows total, 5 increase rows, ending with 8 patt reps, 2 sc.)

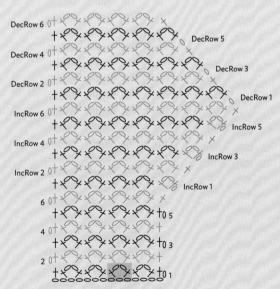

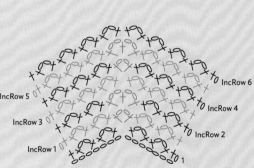

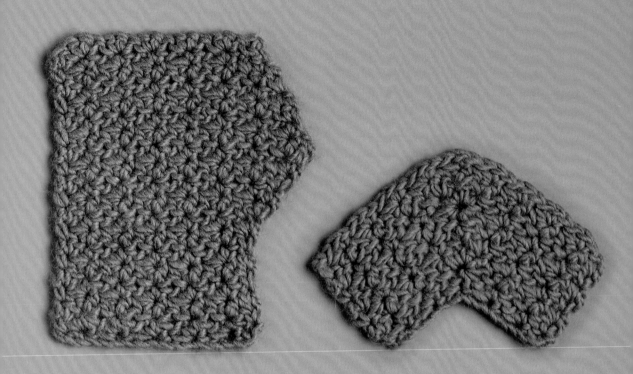

THREESOME

It would be hard to guess from looking at the fabric just how this stitch is composed, but it's simply groups of three single crochet stitches worked into the same stitch and arranged in columns. These little fans create the multidirectional slanted strands, a pleasingly complex surface that's easy to produce.

NUMBER OF STITCHES IN PATTERN REPEAT
3

MULTIPLE
3 + 3

NUMBER OF ROWS IN PATTERN REPEAT
1

REVERSIBLE

BASIC PATTERN

(For swatch, ch 18.)

ROW 1: Sc in 2nd ch from hook, *sk next ch, 3 sc in next ch, sk next ch, rep from * across, sc in last ch, turn.

(Swatch has 5 patt reps, 2 sc.)

ROW 2: Ch 1, sc in first sc, sk next sc, 3 sc in next sc, *sk next 2 sc, 3 sc in next sc, rep from * across to last 2 sc, sk next sc, sc in last sc, turn.

Rep row 2 for patt.

(Swatch has 6 rows in patt.)

Edge Shaping

The rate of shaping is 1 st per row and shaping can begin on any row.

INCREASING

IncRow 1: Ch 1, 2 sc in first sc, sk next sc, 3 sc in next sc, continue in patt across.

IncRow 2: Work in patt to last 3 sc, sk next sc, sc in next sc, 2 sc in last sc, turn.

IncRow 3: Ch 1, sc in first sc, 3 sc in next sc, sk next 2 sc, 3 sc in next sc, continue in patt across.

IncRow 4: Work in patt to last 2 sc, sk next sc, 2 sc in last sc, turn.

IncRow 5: Ch 1, sc in first sc, 3 sc in next sc, sk next sc, 3 sc in next sc, continue in patt across.

IncRow 6: Work in patt across.

Rep IncRows 1–6 to continue increasing.

(Swatch has 6 increase rows, ending with 7 patt reps, 2 sc.)

DECREASING

DecRow 1: Ch 1, sk first 2 sc, 3 sc in next sc, continue in patt across.

DecRow 2: Work in patt to last 4 sc, sk 2 sc, 2 sc in next sc, leave last sc unworked, turn.

DecRow 3: Ch 1, sk first sc, sc in next sc, sk next sc, 3 sc in next sc, continue in patt across.

DecRow 4: Work in patt to last 4 sc, sk next sc, 2 sc in next sc, sk next sc, sc in last sc, turn.

DecRow 5: Ch 1, sk first sc, sc in next 2 sc, sk next sc, 3 sc in next sc, continue in patt across.

DecRow 6: Work in patt to last 3 sc, sk next sc, sc2tog, turn.

Rep DecRows 1–6 to continue decreasing.

(Swatch has 6 decrease rows, ending with 5 patt reps, 2 sc.)

Internal Shaping

Here we increase 3 stitches (one patt rep) over 3 rows. The increase happens in IncRow 1 with IncRows 2 and 3 worked even.

(For swatch, ch 18. Work row 1 of patt. 17 sc: 5 patt reps, 2 sc.)

Place marker in center sc of center 3-sc group.

IncRow 1: Work in patt to marked sc, (3 sc, ch 1, 3 sc) in marked sc, move marker to ch-1 sp just made, sk next 2 sc, 3 sc in next sc, continue in patt across.

IncRow 2: Work in patt to marked ch-1 sp, 3 sc in marked ch-1 sp, move marker to center sc of group just made, continue in patt across.

IncRow 3: Work in patt to marked sc, 3 sc in marked sc, move marker to center sc of group just made, continue in patt across.

Rep IncRows 1–3 to continue increasing.

(Swatch has 7 rows total, 6 increase rows, ending with 9 patt reps, 2 sc.)

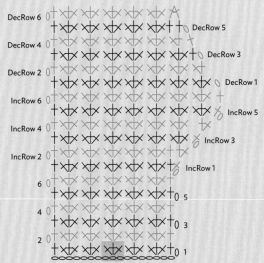

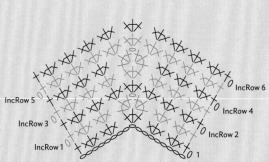

SURFACE TENSION

This pattern can be considered a variation of Seed Stitch as it consists of three rows identical to that stitch, then adds a fourth row of plain double crochet stitches. That extra row gives it a whole new look!

NUMBER OF STITCHES IN PATTERN REPEAT	NUMBER OF ROWS IN PATTERN REPEAT
V	4
MULTIPLE	**NOT REVERSIBLE**
2 + 3	

NOTES

Dc rows have 1 more stitch than seed stitch rows. The resulting slight discrepancy in width at side edges can be corrected with blocking or edging.

In row 2 of patt, to work between stitches, do not insert hook in the top loops of a stitch as you would normally, but rather insert the hook between the posts of the last skipped dc and the next dc.

BASIC PATTERN

(For swatch, ch 17.)

ROW 1: 2 dc in 4th ch from hook (3 sk ch count as first dc), sk next ch, *2 dc in next ch, sk next ch, rep from * across to last 2 ch, 2 dc in next ch, dc in last ch, turn.

(Swatch has 16 dc.)

ROW 2: Ch 1, sc in first dc, *ch 1, sk next 2 dc, sc between last skipped dc and next dc, rep from * across, turn.

ROW 3: Ch 1, sc in first sc, *sc in next ch-1 sp, ch 1, sk next sc, rep from * across, sc in last ch-1 sp, sc in last sc, turn.

ROW 4: Ch 1, sc in first sc, *ch 1, sk next sc, sc in next ch-1 sp, rep from * across to last 2 sts, ch 1, sk next sc, sc in last sc, turn.

ROW 5: Ch 3 (counts as dc throughout), *2 dc in next ch-1 sp, rep from * across, dc in last sc, turn.

Rep rows 2–5 for patt.

(Swatch has 8 rows in patt.)

Edge Shaping

Shaping is at the rate of 1 st every other row, resulting in a gentle slope. It begins in the dc row.

INCREASING

IncRow 1: Ch 3, dc in same sc, 2 dc in next ch-1 sp, continue in row 5 of patt across.

IncRow 2: Work in row 2 of patt to last 2 sts, ch 1, sk next dc, sc in tch, turn.

IncRow 3: Ch 1, sc in first sc, ch 1, sc in first ch-1 sp, ch 1, continue in row 3 of patt across.

IncRow 4: Work in row 4 of patt to last ch-1 sp, sc in last ch-1 sp, sc in last sc, turn.

Rep IncRows 1–4 to continue increasing.

(Swatch has 8 increase rows, ending with 20 sts.)

DECREASING

DecRow 1: Ch 3, sk next sc, dc2tog in next ch-1 sp, continue in row 5 patt across.

DecRow 2: Work in row 2 of patt ending with sc between last dc and dc2tog, sk dc2tog, sc in tch, turn.

DecRow 3: Ch 1, sc in first sc, sk next sc, sc in next ch-1 sp, ch 1, sk next sc, continue in row 3 of patt across.

DecRow 4: Work in row 4 of patt across.

DecRow 5: Ch 3, dc2tog in next ch-1 sp, continue in row 5 patt across.

If decreasing immediately after an increase row, use DecRow 1, then rep DecRows 2–5 thereafter to continue decreasing. If decreasing after row 4 of patt, begin with DecRow 5, then rep DecRows 2–5.

(Swatch has 8 decrease rows, ending with 15 sts.)

Internal Shaping

The increase begins on row 2 of patt. The rate of increase is 10 sts over 4 rows: 2 sts gained in each of the first 3 IncRows and 4 sts in IncRow 4.

Note that in IncRows 1–3 the last st "in pattern" before the marked ch-1 sp is a ch 1. The first st after completing the increase is also a ch 1.

(For swatch, ch 12. Row 1: Dc in 4th ch from hook [3 sk ch count as first dc], dc in each ch across, turn. 10 dc.)

Place marker in sp between 2 center dc.

IncRow 1: Work in row 2 of patt to marked sp, (sc, ch 1, sc) in marked sp, move marker to ch-1 sp just made, continue in patt across.

IncRow 2: Work in row 3 of patt to marked ch-1 sp, (sc, ch 1, sc) in marked ch-1 sp, move marker to ch-1 sp just made, continue in patt across.

IncRow 3: Work in row 4 of patt to marked ch-1 sp, (sc, ch 1, sc) in marked ch-1 sp, move marker to ch-1 sp just made, continue in patt across.

IncRow 4: Work in row 5 of patt to marked ch-1 sp, (2 dc, ch 1, 2 dc) in marked ch-1 sp, move marker to ch-1 sp just made, 2 dc in next ch-1 sp, continue in patt across.

Rep IncRows 1–4 to continue increasing.

(Swatch has 10 rows total, 9 increase rows, ending with 27 sts.)

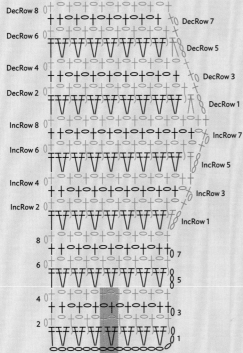

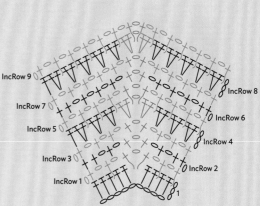

EXTENDED STITCHES

Extended stitches are a bit taller than their plain counterparts. The lengthening is done by adding one chain as you work the stitch. In this stitch pattern two extended stitches—an Extended Single Crochet (Esc) and an Extended Half Double Crochet (Ehdc)—are worked on alternate rows, creating a unique look and lending the fabric good drape.

NUMBER OF STITCHES IN PATTERN REPEAT	NUMBER OF ROWS IN PATTERN REPEAT
1	2
MULTIPLE	**REVERSIBLE**
1 + 2	

NOTE

To make stitches align well vertically, we do not use turning chains in this pattern. Instead we work a ch 1 at the beginning of each row that does not count as a stitch.

Because of the inherent slant of these stitches, as well as the shortened turning chain, it's easy to miss a stitch on the following row. To prevent errors, place a marker in the last stitch of each row right after you make it. This will ensure you know where to place the last stitch of the following row, and is particularly crucial when increasing or decreasing.

SPECIAL STITCHES

Extended Single Crochet (Esc): Insert hook in designated st, yo and draw up loop, ch 1, yo, draw through 2 loops.

Extended Half Double Crochet (Ehdc): Yo, insert hook in designated st, yo and draw up loop, ch 1, yo, draw through 3 loops.

BASIC PATTERN

(For swatch, ch 14.)

ROW 1: Esc in 3rd ch from hook (2 sk ch do not count as st) and in each st across, turn.

(Swatch has 12 sts.)

ROW 2: Ch 1, Ehdc in first st and in each st across, turn.

ROW 3: Ch 1, Esc in first st and in each st across, turn.

Rep rows 2 and 3 for patt.

(Swatch has 6 rows in patt.)

Edge Shaping

Shaping can begin on any row. Instructions below begin increasing on an Esc row, but if you wish to begin on an Ehdc row, simply reverse IncRows 1 and 2. To begin decreasing on an Ehdc row, reverse DecRows 1 and 2.

INCREASING

IncRow 1: Ch 1, 2 Esc in first st, continue in row 3 of patt across.

IncRow 2: Work in row 2 of patt to last st, 2 Ehdc in last st, turn.

Rep IncRows 1 and 2 to continue increasing.

(Swatch has 6 increase rows, ending with 18 sts.)

DECREASING

DecRow 1: Ch 1, insert hook in first st and draw up loop, insert hook in 2nd st and draw up loop, ch 1, yo, draw through 3 loops on hook (Esc dec made), continue in row 3 of patt across.

DecRow 2: Work in row 2 of patt to last 2 sts, yo, insert hook in next st and draw up loop, insert hook in following st and draw up loop, ch 1, yo, draw through 4 loops on hook (Ehdc dec made), turn.

Rep DecRows 1 and 2 to continue decreasing.

(Swatch has 6 decrease rows, ending with 12 sts.)

Internal Shaping

The natural bias of the stitches used here causes problems when increasing on either side of a ch-1; therefore a center stitch is used instead.

(For swatch, ch 15. Work row 1 of patt. 13 sts.)

Place marker in center (7th) st.

IncRow 1: Work in row 2 of patt to marked st, 3 Ehdc in marked st, move marker to center Ehdc just made, continue in patt across.

IncRow 2: Work in row 3 of patt to marked st, 3 Esc in marked st, move marker to center Esc just made, continue in patt across.

Rep IncRows 1 and 2 to continue increasing.

(Swatch has 6 rows total, 5 increase rows, ending with 23 sts.)

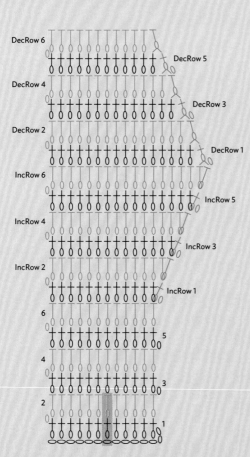

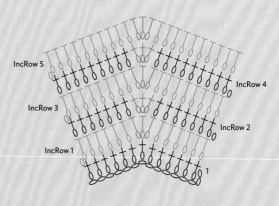

ETCHED HALF DOUBLES

A simple and attractive stitch pattern that alternates rows of half doubles with rows of slip stitches. The slip stitches create a strong line defining each row.

NUMBER OF STITCHES IN PATTERN REPEAT	NUMBER OF ROWS IN PATTERN REPEAT
1	2
MULTIPLE	**REVERSIBLE**
1 + 1	

NOTES

To avoid gaps in the fabric, instead of ch 2 at the starts of rows, we begin hdc rows with ch 1, which does not count as a stitch, then work a hdc in the first stitch of the row.

Work slip stitches loosely throughout so that they match in size the top of the stitch you are working into.

SPECIAL STITCH

Half double crochet decrease (Hdc dec): Yo, insert hook in st, yo and draw up loop, insert hook in next st, yo and draw through 4 loops on hook. This creates a less bulky st than the usual way of working 2 hdc sts together, while maintaining the necessary height to match other hdc sts.

BASIC PATTERN

(For swatch, ch 13.)
ROW 1: Hdc in 2nd ch from hook, hdc in each ch across, turn.
(Swatch has 12 hdc.)
ROW 2: Ch 1, BLsl st in first hdc, BLsl st in each hdc across, turn.
ROW 3: Ch 1, hdc in first st and in each st across, turn.
Rep rows 2 and 3 for patt, ending with an even-numbered row.
(Swatch has 6 rows in patt.)

Edge Shaping

Shaping is at the rate of 1 st every other row on hdc rows only and can begin on any hdc row.

INCREASING

IncRow 1: Ch 1, 2 hdc in first st, continue in row 3 of patt across.
IncRow 2: Work in row 2 of patt across.
Rep IncRows 1 and 2 to continue increasing.
(Swatch has 8 increase rows, ending with 16 sts.)

DECREASING

DecRow 1: Ch 1, Hdc dec, continue in row 3 of patt across.
DecRow 2: Work in row 2 of patt across.
Rep DecRows 1 and 2 to continue decreasing.
(Swatch has 8 decrease rows, ending with 12 sts.)

Internal Shaping

Instead of a ch-1 space at the center, we use a stitch. 2 stitches are increased every other row.
(For swatch, ch 12. Work rows 1 and 2 of patt. 11 sts.)
Place marker in center st.
IncRow 1: Work in row 3 of patt to marked st, 3 hdc in marked st, move marker to center hdc of group just made, continue in patt across.
IncRow 2: Work in row 2 of patt across.
Rep IncRows 1 and 2 to continue increasing.
(Swatch has 8 rows total, 6 increase rows, ending with 17 sts.)

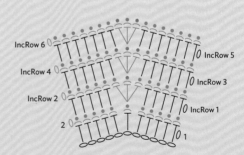

49

FRONT-FACING TREBLES

Treble stitches give lovely drape to fabric, although the space between their long posts means the fabric isn't completely solid. The backs of these tall stitches are not as attractive as their fronts, however. To avoid having the backs of stitches on the right side of the work, I insert an alternate row of slip stitches, which adds no height to the row but supplies a nice horizontal line against the background of tall stitches. This pattern is very similar to Etched Half Doubles.

NOTES

To work into sl sts: After completing row 2 of patt, turn your work to see the RS; you will see two loops typical of the tops of stitches. These are the tops of the tr stitches 2 rows below. Do not work into these 2 loops when working row 3 of patt. Work into the sl sts that are just behind these loops, except for the last tr of the row, which is worked into back loop of the ch 1 of the prev row.

Slip stitch rows should be worked loosely so that the stitches match in size the tops of the stitches below.

Because the ch 1 that begins each sl st row serves as the first sl st of the row, we do not work into the first st of previous row.

NUMBER OF STITCHES IN PATTERN REPEAT	NUMBER OF ROWS IN PATTERN REPEAT
1	2
MULTIPLE	**REVERSIBLE**
1 + 4	

BASIC PATTERN

(For swatch, ch 15.)

ROW 1: Tr in 5th ch from hook (4 sk ch count as tr), tr in each ch across, turn.

(Swatch has 12 sts.)

ROW 2: Ch 1 (counts as first sl st), sk first tr, sl st in each tr across, turn.

ROW 3: Ch 4 (counts as tr throughout), tr in each sl st (see Notes above) across, turn.

Rep rows 2 and 3 for patt.

(Swatch has 6 rows in patt.)

Edge Shaping

The rate of shaping is one st on each tr row; no shaping on sl st rows.

INCREASING

IncRow 1: Ch 4, tr in same st, continue in row 3 of patt across.

IncRow 2: Work in row 2 of patt.

Rep IncRows 1 and 2 to continue increasing.

(Swatch has 8 increase rows, ending with 16 sts.)

DECREASING

DecRow 1: Ch 3, sk first st, tr in next st (counts as tr2tog), continue in row 3 of patt across.

DecRow 2: Work in row 2 of patt.

Rep DecRows 1 and 2 to continue decreasing.

(Swatch has 8 decrease rows, ending with 12 sts.)

Internal Shaping

2 sts are increased on every tr row around a center ch-1 sp. Work sl sts in center ch by inserting hook under 2 loops of ch.

(For swatch, ch 12. Work row 1 of patt. 9 sts.)

Place marker in center tr.

IncRow 1: Work in row 2 of patt across, moving marker up to center sl st.

IncRow 2: Work in row 3 of patt to marked st, (tr, ch 1, tr) in marked st, move marker to ch-1 sp just made, continue in patt across.

IncRow 3: Work in row 2 of patt to marked ch-1 sp, sl st in ch-1 sp, move marker to sl st just made, continue in patt across.

Rep IncRows 2 and 3 to continue increasing.

(Swatch has 8 rows total, 7 increase rows, ending with 15 sts.)

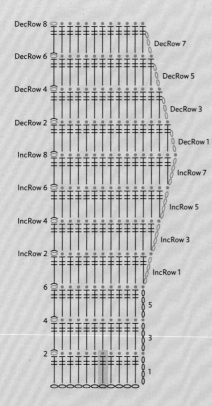

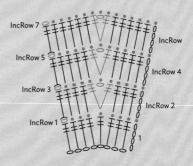

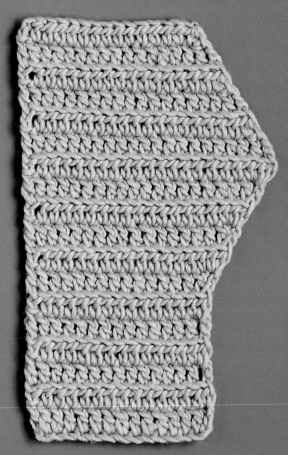

LEDGES

If you want to use rows of plain stitches, two
different ones often make a nice combination.
Here rows of half double crochet stitches
alternate with double crochet stitches, which
are worked into the back loop only, creating the
little ledge on the front of the work.

NUMBER OF STITCHES IN PATTERN REPEAT	NUMBER OF ROWS IN PATTERN REPEAT
1	2
MULTIPLE	**NOT REVERSIBLE**
1 + 2	

BASIC PATTERN

(For swatch, ch 17.)

ROW 1: Dc in 4th ch from hook (3 sk ch count as dc) and in each ch across, turn.

(Swatch has 15 sts.)

ROW 2: Ch 2 (counts as hdc throughout), hdc in each dc across, turn.

ROW 3: Ch 3 (counts as dc throughout), BLdc in each hdc across, turn.

Rep rows 2 and 3 for patt.

(Swatch has 6 rows in patt.)

Edge Shaping

Shaping is at the rate of 1 st per row, beginning on a dc row.

INCREASING

IncRow 1: Ch 3, BLdc in first st, continue in row 3 of patt across.

IncRow 2: Work in row 2 of patt to tch, 2 hdc in tch, turn.

Rep IncRows 1 and 2 to continue increasing.

(Swatch has 6 increase rows, ending with 21 sts.)

DECREASING

DecRow 1: Ch 2, sk first st (counts as dc2tog), BLdc in next st, continue in row 3 of patt across.

DecRow 2: Work in row 2 of patt to last 2 sts, hdc2tog, turn.

Rep DecRows 1 and 2 to continue decreasing.

(Swatch has 6 decrease rows, ending with 15 sts.)

Internal Shaping

2 sts are added per row on either side of a center st.

(For swatch, ch 15. Work row 1 of patt. 13 sts.)

Place marker in center st.

IncRow 1: Work in row 2 of patt to marked st, 3 hdc in marked st, move marker to center st of group just made, continue in patt across.

IncRow 2: Work in row 3 of patt to marked st, 3 BLdc in marked st, move marker to center st of group just made, continue in patt across.

Rep IncRows 1 and 2 to continue increasing.

(Swatch has 6 rows total, 5 increase rows, ending with 23 sts.)

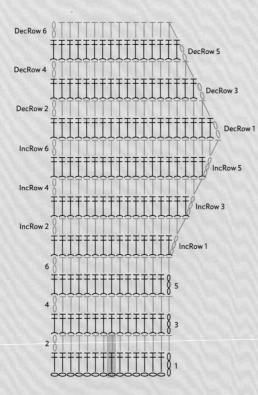

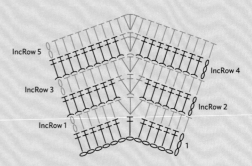

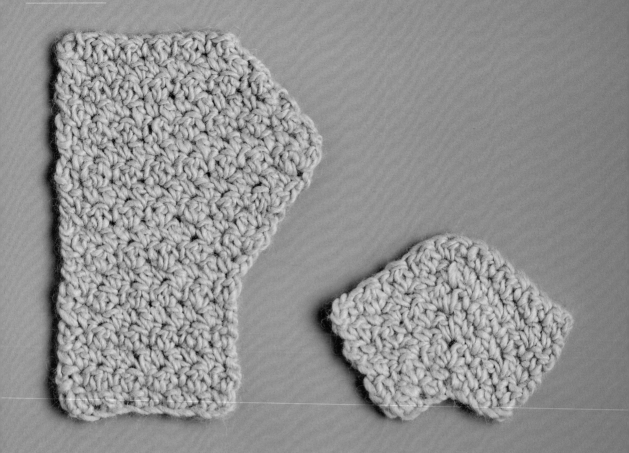

GRIDDLE STITCH

A popular stitch that features adjacent stitches of different heights—a single crochet stitch next to a double crochet stitch—resulting in an attractive nubbly surface.

NUMBER OF STITCHES IN PATTERN REPEAT

2

MULTIPLE

2 + 2

NUMBER OF ROWS IN PATTERN REPEAT

2

REVERSIBLE

SPECIAL STITCH
Work dc and sc together (Dc/sc2tog): Yo, insert hook in next st, yo and draw up loop, yo, draw through 2 loops, insert hook in next st and draw up loop, yo, draw through 3 loops on hook.

BASIC PATTERN

(For swatch, ch 12.)

ROW 1: Sc in 2nd ch from hook, dc in next ch, *sc in next ch**, dc in next ch, rep from * across, ending last rep at **, turn. *(Swatch has 11 sts.)*

ROW 2: Ch 3 (counts as dc throughout), *sc in next dc, dc in next sc, rep from * across, turn.

ROW 3: Ch 1, sc in first dc, *dc in next sc, sc in next dc, rep from * across, turn.

Rep rows 2 and 3 for patt.

(Swatch has 6 rows in patt.)

Edge Shaping

Shaping is at the rate of 1 st per row and can begin on any row.

INCREASING

IncRow 1: Ch 3, sc in first dc, dc in next sc, continue in row 3 of patt across.

IncRow 2: Work in row 2 of patt to tch, (sc, dc) in tch, turn.

Rep IncRows 1 and 2 to continue increasing.

(Swatch has 6 increase rows, ending with 17 sts.)

DECREASING

DecRow 1: Ch 1, sk first dc, dc in next sc, continue in row 3 of patt across.

DecRow 2: Work in row 2 of patt to last 2 sts (which are sc, dc), dc/sc2tog over last 2 sts, turn.

DecRow 3: Ch 1, sk first st, dc in next sc, continue in row 3 of patt across.

Rep DecRows 2 and 3 to continue decreasing.

(Swatch has 6 decrease rows, ending with 11 sts.)

Internal Shaping

2 stitches are added on each row.

(For swatch, ch 10. Work row 1 of patt. 9 sts.)

Place marker in center st.

IncRow 1: Work in row 2 of patt to marked sc, (dc, ch 1, dc) in marked sc, move marker to ch-1 sp just made, sc in next dc, continue in patt across.

IncRow 2: Work in row 3 of patt to marked ch-1 sp, (dc, ch 1, dc) in marked ch-1 sp, move marker to ch-1 sp just made, sc in next dc, continue in patt across.

Rep IncRows 1 and 2 to continue increasing.

To return to patt on last row as in swatch:

LAST ROW: Work in patt to marked ch-1 sp, dc in marked ch-1 sp, sc in next dc, continue in patt across.

(Swatch has 6 rows total, 4 increase rows, ending with 17 sts.)

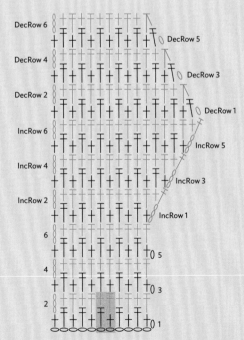

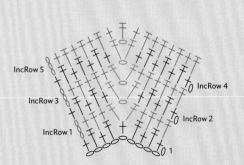

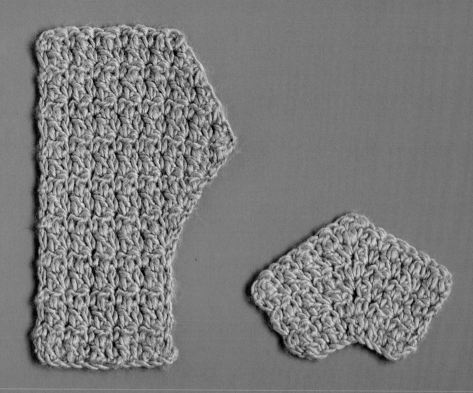

CRUMPLED GRIDDLE

Like the Griddle Stitch, this version produces nice texture on the surface by placing a tall stitch—a double crochet stitch—next to a short one—a single crochet stitch. The only difference between the two is that in Griddle Stitch a double is worked into the single on the following row, while in Crumpled Griddle double crochet stitches are always worked into double crochets and single crochet stitches into singles.

NUMBER OF STITCHES IN PATTERN REPEAT	NUMBER OF ROWS IN PATTERN REPEAT
2	1
MULTIPLE	REVERSIBLE
2 + 2	

BASIC PATTERN

(For swatch, ch 12.)

ROW 1: Sc in 2nd ch from hook, *dc in next ch, sc in next ch, rep from * across, turn.

(Swatch has 11 sts.)

ROW 2: Ch 1, sc in first sc, *dc in next dc, sc in next sc, rep from * across, turn.

Rep row 2 for patt.

(Swatch has 6 rows in patt.)

Edge Shaping

Shaping at the rate of 1 st per row can begin on any row.

INCREASING

IncRow 1: Ch 3 (counts as dc throughout), sc in first sc, dc in next dc, continue in patt across.

IncRow 2: Work in patt to tch, (dc, sc) in tch, turn.

Rep IncRows 1 and 2 to continue increasing.

(Swatch has 6 increase rows, ending with 17 sts.)

DECREASING

DecRow 1: Ch 1, sk first sc, dc in next dc, sc in next sc, continue in patt across.

DecRow 2: Work in patt to last 2 sts, insert hook in next sc and draw up loop, yo, insert hook in next dc and draw up loop (4 loops on hook), yo and draw through all loops on hook, turn.

Rep DecRows 1 and 2 to continue decreasing.

(Swatch has 6 decrease rows, ending with 11 sts.)

Internal shaping

2 sts are added in each row.

(For swatch, ch 12. Work row 1 of patt. 11 sts.)

Place marker in center dc.

IncRow 1: Work in patt to marked st, (dc, ch 1, dc) in marked st, move marker to ch-1 just made, sc in next sc, dc in next dc, continue in patt across.

IncRow 2: Work in patt to marked ch-1 sp, placing dc in dc before marked ch-1 sp, (sc, ch 1, sc) in marked ch-1 sp, move marker to ch-1 just made, dc in next dc, continue in patt across.

Rep IncRows 1 and 2 to continue increasing.

(Swatch has 6 rows total, 5 increase rows, ending with 21 sts.)

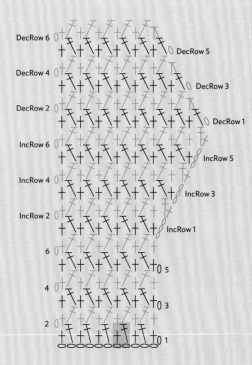

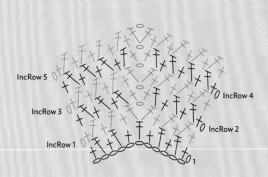

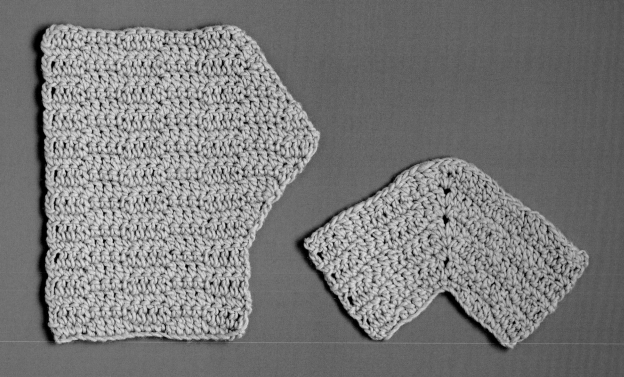

TALL SHORT

This stitch pattern offers an easy way to work with basic stitches and create a lively surface. Two stitches of different heights, single crochet and double crochet, alternate in groups of four across the row.

NUMBER OF STITCHES IN PATTERN REPEAT

8

MULTIPLE

8 + 5

SPECIAL STITCH

Work dc and sc together (Dc/sc2tog): Yo, insert hook in next st and draw up loop, yo, draw through 2 loops on hook, insert hook in next st and draw up loop, yo, draw through 3 loops on hook.

NUMBER OF ROWS IN PATTERN REPEAT

2

REVERSIBLE

BASIC PATTERN

(For swatch, ch 21.)
ROW 1: Sc in 2nd ch from hook, sc in next 3 ch, *dc in next 4 ch, sc in next 4 ch, rep from * across, turn.
(Swatch has 20 sts.)
ROW 2: Ch 3, dc in next 3 sc, *sc in next 4 dc, dc in next 4 sc, rep from * across, turn.
ROW 3: Ch 1, sc in first 4 dc, *dc in next 4 sc, sc in next 4 dc, rep from * across, turn.
Rep rows 2 and 3 for patt.
(Swatch has 6 rows in patt.)

Edge Shaping

When shaping 1 stitch at a time, 8 rows are needed to get to the beginning of a pattern repeat again. It's easy to adapt this so you can begin shaping on any row and on either edge—just pay attention to what stitch is coming next in pattern.

INCREASING

IncRow 1: Ch 3 (counts as dc throughout), sc in first dc, sc in next 3 dc, dc in next 4 sc, continue in row 3 of patt across, turn.
IncRow 2: Work in row 2 of patt to tch, 2 sc in tch, turn.
IncRow 3: Ch 3, dc in first sc, dc in next sc, sc in next 4 dc, continue in row 3 of patt across.
IncRow 4: Work in row 2 of patt to last 3 sts, sc in next 2 dc, 2 sc in tch, turn.
IncRow 5: Ch 1, (sc, dc) in first sc, dc in next 3 sc, continue in row 3 of patt across.
IncRow 6: Work in patt to last sc, 2 dc in last sc, turn.
IncRow 7: Ch 1, 2 sc in first dc, sc in next dc, dc in next 4 sc, continue in patt across.
IncRow 8: Work in patt to last 3 sc, dc in next 2 sc, 2 dc in last sc, turn.
Rep IncRows 1–8 to continue increasing.
(Swatch has 8 increase rows, ending with 28 sts.)

DECREASING

DecRow 1: Ch 1, sk first dc, sc in next 3 dc, dc in next 4 sc, continue in row 3 of patt across.
DecRow 2: Work in row 2 of patt to last 3 sc, dc in next sc, dc2tog, turn.
DecRow 3: Ch 1, sk first dc, sc in next dc, dc in next 4 sc, sc in next 4 dc, continue in row 3 of patt across.
DecRow 4: Work in row 2 of patt to last 5 sts, sc in next 3 dc, sc2tog over last 2 sts, turn.
DecRow 5: Ch 2, dc in next sc (counts as dc2tog), dc in next 2 sc, sc in next 4 dc, continue in row 3 of patt across.
DecRow 6: Work in patt to last 3 dc (note that ch 2 tch does not count as st), sc in next dc, sc2tog, turn.

DecRow 7: Ch 2, dc in next sc (counts as dc2tog), sc in next 4 dc, continue in patt across.
DecRow 8: Work in patt to last 5 sts, dc in next 3 sc, dc/sc2tog.
Rep DecRows 1–8 to continue decreasing.
(Swatch has 8 decrease rows, ending with 20 sts.)

Internal Shaping

Because this pattern consists of 8 sts, if we increase by 2 sts every row around a center ch-1 sp it requires 8 rows to return to pattern. That's because we build the patt rep from the center and need to add 8 sts on each side of the center.
(For swatch ch 21. Work row 1 of patt. 20 sts.)
Place marker in last sc of center group of sc sts, turn.
IncRow 1: Work in row 2 of patt to marked sc, dc in marked sc, 2 dc in next sc, ch 1, 2 dc in next sc, dc in next sc, move marker to last dc made, sc in next 4 dc, continue in patt across.
IncRow 2: Work in row 3 of patt to marked dc, sc in next 3 dc, (sc, ch 1, sc) in next ch-1 sp, sc in next 3 dc, move marker to last sc made, dc in next 4 dc, continue in patt across.
IncRow 3: Work in row 2 of patt to marked sc, dc in marked sc, dc in next 3 dc, (sc, ch 1, sc) in next ch-1 sp, move marker to last sc made, dc in next 4 dc, continue in patt across.
IncRow 4: Work in row 3 of patt to marked sc, dc in marked sc, (dc, ch 1, dc) in next ch-1 sp, dc in next sc, move marker to last dc made, continue in patt across.
IncRow 5: Work in row 2 of patt to marked dc, sc in marked dc, sc in next dc, (sc, ch 1, sc) in next ch-1 sp, sc in next 2 dc, move marker to last sc made, continue in patt across.
IncRow 6: Work in patt to marked sc, dc in marked sc, dc in next 2 sc, (dc, ch 1, dc) in next ch-1 sp, dc in next 3 sc, move marker to last dc made, continue in patt across.
IncRow 7: Work in patt to marked dc, sc in marked dc, sc in next 3 dc, (dc, ch 1, dc) in next ch-1 sp, move marker to last dc made, sc in next 4 dc, continue in patt across.
IncRow 8: Work in patt to marked sc, dc in marked sc, 2 sc in next ch-1 sp, sc in next dc, move marker to sc just made, continue in patt across.
Rep IncRows 1–8 to continue increasing.
(Swatch has 9 rows in total, 8 increase rows, ending with 36 sts.)

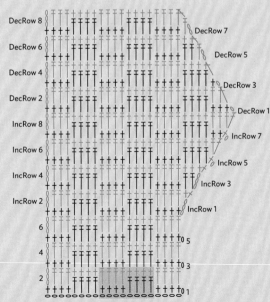

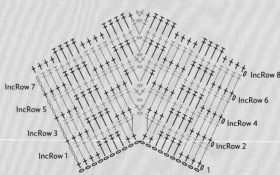

HERRINGBONE DOUBLES

This nifty variation on double crochet stitches yields an effect that some liken to traditional herringbone woven textiles, hence the name. Pay attention to the details of how to work the stitch to get it exactly right!

NUMBER OF STITCHES IN PATTERN REPEAT:

1

MULTIPLE:

1 + 3

NUMBER OF ROWS IN PATTERN REPEAT:

1

REVERSIBLE

NOTES

The tricky thing about this stitch is drawing a loop through the top of the stitch below and also through the first loop on the hook (the yo just made). After a while it gets easier.

There is a natural slant to these stitches. Since the slant is in the opposite direction on alternate rows, the fabric does not bias. However, the side edges are not absolutely straight.

SPECIAL STITCHES

Herringbone dc (HBdc): Yo, insert hook in designated st, yo and draw loop through top of st and first loop on hook, ch 1, yo, draw through 2 loops on hook.

HBdc2tog: *Yo, insert hook in designated st, yo and draw loop through top of st and first loop on hook, ch 1**, rep from * to ** in next st, yo, draw through 3 loops on hook. Work the yo loosely to make it easier to execute. After drawing up loop in top of st, turn the point of your hook down to avoid it catching on first loop on hook.

BASIC PATTERN

(For swatch, ch 14.)
ROW 1: HBdc in 4th ch from hook (3 sk ch count as dc), HBdc in each ch across.
(Swatch has 12 sts.)
ROW 2: Ch 3 (counts as dc throughout), Hbdc in each dc across.
Rep row 2 for patt.
(Swatch has 6 rows in patt.)

Edge Shaping

Shaping at the rate of 1 st per row to begin on any row.

INCREASING

IncRow 1: Ch 3, HBdc in first st, continue in patt across.
IncRow 2: Work in patt to tch, 2 HBdc in tch, turn.
Rep IncRows 1 and 2 to continue increasing.
(Swatch has 6 increase rows, ending with 18 sts.)

DECREASING

DecRow 1: Ch 2, HBdc in next st (counts as dc2tog), continue in patt across.
DecRow 2: Work in patt to last 2 sts, HBdc2tog, turn.
Rep DecRows 1 and 2 to continue decreasing.
(Swatch has 6 decrease rows, ending with 12 sts.)

Internal Shaping

Increasing 2 sts per row around a center st rather than ch-1, to keep solid fabric.
(For swatch, ch 13. Work row 1 of patt. 11 sts.)
Place marker in center st.
IncRow 1: Work in patt to marked st, 3 HBdc in marked st, move marker to center st of group just made, continue in patt across.
Rep IncRow 1 to continue increasing.
(Swatch has 6 rows total, 5 increase rows, ending with 21 sts.)

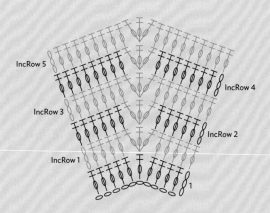

61

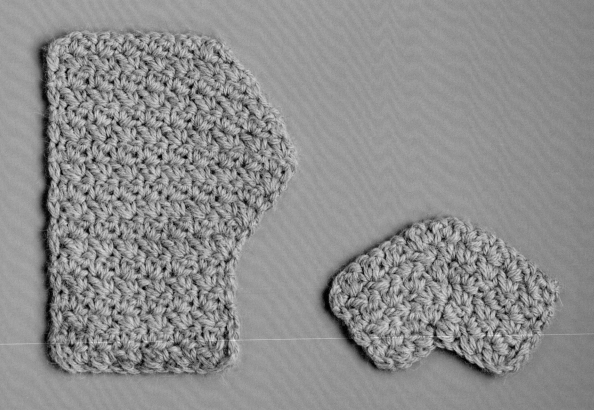

TILTED PAIRS

When two stitches of different heights are worked into the same place, they tilt toward the shorter stitch. The direction of the slant changes as we go from one row to the next, creating a design of angled lines.

NUMBER OF STITCHES IN PATTERN REPEAT:

2

MULTIPLE:

2 + 1

NUMBER OF ROWS IN PATTERN REPEAT:

1

REVERSIBLE

BASIC PATTERN

(For swatch, ch 15.)

ROW 1: Sc in 2nd ch from hook, *(sc, dc) in next ch, sk next ch, rep from * across, sc in last ch, turn.

(Swatch has 14 sts.)

ROW 2: Ch 1, sc in first sc, *(sc, dc) in next dc, sk next sc, rep from * across, sc in last sc, turn.

Rep row 2 for patt.

(Swatch has 6 rows in patt.)

Edge Shaping

Shaping can begin on any row. Shaping is at the rate of 1 full patt rep over 2 rows.

INCREASING

IncRow 1: Ch 1, (sc, dc) in first sc, (sc, dc) in next dc, sk next sc, continue in patt across.

IncRow 2: Work in patt to last 2 sts, (sc, dc) in last dc, sc in last sc, turn.

Rep IncRows 1 and 2 to continue increasing.

(Swatch has 6 increase rows, ending with 20 sts.)

DECREASING

DecRow 1: Ch 1, sk first sc, (sc, dc) in next dc, sk next sc, continue in patt across.

DecRow 2: Work in patt to last 2 sts (which are dc, sc), sc in next dc, leave last sc unworked, turn.

Rep DecRows 1 and 2 to continue decreasing.

(Swatch has 6 decrease rows, ending with 14 sts.)

Internal Shaping

For this internal increase, always place the increase in the unworked sc of a (sc, dc) pair. This method adds 2 stitches—a full pattern repeat—in each row. Note that the "center line" moves one stitch off center on odd-numbered rows, nicely melding the angled stitches. To ensure that work ends symmetrically, work an even number of internal shaping rows.

(For swatch, ch 13. Work row 1 of patt. 12 sts.)

Place marker in sc of center patt rep.

IncRow 1: Work in patt to marked sc, (sc, dc) in marked sc, move marker to sc just made, continue in patt across.

Rep IncRow 1 to continue increasing.

(Swatch has 6 rows total, 5 increase rows, ending with 22 sts.)

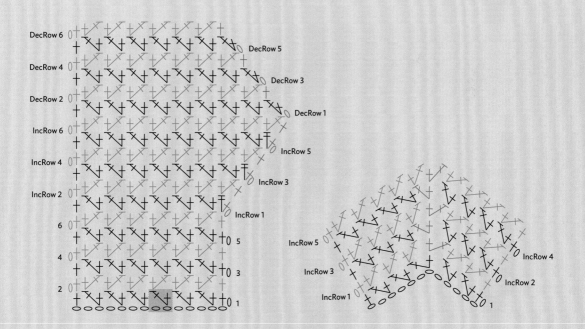

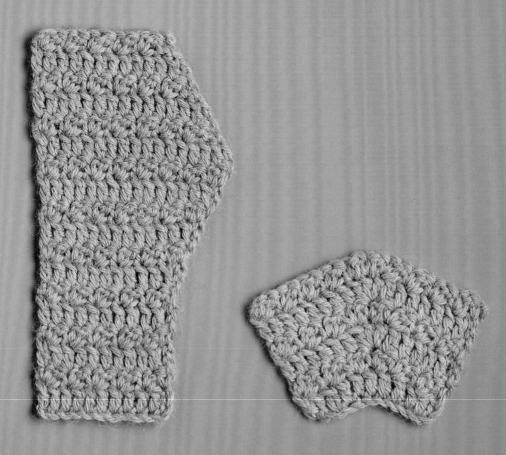

STRAIGHT
AND TILTED

The interesting feature of this pattern is the
alternation of a row of vertical stitches with
another row where the stitches slant.

**NUMBER OF STITCHES
IN PATTERN REPEAT**

2

MULTIPLE

2 + 1

**NUMBER OF ROWS
IN PATTERN REPEAT**

2

REVERSIBLE

SPECIAL STITCH

Special Decrease (Sdec): Insert hook in next st and
draw up loop, yo, insert hook in next st and draw up
loop, yo, draw through 5 loops on hook.

BASIC PATTERN

(For swatch, ch 13.)

ROW 1: Dc in 4th ch from hook (3 sk ch count as first dc), dc in each ch across, turn.

(Swatch has 11 sts.)

ROW 2: Ch 1, (sc, dc) in first dc, *sk next dc, (sc, dc) in next dc, rep from * across, sc in tch, turn.

ROW 3: Ch 3 (counts as dc throughout), dc in each st across, turn.

Rep rows 2 and 3 for patt.

(Swatch has 6 rows in patt.)

Edge Shaping

Shaping is at the rate of 1 st per row beginning on an odd-numbered row, but it can begin on any row by reversing the instructions for IncRows 1 and 2 or DecRows 1 and 2.

INCREASING

IncRow 1: Ch 3, dc in first sc, continue in row 3 of patt across.

IncRow 2: Work in row 2 of patt to last 2 sts, (sc, dc) in next dc, sc in tch, turn.

Rep IncRows 1 and 2 to continue increasing.

(Swatch has 6 increase rows, ending with 17 sts.)

DECREASING

DecRow 1: Ch 2, dc in next st (counts as dc2tog), continue in row 3 of patt across.

DecRow 2: Work in row 2 of patt to last 2 dc, Sdec, leave tch unworked, turn.

Rep DecRows 1 and 2 to continue decreasing.

(Swatch has 6 decrease rows, ending with 11 sts.)

Internal Shaping

Increasing at the rate of 2 sts per row.

(For swatch, ch 13. Work row 1 of patt. 11 sts.)

Place marker in center dc.

IncRow 1: Work in row 2 of patt to marked dc, (sc, dc) in marked dc, move marker to sc just made, (sc, dc) in next dc, continue in patt across.

IncRow 2: Work in row 3 of patt to marked sc, 3 dc in marked sc, move marker to center dc of group, continue in patt across.

Rep IncRows 1 and 2 to continue increasing.

(Swatch has 6 rows total, 5 increase rows, ending with 21 sts.)

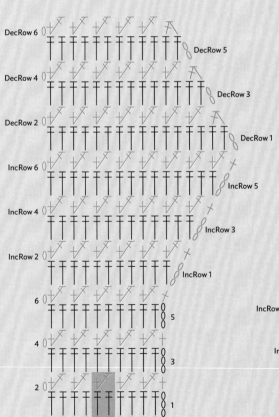

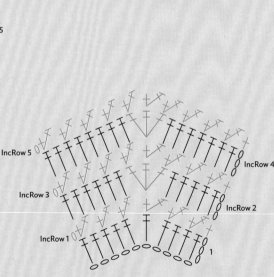

ANGLED BLOCKS

Angled patterns present a pleasing alternative to the usual rectangular grid of many stitch patterns. The angle is created by having blocks of three double crochet stitches worked into the turning chain of a block in the row below.

NUMBER OF STITCHES IN PATTERN REPEAT	**NUMBER OF ROWS IN PATTERN REPEAT**
6	2
MULTIPLE	**REVERSIBLE**
7 + 8	

BASIC PATTERN

(For swatch, ch 29.)

ROW 1: 2 dc in 4th ch from hook (3 sk ch count as dc), *sk next 3 ch, sc in next ch**, ch 2, dc in next 3 ch, rep from * across, ending last rep at **, turn.
(Swatch has 3½ blocks.)

ROW 2: Ch 3, 2 dc in first sc, *sk next 3 dc, sc in top of next ch-2, ch 2, 3 dc in same ch-2 sp, rep from * across, sc in tch, turn.
Rep row 2 for patt.
(Swatch has 6 rows in patt.)

Edge Shaping

One peculiarity of this stitch is the partial pattern repeat that begins each row. It serves to fill in space at the end of the row so that the side edges are flat, but results in a pattern that is not symmetrical. For purposes of shaping, we bring this partial pattern repeat to full size with the use of extra chains. Shaping can begin on any row, but if shaping on both sides, the second side must start on the following row. The shaping is at the rate of ½ patt rep per row.

INCREASING

IncRow 1: Ch 5, dc in 3rd ch, dc in next 2 ch, continue in patt across.

IncRow 2: Work in patt to tch, leave tch unworked, turn.
Rep IncRows 1 and 2 to continue increasing.
(Swatch has 4 increase rows, ending with 5½ blocks.)

DECREASING

DecRow 1: Ch 1, sk first dc, sl st in next 2 dc, [no ch 1], sc in top of next ch-2, ch 2, 3 dc in same ch-2 sp, continue in patt across.

DecRow 2: Work in patt across.

DecRow 3: Ch 1, sk first sc, sl st in next 3 dc, sc in next ch-2 sp, ch 2, 3 dc in same ch-2 sp, continue in patt across.
Rep DecRows 2 and 3 to continue decreasing.
(Swatch has 4 decrease rows, ending with 3½ blocks, and last row to flatten top edge.)

To make work flat at top, work last row as follows: Ch 3, 2 dc in first sc, sk next 3 dc, *(sc, hdc, 2 dc) in next ch-2 sp, rep from * across, sc in tch.

If your last row is a decrease row, work as follows: Ch 1, sk first sc, sl st in next 3 dc, *(sc, hdc, 2 dc) in next ch-2 sp, rep from * across, sc in tch.

Internal Shaping

Because stitches don't align on a vertical axis and due to the asymmetry of the pattern, this stitch is not suitable for internal shaping.

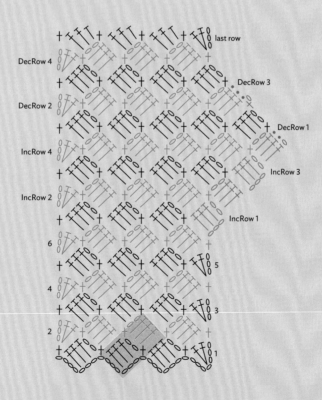

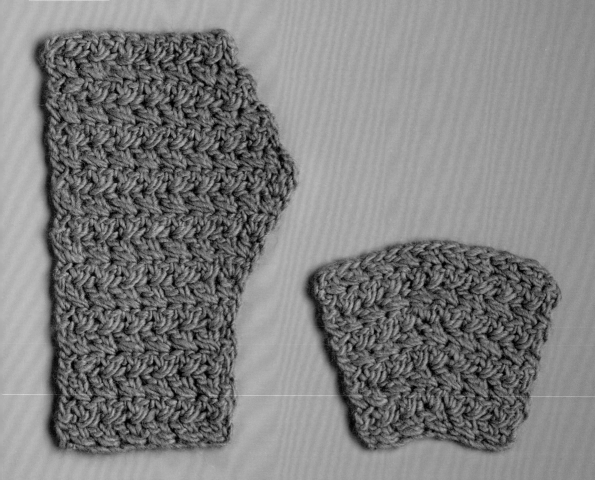

CROSSED SC/DC

The attractive texture in this stitch is caused by crossing a taller stitch over a shorter one. To match the height of these crossed stitches, half double crochet stitches are used at both ends of the row.

NUMBER OF STITCHES IN PATTERN REPEAT

2

MULTIPLE

2 + 3

NUMBER OF ROWS IN PATTERN REPEAT

1

REVERSIBLE

BASIC PATTERN

(For swatch, ch 15.)
ROW 1: Sc in 4th ch from hook, dc in 3rd ch from hook (2 sk ch count as hdc), *sk next ch, sc in next ch, dc in sk ch, rep from * across, hdc in last ch, turn.
(Swatch has 6 patt reps, 2 hdc.)
ROW 2: Ch 2 (counts as hdc throughout), *sk next dc, sc in next sc, dc in sk dc, rep from * across, hdc in tch, turn.
Rep row 2 for patt.
(Swatch has 6 rows in patt.)

Edge Shaping

The patt rep consists of 2 sts—the sc/dc pair that cross each other. Shaping is at the rate of 1 st per row and can begin on any row. Hdc sts are used as filler where necessary.

INCREASING

IncRow 1: Ch 2, hdc in first hdc, sk next dc, sc in next sc, dc in sk dc, continue in patt across.
IncRow 2: Work in patt across to last 2 hdc, 2 hdc in next hdc, hdc in tch, turn.
IncRow 3: Ch 2, hdc in first hdc, sk next hdc, sc in next hdc, dc in sk hdc, continue in patt across.
Rep IncRows 2 and 3 to continue increasing.
(Swatch has 6 increase rows, ending with 8 patt reps, 4 hdc.)

DECREASING

DecRow 1: Ch 2, sk next hdc, hdc in next hdc, sk next dc, sc in next sc, dc in sk dc, continue in patt across.
DecRow 2: Work in patt to last 2 hdc, hdc in next hdc, sk tch, turn.
DecRow 3: Ch 2, hdc2tog over (dc, sc), sk next dc, sc in next sc, dc in sk dc, continue in patt across.
Rep DecRows 2 and 3 to continue decreasing.
(Swatch has 6 decrease rows, ending with 6 patt reps, 2 hdc.)

Internal Shaping

It's not possible to cross stitches when both are worked into the same st; therefore (sc, dc) are worked at increase points. Increases are made every other row, for an increase rate of 1 patt rep (an sc/dc pair) every other row.
(For swatch, ch 13. Work row 1 of patt. 5 patt reps, 2 hdc.)
Place marker in dc of center sc/dc pair.

IncRow 1: Work in patt to marked dc, (sc, dc) in marked dc, (sc, dc) in next sc, move marker to dc just made, continue in patt across.
IncRow 2: Work in patt across. Move marker to dc made in marked dc.
IncRow 3: Work in patt to marked dc, sc in marked dc, dc in sc before marker (already worked into), sk marked dc (already worked into), sc in next sc, dc in sk dc, continue in patt across.
IncRow 4: Work in patt across. Move marker to dc of center sc/dc pair.
Rep IncRows 1–4 to continue increasing.
(Swatch has 9 rows total, 8 increase rows, ending with 9 patt reps, 2 hdc.)

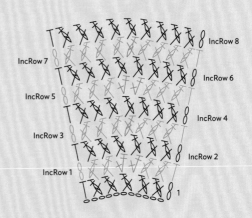

MARGUERITE STITCH

Also known as Star stitches, the Marguerite is a loop stitch, meaning that loops are picked up in several places and drawn together. Marguerites can be done in several ways but always have an alternating row of plain stitches to keep the Marguerites facing the right side.

NUMBER OF STITCHES IN PATTERN REPEAT	NUMBER OF ROWS IN PATTERN REPEAT
2	2
MULTIPLE	**NOT REVERSIBLE**
2 + 3	

NOTES

On Marguerite rows, working into the back bump of starting chains keeps the edge of the work flatter. Note that unlike working into top loops, when inserting into the back bump it is possible to work into the first chain from the hook. On row 1, the first 2 loops are drawn up in the back bump, but the remaining ones in this row can be worked in whatever manner you prefer to work into a foundation chain.

SPECIAL TERMS AND STITCH

Eye: The small hole made after working 6 loops of Marguerite together and ch 1.

Leg: One of the 6 loops of a Marguerite st.

Marguerite: Working loosely throughout, draw up loop in eye just made, draw up back loop in last leg of Marguerite just made, draw up loop in same sc as last leg of Marguerite just made, draw up loop in next 2 sc, yo, draw through 6 loops, ch 1 to close. Counts as 2 sts.

BASIC PATTERN

(For swatch, ch 13.)

ROW 1: Draw up loop in back bump of 1st and 2nd ch from hook, draw up loop in next 3 ch, yo, draw through 6 loops on hook, ch 1 for eye (Marguerite made), *draw up loop in eye just made, draw up loop in last leg of Marguerite just made, draw up loop in same ch as last leg of Marguerite just made, draw up loop in next 2 ch, yo, draw through 6 loops on hook, ch 1, rep from * across, hdc in same ch as last leg of Marguerite just made, turn.

(Swatch has 5 Marguerites, 1 hdc.)

ROW 2: Ch 1, sc in first hdc, sc in first eye, *2 sc in next eye, rep from * across, sc in tch, turn.

ROW 3: Ch 2, draw up loop in back bump of 1st and 2nd ch, draw up loop in next 3 sc, yo, draw through 6 loops on hook, ch 1, work Marguerites across, hdc in same sc as last leg of Marguerite just made, turn.

Rep rows 2 and 3 for patt.

(Swatch has 5 rows in patt.)

Edge Shaping

Shaping Marguerites can be tricky, and it's easier to begin shaping on a sc row rather than a Marguerite row. Shaping is at the rate of 1 Marguerite every other row.

When shaping on the opposite edge, work as follows: 2 sc at the beginning of sc rows and 2 sc in first eye to allow an additional Marguerite to be worked at the end of the next row. To decrease at the opposite edge, work 1 sc in first hdc, 1 sc in the first eye, 1 sc in the next eye, then continue in patt on sc rows. Complete the decrease on the Marguerite row by working hdc2tog at the end of the row, working over the same stitch as last leg of previous Marguerite and the last stitch in the row.

INCREASING

IncRow 1: Work in row 2 of patt to tch, 2 sc in tch, turn.

IncRow 2: Ch 3, draw up loop in back bump of 1st, 2nd, and 3rd ch, draw up loop in first sc, draw up loop in next sc, yo, draw through 6 loops, ch 1, (Marguerite made), continue in row 3 of patt across.

Rep IncRows 1 and 2 to continue increasing.

(Swatch has 6 increase rows, ending with 8 Marguerites, 1 hdc.)

DECREASING

DecRow 1: Work in row 2 of patt to last eye, sc in last eye, sc in tch.

DecRow 2: Ch 2, draw up loop in back bump of 2nd ch from hook, draw up loop in first sc, draw up loop in next 3 sc, yo, draw through 6 loops, ch 1, (Marguerite made), continue in row 3 of patt across.

Rep DecRows 1 and 2 to continue decreasing.

(Swatch has 6 decrease rows, followed by 1 even row, ending with 5 Marguerites, 1 hdc.)

Internal Shaping

This stitch is not suitable for increasing around a center point. However, an increase can be placed on any sc row that is convenient. Every 2 sc added result in one extra Marguerite on the following row. The following sequence is one way of doing it, but the increase can be placed anywhere in the row.

(For swatch, ch 15. Work row 1 of patt. 13 sts: 6 Marguerites, 1 hdc.)

IncRow 1: Ch 1, sc in first hdc, sc in first eye, (2 sc in next eye, 3 sc in next eye) twice, 2 sc in last eye, sc in tch, turn.

IncRow 2: Work in row 3 of patt across.

IncRow 3: Ch 1, sc in first hdc, sc in first eye, 2 sc in next eye, 3 sc in next eye, (2 sc in next eye) twice, 3 sc in next eye, 2 sc in last eye, sc in tch, turn.

IncRow 4: Rep IncRow 2.

IncRow 5: Ch 1, sc in first hdc, sc in first eye, [(2 sc in next eye) twice, 3 sc in next eye] twice, 2 sc in last eye, sc in tch, turn.

IncRow 6: Rep IncRow 2.

To continue increasing, place two 3-sc groups in a row for every additional Marguerite.

(Swatch has 7 rows total, 6 increase rows, ending with 9 Marguerites, 1 hdc.)

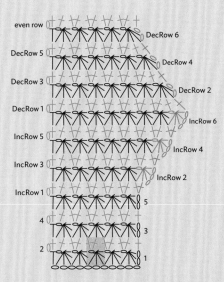

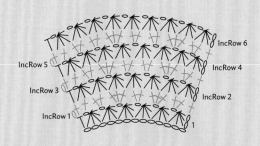

LOOP STITCH VARIATION

This loop stitch is far easier than Marguerites. In fact, it's the same as working a single crochet and half double crochet stitch together. It consists of only two loops, where one loop is preceded by a yarnover. This causes the resulting Loop Stitch to tilt and creates a nice zigzag vertical line.

NUMBER OF STITCHES IN PATTERN REPEAT

2

NUMBER OF ROWS IN PATTERN REPEAT

1

MULTIPLE

2 + 1

NOT REVERSIBLE

SPECIAL STITCH

Loop Stitch (LS): Draw up loop in first designated st, yo, draw up loop in next designated st, yo, draw through 4 loops on hook.

BASIC PATTERN

(For swatch, ch 13.)

ROW 1: Draw up loop in 3rd ch from hook (2 sk ch do not count as st), yo, draw up loop in next ch, yo, draw through 4 loops on hook (first LS made), *ch 1, LS over next 2 ch, rep from * across to last st, ch 1, sc in last ch, turn.
(Swatch has 5 patt reps, 1 sc.)

ROW 2: Ch 2 (does not count as st throughout), LS over first sc and next ch-1 sp, *ch 1, LS over next LS and next ch-1 sp, rep from * across, ch 1, sk last LS, sc in top ch of 2 sk ch, turn.

ROW 3: Ch 2, LS over first sc and next ch-1 sp, *ch 1, LS over next LS and next ch-1 sp, rep from * across, ch 1, sk last LS, sc in tch, turn.

Rep row 3 for patt.
(Swatch has 6 rows in patt.)

Edge Shaping

Shaping is at the rate of 1 st per row and can start on any row of this one-row pattern.

To shape at the opposite edge, make first increase at the end of the row by placing an sc into the skipped stitch before the turning chain. IncRow 2 begins on the next row as follows:

Ch 1, draw up loop in first sc, yo, draw up loop in next sc, yo, and draw through 4 loops on hook, ch 1, draw up loop in same sc, yo, draw up loop in next ch-1 sp, yo, and draw through 4 loops on hook, then continue in pattern.

INCREASING

IncRow 1: Ch 2, sc in first sc, LS over first sc and next ch-1 sp, ch 1, continue in patt across.

IncRow 2: Work in patt to last LS, LS over last LS and last sc, ch 1, sc in top of tch, turn.

Rep IncRows 1 and 2 to continue increasing.
(Swatch has 6 increase rows, ending with 8 patt reps, 1 sc.)

DECREASING

DecRow 1: Ch 3 (counts as st), sk first (sc, ch 1), LS over next LS and next ch-1 sp, ch 1, continue in patt across.

DecRow 2: Work in patt across.

Rep DecRows 1 and 2 to continue decreasing.
(Swatch has 6 decrease rows, ending with 5 patt reps, 1 sc.)

Internal Shaping

All the strategies attempted distorted the stitch pattern, primarily because the angles going from row to row were lost.

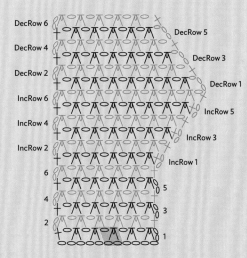

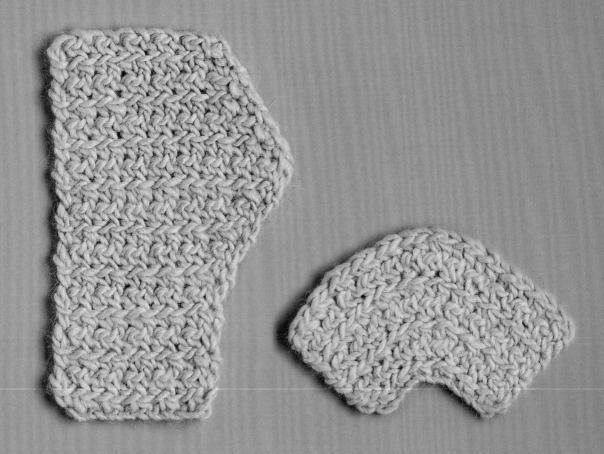

SQUISHED SINGLES

Here's another kind of loop stitch, and this one is exactly the same as working together two single crochet stitches, inserting the hook in the front loop only. The "squished together" singles count as one stitch. The fabric is supple with a very interesting surface.

NUMBER OF STITCHES IN PATTERN REPEAT	NUMBER OF ROWS IN PATTERN REPEAT
2	1
MULTIPLE	REVERSIBLE
2 + 2	

NOTES

Always work the last sc in the row under both loops.

The patt rep consists of 1 Loop Stitch and ch 1.

SPECIAL STITCHES

Single crochet in front loop (FLsc): Insert hook in FL of st, yo and draw up loop, yo, draw through 2 loops.

Loop Stitch (LS): Draw up FL in first designated st, draw up FL in next designated ch-sp, yo, draw through 3 loops on hook.

BASIC PATTERN

(For swatch, ch 12.)

ROW 1: Draw up loop in 2nd and 3rd ch from hook, yo, draw through 3 loops (first LS made), ch 1, *draw up loop in next 2 ch, yo, draw through 3 loops, ch 1, rep from * across, sc in last ch, turn.

(Swatch has 5 patt reps, 1 sc.)

ROW 2: Ch 1, LS over first sc and next ch-1 sp, ch 1, *LS over next st and next ch-1 sp, ch 1, rep from * across, sc in last st, turn.

Rep row 2 for patt.

(Swatch has 6 rows in patt.)

Edge Shaping

To increase we add a LS and 1 ch at the start of a row, then work even in pattern on the next row. For decreasing, the method is slightly different, with a 1-st decrease every row in order to maintain a slant on the shaped edge.

INCREASING

IncRow 1: Ch 1, FLsc in first sc, ch 1, LS over same sc and next ch-1 sp, ch 1, LS over next st and next ch-1 sp, continue in patt across.

IncRow 2: Work in patt across, sc in last sc, turn.

Rep IncRows 1 and 2 to continue increasing.

(Swatch has 6 increase rows, ending with 8 patt reps, 1 sc.)

DECREASING

DecRow 1: Ch 1, sk first sc, sc in next ch-1 sp, LS over next st and next ch-1 sp, ch 1, continue in patt across.

DecRow 2: Work in patt to last 2 sts, sc2tog working in both loops, turn.

Rep DecRows 1 and 2 to continue decreasing.

(Swatch has 6 decrease rows, ending with 5 patt reps, 1 sc2tog.)

Internal Shaping

Center increases are worked in groups of 3 every other row, yielding 2 LS per increase row.

(For swatch, ch 14. Work row 1 of patt. 13 sts: 6 patt reps, 1 sc.)

Place marker in center st (an LS).

IncRow 1: Work in patt to marked st, *LS inserting hook in same ch-1 as last LS worked and in first st of next LS, ch 1, LS inserting hook in same st and in next ch-1 sp**, ch 1, rep from * to ** once, continue in patt across.

IncRow 2: Work in patt across, moving marker to LS worked over marked LS.

Rep IncRows 1 and 2 to continue increasing.

(Swatch has 7 rows total, ending with 12 patt reps, 1 sc.)

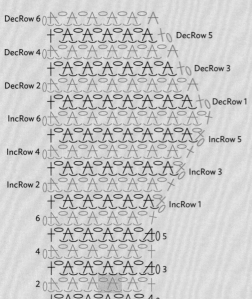

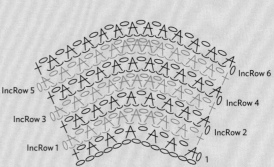

FORKED CLUSTERS

A Forked Cluster is a variation on working two double crochet stitches together that creates interesting texture. The pattern alternates a row of Forked Clusters with a row of single crochet.

NUMBER OF STITCHES IN PATTERN REPEAT	NUMBER OF ROWS IN PATTERN REPEAT
1	2
MULTIPLE	**REVERSIBLE**
1 + 4	

NOTES

For this stitch we insert the hook in 2 adjacent stitches, and we refer to these as 2 "legs" of the same stitch.

This pattern has a natural bias which can be countered with blocking.

SPECIAL STITCH

Forked Cluster (FC): Yo, insert hook in same sc as 2nd leg of last FC and draw up loop, yo, insert hook in next sc and draw up loop (5 loops on hook), (yo, draw through 3 loops) twice.

BASIC PATTERN

(For swatch, ch 14.)

ROW 1: Yo, insert hook in 4th ch from hook and draw up loop, yo, insert hook in next ch and draw up loop (5 loops on hook), (yo, draw through 3 loops) twice (first FC made), *yo, insert hook in same ch as 2nd leg of last FC and draw up loop, yo, insert hook in next ch and draw up loop, (yo, draw through 3 loops) twice, rep from * across, placing last leg in last ch, dc in same ch, turn.
(Swatch has 10 FC, 1 dc.)

ROW 2: Ch 1, sc in first dc, sc in each FC across, leave tch unworked, turn.

ROW 3: Ch 3 (does not count as st throughout), FC over 1st and 2nd sc, FC across placing last leg in last sc, dc in same sc, turn.

Rep rows 2 and 3 for patt.
(Swatch has 5 rows in patt.)

Edge Shaping

Shaping is at the rate of 1 FC every other row. It's easiest to shape on sc rows. Shaping can begin on any even-numbered row. While the ch 3 that begins FC rows does *not* count as a stitch, we will work into it when increasing or decreasing. Note that the dc that ends FC rows *does* count as a stitch.

INCREASING

IncRow 1: Work in row 2 of patt to tch, sc in tch, turn.
IncRow 2: Work in row 3 of patt across.
Rep rows 1 and 2 to continue increasing.
(Swatch has 8 increase rows, ending with 14 FC, 1 dc.)

DECREASING

DecRow 1: Work in row 2 of patt to last 2 FC, sc2tog over 2 FC, turn.
DecRow 2: Work in row 3 of patt across.
Rep DecRows 1 and 2 to continue decreasing.
(Swatch has 8 decrease rows, ending with 10 FC, 1 dc, followed by 1 row worked even.)

Internal Shaping

This stitch lends itself to internal increases placed at regular intervals in a row, not at a center point, and only on sc rows. Here we increase by 3 sts every other row.
(For swatch, ch 14. Work row 1 of patt. 11 sts.)

IncRow 1: Ch 1, sc in first dc, sc in next FC, *2 sc in next FC, sc in next 2 FC, rep from * across, leave tch unworked, turn.
IncRow 2: Work in row 3 of patt across.
IncRow 3: Ch 1, sc in first dc, sc in next 2 FC, *2 sc in next FC**, sc in next 3 FC, rep from * across, ending last rep at **, sc in each FC across, leave tch unworked, turn.
IncRow 4: Rep IncRow 2.
IncRow 5: Ch 1, sc in first dc, sc in next 3 FC, *2 sc in next FC**, sc in next 4 FC, rep from * ending last rep at **, sc in each FC across, leave tch unworked, turn.
IncRow 6: Rep IncRow 2.
To continue increasing 3 sts every other row, add 1 more stitch between increases on every sc row. For example, IncRow 5 has increases every 5th stitch, therefore in IncRow 7 work an increase every 6th stitch, on IncRow 9 work an increase every 7th stitch, and so on.
(Swatch has 7 rows total, 6 increase rows, ending with 19 FC, 1 dc.)

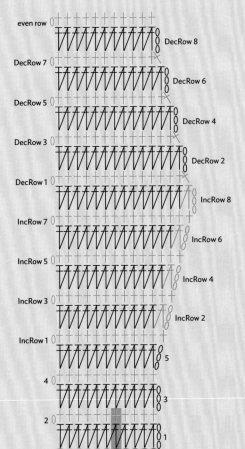

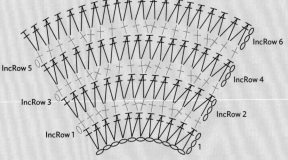

LINKED DOUBLE TREBLES

Linked stitches are unique in how they are made and how they look. They can be viewed as a blend of Tunisian and regular crochet. In this pattern, rows of linked double trebles are alternated with rows of half double crochet stitches.

NUMBER OF STITCHES IN PATTERN REPEAT	NUMBER OF ROWS IN PATTERN REPEAT
1	2
MULTIPLE	**NOT REVERSIBLE**
1 + 4	

NOTES
Linked stitches are connected to one another along the posts. To work them, one turns the work 90 degrees to draw up bars that form over the post of the previous stitch. You will see these vertical bars as you work. For linked double trebles, you will have 5 loops on your hook, which are then worked off as in Tunisian crochet.

Mark the first stitch of each hdc row, as it is difficult to see when working the following row.

For the first Linked Double Treble (Ldtr) in a row, work into the back bump of chains. This makes for a flatter starting edge.

Work the last Ldtr in a row tightly to give it a more finished appearance.

The last stitch in a row is worked into the top of the turning chain, to create a straight edge.

This pattern requires blocking to counter bias.

SPECIAL STITCHES
Beginning Linked Double Treble (Beg Ldtr): Ch 4, draw up loop in bump of 2nd, 3rd, and 4th ch and in first hdc, (yo, draw through 2 loops on hook) 4 times.

Linked Double Treble (Ldtr): Draw up loop in 3 vertical bars of prev st, draw up loop in top of next st in row below (5 loops on hook), (yo, draw through 2 loops) 4 times.

BASIC PATTERN

(For swatch, ch 16.)

ROW 1: Draw up loop in bump of 2nd ch from hook, draw up loop in bump of next 3 ch, (yo, draw through 2 loops on hook) 4 times (Ldtr made); *draw up loop in 3 vertical bars of prev st, draw up loop in next ch of fdn ch, (yo, draw through 2 loops on hook) 4 times, rep from * across, turn.
(Swatch has 12 sts.)

ROW 2: Ch 1 (does not count as st throughout), FLhdc in first and in each Ldtr across to last st, sk last Ldtr, FLhdc in tch, turn.

ROW 3: Beg Ldtr, Ldtr across, work last st tightly, turn.
Rep rows 2 and 3 for patt, ending with even numbered row.
(Swatch has 4 rows in patt.)

Edge Shaping

Shaping is at the rate of 1 st per row and begins at the end of a Ldtr row. To shape at the starting edge of a Ldtr row, work the first stitch as usual, then work a 2nd stitch, pulling up the last loop again in the first stitch.

INCREASING

IncRow 1: Work in row 3 of patt to last st, 2 Ldtr in last hdc, turn.

IncRow 2: Ch 1, 2 FLhdc in first Ldtr, continue in row 2 of patt across.
Rep IncRows 1 and 2 to continue increasing.
(Swatch has 4 increase rows, ending with 16 sts.)

DECREASING

DecRow 1: Work in row 3 of patt to last 2 hdc, draw up loop in 3 vertical bars of prev st, sk next hdc, draw up last loop in last hdc, (yo, draw through 2 loops on hook) 4 times.

DecRow 2: Ch 1, sk first Ldtr, work in row 2 of patt across.
Rep DecRows 1 and 2 to continue decreasing.
(Swatch has 4 decrease rows, ending with 12 sts.)

Internal Shaping

Two stitches are added each row. To work 3 Ldtr in the same st, work 3 sts drawing up the last loop in the same st 3 times.
(For swatch, ch 17. Work row 1 of patt. 13 sts.)
Place marker in center Ldtr.

IncRow 1: Work in row 2 of patt to marked Ldtr, 3 FLhdc in marked st, move marker to center hdc just made, continue in patt across.

IncRow 2: Work in row 3 of patt to marked hdc, 3 Ldtr in marked hdc, move marker to center Ldtr just made, continue in patt across.
Rep IncRows 1 and 2 to continue increasing.
(Swatch has 6 rows total, 5 increase rows, ending with 23 sts.)

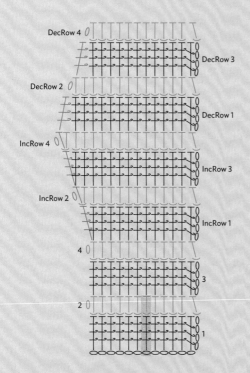

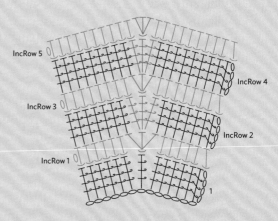

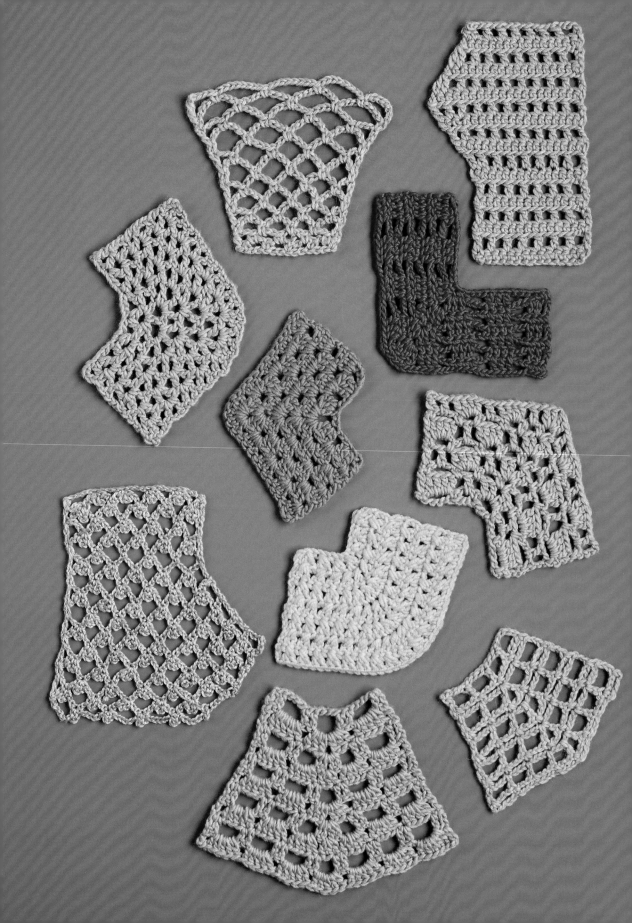

CHAPTER TWO

MESH, FILET, AND EASY LACES

Some of the first crochet stitch patterns developed in the early nineteenth century were simple laces. For example, Traditional Mesh can be found in the very first European printed pattern book (*Penelope*, Dutch needlework magazine, 1824). Filet work also evolved in the nineteenth century as a technique for creating pictures with stitches against a background of plain stitches, with the plain stitches often being double crochet stitches separated by one or two chains. From these simple beginnings, a huge collection of lace stitch patterns developed.

This chapter focuses on simpler openwork stitches. They are plentiful and inviting, not only because they are relatively easy but also because they create clean-looking designs and lend drape to fabric. While the full-blown complex laces of the later chapters are beautiful, they may suggest a "period" feel that simpler laces avoid. Many of the stitches in this chapter will make gorgeous garments with simple lines that appeal to the modern eye.

The same basic elements appear in many of these stitches, including chain spaces anchored by single crochet stitches, blocks of three or four double crochet stitches, and V-stitches. I chose quite a few V-stitches because their angles offer a welcome departure from the grid seen so often in crochet. It's fascinating how these same few elements can be cleverly combined to create an array of interesting and diverse designs.

An important factor to notice in any lace stitch pattern is the degree of openness. Some have small holes in the fabric, others much larger ones, and you can find every degree between extremes. Our swatches show a small sample of each stitch, but do consider how an entire fabric of any stitch will look and behave. Fabric with large holes is very fluid, but can be impractical if, for example, it's at the bottom of a sleeve. The openness of the stitch can also dictate your choice of yarn, because the heavier the weight of the yarn used, the larger will be the holes in your fabric. So for the most open patterns, use thinner yarns, lace or fingering weight being best for such stitches. And if you want to work with worsted weight yarns, choose stitches where the holes are small.

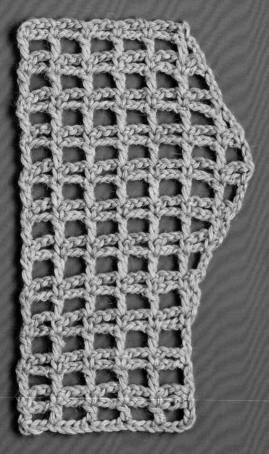

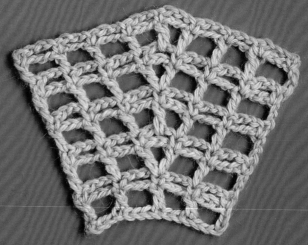

STRING NETWORK

This attractive and easy openwork pattern alternates rows of single crochet and double crochet stitches, always separated by three chains.

NUMBER OF STITCHES IN PATTERN REPEAT	NUMBER OF ROWS IN PATTERN REPEAT
4	2
MULTIPLE	REVERSIBLE
4 + 6	

BASIC PATTERN

(For swatch, ch 26.)

ROW 1: Dc in 10th ch from hook (9 sk ch count as 3 fnd ch, 1 dc, 3 ch of row 1), *ch 3, sk next 3 ch, dc in next ch, rep from * across, turn.
(Swatch has 5 patt reps, 1 dc.)

ROW 2: Ch 1, sc in first dc, *ch 3, sc in next dc, rep from * across, ch 3, sc in 6th ch of beginning ch-9, turn.

ROW 3: Ch 6 (counts as dc, ch 3 throughout), *dc in next sc, ch 3, rep from * across, dc in last sc, turn.

ROW 4: Ch 1, sc in first dc, *ch 3, sc in next dc, rep from * across, placing last sc in 3rd ch of tch, turn.

Rep rows 3 and 4 for patt.
(Swatch has 6 rows in patt.)

Edge Shaping

The simple grid-like lines of this stitch pattern make it easy to shape. Shaping is at the rate of a full patt rep over 4 rows.

INCREASING

IncRow 1: Ch 3 (counts as dc), dc in first sc, ch 3, dc in next sc, continue in row 3 of patt across.

IncRow 2: Work in row 4 of patt to tch, ch 1, sc in tch, turn.

IncRow 3: Ch 5 (counts as dc, ch 2 throughout), dc in next sc, continue in row 3 of patt across.

IncRow 4: Work in row 4 of patt to tch, ch 3, sk 2 ch, sc in 3rd ch of tch, turn.

Rep IncRows 1–4 to continue increasing.

(Swatch has 8 increase rows, ending with 7 patt reps, 1 dc.)

DECREASING

DecRow 1: Ch 5, sk first sc, dc in next sc, continue in row 3 of patt across.

DecRow 2: Work in row 4 of patt to tch, ch 2, sc in 3rd ch of tch

DecRow 3: Ch 3 (counts as dc), dc in next sc, continue in row 3 of patt across.

DecRow 4: Work in row 4 of patt to last 2 sts, sk next dc, sc in tch, turn.

Rep DecRows 1–4 to continue decreasing.

(Swatch has 8 decrease rows, ending with 5 patt reps, 1 sc.)

Internal Shaping

This swatch has increases on dc rows only. It uses two strategies for increasing: on IncRows 1 and 5, a wide V-st (dc, ch 3, dc) at center adds 1 patt rep, and on IncRow 3 a single dc in the center ch-3 also adds 1 patt rep.

(For swatch, ch 18. Work rows 1 and 2 of patt. 4 patt reps, 1 sc.)

Place marker in center sc of row.

IncRow 1: Work in row 3 of patt to marked sc, (dc, ch 3, dc) in marked sc, move marker to ch-3 sp just made, continue in patt across.

IncRow 2: Work in row 4 of patt across, moving marker up to ch-3 sp at center.

IncRow 3: Work in row 3 of patt to marked ch-3 sp, ch 3, dc in marked ch-3 sp, move marker to dc just made, ch 3, continue in patt across.

IncRow 4: Work in row 4 of patt across, moving marker up to center sc.

Rep IncRows 1–4 to continue increasing.

(Swatch has 10 rows total, 8 increase rows, ending with 8 patt reps, 1 sc.)

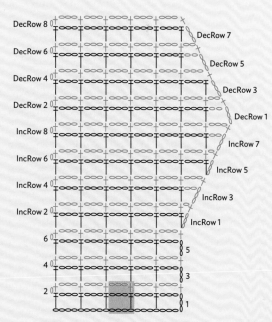

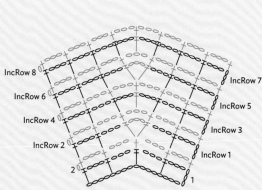

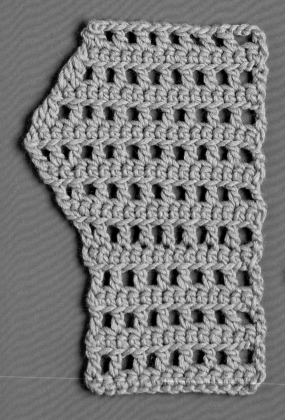

FRAMED FILET

This stitch pattern features rows of "double crochet filet," meaning double crochet stitches alternating with chain-one spaces across the row, with a second row of single crochet stitches worked in the front loop. This leaves the unworked back loop showing as a decorative element on the right side of the work.

NUMBER OF STITCHES IN PATTERN REPEAT

2

NUMBER OF ROWS IN PATTERN REPEAT

2

MULTIPLE

2 + 2

NOT REVERSIBLE

NOTES

For the last sc in the row, work under 2 top loops of the tch for a firm edge.

BASIC PATTERN

(For swatch, ch 16.)

ROW 1 (WS): Sc in 2nd ch from hook, sc in each ch across, turn.

(Swatch has 15 sts.)

ROW 2: Ch 4 (counts as dc, ch 1 throughout), * sk next sc, dc in next sc**, ch 1, rep from * across, ending last rep at **, turn.

ROW 3: Ch 1, FLsc in each dc and in each ch across to ch-4 tch, FLsc in next ch, sc in 3rd ch of tch, turn.

Rep rows 2 and 3 for patt.

(Swatch has 6 rows in patt.)

Edge Shaping

The rate of shaping is 1 st per row and begins on row 2. To begin on row 3, reverse IncRows 1 and 2 and DecRows 1 and 2.

INCREASING

IncRow 1: Ch 1, 2 FLsc in first dc, continue in row 3 of patt across.

IncRow 2: Work in row 2 of patt to last 2 sc, dc in next sc, ch 1, dc in last sc, turn.

Rep IncRows 1 and 2 to continue increasing.

(Swatch has 6 increase rows, ending with 21 sts.)

DECREASING

DecRow 1: Ch 1, sk first dc, FLsc in next ch-1 sp, continue in row 3 of patt across

DecRow 2: Work in row 2 of patt to last 2 sc, dc2tog, turn.

Rep DecRows 1 and 2 to continue decreasing.

(Swatch has 6 decrease rows, ending with 15 sts.)

Internal Shaping

2 sts are added on each row.

(For swatch, ch 16. Work row 1 of patt. 15 sts.)

Place marker in center sc.

IncRow 1: Work in row 2 of patt to marked st, (dc, ch 1, dc) in marked st, move marker to ch-1 sp just made, dc in next sc, continue in patt across.

IncRow 2: Work in row 3 of patt to marked ch-1 sp, 3 sc in marked ch-1 sp, move marker to center sc just made, continue in patt across.

Rep IncRows 1 and 2 to continue increasing.

(Swatch has 7 rows total, 6 increase rows, ending with 27 sts.)

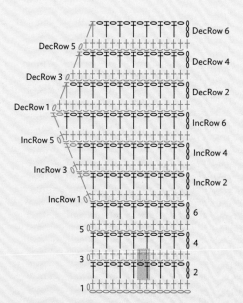

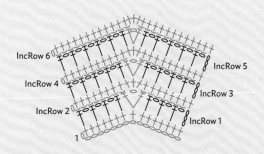

ZIGZAG MESH

Groups of 2 chains separate stitches of different heights—a single crochet and a double crochet—alternating across the row. This causes the chains to move up and down for the zigzag effect.

NUMBER OF STITCHES IN PATTERN REPEAT

6

MULTIPLE

4 + 2

NUMBER OF ROWS IN PATTERN REPEAT

2

REVERSIBLE

BASIC PATTERN

(For swatch, ch 18.)

ROW 1: Sc in 2nd ch from hook, *ch 2, sk next ch, dc in next ch, ch 2, sk next ch, sc in next ch, rep from * across, turn.
(Swatch has 4 patt reps, 1 sc.)

ROW 2: Ch 5 (counts as dc, ch 2), *sc in next dc, ch 2**, dc in next sc, ch 2, rep from * across, ending last rep at **, dc in last sc, turn.

ROW 3: Ch 1, sc in first dc, *ch 2, dc in next sc, ch 2, sc in next dc, rep from * across, placing last sc in 3rd ch of tch.
Rep rows 2 and 3 for patt.
(Swatch has 7 rows in patt.)

Edge Shaping

The most natural way to shape this stitch pattern is by increasing half a pattern repeat per row. The zigzag lines present an opportunity for shaping, with increases beginning on an even-numbered row, where the taller stitch is at the edge. Decreasing begins on an odd-numbered row.

INCREASING

IncRow 1: Ch 5 (counts as dc, ch 2), dc in first sc, ch 2, sc in next dc, continue in row 2 of patt across.

IncRow 2: Work in row 3 of patt to tch, ch 2, dc in 3rd ch of tch, ch 2, sc in same st, turn.
Rep IncRows 1 and 2 to continue increasing.
(Swatch has 6 increase rows followed by 1 even row, ending with 7 patt reps, 1 sc. Then one row is worked even before beginning decreases.)

DECREASING

DecRow 1: Work in row 3 of patt to last sc, ending with ch 2, dc2tog over (last sc, 3rd ch of tch), turn.

DecRow 2: Ch 3, dc in next sc (count as dc2tog), ch 2, sc in next dc, continue in row 2 of patt across.
Rep DecRows 1 and 2 to continue decreasing.
(Swatch has 6 decrease rows followed by 1 even row, ending with 4 patt reps, 1 sc.)

Internal Shaping

The rate of shaping is 1 full patt rep per row, except for IncRow1, which adds ½ patt rep.
(For swatch, ch 18. Work row 1 of patt. 4 patt reps, 1 sc.)
Place marker in center sc of row.

IncRow 1: Work in row 2 of patt to marked sc, ch 2, (dc, ch 2, dc) in marked sc, move marker to ch-2 sp just made, ch 2, continue in patt across.

IncRow 2: Work in row 3 of patt to marked ch-2 sp, ch 2, (dc, ch 2, dc) in marked ch-2 sp, ch 2, sc in next dc, continue in patt across.

IncRow 3: Work in row 2 of patt to marked ch-2 sp, ch 2, (dc, ch 2, dc) in marked ch-2 sp, move marker to ch-2 just made, ch 2, sc in next dc, continue in patt across.
Rep IncRows 2 and 3 to continue increasing.
To return to patt after increasing (as on last row of swatch): work in row 2 of patt to marked ch-2 sp, dc in marked ch-2 sp, continue in patt across.
(Swatch has 6 rows total, 4 of them increase rows, ending with 8 patt reps, 1 dc.)

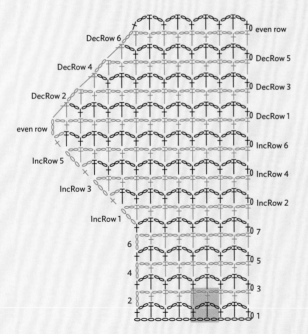

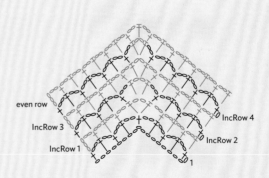

ZIGZAG BLOCKS

The blocks here are alternating groups of three single crochet and three double crochet, with three chains between them. The chains zigzag because of the different heights of stitches across the row.

NUMBER OF STITCHES IN PATTERN	NUMBER OF ROWS IN PATTERN
12	2
MULTIPLE	**REVERSIBLE**
12 + 4	

BASIC PATTERN

(For swatch, ch 28.)

ROW 1: Sc in 2nd ch from hook, sc in next 2 ch, *ch 3, sk 3 ch, dc in next 3 ch, ch 3, sk 3 ch, sc in next 3 ch, rep from * across, turn.

(Swatch has 2 patt reps, 3 sc.)

ROW 2: Ch 3 (counts as dc throughout), dc in next 2 sc, *ch 3, sc in next 3 dc, ch 3, dc in next 3 sc, rep from * across, turn.

ROW 3: Ch 1, sc in first 3 dc, *ch 3, dc in next 3 sc, ch 3, sc in next 3 dc, rep from * across, placing last sc in tch, turn.

Rep rows 2 and 3 for patt.

(Swatch has 6 rows in patt.)

Edge shaping

Because there are stitches of different heights and chain stitches running at various angles, shaping is handled a bit differently when increasing and decreasing to keep the edge at a nice slant. For increasing, we add 6 stitches over 4 rows by adding 2 stitches per row for 3 increase rows and working even on the 4th increase row. For decreasing, the 6-stitch decrease is spread over all 4 rows.

INCREASING

IncRow 1: Ch 4 (counts as dc, ch 1), sc in same dc, sc in next 2 dc, continue in row 3 of patt across.

IncRow 2: Work in row 2 of patt to tch, ch 3, sc in 3rd of tch, turn.

IncRow 3: Ch 3, 2 dc in same sc, ch 3, sc in next 3 dc, continue in row 3 of patt across.

IncRow 4: Work in row 2 of patt across.

IncRow 5: Ch 1, sc in first sc, ch 1, dc in same sc, dc in next 2 sc, continue in row 3 of patt across.

IncRow 6: Work in row 2 of patt to last 5 sts, sc in next 3 dc, ch 3, sk ch -1 sp, dc in last sc, turn.

IncRow 7: Ch 1, 3 sc in first dc, ch 3, continue in patt across.

IncRow 8: Rep row 2 of patt.

Rep IncRows 1–8 to continue increasing.
(Swatch has 8 increase rows, followed by one row worked even, ending with 3 patt reps, 3 sc.)

DECREASING

DecRow 1: Work in row 2 of patt to last 3 sts, dc3tog, turn.

DecRow 2: Ch 1, sc in first st, ch 2, dc in next 3 sc, continue in row 3 of patt across.

DecRow 3: Work in row 2 of patt to last ch-2 sp, sk ch-2 sp, dc in last sc, turn.

DecRow 4: Ch 1, dc in next 3 sc, continue in row 3 of patt across.

DecRow 5: Work in row 2 of patt to last 3 sts, sc3tog, turn.

DecRow 6: Ch 5 (counts as dc, ch 2), sc in next 3 dc, continue in row 3 of patt across.

DecRow 7: Work in row 2 of patt to tch, sc in 3rd ch of tch, turn.

DecRow 8: Ch 1, sk first sc, sc in next 3 dc, continue in row 3 of patt across, turn.

Rep DecRows 1–8 to continue decreasing.
(Swatch has 8 decrease rows, ending with 2 patt reps, 3 sc).

Internal Shaping

A full patt rep is added over 3 rows.
(For swatch, ch 28. Work row 1 of patt. 2 patt reps, 3 sc.)
Place marker in center sc of center 3-sc group.

IncRow 1: Work in row 2 of patt to marked sc, ending with dc in sc before marked sc, (2 dc, ch 1, 2 dc) in marked sc, move marker to ch-1 sp just made, dc in next sc, ch 3, sc in next 3 dc, continue in patt across.

IncRow 2: Work in row 3 of patt to marked ch-1 sp, ch 2, 3 dc in marked ch-1 sp, move marker to center dc of 3-dc group just made, ch 2, sc in next 3 dc, continue in patt across.

IncRow 3: Work in row 2 of patt across, moving marker up to sc worked into marked dc.

Rep IncRows 1–3 to continue increasing.
(Swatch has 7 rows total, 6 increase rows, ending with 4 patt reps, 3 sc.)

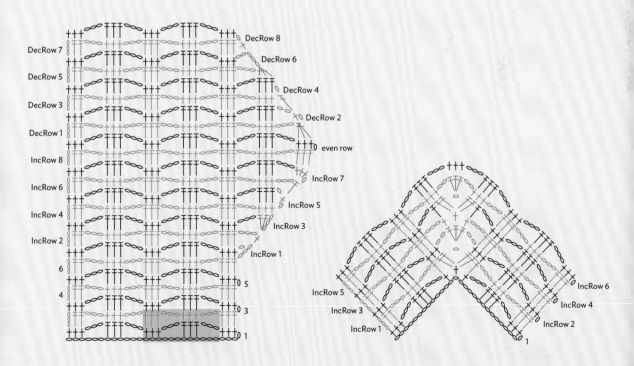

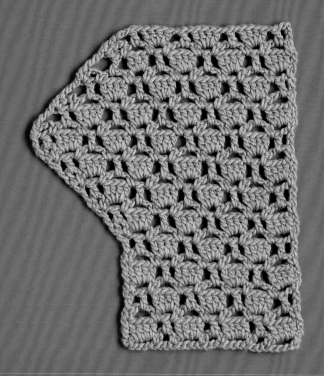

STAGGERED BLOCKS

This stitch alternates two elements, one being blocks of four double crochet stitches and the second consisting of (chain one, double crochet, chain one), which together make up the pattern repeat. Note that the two elements are not equal in width, since one has four stitches and the other three. The widths are "equalized" in the row alternating single crochet stitches with chain-three spaces.

NUMBER OF STITCHES IN PATTERN REPEAT	NUMBER OF ROWS IN PATTERN REPEAT
V	4
MULTIPLE	**REVERSIBLE**
7 + 6	

BASIC PATTERN

(For swatch, ch 27.)

ROW 1 (WS): Sc in 2nd ch from hook, *ch 3, sk next 3 ch, sc in next ch**, ch 3, sk next 2 ch, sc in next ch, rep from * across, ending last rep at **, turn.
(Swatch has 3½ patt reps.)

ROW 2: Ch 3 (counts as dc throughout), 4 dc in first ch-3 sp, *ch 1, dc in next ch-3 sp, ch 1, 4 dc in next ch-3 sp, rep from * across, dc in last sc, turn.

ROW 3: Ch 1, sc in first dc, *ch 3, sk next 4 dc**, sc in next ch-1 sp, ch 3, sk next dc, sc in next ch-1 sp, rep from * across, ending last rep at **, sc in tch, turn.

ROW 4: Ch 4 (counts as dc, ch 1 throughout), *dc in next ch-3 sp, ch 1**, 4 dc in next ch-3 sp, ch 1, rep from * across, ending last rep at **, dc in last sc, turn.

ROW 5: Ch 1, sc in first dc, *ch 3, sk next dc, sc in next ch-1 sp, ch 3, sk next 4 dc, sc in next ch-1 sp, rep from * across, ch 3, sc in 3rd ch of tch, turn.

Rep rows 2–5 for patt.
(Swatch has 8 rows in patt.)

Edge Shaping

Shaping at the rate of ½ patt rep every other row begins in row 5 of patt. Decreasing begins on row 2.

INCREASING

IncRow 1: Ch 1, (sc, ch 3, sc) in first dc, ch 3, sk next dc, sc in next ch-1 sp, continue in row 5 of patt across.

IncRow 2: Work in row 2 of patt placing dc in last ch-3 sp, dc in last sc, turn.

IncRow 3: Rep IncRow 1.

IncRow 4: Work in row 4 of patt placing dc in last ch-3 sp, dc in last sc, turn.

Rep IncRows 1–4 to continue increasing.

(Swatch has 9 rows total, 8 increase rows followed by one row worked even, ending with 5½ patt reps.)

DECREASING

DecRow 1: Work in row 2 of patt to last 2 ch-3 sps, ch 1, dc in next ch-3 sp, sk last ch-3 sp, tr in last sc, turn.

DecRow 2: Ch 1, sc in first tr, ch 3, sk next dc, sc in next ch-1 sp, ch 3, sk next 4 dc, continue in row 3 of patt across.

DecRow 3: Work in row 4 of patt to last 2 ch-3 sps, ch 1, dc in next ch-3 sp, sk last ch-3 sp, tr in last sc, turn.

DecRow 4: Rep DecRow 2.

Rep DecRows 1–4 to continue decreasing.

To return to patt work last DecRow 4 as follows:

Last DecRow 4: Work row 4 of patt to last ch-3 sp, ch 1, tr in last sc.

(Swatch has 7 decrease rows, ending with 3½ patt reps.)

Internal Shaping

The rate of shaping is 1 patt rep every 2 rows.

(For swatch, ch 20. Work row 1 of patt. 2½ patt reps.)

Place marker in center ch-3 sp.

IncRow 1: Work in row 2 of patt to marked ch-3 sp, ch 1, (2 dc, ch 1, 2 dc) in marked ch-3 sp, move marker to ch-1 sp just made, ch 1, dc in next ch-3 sp, continue in patt across.

IncRow 2: Work in row 3 of patt to marked ch-1 sp, ch 3, (sc, ch 3, sc) in marked ch-1 sp, move marker to ch-3 sp just made, ch 3, sk next 2 dc, sc in next ch-1 sp, continue in patt across.

IncRow 3: Work in row 4 of patt to marked ch-3 sp, ch 1, (2 dc, ch 1, 2 dc) in marked ch-3 sp, move marker to ch-1 sp just made, ch 1, dc in next ch-3 sp, continue in patt across.

IncRow 4: Work in row 5 of patt to marked ch-1 sp, ch 3, (sc, ch 3, sc) in marked ch-1 sp, move marker to ch-3 sp just made, ch 3, sk next 2 dc, sc in next ch-1 sp, continue in patt across.

Rep IncRows 1–4 to continue increasing.

To return to patt work last row as follows: Work in row 4 of patt to marked ch-3 sp, ch 1, 4 dc in marked ch-3 sp, ch 1, dc in next ch-1 sp, continue in patt across.

(Swatch has 8 rows total, 6 increase rows, ending with 5½ patt reps.)

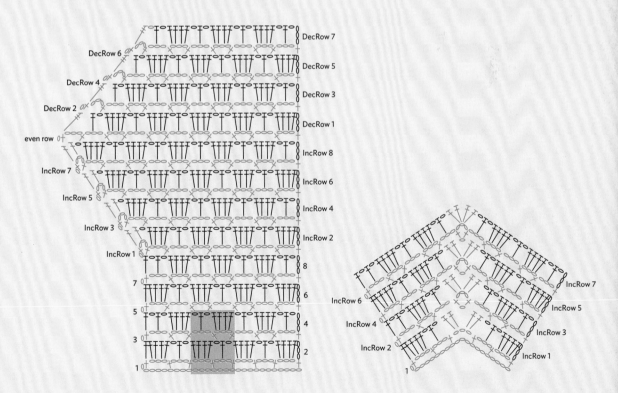

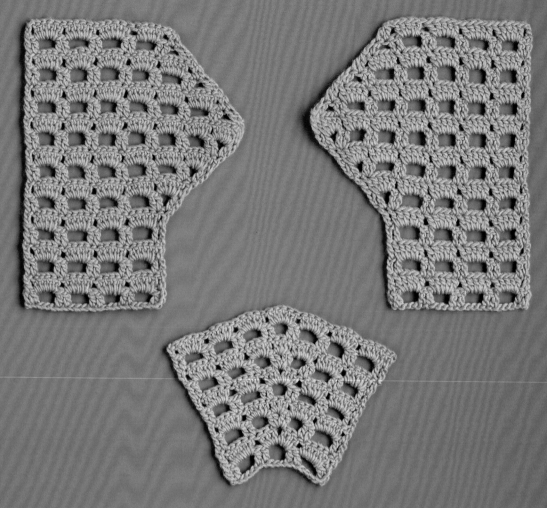

BOXED BLOCKS

The clean lines of this pattern give it modern appeal, and the large spaces lend drape to fabric. The blocks consist of five double crochet stitches worked into chain-three spaces.

NUMBER OF STITCHES IN PATTERN REPEAT

5

MULTIPLE

5 + 4

NUMBER OF ROWS IN PATTERN REPEAT

2

REVERSIBLE, 2 SIDES DIFFERENT

BASIC PATTERN

(For swatch, ch 24.)
ROW 1: Dc in 4th ch from hook (3 sk ch count as dc), *ch 3, sk 3 ch, dc in next 2 ch, rep from * across, turn.
(Swatch has 4 patt reps, 2 dc.)
ROW 2: Ch 3 (counts as dc throughout), sk next dc, *5 dc in next ch-3 sp, rep from * across to last 2 sts, sk next dc, dc in tch, turn.
ROW 3: Ch 3, dc in next dc, *ch 3, sk next 3 dc, dc in next 2 dc, rep from * across, placing last dc in tch, turn.
Rep rows 2 and 3 for patt.
(Swatch has 6 rows in patt.)

Edge Shaping

The rate of shaping is ½ patt per row, beginning on an odd-numbered row. Note that the (ch 2, dc) that begins DecRow 1 counts as dc2tog. At end of next row, work into the dc and leave ch-2 unworked.

INCREASING

IncRow 1: Ch 3, dc in first dc, ch 2, 2 dc in next dc, continue in row 3 of patt across.
IncRow 2: Work in row 2 of patt to last ch-2 sp, 5 dc in last ch-2 sp, sk next dc, dc in tch, turn.
Rep IncRows 1 and 2 to continue increasing.
(Swatch has 6 increase rows, ending with 7 patt reps, 2 dc.)

DECREASING

DecRow 1: Ch 2, dc in next dc (counts as dc2tog), sk next 3 dc, dc in next 2 dc, continue in row 3 of patt across.
DecRow 2: Work in row 2 of patt to last 3 sts (which are 2 dc, dc2tog), sk next dc, dc2tog (see note), turn.
Rep DecRows 1 and 2 to continue decreasing.
(Swatch has 6 decrease rows, ending with 4 patt reps, 2 dc.)

Internal Shaping

1 patt rep is added over 2 rows.
(For swatch, ch 19. Work row 1 of patt. 3 patt reps, 2 dc.)
Place marker in center ch-3 sp.
IncRow 1: Work in row 2 of patt to marked ch-3 sp, (3 dc, ch 1, 3 dc) in marked ch-3 sp, move marker to ch-1 sp just made, continue in patt across.
IncRow 2: Work in row 3 of patt to marked ch-1 sp, ch 3, sk next 2 dc, (2 dc, ch 1, 2 dc) in marked ch-1 sp, move marker to ch-1 sp just made, ch 3, sk next 2 dc, dc in next 2 dc, continue in patt across.
IncRow 3: Work in row 2 of patt to marked ch-1 sp, 3 dc in marked ch-1 sp, move marker to center dc of 3-dc group just made, continue in patt across.
IncRow 4: Work in row 3 of patt to marked dc, ch 3, sk marked dc, dc in next 2 dc, move marker to ch-3 sp just made, continue in patt across.
Rep IncRows 1–4 to continue increasing.
(Swatch has 10 rows total, 8 increase rows, ending with 7 patt reps, 2 dc.)

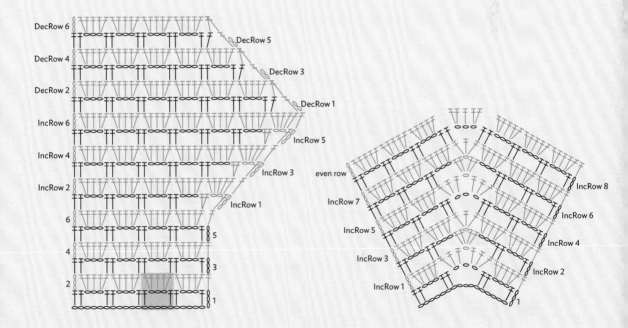

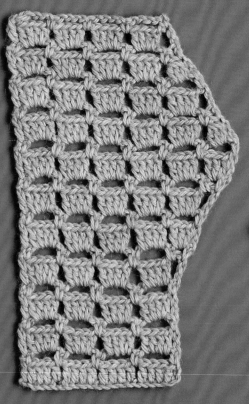

BRICKS

I've seen this simple stitch used in high
fashion pieces, perhaps because it is almost
solid but makes a very fluid fabric. It consists
of alternating rows of four–double crochet
groups and chain-four spaces anchored by
single crochet stitches.

**NUMBER OF STITCHES
IN PATTERN REPEAT**

5

MULTIPLE

5 + 3

**NUMBER OF ROWS
IN PATTERN REPEAT**

2

NOT REVERSIBLE

NOTE
Work row 1 more tightly than usual so it will match
subsequent rows.

94

BASIC PATTERN

(For swatch, ch 23.)

ROW 1: Dc in 4th ch from hook (3 sk ch count as dc), dc in next 3 ch, *ch 1, sk next ch, dc in next 4 ch, rep from * across, dc in last ch, turn.

(Swatch has 4 patt reps, 1 dc.)

ROW 2: Ch 1, sc in first dc, *ch 4, sc in next ch-1 sp, rep from * across, placing last sc in tch, turn.

ROW 3: Ch 3 (counts as dc throughout), *4 dc in next ch-4 sp**, ch 1, rep from * across, ending last rep at **, dc in tch, turn.

Rep rows 2 and 3 for patt.

(Swatch has 6 rows in patt.)

Edge Shaping

1 patt rep is added or subtracted over 4 rows.

INCREASING

IncRow 1: Ch 5 (counts as dc, ch 2), 4 dc in next ch-4 sp, continue in row 3 of patt across.

IncRow 2: Work in row 2 of patt across, placing sc in last ch-5 sp, ch 2, sc in 3rd ch of ch-5 tch, turn.

IncRow 3: Ch 3, 3 dc in first ch-2 sp, ch 1, 4 dc in next ch-4 sp, continue in row 3 of patt across.

IncRow 4: Work in row 2 of patt across placing last sc in tch.

Rep IncRows 1–4 to continue increasing.

(Swatch has 8 increase rows, ending with 6 patt reps, 1 sc.)

DECREASING

DecRow 1: Ch 3, dc3tog in first ch-4 sp, ch 1, 4 dc in next ch-4 sp, continue in row 3 of patt across.

DecRow 2: Work in row 2 of patt to last ch-1 sp, sc in last ch-1 sp, sk dc3tog, sc in tch, turn.

DecRow 3: Ch 4 (counts as dc, ch 1), sk next sc, 4 dc in next ch-4 sp, continue in row 3 of patt across.

DecRow 4: Work in row 2 of patt to tch, sk next ch, sc in 3rd ch of tch, turn.

Rep DecRows 1–4 to continue decreasing.

(Swatch has 8 decrease rows, ending with 4 patt reps, 1 sc.)

Internal Shaping

2 patt reps are gained over 4 rows.

(For swatch, ch 23. Work row 1 of patt. 4 patt reps, 1 dc.)

Place marker in center ch-1 sp.

IncRow 1: Work in row 2 of patt to marked ch-1 sp, ch 4, (sc, ch 1, sc) in marked ch-1 sp, move marker to ch-1 sp just made, ch 4, continue in patt across.

IncRow 2: Work in row 3 of patt to marked ch-1 sp, ch 1, (2 dc, ch 1, 2 dc) in marked ch-1 sp, move marker to ch-1 sp just made, ch 1, continue in patt across.

IncRow 3: Work in row 2 of patt to marked ch-1 sp, ch 4, sc in marked ch-1 sp, move marker to sc just made, ch 4, continue in patt across.

IncRow 4: Work in row 3 of patt across, placing marker in center ch-1 sp.

Rep IncRows 1–4 to continue increasing.

(Swatch has 10 rows total, 8 increase rows, ending with 8 patt reps, 1 sc.)

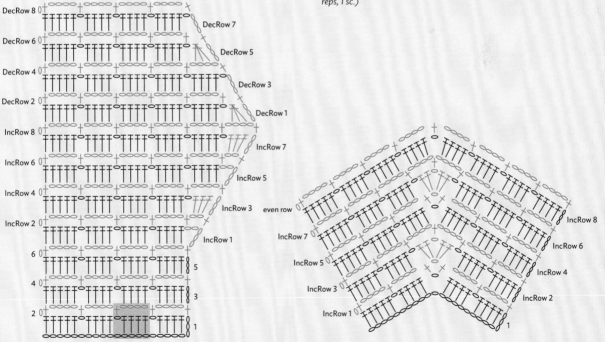

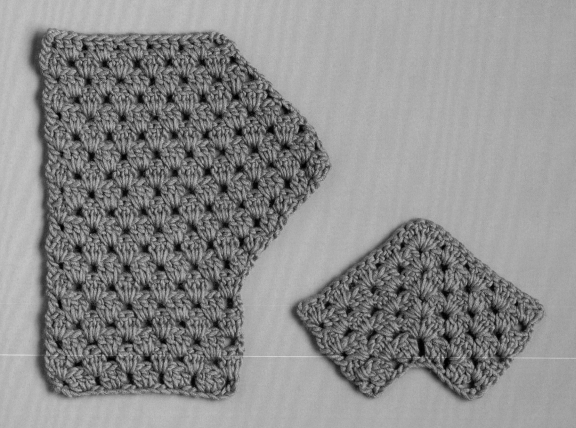

GRANNY STITCH

This stitch is familiar as the basis for Granny Squares, where three–double crochet blocks are worked in the round, with blocks worked between two blocks on subsequent rounds. It's perfectly nice when worked in rows as well.

NOTES

To work between stitches, do not work into the tops of a stitch but rather insert the hook between the posts of 2 designated stitches.

In instructions below, "last dc" refers to the last skipped dc in previous row.

Even-numbered rows have one more stitch than do odd-numbered rows.

NUMBER OF STITCHES IN PATTERN REPEAT	NUMBER OF ROWS IN PATTERN REPEAT
V	2
MULTIPLE	**REVERSIBLE**
3 + 5	

BASIC PATTERN

(For swatch, ch 20.)

ROW 1: Dc in 6th ch from hook (5 sk ch count as dc and 2 fnd ch), 2 dc in same ch, *sk 2 ch, 3 dc in next ch, rep from * across, dc in last ch, turn.

(Swatch has 17 dc.)

ROW 2: Ch 3 (counts as dc throughout), 2 dc between first dc and next dc, *sk next 3 dc, 3 dc between last dc and next dc, rep from * across, sk next 3 dc, 2 dc between last dc and tch, dc in tch, turn.

ROW 3: Ch 3, sk next 2 dc, *3 dc between last dc and next dc**, sk next 3 dc, rep from * across, ending last rep at **, sk next 2 dc, dc in tch, turn.

Rep rows 2 and 3 for patt.

(Swatch has 6 rows in patt.)

Edge Shaping

The oddity in this very simple stitch is that the number of stitches is not the same in each row, yet the edges are even. For this reason we give stitch counts for the total number of dc rather than patt reps. Shaping is easily done at the rate of 3 sts over 2 rows and can begin on any row. However, because of the discrepancy between stitch counts, decreasing must begin on an odd-numbered row.

INCREASING

IncRow 1: Ch 3, 2 dc in same dc, sk next 2 dc, 3 dc between last dc and next dc, continue in row 3 of patt across.

IncRow 2: Work in row 2 of patt to last 3 sts, sk next 2 dc, 3 dc in tch, turn.

Rep IncRows 1 and 2 to continue increasing.

(Swatch has 6 increase rows, ending with 27 dc, followed by 1 row worked even which has 26 sts.)

DECREASING

DecRow 1: Work in row 2 of patt to last 4 sts, sk next 3 dc, dc in tch, turn.

DecRow 2: Ch 3, sk next 3 dc, 3 dc between last dc and next dc, continue in row 3 of patt across.

Rep DecRows 1 and 2 to continue decreasing.

(Swatch has 6 decrease rows, ending with 17 sts.)

Internal Shaping

IncRow 1 adds 4 sts and IncRow 2 adds 2 sts, for a total of 6 sts over 2 rows.

(For swatch, ch 17. Work row 1 of patt. 14 dc.)

Place marker between 2 center 3-dc groups.

IncRow 1: Work in row 2 of patt to marker, 6 dc between last dc and next dc, move marker between 3rd and 4th dc just made, sk next 3 dc, 3 dc between last dc and next dc, continue in patt across.

IncRow 2: Work in row 3 of patt to marker, 6 dc between 3rd and 4th dc, move marker between 3rd and 4th dc just made, sk next 3 dc, continue in patt across.

Rep IncRows 1 and 2 to continue increasing.

(Swatch has 6 rows total, 5 increase rows, ending with 30 sts.)

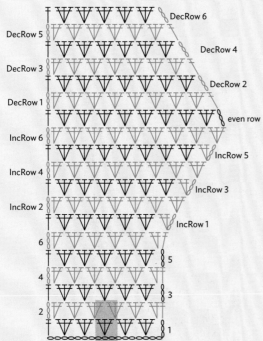

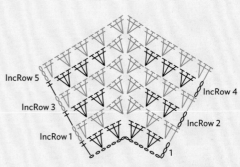

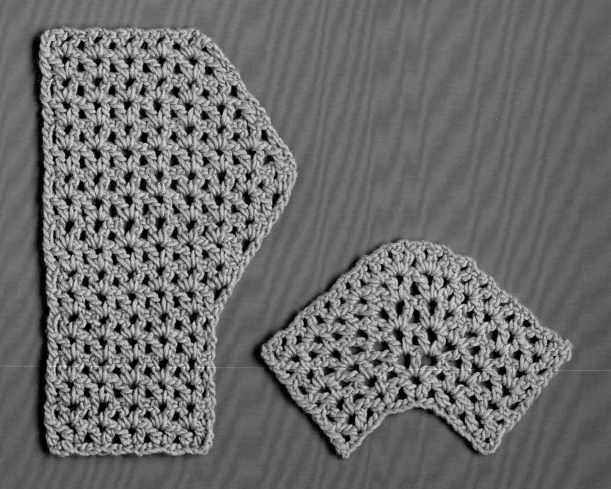

WIDE V-STITCH

Another simple lace that has the attractive feature of small and evenly spaced holes. The simple pattern repeat consists of two double crochet stitches separated by a chain-two space.

NOTE

Work the initial chains tightly so that they match subsequent rows in width.

SPECIAL STITCHES

V-stitch (V-st): (Dc, ch 2, dc) in designated sp.

Increase V-stitch (Inc V-st): (Dc, ch 2, dc, ch 2, dc) in designated st.

NUMBER OF STITCHES IN PATTERN REPEAT

4

MULTIPLE

4 + 5

NUMBER OF ROWS IN PATTERN REPEAT

1

REVERSIBLE

BASIC PATTERN

(For swatch, ch 28.)
ROW 1: V-st in 6th ch from hook (5 sk ch count as 2 fnd ch and dc), *sk 3 ch, V-st in next ch, rep from * to last 3 ch, dc in last ch, turn.
(Swatch has 5 V-sts, 2 dc.)
ROW 2: Ch 3, V-st in first ch-2 sp, V-st in each ch-2 sp across, dc in tch, turn.
Rep row 2 for patt.
(Swatch has 6 rows in patt.)

Edge Shaping

Shaping is at the rate of 1 patt rep over 2 rows.

INCREASING

IncRow 1: Ch 5 (counts as dc, ch 2), dc in first dc, V-st in next ch-2 sp, continue in patt across.
IncRow 2: Work in patt across to tch, V- st in ch-5 tch, dc in 3rd ch of tch, turn.
Rep IncRows 1 and 2 to continue increasing.
(Swatch has 6 increase rows, ending with 8 V-sts, 2 dc.)

DECREASING

DecRow 1: Ch 3, dc in first dc, sk first ch-2 sp, V-st in next ch-2 sp, continue in patt across.
DecRow 2: Work in patt across to last 2 dc, sk next dc, dc in tch, turn.
Rep DecRows 1 and 2 to continue decreasing.
(Swatch has 6 decrease rows, ending with 5 V-sts, 2 dc.)

Internal Shaping

The rate of increase is 1 V-st per row.
(For swatch, ch 28. Work row 1 of patt. 5 V-sts, 2 dc.)
Place marker in ch-2 sp of center V-st.
IncRow 1: Work in patt to marked sp, Inc V-st in marked sp, move marker to last ch-2 space made, continue in patt across.
IncRow 2: Work in patt to marked sp, (Inc V-st in next ch-2 sp) twice, move marker to last ch-2 sp made, continue in patt across.
IncRow 3: Work in patt to marked sp, V-st in marked ch-2 sp, (Inc V-st in next ch-2 sp) twice, move marker to last ch-2 sp made, continue in patt across.
Rep IncRow 3 to continue increasing.
(Swatch has 6 rows total, 5 increase rows, ending with 14 V-sts, 2 dc.)

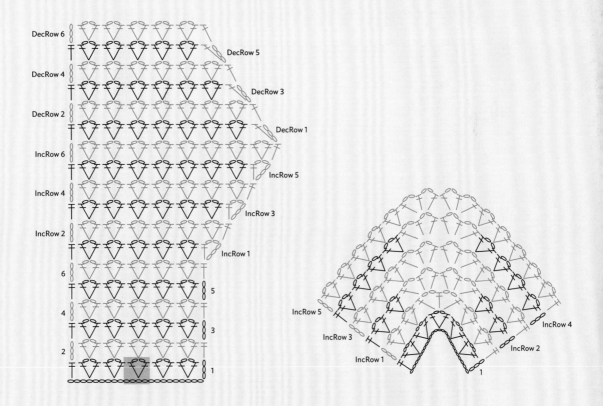

Vs AND BLOCKS

This stitch features alternating rows of V-stitches and three–double crochet blocks. The resulting design presents an energetic flow of curved, slanted, and vertical lines.

NUMBER OF STITCHES IN PATTERN REPEAT	NUMBER OF ROWS IN PATTERN REPEAT
V	4
MULTIPLE	REVERSIBLE
3 + 5	

NOTE

In odd-numbered rows a patt rep is a 3-dc block and 1 ch. In V-st (even-numbered) rows a patt rep is a V-st.

SPECIAL STITCHES

V-stitch (V-st): (Dc, ch 3, dc) in designated st.

Double V-stitch (Double V-st): (dc, ch 3, dc, ch 3, dc) in designated sp.

BASIC PATTERN

(For swatch, ch 17.)

ROW 1: 3 dc in 6th ch from hook (5 sk ch count as 1 fnd ch, dc, ch 1), *ch 1**, sk 2 ch, 3 dc in next ch, rep from * across, ending last rep at **, sk 1 ch, dc in last ch, turn.
(Swatch has 4 patt reps, 2 dc, 1 ch.)

ROW 2: Ch 5 (counts as dc, ch 2 of V-st), dc in first ch-1 sp, *sk next 3 dc, V-st in next ch-1 sp, rep from * across, (dc, ch 2) in ch-4 tch, sk 1 ch, dc in 3rd ch of tch, turn.

ROW 3: Ch 3, 2 dc in first ch-2 sp, ch 1, (3 dc, ch 1) in each ch-3 sp to ch-5 tch, 2 dc in ch-5 tch, dc in 3rd ch of tch, turn.

ROW 4: Ch 3, V-st in first ch-1 sp, V-st in each ch-1 sp across, dc in tch, turn.

ROW 5: Ch 4 (counts as dc, ch 1), (3 dc, ch 1) in each ch-3 sp across, dc in tch, turn.

Rep rows 2–5 for patt.
(Swatch has 6 rows in patt.)

Edge Shaping

Shaping is at the rate of 1 patt rep every 2 rows.

When decreasing, taller stitches are placed at the outside edge to cover the steep angle formed by the 3-st decrease.

On the last decrease row the 2nd dc of the last V-st is worked together with a dc made in the tch to finish the edge.

INCREASING

IncRow 1: Ch 3, 2 dc in first dc, ch 1, 3 dc in first ch-sp, continue in row 3 of patt across.

IncRow 2: Work in row 4 of patt to tch, V-st in tch, turn.

IncRow 3: Ch 3, 2 dc in first dc, ch 1, (3 dc, ch 1) in first ch-3 sp, continue in row 5 of patt across.

IncRow 4: Work in row 2 of patt to tch, V-st in tch, turn.

Rep IncRows 1–4 to continue increasing.

(Swatch has 5 increase rows, ending with 9 patt reps, followed by one row worked even.)

DECREASING

DecRow 1: Ch 4 (counts as tr throughout), dc3tog in next ch-3 sp, ch 1, (3 dc, ch 1) in next ch-3 sp, continue in row 5 of patt across.

DecRow 2: Work in row 2 of patt to last ch-1 sp, sk last ch-1 sp, tr in tch, turn.

DecRow 3: Ch 4, dc3tog in next ch-3 sp, ch 1, (3 dc, ch 1) in next ch-3 sp, continue in row 3 of patt across.

DecRow 4: Work in row 4 of patt to last ch-1 sp, sk last ch-1 sp, tr in tch, turn.

Rep DecRows 1–4 to continue decreasing.

To return to patt, work last DecRow2 as follows: Work in row 2 of patt to last ch-1 sp, (dc, ch 2) in last ch-1 sp, dc2tog over (same ch-1 sp, sk dc3tog, tch), turn.

(Swatch has 5 decrease rows, followed by 1 even row, ending with 5 patt reps.)

Internal Shaping

Internal increases in V-st rows are easier and more attractive than increases on blocks rows. IncRow 1 has an increase at the center, which adds a patt rep to the row. IncRows 3 and 5 have an increase at the center and also in the ch-1 sp on either side of the center, adding 3 patt reps on these rows.

(For swatch, ch 17. Work row 1 of patt. 4 patt reps, 2 dc, 1 ch.)

Place marker in center ch-1 sp.

IncRow 1: Work in row 2 of patt to marker, Double V-st in marked ch-1 sp, move marker to center dc just made, V-st in next ch-1 sp, continue in patt across.

IncRow 2: Work in row 3 of patt across. Move marker up to center ch-1 sp.

IncRow 3: Work in row 4 of patt to one ch-1 sp before marked ch-1 sp, Double V-st in next ch-1 sp, Double V-st in marked ch-1 sp, move marker to center dc just made, Double V-st in next ch-1 sp, V-st in next ch-1 sp, continue in patt across.

IncRow 4: Work in row 5 of patt across. Move marker up to center ch-1 sp.

IncRow 5: Work in row 2 of patt to one ch-1 sp before marked ch-1 sp, Double V-st in next ch-1 sp, Double V-st in marked ch-1 sp, move marker to center dc just made, Double V-st in next ch-1 sp, V-st in next ch-1 sp, continue in patt across.

Rep IncRows 2 and 3 or IncRows 4 and 5 as needed to continue increasing.

(Swatch has 7 rows total, 6 increase rows, ending with 12 patt reps.)

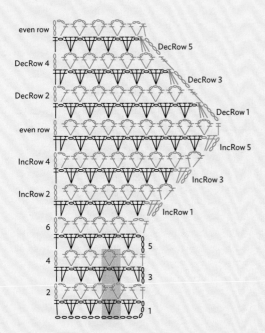

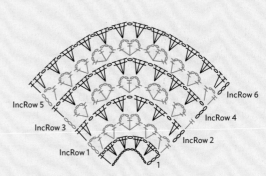

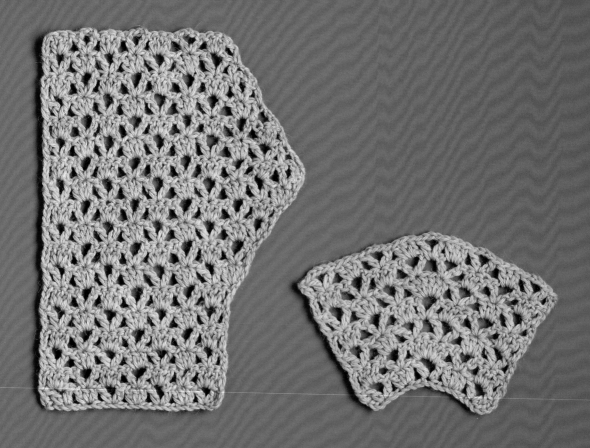

STAGGERED Vs AND BLOCKS

In this stitch pattern two elements—V-stitches and blocks—alternate within the row. The pattern repeat consists of one V-stitch and one three–double crochet block.

NUMBER OF STITCHES IN PATTERN REPEAT

8

MULTIPLE

6 + 9

NUMBER OF ROWS IN PATTERN REPEAT

2

REVERSIBLE

SPECIAL STITCH
V-Stitch (V-st): (dc, ch 3, dc) in designated st.

BASIC PATTERN

(For swatch, ch 27.)

ROW 1: Dc in 6th ch from hook (5 sk ch count as dc and 2 fnd ch), ch 3, dc in same ch, *sk 2 ch, 3 dc in next ch, sk 2 ch, V-st in next ch, rep from * across, sk 2 ch, dc in last ch, turn.
(Swatch has 3½ patt reps, 2 dc.)

ROW 2: Ch 3 (counts as dc at start of row), *3 dc in next ch-3 sp**, V-st in center dc of next 3-dc group, rep from * across, ending last rep at **, dc in tch, turn.

ROW 3: Ch 3, *V-st in center dc of next 3-dc group**, 3 dc in next ch-3 sp, rep from * across, ending last rep at **, dc in tch, turn.

Rep rows 2 and 3 for patt.
(Swatch has 6 rows in patt.)

Edge Shaping

Shaping is at the rate of ½ patt rep every 2 rows.

INCREASING

IncRow 1: Ch 3, 3 dc in same dc, V-st in center dc of next 3-dc group, continue in row 3 of patt across.

IncRow 2: Work in row 2 of patt to last 3-dc group, V-st in center dc of last 3-dc group, dc in tch, turn.

IncRow 3: Ch 3, V-st in same dc, 3 dc in next ch-3 sp, continue in row 3 of patt across.

IncRow 4: Work in row 2 of patt to last V-st, 3 dc in last ch-3 sp, dc in tch, turn.

Rep IncRows 1–4 to continue increasing.
(Swatch has 6 increase rows, ending with 5 patt reps, 2 dc.)

DECREASING

DecRow 1: Ch 3, sk next (dc, ch 3), dc in next dc, V-st in center dc of next 3-dc group, continue in row 3 of patt across.

DecRow 2: Work in row 2 of patt across, dc in last dc, leave tch unworked, turn.

DecRow 3: Ch 3, sk next 3 dc, dc in next dc, 3 dc in next ch-3 sp, continue in row 3 of patt across.

DecRow 4: Rep DecRow 2.

Rep DecRows 1–4 to continue decreasing.
(Swatch has 6 decrease rows, ending with 3½ patt reps, 2 dc.)

Internal Shaping

The rate of increase is 1 patt rep every 3 rows.
(For swatch, ch 21. Work row 1 of patt. 2½ patt reps.)
Place marker in ch-3 sp of center V-st.

IncRow 1: Work in row 2 of patt to marked ch-3 sp, 6 dc in marked ch-3 sp, V-st in center dc of next 3-dc group, continue in patt across, remove marker.

IncRow 2: Work in row 3 of patt to 6-dc group, V-st in 2nd dc of group, ch 1, sk next 2 dc, V-st in next dc, place marker in ch-1 sp just made, 3 dc in next ch-3 sp, continue in patt across.

IncRow 3: Work in row 2 of patt across to marked ch-1 sp, V-st in marked ch-1 sp, move marker to ch-3 sp just made, 3 dc in next ch-3 sp, continue in patt across.

IncRow 4: Work in row 3 of patt to marked ch-3 sp, 6 dc in marked ch-3 sp, continue in patt across, remove marker.

IncRow 5: Work in row 2 of patt to 6-dc group, V-st in 2nd dc of group, ch 1, sk next 2 dc, V-st in next dc, place marker in ch-1 sp just made, 3 dc in next ch-3 sp, continue in patt across.

IncRow 6: Work in row 3 of patt to marked ch-1 sp, V-st in marked ch-1 sp, move marker to ch-3 sp just made, continue in patt across.

Rep IncRows 1–6 to continue increasing.
(Swatch has 7 rows total, 6 increase rows, ending with 4½ patt reps.)

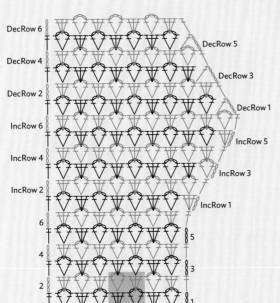

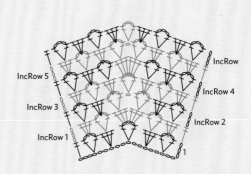

CLUSTER Vs

This stitch features an unusual use of picots, which are usually seen as a decorative embellishment. Here the picots are worked into and so are not obvious to the eye. They provide a midway point between Cluster Vees, allowing Vees to be staggered from one row to the next and making them stand out more clearly since no stitches are worked into them.

NOTE
To work into picot, insert hook into ch-4 space of picot.

SPECIAL STITCHES
Cluster (Cl): (Yo, insert hook in designated st and draw up loop, yo, draw through 2 loops) twice.

Cluster V-Stitch (Cl V-st): (Cl, ch 3, Cl) in designated st or sp.

Picot: Ch 4, sl st in 4th ch from hook. Note that picot counts as 1 st.

NUMBER OF STITCHES IN PATTERN REPEAT	NUMBER OF ROWS IN PATTERN REPEAT
6	2
MULTIPLE	**REVERSIBLE**
4 + 9	

BASIC PATTERN

(For swatch, ch 21.)

ROW 1: Sl st in 4th ch (picot made), sk 5 ch (counts as dc, 2 fnd ch), *Cl V-st in next ch, picot**, sk 3 ch, rep from * across, ending last rep at **, sk 2 ch, dc in last ch, turn.
(Swatch has 4 Cl V-sts, 2 dc.)

ROW 2: Ch 4 (counts as dc, ch 1), Cl in first picot, *picot, Cl V-st in next picot, rep from * across to last picot, picot, (Cl, ch 1, dc) in last picot, turn.

ROW 3: Ch 3, *picot, Cl V-st in next picot, rep from * across, picot, tr in tch, turn.
Rep rows 2 and 3 for patt.
(Swatch has 5 rows in patt.)

Edge Shaping

The single Cluster that begins even-numbered rows is expanded to a full V-st, allowing shaping at ½ patt rep per row, beginning on an even-numbered row. The first decrease row is shaped at the end of the row.

INCREASING

IncRow 1: Ch 3, picot, Cl V-st in first picot, picot, continue in row 2 of patt across.

IncRow 2: Work in row 3 of patt to last picot, Cl V-st in last picot, picot, turn.
Rep IncRows 1 and 2 to continue increasing.
(Swatch has 4 increase rows, ending with 6 Cl V-sts, 1 dc, followed by 1 row worked even.)

DECREASING

DecRow 1: Work in row 3 of patt to last picot, Cl in last picot, turn.

DecRow 2: Ch 4 (counts as dc, ch 1), Cl in first picot, picot, continue in row 2 of patt across.
Rep DecRows 1 and 2 to continue decreasing.
(Swatch has 4 decrease rows, ending with 4 Cl V-sts, 2 dc.)

Internal Shaping

1 patt rep (Cl V-st and picot) Cl V-st is added in each row in the center ch-3 sp.
(For swatch, ch 17. Work row 1 of patt. 3 Cl V-sts, 2 dc.)
Place marker in ch-3 sp of center Cl V-st.

IncRow 1: Work in row 2 of patt across to marker, Cl V-st in marked ch-3 sp, move marker to ch-3 sp just made, picot, Cl V-st in next picot, continue in patt across.

IncRow 2: Work in row 3 of patt across to marked ch-3 sp, Cl V-st in marked ch-3 sp, move marker to ch-3 sp, picot, Cl V-st in next picot, continue in patt across.
Rep IncRows 1 and 2 to continue increasing.
(Swatch has 6 rows total, 4 increase rows, ending with 7 Cl V-sts counting ½ Cl V-sts at edges.)

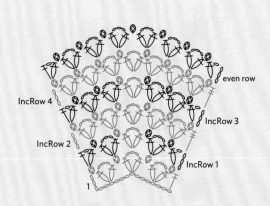

OVERLAPPING Vs

The V-stitches here are made with two
double crochet stitches with a chain-three
space between them. The overlapping is
accomplished by working into the chain-three
space of a V-stitch two rows below. It's a bit
tricky to find the insertion point, but the effect
is well worth the effort.

NOTES
The ch-3 2 rows below is covered by the 2 legs of
the V-st. Spread them apart to see the ch-3, and
insert hook below ch-3.

When working an Overlapping V-stitch (OV), it's
easy to inadvertently pick up other strands on your
work, so turn to the opposite side to check your
work at the end of each row.

SPECIAL STITCH
Overlapping V-stitch (OV): (Dc, ch 3, dc) into next
ch-3 sp 2 rows below and drawing up stitches taller
than normally. On row 2 only, work into skipped
foundation ch between legs of V-st below.

NUMBER OF STITCHES IN PATTERN REPEAT	NUMBER OF ROWS IN PATTERN REPEAT
6	1
MULTIPLE	**REVERSIBLE**
6 + 2	

BASIC PATTERN

(For swatch, ch 26.)

ROW 1: Dc in 4th ch from hook (3 sk ch count as hdc, 1 fnd ch), *ch 3, sk 1 ch, dc in next ch**, ch 1, sk 3 ch, dc in next ch, rep from * across, ending last rep at **, sk next ch, hdc in last ch, turn.

(Swatch has 4 patt reps.)

ROW 2: Ch 2 (counts as hdc throughout), *OV in center fnd ch between 2 dc**, ch 1, rep from * across, ending last rep at **, hdc in tch, turn.

ROW 3: Ch 2, *OV**, ch 1, rep from * across, ending last rep at **, hdc in tch, turn.

Rep row 3 for patt. To avoid gaps on last row, work it as follows: Ch 1, sc in first hdc, *(hdc, ch 3, hdc) working into ch-3 sp 2 rows below**, ch 1, rep from * across, ending last rep at **, sc in tch.

(Swatch has 13 rows in pattern, with last row worked as above.)

Edge Shaping

This stitch is not conducive to edge shaping because of the need to work 2 rows below, nor do the natural angles of the pattern lend themselves to it.

Internal Shaping

We enlarge the patt by increasing the number of chains between V-sts. The number of patt reps remains the same throughout, but each V-st is one more chain apart from its neighbors.

(For swatch, ch 26. Work rows 1 and 2 of patt. 4 patt reps.)

IncRow 1: Ch 2, *OV, ch 2, rep from * across to last ch-3 sp, OV, hdc in tch, turn.

IncRow 2: Ch 2, *OV, ch 3, rep from * across to last ch-3 sp, OV, hdc in tch, turn.

IncRow 3: Ch 2, *OV, ch 4, rep from * across to last ch-3 sp, OV, hdc in tch, turn.

Continue adding one more chain between OV on each row.

(Swatch has 9 rows total, 7 increase rows, ending with 4 patt reps with ch-8 spaces between OVs.)

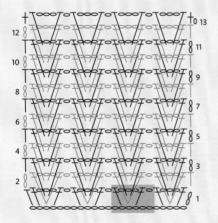

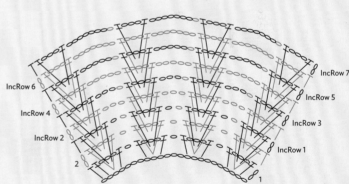

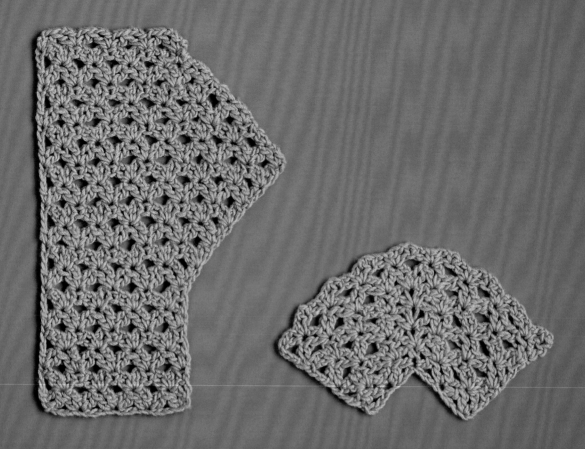

DIAMONDS

In this stitch pattern we work two double crochet stitches together with a space between the two legs of the stitch. The resulting upside-down V creates the diamond shape, which is accented by groups of chains that align with the slanted angles of the V-shape.

NUMBER OF STITCHES IN PATTERN REPEAT	NUMBER OF ROWS IN PATTERN REPEAT
6	2
MULTIPLE	**REVERSIBLE**
4 + 2	

NOTES

Pay careful attention to where the 2 insertion points are when working dc2tog. In most cases both legs are worked into a dc2tog on the previous row, but at the edges they are not. There are also exceptions when shaping. The wording will say to work the dc2tog "over" 2 stitches, which are the 2 insertion points. Each partial dc is considered one "leg" of the stitch.

The diamond shape is not always evident while the stitch is being worked, which in turn affects how well one can read stitches. Check that you are inserting the hook in the intended stitch.

On even-numbered rows the first (ch 3) and last (2nd leg of dc2tog) stitches form a straight edge for the work. For purposes of counting patt reps, these end stitches are not included.

When the term "same st" is used, it always means the same stitch where the previous stitch was made.

BASIC PATTERN

(For swatch, ch 18.)
ROW 1: Sc in 2nd ch from hook, *ch 2, dc2tog over (same st, sk 3 ch, next ch), ch 2, sc in same ch, rep from * across.
(Swatch has 4 patt reps.)
ROW 2: Ch 3, dc in first dc2tog, *ch 2, sc in same st, ch 2, dc2tog over (same st, next dc2tog), rep from * across, ch 2, sc in same st, dc2tog over (same st, last sc), turn.
ROW 3: Ch 1, sc in first dc2tog, *ch 2, dc2tog over (same st, next dc2tog), ch 2, sc in same st, rep from * across, placing last leg in tch, ch 2, sc in tch, turn.
Rep rows 2 and 3 for patt.
(Swatch has 6 rows in patt.)

Edge Shaping

The rate of shaping is 1 patt rep over 2 rows and begins on an odd-numbered row.

INCREASING

IncRow 1: Ch 5 (counts as dc, ch 2 throughout), sc in first st, continue in row 3 of patt across.
IncRow 2: Work in row 2 of patt, placing last leg in 3rd ch of tch, ch 2, sc in same ch, ch 2, dc in same ch, turn.
IncRow 3: Ch 5, sc in first dc, continue in row 3 of patt across.
Rep IncRows 2 and 3 to continue increasing.
(Swatch has 6 increase rows, ending with 7 patt reps counting ½ patts at edges.)

DECREASING

DecRow 1: Ch 1, sc in first st, continue in row 3 of patt across.
DecRow 2: Work in row 2 of patt to last 2 dc2tog, sc in same st, ch 2, dc3tog over (same st, next dc2tog, same dc2tog), turn.
Rep DecRows 1 and 2 to continue decreasing.
(Swatch has 7 decrease rows, ending with 4 patt reps.)

Internal Shaping

The rate of shaping is 1 patt rep per row. When increasing, the sc lies at the bottom of a diamond and is pulled up to the level of the top of the diamond, causing the sc stitch to stretch.
(For swatch, ch 18. Work row 1 of patt. 4 patt reps.)
Place marker in center (3rd) sc of row.
IncRow 1: Work in row 2 of patt to dc2tog before marked sc, dc2tog over (same st, marked sc), ch 2, sc in same st, ch 2, dc2tog over (same marked sc, next dc2tog), move marker to dc2tog just made, continue in patt across.
IncRow 2: Work in row 3 of patt, placing sc in marked dc2tog, ch 2, dc2tog over (same marked st, next sc), ch 2, sc in same sc, ch 2, dc2tog over (same sc, next dc2tog), move marker to dc2tog just made, continue in patt across.
IncRow 3: Work in row 2 of patt, placing sc in marked dc2tog, ch 2, dc2tog over (same marked st, next sc), ch 2, sc in same sc, ch 2, dc2tog over (same sc, next dc2tog), move marker to dc2tog just made, continue in patt across.
Rep IncRows 2 and 3 to continue increasing.
To return to patt, work last IncRow 3 as in row 2 of patt (as on swatch).
(Swatch has 6 rows total, 4 increase rows, ending with 8 patt reps.)

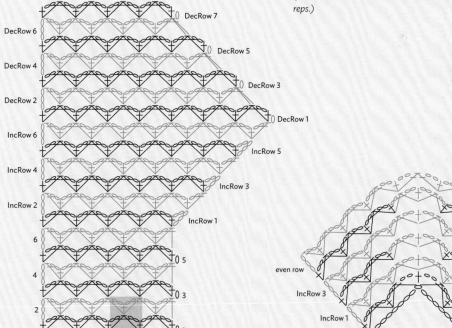

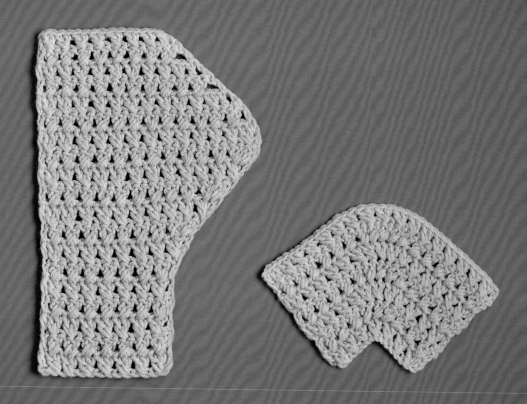

CROSSED DOUBLES

The distinction of this stitch is its unique texture, a result of crossing one stitch over the other.

NUMBER OF STITCHES IN PATTERN REPEAT	NUMBER OF ROWS IN PATTERN REPEAT
2	1

MULTIPLE	REVERSIBLE
2 + 4	

NOTE
When working even, rows start and end with hdc sts except for first row of patt.

SPECIAL STITCH
Crossed double crochet (Crdc): Sk next st, dc in next st, dc in sk st.

BASIC PATTERN

(For swatch, ch 18.)

ROW 1: Dc in 5th ch from hook (4 sk ch count as dc and 1 fdn ch), dc in sk fnd ch, work Crdc across to last ch, dc in last ch, turn.
(Swatch has 7 Crdc, 2 hdc.)

ROW 2: Ch 2 (counts as hdc throughout), Crdc across, hdc in tch, turn.
Rep row 2 for patt.
(Swatch has 6 rows in patt.)

Edge Shaping

Shaping is at the rate of 1 patt rep per row. When increasing at the starts of rows a full patt rep is added, but the stitches appear close together. They open up on the following row. Decreasing begins on an even-numbered row. To begin decreasing on an odd-numbered row, reverse instructions for DecRows 1 and 2.

To increase at the beginning of rows we make a ch 4, which counts as a dc and its fdn ch. For the following Crdc, begin in the next hdc and work the crossed dc into this fdn ch.

To increase at the end of IncRow 2, we work twice in 2nd to last dc and twice in tch.

In decrease section longer turning chains are used at decrease edge on some rows due to the steep angle at the edge. Feel free to lengthen or shorten these tch as needed to keep edge from curling.

At the end of DecRow 1, the last 5 sts are 2 pairs of Crdc and a tch.

INCREASING

IncRow 1: Ch 4 (counts as 1 fnd ch, dc), dc in first hdc, dc in beginning fnd ch, continue in patt across.

IncRow 2: Work in patt across, dc in tch, dc in dc before tch, hdc in tch, turn.

Rep IncRows 1 and 2 to continue increasing.

(Swatch has 6 increase rows, ending with 13 Crdc, 2 hdc, followed by 1 row worked even.)

DECREASING

DecRow 1: Work in patt to last Crdc, sk last Crdc, dc in tch, turn.

DecRow 2: Ch 2 (does not count as a st), sk next dc, dc in next dc, continue in patt across.

DecRow 3: Work in patt to last Crdc, sk last Crdc and next dc, dc in tch, turn.

Rep DecRows 2 and 3 to continue decreasing.

(Swatch has 6 decrease rows, ending with 7 Crdc, 2 sts.)

Internal Shaping

2 Crdc are added each row. This requires working into 4 sts twice, as instructed.

(For swatch, ch 18. Work row 1 of patt. 7 Crdc, 2 dc.)

Place marker in 1st dc of center (4th) Crdc pair.

IncRow 1: Work in patt to marked dc, (dc in next dc, dc in 1 st before dc just made) 2 times, move marker to last dc just made, (dc in next dc, dc in 1 st before dc just made) 2 times, continue in patt across.

Rep IncRow 1 to continue increasing.

(Swatch has 7 rows total, 5 increase rows, ending with 17 Crdc, 2 hdc.)

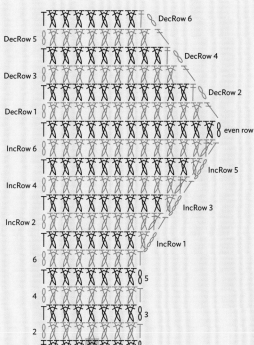

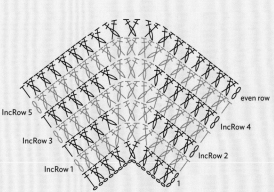

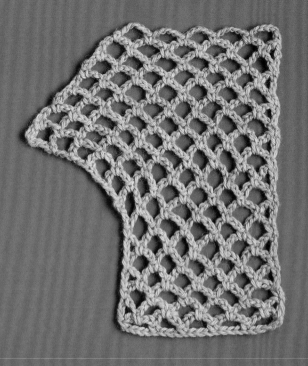

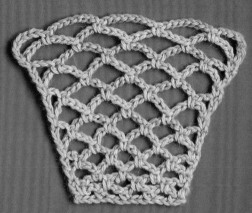

TRADITIONAL MESH

This basic mesh appears in the earliest printed patterns of 1824 and remains a favorite lace stitch that's easily combined with other stitches.

NUMBER OF STITCHES IN PATTERN REPEAT
6

MULTIPLE
4 + 2

NUMBER OF ROWS IN PATTERN REPEAT
2

REVERSIBLE

BASIC PATTERN

(For swatch, ch 22.)
ROW 1: Sc in 2nd ch from hook, *ch 5, sk 3 ch, sc in next ch, rep from * across, turn.
(Swatch has 5 patt reps, 1 sc.)
ROW 2: Ch 5 (counts as dc, ch 2), *sc in next ch-5 sp, ch 5, rep from * across, ch 2, dc in last sc, turn.
ROW 3: Ch 1, sc in first dc, *ch 5, sc in next ch-5 sp, rep from * across, placing last sc in 3rd ch of tch.
Rep rows 2 and 3 for patt.
(Swatch has 7 rows in patt.)

Edge Shaping
The patt rep consists of a sc and ch-5 sp. On even-numbered row there are half patterns—that is, 2 ch—at the edges. Shaping is at the rate of ½ patt per row, beginning on an even-numbered row.

INCREASING

IncRow 1: Ch 4, BLsc in 2nd ch from hook, ch 5, sc in next ch-5 sp, continue in row 2 of patt across.

IncRow 2: Work in row 3 of patt across, ch 5, dc in last sc, turn.

Rep IncRows 1 and 2 to continue increasing.

(Swatch has 6 increase rows, ending with 8 patt reps, 1 dc.)

DECREASING

DecRow 1: Ch 1, sl st over next 2 ch, sc in same ch-5 sp, ch 5, sc in next ch-5 sp, continue in row 2 of patt across.

DecRow 2: Work in row 3 of patt across.

Rep DecRows 1 and 2 to continue decreasing.

(Swatch has 6 decrease rows, ending with 5 patt reps, 1 sc.)

Internal Shaping

This is an example of increasing by enlarging the stitch pattern, in this case by adding 1 chain to the ch-sps between sc every other row. We begin with a smaller version of the main pattern that has ch-3 sps instead of ch-5.

*(For swatch, ch 14. Row 1: Sc in 2nd ch from hook, *ch 3, sk 2 ch, sc in next ch, rep from * across, turn. 4 patt reps with ch-3 sps.)*

IncRow 1: Ch 3 (counts as hdc, ch 1), sc in first ch-3 sp, *ch 3, sc in next ch-3 sp, rep from * across, ch 1, hdc in last sc, turn.

IncRow 2: Ch 1, sc in first hdc, *ch 4, sc in next ch-3 sp, rep from * across, ch 4, sc in 2nd ch of tch.

IncRow 3: Ch 4 (counts as hdc, ch 2), sc in first ch-4 sp, *ch 4, sc in next ch-4 sp, rep from * across, ch 2, hdc in last sc, turn.

IncRow 4: Ch 1, sc in first hdc, *ch 5, sc in next ch-4 sp, rep from * across, ch 5, sc in 2nd ch of tch, turn.

IncRow 5: Ch 5 (counts as dc, ch 2), sc in first ch-5 sp, *ch 5, sc in next ch-5 sp, rep from * across, ch 2, dc in last sc, turn.

IncRow 6: Ch 1, sc in first dc, *ch 6, sc in next ch-5 sp, rep from * across, ch 6, sc in 3rd ch of tch, turn.

IncRow 7: Ch 5 (counts as dc, ch 2), sc in first ch-6 sp, *ch 6, sc in next ch-6 sp, rep from * across, ch 2, dc in last sc, turn.

To continue increasing, add 1 more ch every 2 rows, making sts at ends of odd-numbered rows taller as needed.

(Swatch has 12 rows in total, 11 increase rows, ending with 9 sts per patt rep.)

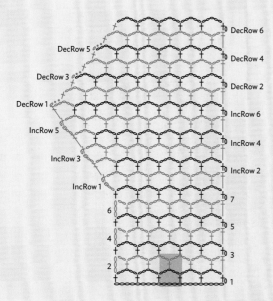

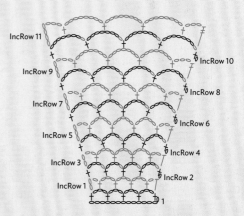

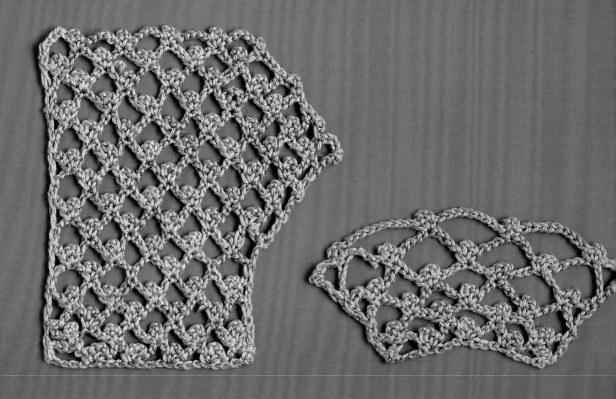

PICOT MESH

The familiar basic mesh pattern is elaborated with picots. Note that the picots in this case do not involve slip stitching into a chain, which makes them easier to work.

NUMBER OF STITCHES IN PATTERN REPEAT	NUMBER OF ROWS IN PATTERN REPEAT
6	2
MULTIPLE	**REVERSIBLE**
4 + 2	

NOTES

For this stitch it's necessary to work into the center chain of ch-5 spaces, a bit trickier than inserting in the space under it.

Picots are avoided at the edges of the work, with sc used instead.

SPECIAL STITCH
Picot: (sc, ch 3, sc) in designated ch. Picot counts as one stitch.

BASIC PATTERN

(For swatch, ch 22.)
ROW 1: Sc in 2nd ch from hook, *ch 5, sk 3 ch, picot in next ch, rep from * across, ch 5, sc in last ch, turn.
(Swatch has 5 patt reps, 1 sc.)
ROW 2: Ch 5 (counts as dc, ch 2), *picot in 3rd ch of next ch-5 sp, ch 5, rep from * across, ch 2, dc in last sc, turn.
ROW 3: Ch 1, sc in first dc, *ch 5, picot in 3rd ch of next ch-5 sp, rep from * across, ch 5, sc in 3rd ch of tch, turn.
Rep rows 2 and 3 for patt.
(Swatch has 7 rows in patt.)

Edge Shaping

Shaping is at the rate of ½ patt per row—a dc is used at the shaping edge on some rows to maintain a smooth slant.

INCREASING

IncRow 1: Ch 4, BLsc in 2nd ch from hook, ch 5, picot in 3rd ch of next ch-5 sp, continue in row 2 of patt across.

IncRow 2: Work in row 3 of patt across, ch 5, dc in last sc, turn. Rep IncRows 1 and 2 to continue increasing.
(Swatch has 6 increase rows, ending with 8 patt reps, 1 dc.)

DECREASING

DecRow 1: Ch 1, sl st over next 2 ch, sc in next ch, ch 5, picot in 3rd ch of next ch-5 sp, continue in row 2 of patt across.

DecRow 2: Work in row 3 of patt across, placing last sc in last ch-5 sp.
Rep DecRows 1 and 2 to continue decreasing.
(Swatch has 6 decrease rows, ending with 5 patt reps, 1 sc.)

Internal Shaping

This pattern is suitable for internal shaping by enlarging the pattern. It's necessary to have an odd number of chains in each patt rep, since picots are worked in the center chain of a group. Therefore we add 2 chains in each patt rep every other row.

(For swatch, ch 18. Work rows 1 and 2 of patt. 4 patt reps, 1 sc.)

IncRow 1: Ch 1, sc in first dc, *ch 7, picot in 3rd ch of next ch-5 sp, rep from * across, ch 7, sc in 3rd ch of tch, turn.

IncRow 2: Ch 6 (counts as dc, ch 3), *picot in 4th ch of next ch-7 sp, ch 7, rep from * across, ch 3, dc in last sc, turn.

IncRow 3: Ch 1, sc in first dc, *ch 9, picot in 4th ch of next ch-7 sp, rep from * across, ch 9, sc in 3rd ch of tch, turn.

IncRow 4: Ch 7 (counts as dc, ch 4), *picot in 5th ch of next ch-9 sp, rep from * across, ch 4, dc in last sc, turn.

Depending on preference, this may be the limit for internal increasing.

(Swatch has 6 rows total, 4 patt reps counting half patt 5 at edges.)

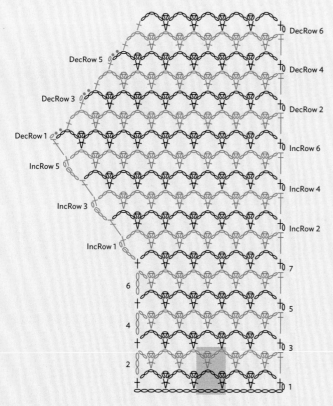

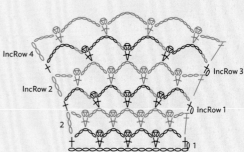

CLUSTERED ARCHES

In this pattern traditional mesh is combined with Clusters. On even-numbered rows the arches formed by chain-five spaces are filled in with four–double crochet Clusters. The clustered arches are staggered from one even row to the next. The pattern repeat consists of two arches, whether open or filled.

NUMBER OF STITCHES IN PATTERN REPEAT	NUMBER OF ROWS IN PATTERN REPEAT
V	4
MULTIPLE	**REVERSIBLE**
8 + 6	

SPECIAL STITCH
Cluster (Cl): (Yo, insert hook in designated sp, yo and draw up loop, yo, draw through 2 loops) 4 times, yo, draw through 5 loops on hook.

BASIC PATTERN

(For swatch, ch 22.)
ROW 1: Sc in 2nd ch from hook, * ch 5, sk 3 ch, sc in next ch, rep from * across, turn.
(Swatch has 5 ch-5 arches.)
ROW 2: Ch 5 (counts as dc, ch 2), *sc in next ch-5 sp**, ch 4, Cl in next ch-5 sp, ch 4, rep from * across, ending last rep at **, ch 2, dc in last sc, turn.
ROW 3: Ch 1, sc in first dc, *ch 5, sc in next ch-4 sp, rep from * across, ch 5, sc in 3rd ch of ch-5 tch, turn.
ROW 4: Ch 5 (counts as dc, ch 2), Cl in first ch-5 sp, *ch 4, sc in next ch 5 sp, ch 4, Cl in next ch-5 sp, rep from * across to last st, ch 2, dc in last sc, turn.
ROW 5: Rep row 3.
Rep rows 2–5 for patt.
(Swatch has 9 rows in patt.)

Edge Shaping

The natural slant of the arches dictates that shaping is best done beginning on an even-numbered row. Since this mesh is double the length of previous mesh stitches, we are adding ¼ of a patt rep on each increase.

INCREASING

IncRow 1: Ch 4, sc in 2nd ch from hook, ch 4, sc in next ch-5 sp, continue in row 2 of patt across.
IncRow 2: Work in row 3 of patt across, ch 5, dc in last sc, turn.
IncRow 3: Ch 4, sc in 2nd ch from hook, ch 4, sc in next ch-5 sp, continue in row 4 of patt across.
IncRow 4: Rep IncRow 2.
Rep IncRows 1–4 to continue increasing.
(Swatch has 8 increase rows, ending with 10 ch-5 arches.)

DECREASING

DecRow 1: Ch 1, sl st over next 2 ch, sc in same ch-5 sp, ch 4, Cl in next ch-5 sp, continue in row 2 of patt across.
DecRow 2: Work in row 3 of patt across placing last sc in last ch-4 sp, turn.
DecRow 3: Ch 1, sl st over next 2 ch, sc in same ch-5 sp, ch 4, Cl in next ch-5 sp, continue in row 4 of patt across.
DecRow 4: Rep DecRow 2.
Rep DecRows 1–4 to continue decreasing.
(Swatch has 8 decrease rows, ending with 5 ch-5 arches.)

Internal Shaping

The rate of increase is 1 patt rep over 2 rows.
(For swatch, ch 22. Work rows 1 and 2 of patt. First row has 5 ch-5 arches.)
Place marker in center sc in row 2 of patt.
IncRow 1: Work in row 3 of patt to marked sc, ch 5, sc in marked sc, move marker to sc just made, ch 5, continue in patt across.
IncRow 2: Work in row 4 of patt to marked sc, ch 4, sc in marked sc, move marker to sc just made, ch 4, continue in patt across.
IncRow 3: Work in row 5 of patt to marked sc, ch 5, sc in marked sc, move marker to sc just made, ch 5, continue in patt across.
IncRow 4: Work in row 2 of patt to marked sc, ch 4, sc in marked sc, move marker to sc just made, ch 4, continue in patt across.
Rep IncRows 1–4 to continue increasing. To return to patt, work row 3 of patt instead of IncRow 1 or row 5 of patt instead of IncRow 3.
(Swatch has 10 rows total, 6 increase rows, ending with 5 patt reps, 4 ch, 2 dc.)

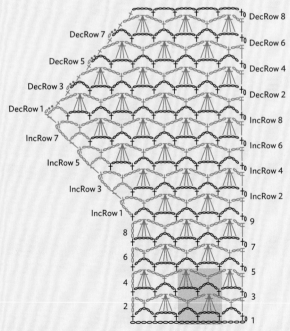

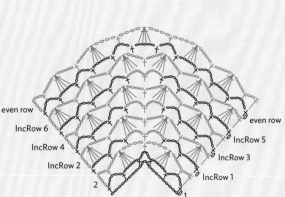

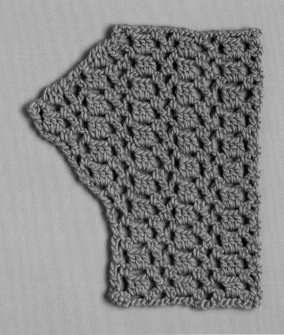

BLOCKS AND DIAMONDS

This clever stitch creates vertical columns of blocks alternating with columns of a diamond-like shape created with chain-three spaces and single crochet stitches.

NUMBER OF STITCHES IN PATTERN REPEAT	NUMBER OF ROWS IN PATTERN REPEAT
V	2
MULTIPLE	**REVERSIBLE**
8 + 2	

BASIC PATTERN

(For swatch, ch 26.)

ROW 1: Sc in 2nd ch from hook, ch 1, sk next ch, *sc in next ch, ch 3, sk 3 ch, rep from * across to last 3 ch, sc in next ch, ch 1, sk next ch, sc in last ch, turn.

(Swatch has 25 sts.)

ROW 2: Ch 1, sc in first st, *ch 3, 3 dc in next ch-3 sp, ch 3**, sc in next ch-3 sp, rep from * across, ending last rep at **, sc in last sc, turn.

(Swatch has 3 patt reps.)

ROW 3: Ch 4 (counts as dc, ch 1), sc in first ch-3 sp, *ch 3, sc in next ch-3 sp, rep from * across to last st, ch 1, dc in last sc, turn. Rep rows 2 and 3 for patt.

(Swatch has 6 rows in patt.)

Edge Shaping

Shaping is at the rate of a full patt rep over 4 rows.

INCREASING

IncRow 1: Ch 6 (counts as dc, ch 3), sc in first ch-3 sp, continue in row 3 of patt across.

IncRow 2: Work in row 2 of patt across to ch-6 tch, sc in tch, ch 3, dc in 3rd ch of tch, turn.

IncRow 3: Rep IncRow 1.

IncRow 4: Work in row 2 of patt across to ch-6 tch, 3 dc in tch, ch 3, dc in 3rd ch of tch, turn.

Rep IncRows 1–4 to continue increasing.

(Swatch has 8 increase rows, ending with 5 patt reps.)

DECREASING

DecRow 1: Ch 1, sl st over next 2 ch, sc in first ch-3 sp, continue in row 3 of patt across.

DecRow 2: Work in row 2 of patt across to last ch-3 sp, ch 3, dc3tog over (next ch-3 sp, same ch-3 sp, last sc), turn.

DecRow 3: Ch 1, sc in dc3tog, ch 3, sk first ch-3 sp, sc in next ch-3 sp, continue in row 3 of patt across.

DecRow 4: Work in row 2 of patt across to last ch-3 sp, ch 3, sk last ch-3 sp, dc in last sc, turn.

Rep DecRows 1–4 to continue decreasing.

When ending decrease, work DecRow 4 as follows: Work in row 2 of patt across to last ch-3 sp, sc in last sc, turn.

(Swatch has 8 decrease rows, ending with 3 patt reps, and one more row worked even.)

Internal Shaping

To increase gradually over 6 rows, increases are made on 4 rows and 2 rows are worked even.

(For swatch, ch 26. Work rows 1 and 2 of patt. 25 sts.)

Place marker in center dc of 3-dc group.

IncRow 1: Work in row 3 of patt to marked dc, ch 3, sc in marked dc, move marker to sc just made, ch 3, sc in next ch-3 sp, continue in patt.

IncRow 2: Work in row 2 of patt to marked sc, ch 3, sc in marked sc, move marker to sc just made, ch 3, 3 dc in next ch-3 sp, continue in patt across.

(Swatch has 4 patt reps.)

IncRow 3: Work in row 3 of patt, moving marker to center ch-3 sp.

IncRow 4: Work in row 2 of patt moving marker to center sc.

IncRow 5: Work in row 3 of patt across to marked sc, ch 3, sc in marked sc, move marker to sc just made, ch 3, sc in next ch-3 sp, continue in patt across.

IncRow 6: Work in row 2 of patt to marked sc, ch 3, 3 dc in marked sc, move marker to center dc of 3-dc group just made, ch 3, sc in next ch-3 sp, continue in patt across.

(Swatch has 5 patt reps.)

Rep IncRows 1–6 to continue increasing.

(Swatch has 11 rows total, 9 increase rows, ending with 6 patt reps.)

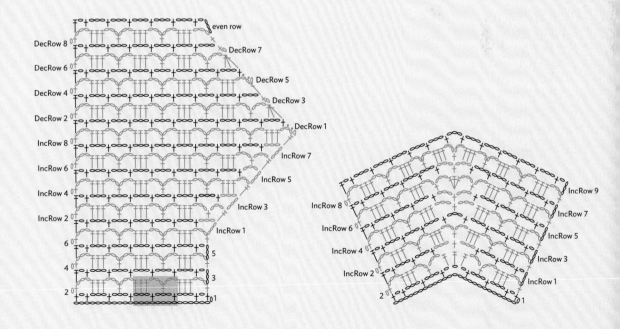

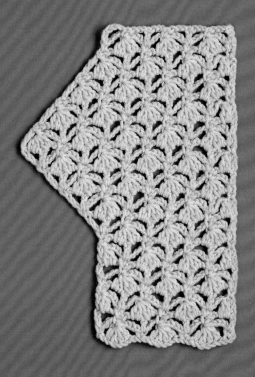
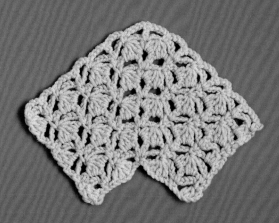

CLUSTER MESH

Clusters are worked over two chain-three spaces with eight chains and a single crochet stitch between the Clusters. Alternate rows are Zigzag Mesh (see page 86), which nicely frames the Clusters.

NUMBER OF STITCHES IN PATTERN REPEAT	NUMBER OF ROWS IN PATTERN REPEAT
V	4

MULTIPLE	NOT REVERSIBLE
8 + 2	

SPECIAL STITCHES

Cluster (Cl): (Yo, insert hook in designated ch-3 sp and draw up loop, yo, draw through 2 loops) twice, sk next dc, (yo, insert hook in next ch-3 sp and draw up loop, yo, draw through 2 loops) twice, yo, draw through 5 loops.

Half Cluster (Hcl): (Yo, insert hook in designated ch-3 sp and draw up loop, yo, draw through 2 loops) twice, yo, draw through 3 loops.

BASIC PATTERN

(For swatch, ch 26.)

ROW 1: Sc in 2nd ch from hook, *ch 4, sk next ch, (yo, insert hook in next ch and draw up loop, yo, draw through 2 loops) twice (Cl made), sk next ch, (yo, insert hook in next ch and draw up loop, yo, draw through 2 loops) twice, yo, draw through 5 loops, ch 4, sk next ch, sc in next ch, rep from * across, placing last sc in last ch, turn.

(Swatch has 3 patt reps, 1 sc.)

ROW 2: Ch 6 (counts as dc, ch 3 throughout), *sc in next Cl, ch 3, dc in next sc, ch 3, rep from * across, placing last dc in last sc, turn.

ROW 3: Ch 3 (counts as dc throughout), Hcl in first ch-3 sp, ch 4, sc in next sc, *ch 4, Cl over next 2 ch-3 sps, ch 4, sc in next sc, rep from * across, ch 4, Hcl in ch-6 tch, dc in 3rd ch of tch, turn.

ROW 4: Ch 1, sc in first dc, *ch 3, dc in next sc, ch 3, sc in next Cl, rep from * across, placing last sc in tch, turn.

ROW 5: Ch 1, sc in first sc, *ch 4, Cl over next 2 ch-3 sps, ch 4, sc in next sc, rep from * across, turn.

Rep rows 2–5 for patt.

(Swatch has 9 rows in patt.)

Edge Shaping

Shaping is at the rate of ½ patt rep over 2 rows beginning on row 2 of patt. Decreasing begins at row 5 at the end of the row.

INCREASING

IncRow 1: Ch 6 (counts as dc, ch 3 throughout), dc in first sc, ch 3, sc in next Cl, continue in row 2 of patt across.

IncRow 2: Work in row 3 of patt to last 2 ch-3 sps, ch 4, Cl over last 2 ch-3 sps, ch 4, sc in 3rd ch of 6-ch tch, turn.

IncRow 3: Ch 6, dc in first sc, ch 3, sc in next Cl, continue in row 4 of patt across.

IncRow 4: Work in row 5 of patt to last 2 ch-3 sps, Cl over last 2 ch-3 sp, ch 4, sc in 3rd ch of ch-6 tch, turn.

Rep IncRows 1–4 to continue increasing.

(Swatch has 7 increase rows ending with IncRow 3, and 5 patt reps.)

DECREASING

DecRow 1: Work in row 5 of patt to last 2 ch-3 sps, ch 4, Cl over last 2 ch-3 sp, tr in last sc (counts as ch-4 when decreasing), turn.

(For swatch, work last tr in 3rd ch of tch.)

DecRow 2: Ch 1, sc in first Cl, continue in row 2 of patt across.

DecRow 3: Work in row 3 of patt to last 2 ch-3 sps, ch 4, Cl over last 2 ch-3 sps, tr in last sc, turn.

DecRow 4: Ch 1, sc in first Cl, continue in row 4 of patt across.

Rep DecRows 1–4 to continue decreasing.

(Swatch has 8 decrease rows ending with DecRow 4, and 3 patt reps.)

Internal Shaping

Shaping is at the rate of ½ patt per row and begins on row 4 of patt; therefore row 1 below is row 3 of patt. Note that in odd-numbered increase rows the marker is not placed at the center. *(For swatch, ch 29.)*

ROW 1: Yo, insert hook in 5th ch from hook and draw up loop, yo, draw through 2 loops, yo, insert hook in next ch and draw up loop, yo, draw through 2 loops, yo, draw through 3 loops (Hcl made), ch 4, sk next ch, sc in next ch, *ch 4, sk next ch, (yo, insert hook in next ch and draw up loop, yo, draw through 2 loops) twice, sk next ch, (yo, insert hook in next ch and draw up loop, yo, draw through 2 loops) twice, yo, draw through 5 loops, ch 4, sk next ch, sc in next ch, rep from * across, ch 4, sk next ch, (yo, insert hook in next ch and draw up loop, yo, draw through 2 loops) twice, yo, draw through 3 loops (Hcl mad), dc in last ch, turn. (3 patt reps, counting half patts at edges) *(Swatch has 3 patt reps.)*

Place marker in center sc between 2 Cl.

IncRow 1: Work in row 4 of patt to marked sc, ch 3, (dc, ch 3, dc) in marked sc, move marker to ch-3 sp just made, ch 3, sc in next Cl, continue in patt across.

IncRow 2: Work in row 5 of patt to marked ch-3 sp, ch 4, work Cl over marked ch-3 sp and next ch-3 sp, ch 2, sc in same ch-3 sp, move marker to sc just made, ch 2, work Cl over same ch-3 sp and next ch-3 sp, ch 4, sc in next sc, continue in patt across.

IncRow 3: Work in row 2 of patt to marked sc, ch 3, (dc, ch 3, dc) in marked sc, move marker to ch-3 sp just made, ch 3, sc in next Cl, continue in patt across.

IncRow 4: Work in row 3 of patt to marked ch-3 sp, ch 4, Cl over marked ch-3 sp and next ch-3 sp, ch 2, sc in same ch-3 sp, move marker to sc just made, ch 2, Cl over same ch-3 sp and next ch-3 sp, ch 4, sc in next sc, continue in patt across.

Rep IncRows 1–4 to continue increasing.

To return to patt, work IncRow 1 as follows: Work in row 4 of patt to marked sc, ch 3, dc in marked sc, ch 3, sc in next Cl, continue in patt across.

(Swatch has 10 rows total, 8 increase rows, ending with 7 patt reps, 1 sc.)

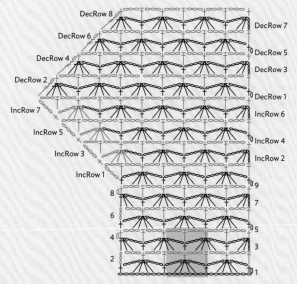

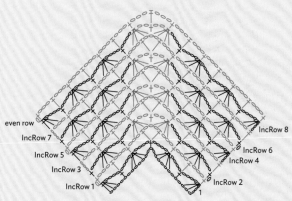

CHAPTER THREE

POPPING OUT: TEXTURED STITCHES

There are many ways to create texture in crochet. By texture, we mean fabric that is not completely flat and smooth, but rather has noticeable protrusions. It makes the fabric lively and interesting, but it also tends to make it heavier and more dense. That's why we've included textured lace stitches, to counter these tendencies.

Textured stitches include Bobbles, Puffs, and Popcorns, all done by inserting the hook multiple times into one stitch and working partial stitches together on the last loop. Bobbles and Popcorns use double crochet stitches, while Puffs use half doubles. Popcorns and Puffs are worked with the front side facing, but Bobbles pop out on the opposite side so are worked with the wrong side facing. Any of these can be made with more or fewer stitches depending on how much you want them to pop. Regardless of the number of partial stitches used to form these stitches, they are still one stitch for purposes of counting.

Post stitches—where you insert the hook not into the top of a stitch but around its post—are also a key way to create texture in crochet. They can be done with stitches of any height, on both the front and the back or on the front only. Here are a few points to consider about post stitches: First, because post stitches are worked into the middle of a stitch below, they

will sit a bit lower in the row than normal stitches. We want to avoid the bulk of a post stitch at the edges, so plain stitches are used at both ends of rows. These edge stitches will be shorter than the post stitch in order to match the height of the post stitches. So, for example, where post stitches are double crochet, the edge stitches will be half double crochet.

Here's a trick that will make back post stitches easier: Turn the work so you are looking at the back and insert your hook from the back to the front around the post. Try it! For stitch patterns using post stitches, the first row of work must be plain stitches, since there are no posts to work into. They are labeled as setup rows, and are not repeated as part of the stitch pattern.

Textured stitches can be used in so many different projects, and the only places they may cause trouble is where a very flat surface is required, such as on a table mat, coaster or the bottom of socks. If you'd like to use textured stitches in garments, use thinner yarns and a larger gauge to keep the fabric supple.

Very smooth yarn—such as a single ply—will produce a crisp texture that clearly pops from the surface. Fuzzier yarns will have a softer effect. Why not delve into your stash and do some exploring?

BILLOWS

This interesting surface is created using long post stitches that extend over two rows. All posts are worked on the front side of the fabric, which makes them easier to execute, and also means the pattern is not reversible.

NUMBER OF STITCHES IN PATTERN REPEAT

2

MULTIPLE

2 + 1

NOTE

When working even-numbered rows the alignment of sts can make it tricky to find the next st. Check the back of your work to be sure you are skipping only 1 st after working Front Post treble (FPtr).

NUMBER OF ROWS IN PATTERN REPEAT

4

NOT REVERSIBLE

BASIC PATTERN

(For swatch, ch 15.)

SETUP ROW: Dc in 4th ch from hook (3 sk ch count as dc), dc in each ch across, turn.

(Swatch has 13 sts.)

ROW 1: Ch 1, sc in first st and in each st across.

ROW 2: Ch 3 (counts as dc throughout), *FPtr in next dc 2 rows below, dc in next sc, rep from * across, turn.

ROW 3: Rep row 1.

ROW 4: Ch 3, dc in next sc, *FPtr in next dc 2 rows below, dc in next sc, rep from * across, dc in last sc, turn.

Rep rows 1–4 for patt.

(Swatch has 9 rows, 1 setup row and 8 rows in patt.)

Edge Shaping

Shaping can begin on any row, and is at the rate of 1 st per row.

INCREASING

IncRow 1: Ch 1, 2 sc in first dc, continue in row 1 of patt across.
IncRow 2: Work in row 2 of patt to last sc, 2 dc in last sc, turn.
IncRow 3: Rep IncRow 1.
IncRow 4: Work in row 4 of patt to last 2 sc, dc in next sc, 2 dc in last sc.
Rep IncRows 1–4 to continue increasing.
(Swatch has 8 increase rows, ending with 21 sts.)

DECREASING

DecRow 1: Ch 1, sk first dc, continue in row 1 of patt across.
DecRow 2: Work in row 2 of patt to last 2 sc, dc2tog, turn.
DecRow 3: Rep DecRow 1.
DecRow 4: Work in row 4 of patt to last 2 sc, dc2tog, turn.
Rep DecRows 1–4 to continue decreasing.
(Swatch has 8 decrease rows, ending with 13 sts, followed by 1 row worked even.)

Internal Shaping

Two sts are added each row. At the center of the increase, instead of a ch-1 we use a stitch, to make it easier to return to patt after increasing. When working 2nd FPtr into same dc, insert hook around post above where prev st was worked. Use 2 markers for this patt.
(For swatch, ch 15. Work setup row of patt. 13 sts.)
Place marker in center dc.

IncRow 1: Work in row 1 of patt to marked dc, 3 sc in marked sc, place 2nd marker in center sc of group just made, continue in patt across. Leave first marker in place.
IncRow 2: Work in row 2 of patt to marked sc, placing last FPtr in dc before marked dc 2 rows below, 3 dc in marked sc, FPtr in dc after marked dc 2 rows below, move first marker to center dc of group just made, continue in patt across.
IncRow 3: Rep IncRow 1.
IncRow 4: Work in row 4 of patt to marked sc, placing last FPtr in marked dc 2 rows below, 3 dc in marked sc, FPtr in same marked dc 2 rows below, move 1st marker to center dc of group just made, continue in patt across.
Rep IncRows 1–4 to continue increasing.
(Swatch has 10 rows total, 1 setup row, 8 increase rows, ending with 29 sts.)

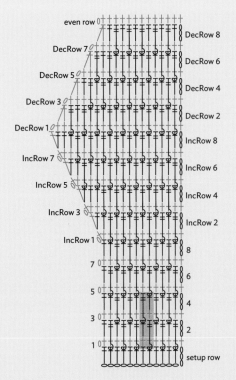

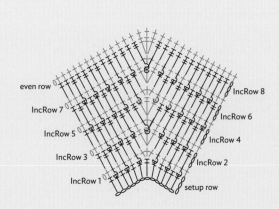

PLUMP POSTS

To create the bulk for this stitch, a double-thick stitch is worked into the post of the stitch two rows below. These post stitches are four stitches apart and are staggered every other row, with single crochet rows between.

NUMBER OF STITCHES IN PATTERN REPEAT	NUMBER OF ROWS IN PATTERN REPEAT
4	4
MULTIPLE	**NOT REVERSIBLE**
4 + 5	

NOTES

This pattern requires a stitch we are calling Double Post (DP)—which is essentially a dc2tog worked around the post of a dc 2 rows below. It can be tricky to work into the correct stitch. In row 1, make the first DP in the 4th dc of row 1, and for the next DP sk 3 dc in row 1 and work the DP into the next dc. In subsequent rows, the DP is placed in the center dc between DP stitches 2 rows below.

When working DP stitches, loops must be long enough that the work doesn't buckle. The precise height of the DP loops depends on the yarn and the gauge being worked. Experiment to see what produces the most attractive effect.

When increasing, we do not work DP stitches into stitches at edge, but use plain dc stitches instead.

SPECIAL STITCH
Double Post (DP): (Yo, insert hook in post of dc 2 rows below, yo and draw up loop to 1" [see Note]) twice (5 loops on hook), yo, draw through 4 loops on hook, yo, draw through 2 loops on hook.

BASIC PATTERN
(For swatch, ch 17.)
SETUP ROW: Dc in 4th ch from hook (3 sk ch count as dc) and in each ch across, turn.
(Swatch has 15 sts.)
ROW 1: Ch 1, sc in each st across, turn.
ROW 2: Ch 3 (counts as dc throughout), dc in next 2 sc, *DP, sk sc behind st just made, dc in next 3 sc, rep from * across, turn.
ROW 3: Rep row 1.
ROW 4: Ch 3, DP in 2nd dc 2 rows below, *dc in next 3 sc, DP, sk sc behind st just made, rep from * across to last st, dc in last sc, turn.
Rep rows 1–4 for patt.
(Swatch has 8 rows in patt.)

Edge Shaping

The rate of shaping is 1 st per row, adding a full patt rep over 4 rows.

INCREASING

IncRow 1: Ch 1, 2 sc in first dc, continue in row 1 of patt.
IncRow 2: Work in row 2 of patt to last sc, 2 dc in last sc, turn.
IncRow 3: Rep IncRow 1.
IncRow 4: Work in row 4 of patt to last sc, 2 dc in last sc, turn.
Rep IncRows 1–4 to continue increasing.
(Swatch has 8 increase rows, ending with 23 sts.)

DECREASING

DecRow 1: Ch 1, sk first sc, sc in next sc, continue in row 1 of patt across.
DecRow 2: Work in row 2 of patt to last 2 sts, dc2tog, turn.
DecRow 3: Rep DecRow 1.
DecRow 4: Work in row 4 of patt to last 2 sts, dc2tog, turn.
Rep DecRows 1–4 to continue decreasing.
(Swatch has 8 decrease rows, ending with 15 sts.)

Internal Shaping

2 sts are added in each row, with filler dc sts used until there are sufficient number of sts 2 rows below to work DP.
(For swatch, ch 17. Work setup row and row 1. 15 sts.)
Place marker in center sc.

IncRow 1: Work in row 2 of patt to marked sc, 3 dc in marked sc, move marker to center dc of group just made, dc in next 3 dc, sk 7 dc 2 rows below, DP in next dc 2 rows below, continue in patt across.

IncRow 2: Work in row 3 of patt to marked dc, 3 sc in marked dc, move marker to center sc of group just made, continue in patt across.

IncRow 3: Work in row 4 of patt to marked sc, 3 dc in marked sc, move marker to center dc of group just made, dc in next 3 sc, sk 5 dc 2 rows below, DP in next dc 2 rows below, continue in patt across.

IncRow 4: Rep IncRow 2.

IncRow 5: Work in row 2 of patt to marked sc, 3 dc in in marked sc, move marker to center dc of 3 just made, dc in next 3 sc, sk 5 dc 2 rows below, DP in next dc 2 rows below, continue in patt across.

Rep IncRows 2–5 to continue increasing.
(Swatch has 10 rows total, 7 increase rows, ending with 29 sts.)

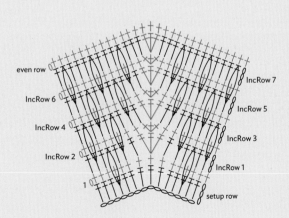

BASKET-WEAVE

This classic post stitch pattern uses alternating groups of front and back post stitches. Every four rows the order of groups changes. The woven effect is produced by the appearance of front post groups emerging from "underneath" back post groups. Here we use groups of four stitches over four rows, but this can be modified to use as many stitches and rows as you like.

NUMBER OF STITCHES IN PATTERN REPEAT

8

MULTIPLE

8 + 8

NUMBER OF ROWS IN PATTERN REPEAT

8

BASIC PATTERN

(For swatch, ch 24.)

SETUP ROW: Dc in 4th ch from hook (3 sk ch count as dc), dc in each ch across, turn.

(Swatch has 22 sts.)

ROW 1: Ch 2 (counts as hdc throughout), *FPdc in next 4 dc**, BPdc in next 4 dc, rep from * across, ending last rep at **, hdc in tch, turn.

ROW 2: Ch 2, *BPdc in next 4 dc**, FPdc in next 4 dc, rep from * ending last rep at **, hdc in tch, turn.

ROWS 3 AND 4: Rep rows 1 and 2.

ROW 5: Rep row 2.

ROW 6: Rep row 1.

ROWS 7 AND 8: Rep rows 2 and 1.

Rep rows 1–8 for patt.

(Swatch has 9 rows, 1 setup row and 8 rows in patt.)

Edge Shaping

Shaping is at the rate of 1 st per row. No post sts are worked at edges. When working 2 FPdc sts together in DecRow3 and subsequent decrease rows, work the first leg around the 2nd of the 2 posts worked together previously. When working 2 BPdc together in DecRow 4, work the 2nd leg around the 1st of the 2 posts worked together previously.

INCREASING

IncRow 1: Ch 2, dc in same st, continue in row 1 of patt across.

IncRow 2: Work in row 2 of patt to last 2 sts, FPdc in next dc, (dc, hdc) in tch, turn.

IncRow 3: Ch 2, dc in same st, BPdc in next 2 dc, FPdc in next 4 dc, continue in row 1 of patt across.

IncRow 4: Work in row 2 of patt to last 4 sts, FPdc in next 3 dc, (dc, hdc) in tch, turn.

IncRow 5: Ch 2, dc in same st, FPdc in next 4 dc, continue in row 2 of patt across.

IncRow 6: Work in row 1 of patt to last 6 sts, BPdc in next 4 dc, FPdc in next dc, (dc, hdc) in tch, turn.

IncRow 7: Ch 2, dc in same st, BPdc in next 2 dc, FPdc in next 4 dc, continue in row 2 of patt across.

IncRow 8: Work in patt to last 8 sts, BPdc in next 4 dc, FPdc in next 3 dc, (dc, hdc) in tch, turn.

Rep IncRows 1–8 to continue increasing.
(Swatch has 8 increase rows, ending with 30 sts.)

DECREASING

DecRow 1: Ch 2, FPdc2tog, FPdc in next 2 dc, BPdc in next 4 dc, continue in row 1 of patt across.

DecRow 2: Work in row 2 of patt to last 8 sts, FPdc in next 4 dc, BPdc in next dc, BPdc2tog, hdc in tch, turn.

DecRow 3: Ch 2, FPdc2tog, BPdc in next 4 dc, continue in row 1 of patt across.

DecRow 4: Work in row 2 of patt to last 6 sts, FPdc in next 4 sts, sk next st, hdc in tch, turn.

DecRow 5: Ch 2, FPdc2tog, FPdc in next 2 dc, continue in row 2 of patt across.

DecRow 6: Work in row 1 of patt to last 4 sts, BPdc in next dc, BPdc2tog, hdc in tch.

DecRow 7: Ch 2, FPdc2tog, BPdc in next 4 dc, continue in row 2 of patt across.

DecRow 8: Work in row 1 of patt to last 2 sts, sk next st, hdc in tch, turn.

Rep DecRows 1–8 to continue decreasing.
(Swatch has 8 decrease rows, ending with 22 sts.)

Internal Shaping

Increasing is at the rate of 2 sts per row after IncRow 1, which adds only 1 ch.

(For swatch, ch 24. Work setup row. 22 dc.)

Place marker between 2nd and 3rd st of center 4-FPdc group. Always move marker to ch-1 sp at center.

IncRow 1: Work row 1 of patt to marker, ch 1, continue in patt across.

IncRow 2: Work in row 2 of patt to marked ch-1 sp and ending with 2 BPdc, (dc, ch 1, dc) in marked ch-1 sp, BPdc in next 2 dc, continue in patt across.

IncRow 3: Work in row 1 of patt to marked ch-1 sp and ending with 3 FPdc, (dc, ch 1, dc) in marked ch-1 sp, FPdc in next 3 dc, continue in patt across.

IncRow 4: Work in row 2 of patt to marked ch-1 sp and ending with 4 BPdc, (dc, ch 1, dc) in marked ch-1 sp, BPdc in next 4 dc, continue in patt across.

IncRow 5: Work in row 2 of patt to marked ch-1 sp and ending with FPdc in next dc, (dc, ch 1, dc) in marked ch-1 sp, FPdc in next dc, continue in patt across.

IncRow 6: Work in row 1 of patt to marked ch-1 sp and ending with 2 BPdc, (dc, ch 1, dc) in marked ch-1 sp, BPdc in next 2 dc, continue in patt across.

IncRow 7: Work in row 2 of patt to marked ch-1 sp and ending with 3 FPdc, (dc, ch 1, dc) in marked ch-1 sp, FPdc in next 3 dc, continue in patt across.

IncRow 8: Work in row 1 of patt to marked ch-1 sp and ending with 4 BPdc, (dc, ch 1, dc) in marked ch-1 sp, BPdc in next 4 dc, continue in patt across.

Rep IncRows 1–8 to continue increasing.

To return to patt, work last IncRow 8 as follows (as on swatch): Work in row 1 of patt to marked ch-1 sp and ending with 4 BPd, 4 dc in marked ch-1 sp, BPdc in next 4 dc, continue in patt across. Note that this adds one more stitch to total st count.

NEXT ROW: Work in row 1 of patt across.
(Swatch has 9 rows total, 7 increase rows, ending with 38 sts.)

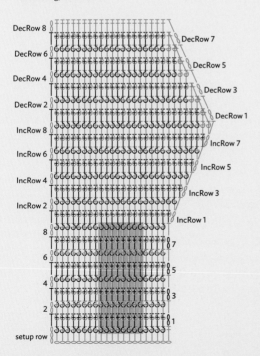

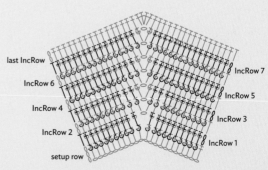

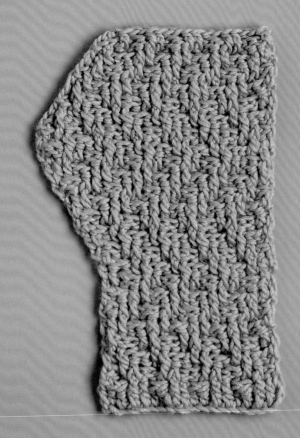

FLOATING RIB

This clever stitch features front and back post stitches that move right and then left in pairs.

NUMBER OF STITCHES IN PATTERN REPEAT	NUMBER OF ROWS IN PATTERN REPEAT
4	8
MULTIPLE	**REVERSIBLE**
4 + 4	

BASIC PATTERN

(For swatch, ch 20.)

SETUP ROW: Dc in 4th ch from hook (3 sk ch count as dc) and in each ch across, turn.
(Swatch has 18 sts.)

ROW 1: Ch 2 (counts as hdc throughout), *FPdc in next 2 dc, BPdc in next 2 dc, rep from * across, hdc in tch, turn.

ROW 2: Ch 2, BPdc in first st, *FPdc in next 2 dc**, BPdc in next 2 dc, rep from * across to last 2 sts, ending last rep at **, BPdc in next dc, hdc in tch, turn.

ROW 3: Ch 2, *BPdc in next 2 dc, FPdc in next 2 dc, rep from * across, hdc in tch, turn.

ROW 4: Ch 2, FPdc in next dc, *BPdc in next 2 dc**, FPdc in next 2 dc, rep from * across to last 2 sts, ending last rep at **, FPdc in next dc, hdc in tch, turn.

ROW 5: Rep row 3.

ROW 6: Rep row 2.

ROW 7: Rep row 1.

ROW 8: Rep row 4.

Rep rows 1–8 for patt.

(Swatch has 9 rows in patt.)

Edge Shaping

The rate of shaping is 1 st per row and can begin on any row by adjusting the order of shaping rows.

INCREASING

IncRow 1: Ch 2, dc in first hdc, FPdc in next 2 dc, continue in row 1 of patt.

IncRow 2: Work in row 2 of patt across to last 2 sts, BPdc in next dc, (dc, hdc) in tch, turn.

IncRow 3: Ch 2, dc in first hdc, FPdc in next 2 dc, BPdc in next 2 dc, continue in row 3 of patt across.

IncRow 4: Work in row 4 of patt, ending at **, (dc, hdc) in tch turn.

IncRow 5: Ch 2, dc in first hdc, BPdc in next 2 dc, FPdc in next 2 dc, continue in row 3 of patt across.

IncRow 6: Work in row 2 of patt, ending at **, BPdc in next 2 dc, (dc, hdc) in tch, turn.

IncRow 7: Ch 2, dc in first hdc, BPdc in next 2 dc, FPdc in next 2 dc, continue in row 1 of patt across.

IncRow 8: Work in row 4 of patt, ending at **, (dc, hdc) in tch, turn.

Rep IncRows 1–8 to continue increasing.
(Swatch has 8 increase rows, ending with 26 sts.)

DECREASING

DecRow 1: Ch 2, sk next dc, FPdc in next dc, BPdc in next 2 dc, continue in row 1 of patt across.

DecRow 2: Work in row 2 of patt to last 5 sts, BPdc in next 2 dc, FPdc in next dc, sk next dc, hdc in tch, turn.

DecRow 3: Ch 2, sk next dc, FPdc in next dc, BPdc in next 2 dc, FPdc in next 2 dc, continue in row 3 of patt across.

DecRow 4: Work in row 4 of patt, ending at **, FPdc in next dc, sk next dc, hdc in tch, turn.

DecRow 5: Ch 2, sk next dc, BPdc in next dc, FPdc in next 2 dc, BPdc in next 2 dc, continue in row 3 of patt across.

DecRow 6: Work in row 2 of patt to last 5 sts, BPdc in next 2 dc, FPdc in next dc, sk next dc, hdc in tch, turn.

DecRow 7: Ch 2, sk next dc, BPdc in next dc, FPdc in next 2 dc, BPdc in next 2 dc, continue in row 1 of patt.

DecRow 8: Work in row 4 of patt, ending at **, FPdc in next dc, sk next dc, hdc in tch, turn.

Rep DecRows 1–8 to continue decreasing.
(Swatch has 8 decrease rows, ending with 18 sts.)

Internal Shaping

The movement of post stitches makes this difficult to shape internally.

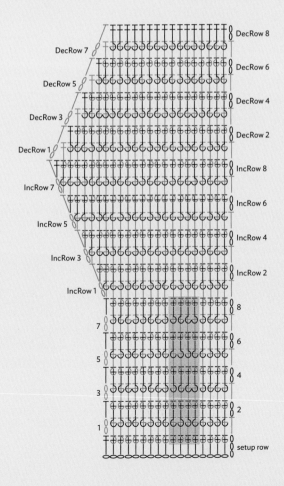

CROSSED CABLE

Here's a bold cable that uses front and back post stitches. The crossing of the cable is achieved by skipping two stitches then working post stitches into the skipped stitches. To make all stitches and rows even in height, three different heights of stitches are used: half double crochet as background stitches, double crochet for post stitches, and trebles for crossed stitches. The distance between cables can be as many stitches as you like.

NUMBER OF STITCHES IN PATTERN REPEAT	NUMBER OF ROWS IN PATTERN REPEAT
8	4
MULTIPLE	REVERSIBLE
8 + 5	

NOTE

When working the hdc immediately after the 4th cable stitch, it is easy to mistake the top of the post stitch below as the next hdc. To help, place a marker in the hdc made right after finishing the cable.

BASIC PATTERN

(For swatch, ch 21.)

SETUP ROW: Hdc in 3rd ch from hook (2 sk ch count as hdc), hdc in each ch across, turn. *(Swatch has 20 sts.)*

ROW 1 (WS): Ch 2, hdc in next 3 hdc, *BPdc in next 4 hdc, hdc in next 4 hdc, rep from * across.

ROW 2: Ch 2, hdc in next 3 hdc, *FPdc in next 4 dc, hdc in next 4 hdc, rep from * across.

ROW 3: Ch 2, hdc in next 3 hdc, *BPdc in next 4 dc, hdc in next 4 hdc, rep from * across.

ROW 4: Ch 2, hdc in next 3 hdc, *sk 2 dc, FPtr in next 2 dc, working in front of sts just made FPtr in 2 sk sts, hdc in next 4 hdc, rep from * across.

ROW 5: Ch 2, hdc in next 3 hdc, *BPdc in next 4 tr, hdc in next 4 hdc, rep from * across.

Rep rows 2–5 for patt.

(Swatch has 5 rows in patt, set up row and rows 1–4.)

Edge Shaping

Shaping at the rate of 1 st per row, using filler stitches as necessary.

INCREASING

IncRow 1: Ch 2, hdc in first st, hdc in next 3 hdc, continue in row 5 of patt across.

IncRow 2: Work in row 2 of patt to tch, 2 hdc in tch, turn.

IncRow 3: Ch 2, hdc in first st, hdc in next 5 hdc, continue in row 3 of patt across.

IncRow 4: Work in row 4 of patt to last 3 sts, FPdc in next 2 sts, 2 dc in tch, turn.

IncRow 5: Ch 2, hdc in first st, BPdc in next 3 dc, hdc in next 4 hdc, continue in row 5 of patt across.

IncRow 6: Work in row 2 of patt to last 5 sts, FPdc in next 4 sts, 2 hdc in tch, turn.

IncRow 7: Ch 2, hdc in first 2 sts, BPdc in next 4 dc, hdc in next 4 hdc, continue in row 3 of patt across.

IncRow 8: Work in row 4 of patt to last 7 sts, sk 2 dc, FPtr in next 2 dc, working in front of sts just made FPtr in 2 sk sts, hdc in next 2 sts, 2 hdc in tch, turn.

Rep IncRows 1–8 to continue increasing.
(Swatch has 8 increase rows, ending with 28 stitches.)

DECREASING

DecRow 1: Ch 1, sk first st, hdc in next 3 hdc, BPdc in next 4 tr, hdc in next 4 hdc, continue in row 5 of patt across.

DecRow 2: Work in row 2 of patt to last 2 hdc, hdc2tog, turn.

DecRow 3: Ch 1, sk first st, hdc in next hdc, BPdc in next 4 dc, hdc in next 4 hdc, continue in row 3 of patt across.

DecRow 4: Work in row 4 of patt to last 5 sts, sk 2 dc, FPtr in next dc, working in front of st just made FPtr in 2 sk sts, hdc2tog over (last tr, hdc), turn.

DecRow 5: Ch 1, sk first st, BPdc in next 3 tr, hdc in next 4 hdc, continue in row 5 of patt across.

DecRow 6: Work in row 2 of patt to last 3 sts, FPdc in next dc, hdc2tog, turn.

DecRow 7: Ch 1, sk first st, hdc in next dc, hdc in next 4 hdc, continue in row 3 of patt across.

DecRow 8: Work in row 4 of patt to last 5 sts, hdc in next 3 hdc, hdc2tog, turn.

Rep DecRows 1–8 to continue decreasing.
(Swatch has 8 decrease rows, ending with 20 sts, followed by row 5 worked even.)

Internal Shaping

The rate of increase is 2 stitches per row.
(For swatch, ch 21. Work setup row. 20 sts.)
Place marker between 2 center hdc. Always move marker to center ch-1 sp unless instructed otherwise.

IncRow 1: Work in row 1 of patt to marker, (hdc, ch 1, hdc) between 2 center hdc, hdc in next 2 hdc, continue in patt across.

IncRow 2: Work in row 2 of patt to marked ch-1 sp, (hdc, ch 1, hdc) in marked ch-1 sp, hdc in next 3 hdc, continue in patt across.

IncRow 3: Work in row 3 of patt to marked ch-1 sp, (hdc, ch 1, hdc) in marked ch-1 sp, hdc in next 4 hdc, continue in patt across.

IncRow 4: Work in row 4 of patt to marked hdc, FPdc in marked hdc, (dc, ch 1, dc) in next ch-1 sp, FPdc in next hdc, hdc in next 4 hdc, continue in patt across.

IncRow 5: Work in row 5 of patt to marked st, BPdc in marked st, BPdc in next dc, (dc, ch 1, dc) in next ch-1 sp, BPdc in next 2 dc, hdc in next 4 hdc, continue in patt across.

IncRow 6: Work in row 2 of patt to marked dc, FPdc in next 3 dc, (dc, ch 1, dc) in next ch-1 sp, FPdc in next 3 dc, hdc in next 4 hdc, continue in patt across.

IncRow 7: Work in row 3 of patt to marked dc, BPdc in next 4 dc, (hdc, ch 1, hdc) in next ch-1 sp, BPdc in next 4 dc, continue in patt across.

IncRow 8: Work in row 4 of patt to marked hdc, hdc in marked hdc, (hdc, ch 1, hdc) in next ch-1 sp, hdc in next hdc, continue in patt across.

IncRow 9: Work in row 5 of patt to marked ch-1 sp, (hdc, ch 1, hdc) in marked ch-1 sp, hdc in next 2 hdc, continue in patt across. To return to patt, work last IncRow 8 as follows: Work in row 4 of patt to marked hdc, hdc in marked hdc, 2 hdc in next ch-1 sp, hdc in next hdc, continue in patt across.

Rep IncRows 2–9 to continue increasing.
(Swatch has 9 rows total, 7 increase rows, last IncRow 8 worked as described above, ending with 36 sts.)

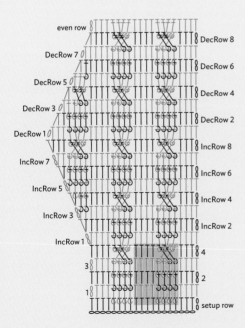

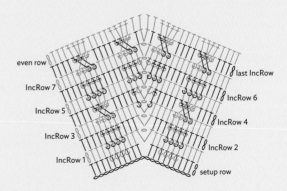

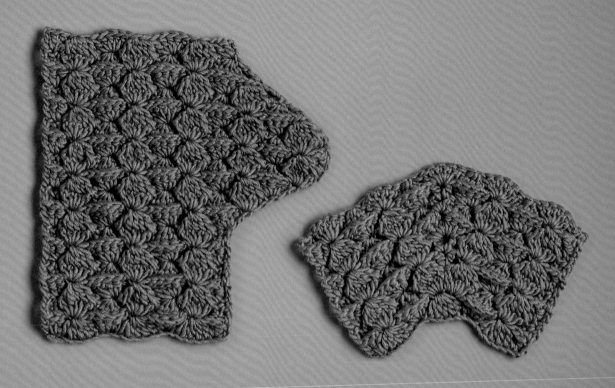

RAISED DISCS

The discs in this stitch pattern are made over two rows with a five-stitch Shell followed in the next row by a Cluster that works all the stitches of the Shell together. All the Cluster stitches are worked into the front post, creating the highly textured surface pattern. The pattern repeat consists of the five double crochet stitches in each Shell plus the FPdc5tog, which counts as only one stitch.

NUMBER OF STITCHES IN PATTERN REPEAT	NUMBER OF ROWS IN PATTERN REPEAT
6	2
MULTIPLE	REVERSIBLE
6 + 4	

NOTES
There is a ch-1 sp after working 3 or 5 stitches together that will be worked into in the following row. It does not have the usual look of a ch-1 sp but rather sits atop and slightly to the right of the worked-together group of sts. We will work into this ch-1 sp and skip the top of the worked-together sts. If you find it hard to identify the ch-1 sp, place a marker in it after completing it.

BASIC PATTERN

(For swatch, ch 22.)
ROW 1: 2 dc in 4th ch from hook, (3 sk ch count as dc), *dc5tog, ch 1**, 5 dc in next ch, rep from * across, ending last rep at **, 3 dc in last ch, turn.
(Swatch has 3 patt reps, counting ½ shells at each edge.)
ROW 2: Ch 3 (counts as dc throughout), FPdc2tog, *ch 1, 5 dc in next ch-1 sp**, sk dc5tog, FPdc5tog, rep from * across, ending last rep at **, FPdc2tog, dc in tch, turn.
ROW 3: Ch 3, 2 dc in next st, *FPdc5tog, ch 1**, 5 dc in next ch-1 sp, rep from * across, ending last rep at **, 2 dc in next ch-1 sp, dc in tch, turn.
Rep rows 2 and 3 for patt.
(Swatch has 6 rows in patt.)

Edge Shaping

Shaping begins by expanding a half shell at the edge to a full shell. Decreasing begins on a row that starts with a Cluster (FPdc5tog) to take advantage of the natural slant of the sts. Shaping is at the rate of 1 patt rep per row (after the first increase row, which adds 2 sts), resulting in a steep angle.

INCREASING

IncRow 1: Ch 3, 5 dc in next dc, FPdc5tog, ch 1, continue in row 3 of patt across.

IncRow 2: Work in row 2 of patt to last 6 sts, FPdc5tog, ch 1, 6 dc in tch, turn.

IncRow 3: Ch 3, 5 dc in first dc, FPdc5tog, ch 1, continue in row 3 of patt across.

Rep IncRows 2 and 3 to continue increasing.

To return to patt, work last IncRow 3 as follows:

Ch 3, 2 dc in first dc, FPdc5tog, ch 1, continue in row 3 of patt across.

(Swatch has 4 increase rows followed by last IncRow 3, followed by row 2 of patt worked even, ending with 5 patt reps.)

DECREASING

DecRow 1: Ch 3, sk next st, FPdc5tog, ch 1, continue in row 3 of patt across.

DecRow 1: Work in row 2 of patt to last 6 dc, FPdc5tog, dc in tch, turn.

Rep DecRows 1 and 2 to continue decreasing.

(Swatch has 5 decrease rows followed by row 3 of patt worked even, ending with 3 patt reps.)

Internal Shaping

To shape gradually, the increase happens on every 3rd row. 1 patt rep is added by IncRow 4 and another patt rep is added by IncRow 7.

(For swatch, ch 22. Work row 1 of patt. 3 patt reps, counting ½ shells at edges.)

Place marker in center dc5tog.

IncRow 1: Work in row 2 of patt to ch-1 sp before marked st, 5 dc in next ch-1 sp, ch 1, 5 dc in marked st, move marker to ch-1 sp just made, continue in patt across.

IncRow 2: Work in row 3 of patt to marked ch-1 sp, (dc, ch 1, dc) in marked ch-1 sp, move marker to last dc made, FPdc5tog, continue in patt across.

IncRow 3: Work in row 2 of patt to marked dc, sk marked dc, (dc, ch 1, dc) in next ch-1 sp, move marker to last dc made, sk next dc, 5 dc in next ch-1 sp, continue in patt across.

IncRow 4: Work in row 3 of patt to marked dc, sk marked dc, (5 dc, ch 1, 5 dc) in next ch-1 sp, move marker to ch-1 sp just made, sk next dc, continue in patt across.

IncRow 5: Work in row 2 of patt to marked ch-1 sp, (dc, ch 1, dc) in marked ch-1 sp, move marker to last dc just made, FPdc5tog, continue in patt across.

IncRow 6: Work in row 3 of patt to marked dc, sk marked dc, (dc, ch 1, dc) in next ch-1 sp, move marker to last dc made, sk next dc, 5 dc in next ch-1 sp, continue in patt across.

IncRow 7: Work in row 2 of patt to marked dc, sk marked dc, (5 dc, ch 1, 5 dc) in next ch-1 sp, move marker to ch-1 sp just made, sk next dc, continue in patt across.

Rep IncRows 2–7 to continue increasing.

To return to patt work last IncRow 4 or 7 as follows: Work in patt to marked dc, sk marked dc, 5 dc in next ch-1 sp, sk next dc, continue in patt across.

(Swatch has 8 rows in total, 6 increase rows and last row worked as described above, ending with 5 patt reps.)

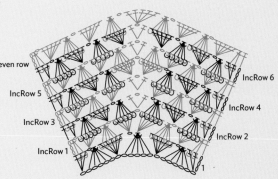

TRIPLETS

Front and back post stitches in groups of three are alternated across the row. The result is strong texture on a small scale.

NUMBER OF STITCHES IN PATTERN REPEAT	NUMBER OF ROWS IN PATTERN REPEAT
6	1
MULTIPLE	**REVERSIBLE**
6 + 5	

NOTE
Working in patt means to continue alternating groups of 3 FPdc and 3 BPdc across.

SPECIAL STITCHES
Below is a series of 2 sts worked together that will be used in the decrease section.

FPdc/hdc2tog: Yo, insert hook from front to back around next post, yo and draw up loop, yo, draw through 2 loops, yo, insert hook in next st and draw up loop, yo, draw through 4 loops on hook.

FPdc/BPdc2tog: Yo, insert hook from front to back around next post, yo and draw up loop, yo, draw through 2 loops, yo, insert hook from back to front around next post, yo and draw up loop, yo, draw through 2 loops, yo, draw through 3 loops on hook.

BPdc/hdc2tog: Yo, insert hook from back to front around next post, yo and draw up loop, yo, draw through 2 loops, yo, insert hook in next st and draw up loop, yo, draw through 4 loops on hook. Note that if the first st below is a BPdc2tog (as in DecRow 5) you can work around one or both posts below, whichever is easier.

BASIC PATTERN

(For swatch, ch 23.)
SETUP ROW: Dc in 4th ch from hook (3 sk ch count as dc), dc in each ch across, turn.
(Swatch has 21 dc.)
ROW 1: Ch 2 (counts as hdc throughout), FPdc in next 2 dc, *BPdc in next 3 dc**, FPdc in next 3 dc, rep from * across, ending last rep at **, FPdc in next 2 dc, hdc in tch, turn. Repeat row 1 for patt.
(Swatch has 7 rows in patt.)

Edge Shaping
Shaping is at the rate of 1 st per row and can begin on any row.

INCREASING

IncRow 1: Ch 2, dc in same st, FPdc in next 2 dc, continue in patt across.

IncRow 2: Work in patt to last 2 sts, FPdc in next dc, (dc, hdc) in tch, turn.

IncRow 3: Ch 2, dc in same st, BPdc in next dc, FPdc in next 3 dc, continue in patt across.

IncRow 4: Work in patt to last 3 sts, BPdc in next 2 dc, (dc, hdc) in tch, turn.

IncRow 5: Ch 2, dc in same st, BPdc in next 3 dc, continue in patt across.

IncRow 6: Rep IncRow 2.

Rep IncRows 1–6 to continue increasing.

(Swatch has 6 increase rows, ending with 27 sts, followed by 1 row worked even.)

DECREASING

DecRow 1: Work in patt to last 3 sts, FPdc in next dc, FPdc/hdc2tog, turn.

DecRow 2: Ch 2, FPdc/BPdc2tog, BPdc in next 2 dc, continue in patt across.

DecRow 3: Work in patt to last 4 sts, BPdc in next 2 dc, BPdc/hdc2tog, turn.

DecRow 4: Ch 2, BPdc2tog, FPdc in next 3 dc, continue in patt across.

DecRow 5: Work in patt to last 2 sts, BPdc/hdc2tog, turn.

DecRow 6: Ch 2, FPdc2tog, FPdc in next dc, continue in patt across.

Rep DecRows 1–6 to continue decreasing.

(Swatch has 6 decrease rows, ending with 21 dc.)

Internal Shaping

The rate of increase is 2 sts per row.

(For swatch, ch 23. Work setup row and row 1 of patt. 21 sts.)

With RS facing, place marker in center dc. Always move marker to center ch-1 sp.

IncRow 1: Work in patt, placing BPdc in dc before marked dc, (dc, ch 1, dc) in marked dc, move marker, BPdc in next dc, continue in patt across.

IncRow 2: Work in patt, placing BPdc in dc before marked ch-1 sp, (dc, ch 1, dc) in marked ch-1 sp, move marker, BPdc in next 2 dc, continue in patt across.

IncRow 3: Work in patt, placing BPdc in dc before marked ch-1 sp, (dc, ch 1, dc) in marked ch-1 sp, move marker, BPdc in next 3 dc, continue in patt across.

IncRow 4: Work in patt, placing FPdc in dc before marked ch-1 sp, (dc, ch 1, dc) in marked ch-1 sp, move marker, FPdc in next dc, continue in patt across.

IncRow 5: Work in patt, placing FPdc in dc before marked ch-1 sp, (dc, ch 1, dc) in marked ch-1 sp, move marker, FPdc in next 2 dc, continue in patt across.

IncRow 6: Work in patt, placing FPdc in dc before marked ch-1 sp, (dc, ch 1, dc) in marked ch-1 sp, move marker, FPdc in next 3 dc, continue in patt across.

Rep IncRows 1–6 to continue increasing.

To return to patt, work last IncRow 1 as follows: Work in patt to marked ch-1 sp, BPdc in dc before marked ch-1 sp, dc in marked ch-1 sp, BPdc in next dc, continue in patt across.

(Swatch has 10 rows, first 2 rows in patt, 6 increase rows, next row to return to patt, ending with 33 sts.)

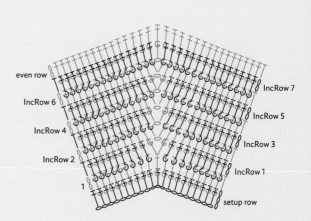

V CABLE

This stitch pattern uses post stitches that are worked at an angle from two directions, forming a V at the center of a five–double crochet group. The post stitches are worked into stitches two rows below and are worked together with double crochet stitches. This is not difficult after a bit of practice. Chain-one spaces between groups of double crochet add a lacy element.

SPECIAL STITCHES

Work double crochet and front post double crochet together (Dc/FPdc2tog): Yo, insert hook in next st, yo and draw up loop, yo, draw through 2 loops, yo, insert hook in post of 3rd dc of group 2 rows below and draw up loop, yo, draw through 2 loops, yo, draw through 3 loops on hook.

Work front post double crochet and double crochet together (FPdc/dc2tog): Yo, insert hook in post of 3rd dc of group 2 rows below, yo, draw up loop, yo, draw through 2 loops, yo, insert hook in next dc, yo, draw through 2 loops, yo, draw through 3 loops on hook.

NUMBER OF STITCHES IN PATTERN REPEAT	**NUMBER OF ROWS IN PATTERN REPEAT**
6	2
MULTIPLE	**NOT REVERSIBLE**
6 + 3	

BASIC PATTERN

(For swatch, ch 21.)

ROW 1: Dc in 4th ch from hook (3 sk ch count as dc), dc in next 4 ch, *ch 1, sk next ch, dc in next 5 ch, rep from * across, dc in last ch, turn.

(Swatch has 19 sts.)

ROW 2: Ch 1, sc in each st and in each ch across, turn.

ROW 3: Ch 2 (counts as hdc throughout), *dc/FPdc2tog, dc in next 3 dc, FPdc/dc2tog**, ch 1, rep from * across, ending last rep at **, hdc in tch.

Rep rows 2 and 3 for patt.

(Swatch has 7 rows in patt.)

Edge Shaping

Shaping is at the rate of 1 st per row, beginning on even-numbered row. Post stitches are avoided at the edges.

INCREASING

IncRow 1: Ch 1, 2 sc in first hdc, continue in row 2 of patt across.

IncRow 2: Work in row 3 of patt to last 2 sc, ch 1, sk next sc, 2 dc in last sc, turn.

IncRow 3: Ch 1, 2 sc in first dc, continue in row 2 of patt across.

IncRow 4: Work in row 3 of patt to last 3 sts, dc in next 2 sc, 2 dc in last sc, turn.

IncRow 5: Rep IncRow 3.

IncRow 6: Work in row 3 of patt to last sc, FPdc/dc2tog in last sc, dc in same sc, turn.

IncRow 7: Rep IncRow 3.

Rep IncRows 2–7 to continue increasing.

(Swatch has 6 increase rows, ending with 25 sts, followed by 2 rows worked even.)

DECREASING

DecRow 1: Ch 1, sk first st, work in row 2 of patt across.

DecRow 2: Work in row 3 of patt to last 5 sc, dc/FPdc2tog, dc in next 2 sc, dc2tog, turn.

DecRow 3: Rep DecRow 1.

DecRow 4: Work in row 3 of patt to last 3 sc, dc/FPdc2tog, dc2tog, turn.

DecRow 5: Rep DecRow 1.

DecRow 6: Work in row 3 of patt to last 2 sc, dc2tog, turn.

Rep DecRows 1–6 to continue decreasing.

(Swatch has 6 decrease rows, ending with 19 sts.)

Internal Shaping

Shaping at the center disrupts the V cable and makes this stitch pattern not suitable for internal shaping.

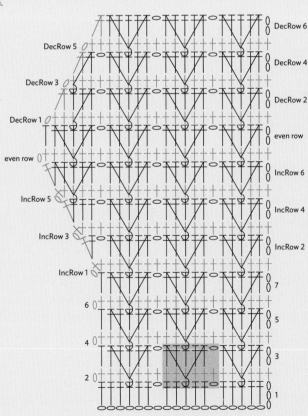

SIDEWAYS BOBBLES

An unusual closed stitch where rows of single crochet are studded with bobbles that lie on their sides.

NUMBER OF STITCHES IN PATTERN REPEAT	NUMBER OF ROWS IN PATTERN REPEAT
6	8
MULTIPLE	**REVERSIBLE**
6 + 3	

NOTE
This pattern consists of rows of sc stitches with Sideways Bobbles worked every 4th row,. The Sideways Bobbles are always separated by 3 sc.

SPECIAL STITCH
Sideways Bobble (SB): (Yo, insert hook under 2 loops at side of sc and draw up loop, yo, draw through 2 loops) 4 times, yo, draw through 5 loops on hook. Counts as 3 sts throughout.

BASIC PATTERN

(For swatch, ch 21.)
ROW 1: Sc in 2nd ch from hook and in each ch across, turn.
(Swatch has 20 sts.)
ROW 2: Ch 1, sc in each sc across, turn.
ROW 3: Ch 1, sc in first sc, *ch 3, SB, sk next 3 sc, sc in next 3 sc, rep from * across, sc in last sc, turn.
ROW 4: Ch 1, sc in first sc, *sc in next 3 sc, 3 sc in next ch-3 sp, rep from * across, sc in last sc, turn.
ROWS 5 AND 6: Rep row 2.
ROW 7: Ch 1, sc in first sc, *sc in next 3 sc, ch 3, SB, sk next 3 sc, rep from * across, sc in last sc, turn.
ROW 8: Ch 1, sc in first sc, *3 sc in next ch-3 sp, sc in next 3 sc, rep from * across, sc in last sc, turn.
ROW 9: Rep row 2.
(Swatch has 8 rows in patt, with increasing beginning on row 9 of patt.)

Edge Shaping

This is a good example of using "filler" stitches for shaping. When the Sideways Bobble would be placed at an edge you wish to shape, substitute 3 sc stitches in its place.
Shaping is at the rate of 1 st per row and can begin on any row. Note, however, that the exact sequence of shaping rows will be different as you continue shaping. Use the same strategy of substituting sc stitches for Sideways Bobbles when the latter would otherwise occur at a shaping edge.

INCREASING

IncRow 1: Ch 1, 2 sc in first sc, work in row 9 of patt across.
IncRow 2: Work in row 2 of patt to last sc, 2 sc in last sc, turn.
IncRow 3: Ch 1, 2 sc in first sc, sc in next 2 sc, ch 3, SB, continue in row 3 of patt across.
IncRow 4: Work in row 4 of patt across.
IncRows 5 AND 6: Rep IncRows 1 and 2.
IncRow 7: Ch 1, 2 sc in first sc, sc in next 2 sc, ch 3, SB, continue in row 7 of patt across.
IncRow 8: Work in row 8 of patt across.
Rep IncRows 1–8 to continue increasing, adding filler sts as needed.
(Swatch has 8 increase rows, ending with 26 sts.)

DECREASING

DecRow 1: Ch 1, sk first sc, work in row 9 of patt across.
DecRow 2: Work in row 2 of patt to last 2 sc, sc2tog, turn.
DecRow 3: Ch 1, sk first sc, sc in next 4 sc, ch 3, SB, continue in row 3 of patt across.
DecRow 4: Work in row 4 of patt across.
DecRows 5 AND 6: Rep DecRows 1 and 2
DecRow 7: Ch 1, sk first sc, sc in next 4 sc, ch 3, SB, continue in row 7 of patt across.
DecRow 8: Work in row 8 of patt across.
Rep DecRows 1–8 to continue decreasing.
(Swatch has 8 decrease rows, ending with 20 sts.)

Internal shaping

The intricate alignment of stitches in this stitch pattern makes it unsuitable for internal shaping.

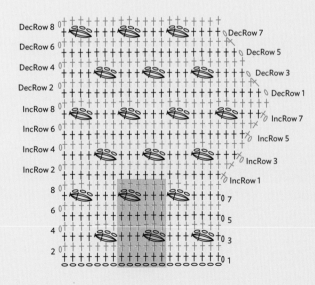

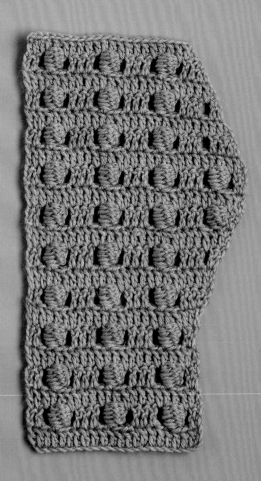

BOBBLE ON POST

The Bobbles in this stitch are worked around the posts of the previous stitches, and are offset by chain-one spaces on either side. Alternate rows are plain rows of double crochet stitches.

NOTE

In the dc rows make sure you work into the Bobble and also into the dc under it. The tops of both sts should be visible along the row.

SPECIAL STITCH

Bobble on Post (Bobble): Dc5tog around post of dc just made, inserting hook from front to back and to the right of post just made. Left-handers work to the left of post just made.

NUMBER OF STITCHES IN PATTERN REPEAT

7

NUMBER OF ROWS IN PATTERN REPEAT

2

MULTIPLE

7 + 3

REVERSIBLE

BASIC PATTERN

(For swatch, ch 24.)
ROW 1: Dc in 4th ch from hook (3 sk ch count as dc), dc in each ch across, turn.
(Swatch has 22 dc.)
ROW 2: Ch 3 (counts as dc throughout), dc in next dc, *ch 1, sk next dc, dc in next dc, Bobble, ch 1, sk next 2 dc**, dc in next 3 dc, rep from * across, ending last rep at **, dc in last 2 sts, turn.
ROW 3: Ch 3, dc in each st and each ch-1 sp across.
Rep rows 2 and 3 for patt.
(Swatch has 6 rows in patt.)

Edge Shaping

Shaping at the rate of 1 st per row except for IncRow 6 and DecRow 6, when we change the count by 2 sts. This permits a repeatable shaping strategy, adding or subtracting a full patt rep of 7 sts over 6 rows. Note that in IncRow 6 we only skip 1 dc after last Bobble.

INCREASING

IncRow 1: Ch 3, dc in same st, continue in row 3 of patt across.
IncRow 2: Work in row 2 of patt to tch, 2 dc in tch.
IncRow 3: Rep IncRow 1.
IncRow 4: Work in row 2 of patt to last 5 sts, dc in next 3 dc, ch 1, sk next dc, 2 dc in tch, turn.

IncRow 5: Rep IncRow 1.
IncRow 6: Work in row 2 of patt to last 3 sts, dc in next dc, Bobble, ch 1, 2 dc in tch, turn.
Rep IncRows 1–6 to continue increasing.
(Swatch has 6 increase rows, ending with 29 sts, followed by rows 3 and 2 worked even in patt.)

DECREASING

DecRow 1: Ch 2, dc in next st (counts as dc2tog), continue in row 3 of patt across.
DecRow 2: Work in row 2 of patt to last 5 sts, ch 1, sk next dc, dc in next 2 dc, dc2tog, turn.
DecRow 3: Rep DecRow 1.
DecRow 4: Work in row 2 of patt to last 3 sts, ch 1, sk next dc, dc2tog, turn.
DecRow 5: Rep DecRow 1.
DecRow 6: Work in row 2 of patt to last 4 sts, dc in next dc, dc3tog, turn.
Rep DecRows 1–6 to continue decreasing.
(Swatch has 6 decrease rows, ending with 22 sts, followed by 1 even row.)

Internal Shaping

The unusual formation of this Bobble makes internal shaping impractical.

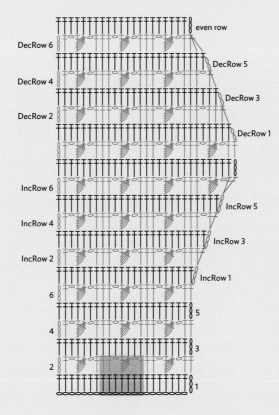

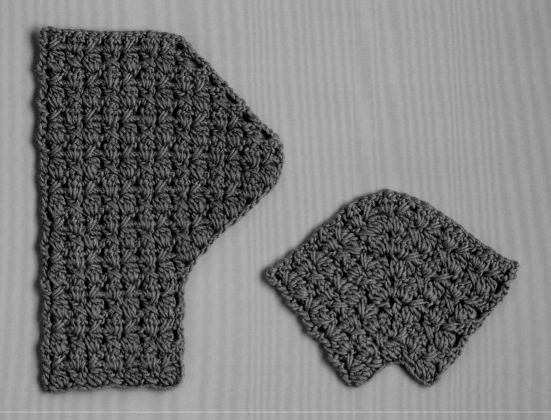

BOBBLED AND CROSSED

Two elements alternate in each row, a three–double crochet Bobble and a pair of double crochet stitches that cross each other. In the next row the two elements switch places, with the crossed stitches worked on either side of the Bobble and the Bobbles sprouting from the center of the two crossed double crochet stitches.

NOTE
Row 2 of patt is as written except for the first time it is worked, when the dc is worked into the 4th ch of tch.

SPECIAL STITCH
Bobble: (Yo, insert hook in designated st or sp and draw up loop, yo and draw through 2 loops) 3 times, yo, draw through 4 loops on hook.

NUMBER OF STITCHES IN PATTERN REPEAT
5

NUMBER OF ROWS IN PATTERN REPEAT
2

MULTIPLE
5 + 3

REVERSIBLE

BASIC PATTERN

(For swatch, ch 23.)

ROW 1: Bobble in 6th ch from hook (5 sk ch count as 1 fnd ch, dc, ch 1 of Row 1), *ch 1, sk 2 ch, dc in next ch, dc in last sk ch, ch 1, sk next ch, Bobble in next ch, rep from * across, ch 1, sk next ch, dc in last ch, turn.

(Swatch has 4 patt reps, counting dcs at edges.)

ROW 2: Ch 4 (counts as dc, ch 1 throughout), sk first ch-1 sp, dc in next ch-1 sp, dc in sk ch-1 sp, *ch 1, Bobble inserting hook in sp between next 2 dc, ch 1, sk next ch-1 sp, dc in next ch-1 sp, dc in sk ch-1 sp, rep from * across, ch 1, dc in 3rd ch of tch (see Note above), turn.

ROW 3: Ch 4, *Bobble between next 2 dc, ch 1**, sk next ch-1 sp, dc in next ch-1 sp, dc in sk ch-1 sp, ch 1, rep from * across, ending last rep at **, dc in 3rd ch of tch, turn.

Rep rows 2 and 3 for patt.

(Swatch has 6 rows in patt.)

Edge Shaping

One patt rep (5 sts: Bobble, crossed dcs, 2 ch) is added or subtracted over 2 rows.

INCREASING

IncRow 1: Ch 3, dc in same st, ch 1, Bobble between next 2 dc, ch 1, continue in row 3 of patt across.

IncRow 2: Work in row 2 of patt across, Bobble between last 2 dc, ch 1, 2 dc in tch, turn.

IncRow 3: Ch 3, dc in same st, ch 1, Bobble between first 2 dc, ch 1, continue in row 3 of patt across.

Rep IncRows 2 and 3 to continue increasing.

(Swatch has 6 increase rows, ending with 6 patt reps, 3 dc, 1 ch, followed by 2 rows worked even in patt.)

DECREASING

DecRow 1: Ch 4 (counts as tr), sk next 2 dc and next ch-1 sp, dc in next ch-1 sp, dc in sk ch-1 sp, continue in row 3 of patt across.

DecRow 2: Work in row 2 of patt, placing last 2 crossed dc over last Bobble, (do not ch 1) sk next 2 sts, dc in tch, turn.

Rep DecRows 1 and 2 to continue decreasing.

To return to patt, work last DecRow 2 as follows:

Work in row 2 of patt across, placing last 2 crossed dc over last Bobble, ch 1, sk next 2 sts, dc in tch, turn.

(Swatch has 6 decrease rows, ending with 4 patt reps.)

Internal Shaping

(For swatch, ch 18. Work row 1 of patt. 3 patt reps.)

Place marker in center Bobble.

IncRow 1: Work in row 2 of patt to marked Bobble, sk next ch-1 sp, dc in marked Bobble, dc in sk ch-1 sp, (dc, ch 1, dc) in marked Bobble, dc in next ch-1 sp, dc in marked Bobble, move marker to ch-1 sp just made, ch 1, continue in patt across.

IncRow 2: Work in row 3 of patt, ending with (Bobble, ch 1) before marked ch-1 sp, (dc, ch 1, dc) in marked ch-1 sp, move marker to last dc made, ch 1, Bobble, continue in patt across.

IncRow 3: Work in row 2 of patt, ending with (2 crossed dc, ch 1) before marked dc, Bobble in marked dc, ch 1, (dc, ch 1, dc) in next ch-1 sp, move marker to last dc made, ch 1, Bobble in next dc, ch 1, continue in patt across.

IncRow 4: Work in row 3 of patt, ending with (2 crossed dc, ch 1) before marked dc , Bobble in marked dc, ch 1, (dc, ch 1, dc) in next ch-1 sp, move marker to last dc made, ch 1, Bobble in next dc, ch 1, continue in patt across.

Rep IncRows 3 and 4 to continue increasing.

To return to patt, on last IncRow 4 work 2 dc at center instead of (dc, ch 1, dc).

(Swatch has 8 rows total, 5 increase rows, next row worked as described above, last row worked even, ending with 8 patt reps.)

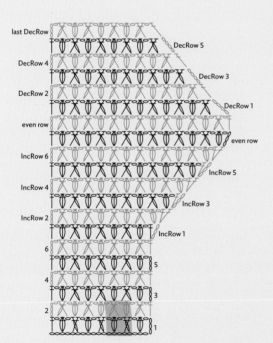

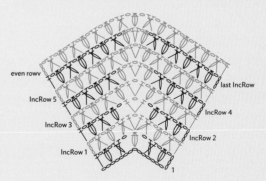

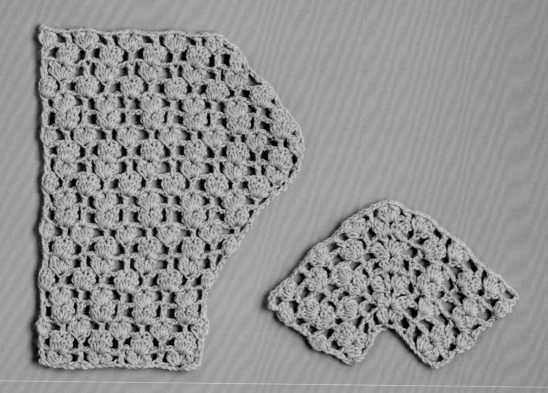

BOBBLES ON STEMS

This easy and pretty lace consists of pairs of three-double crochet Bobbles aligned over each other for two rows, then aligned over double crochet stitches on the third row. The pattern repeat consists of two Bobbles separated by a chain, plus two chains on either side of the Bobble, and one double crochet stitch.

NUMBER OF STITCHES IN PATTERN REPEAT	NUMBER OF ROWS IN PATTERN REPEAT
8	3
MULTIPLE	**REVERSIBLE**
8 + 5	

SPECIAL STITCHES

Bobble: (Yo, insert hook in designated st, yo and draw up loop, yo, draw through 2 loops) 3 times in same st, yo, draw through 4 loops on hook.

Bobble Shell (BShell): (Bobble, ch 1, Bobble) in designated st or sp.

BASIC PATTERN

(For swatch, ch 37.)

ROW 1: BShell in 9th ch from hook (8 sk ch count as 3 fnd ch, dc, ch 2), *ch 2, sk 3 ch, dc in next ch**, ch 2, sk 3 ch, BShell in next ch, rep from * across, ending last rep at **, turn.
(Swatch has 4 patt reps, 1 dc.)

ROW 2: Ch 5 (counts as dc, ch 2 throughout), *BShell in ch-1 sp of next BShell, ch 2, dc in next dc**, ch 2, rep from * across, ending last rep at **, turn.

ROW 3: Ch 3, Bobble in same st, ch 2, dc in ch-1 sp of next BShell, ch 2, rep form * across, Bobble in tch, turn.

ROW 4: Ch 5, *BShell in next dc, ch 2, dc in ch-1 sp of next BShell, ch 2, rep from * across, dc in tch, turn.

Rep rows 2–4 for patt.
(Swatch has 6 rows in patt.)

Edge Shaping

Shaping for this large patt is at the rate of 1 patt rep over 3 rows, beginning on the first row of the 3-row repeat.

INCREASING

IncRow 1: Ch 5, dc in same st, ch 2, BShell in next dc, continue in row 4 of patt across.
IncRow 2: Work in row 2 of patt across, ch 2, Bobble in 3rd ch of tch, turn.
IncRow 3: Ch 5, dc in same st, ch 2, BShell in next dc, continue in row 3 of patt across.
IncRow 4: Work in row 4 of patt across, placing last dc in 3rd ch of tch, turn.
IncRow 5: Ch 5, dc in first dc, ch 2, work in row 2 of patt across, turn.
IncRow 6: Work in row 3 of patt across to tch, (dc, ch 2, dc) in 3rd ch of tch, turn.
Rep IncRows 1–6 to continue increasing.
(Swatch has 6 increase rows, ending with 6 patt reps, followed by 3 rows worked even in patt.)

DECREASING

DecRow 1: Work in row 4 of patt to last dc, BShell in last dc, sk next Bobble, dc in tch, turn.
DecRow 2: Ch 3, Bobble in ch-1 sp of next BShell, ch 2, dc in next dc continue in row 2 of patt across.
DecRow 3: Work in row 3 of patt to last dc, BShell in last dc, sk next Bobble, dc in tch, turn.

DecRow 4: Ch 4, sk next BShell, BShell in next dc, ch 2, dc in ch-1 sp of next BShell, continue in row 4 of patt across.
DecRow 5: Work in row 2 of patt to last BShell, Bobble in ch-1 sp of last BShell, dc in tch, turn.
DecRow 6: Ch 3, sk next Bobble, Bobble in next dc, ch 2, dc in ch-1 sp of next BShell, continue in row 3 of patt across.
Rep DecRows 1–6 to continue decreasing.
(Swatch has 6 decrease rows, ending with 4 patt reps, 1 Bobble.)

Internal Shaping

The rate of shaping is 2 patt reps every 3 rows.
(For swatch, ch 29. Work row 1 of patt. 3 patt reps, 1 dc.)
Place marker in ch-1 sp of center BShell.
IncRow 1: Work in row 2 of patt to marked ch-1 sp, (Bobble, ch 2, dc, ch 1, dc, ch 2, Bobble) in marked ch-1 sp, move marker to Bobble just made, ch 2, dc in next dc, continue in patt across.
IncRow 2: Work in row 3 of patt, placing dc in marked Bobble, ch 2, Bobble in next dc, ch 2, (dc, ch 1, dc) in next ch-1 sp, move marker to ch-1 sp just made, ch 2, Bobble in next dc, ch 2, dc in next Bobble, continue in patt across.
IncRow 3: Work in row 4 of patt to marked ch-1 sp, BShell in marked ch-1 sp, move marker to ch-1 sp just made, continue in patt across.
Rep IncRows 1–3 to continue increasing.
(Swatch has 7 rows total, 6 increase rows, ending with 7 patt reps, 1 dc.)

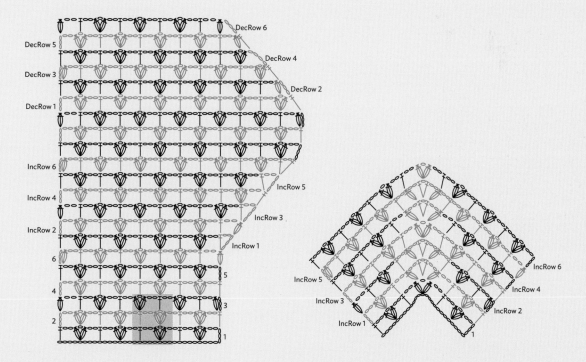

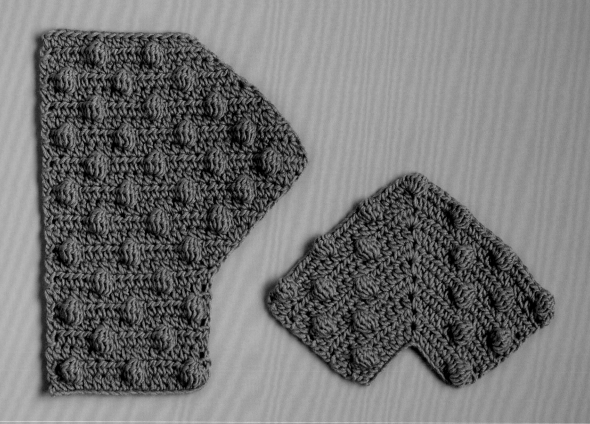

SOFT BOBBLE

A fabric of solid half double crochet stitches is
dotted with Bobbles. The Bobbles are worked
every other row and are staggered.

NUMBER OF STITCHES IN PATTERN REPEAT	NUMBER OF ROWS IN PATTERN REPEAT
6	4
MULTIPLE	**NOT REVERSIBLE**
6 + 6	

SPECIAL STITCHES

Bobble: (Yo, insert hook in designated st, yo and
draw up loop, yo, draw through 2 loops) 5 times, yo,
draw through 6 loops on hook.

Special half double crochet decrease (Shdc2tog):
Yo, insert hook in designated st and draw up loop,
insert hook in next designated st and draw up loop,
yo, draw through 3 loops on hook. This forms a
more compact decrease.

BASIC PATTERN

(For swatch, ch 18.)
ROW 1: Hdc in 3rd ch from hook (2 sk ch count as hdc) and in
each ch across, turn.
(Swatch has 17 sts.)
ROW 2: Ch 2 (counts as hdc throughout), hdc in next hdc,
*Bobble in next hdc**, hdc in next 5 hdc, rep from * across,
ending last rep at **, hdc in last 2 hdc, turn.
ROW 3: Ch 2, hdc in each st across, turn.
ROW 4: Ch 2, hdc in next 4 hdc, *Bobble in next hdc, hdc in
next 5 hdc, rep from * across, turn.
ROW 5: Rep row 3.
Rep rows 2–5 for patt.
(Swatch has 8 rows in patt.)

Edge Shaping

To make this a repeatable pattern, we must increase 6 sts—
that is, a full patt rep, over the 4 rows of the pattern. Therefore,
we increase or decrease 2 sts on 1 row then increase or
decrease by 1 st on the following row.

INCREASING

IncRow 1: Ch 2, 2 hdc in same st, continue in row 3 of patt
across.
IncRow 2: Work in row 2 of patt to tch, 2 hdc in tch, turn.
IncRow 3: Rep IncRow 1.
IncRow 4: Work in row 4 of patt to tch, 2 hdc in tch, turn.
Rep IncRows 1–4 to continue increasing.
(Swatch has 8 increase rows, ending with 29 sts.)

DECREASING

DecRow 1: Ch 1, sk first st, Shdc2tog, hdc in next st, work in
row 5 of patt across.
DecRow 2: Work in row 2 of patt to last 2 hdc, Shdc2tog, turn.
DecRow 3: Rep DecRow 1.
DecRow 4: Work in row 4 of patt to last 2 hdc, Shdc2tog, turn.
Rep DecRows 1–4 to continue decreasing.
*(Swatch has 8 decrease rows, ending with 17 sts, followed by 1 row
worked even.)*

Internal Shaping

6 sts are added every 2 rows. To help maintain patt while
increasing, we specify how many hdc are worked in patt before
the ch-1 sp at center.
(For swatch, ch 18. Work row 1 of patt. 17 sts.)
Place marker in center hdc. Always move marker to ch-1 sp at
center.
IncRow 1: Work in row 2 of patt, ending with 5 hdc before
marked hdc, (2 hdc, ch 1, 2 hdc) in marked hdc, move marker,
hdc in next 5 hdc, Bobble in next hdc, continue in patt across.
IncRow 2: Work in row 3 of patt to marked ch-1 sp, (hdc, ch 1,
hdc) in marked ch-1 sp, move marker, continue in patt across.
IncRow 3: Work in row 4 of patt ending with 5 hdc before
marked ch-1 sp, (2 hdc, ch 1, 2 hdc) in marked ch-1 sp, move
marker, hdc in next 5 hdc, Bobble in next hdc, continue in patt
across.
IncRow 4: Rep IncRow 2.
Rep IncRows 1–4 to continue increasing.
To return to patt, work last IncRow 1 as follows: Work in row
2 of patt, ending with 5 hdc before marked ch-1 sp, Bobble in
marked ch-1 sp, hdc in next 5 hdc, Bobble in next hdc, continue
in patt across.
*(Swatch has 10 rows total, 8 increase rows, last row worked as
described above ending with 41 sts.)*

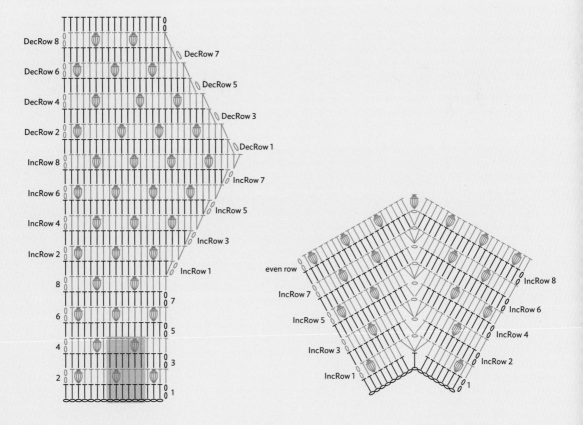

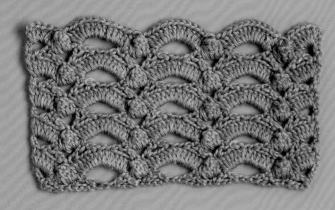

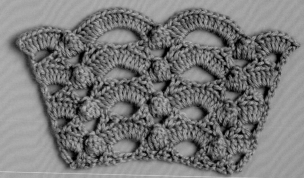

BROAD BAND

A dramatic stitch that uses a thirteen–double crochet Shell worked over a chain-seven space and a five–double crochet Popcorn worked over a chain-three space. In the alternate row we make the chain spaces for the large Shell and Popcorn to be worked into. This alternate row makes the stitch unsuitable for edge shaping.

NUMBER OF STITCHES IN PATTERN REPEAT	NUMBER OF ROWS IN PATTERN REPEAT
V	2

MULTIPLE	NOT REVERSIBLE
11 + 6	

NOTE

When working dc together in this patt, there are always sts skipped between the 2 legs of the dc2tog.

SPECIAL STITCHES

Popcorn: 5 dc in designated sp, remove hook from work and insert it in first st of group, draw unworked loop through.

Shell: 13 dc in designated ch-sp.

BASIC PATTERN

(For swatch, ch 50.)
ROW 1 (WS): Dc2tog over (7th ch from hook, sk 3 ch, next ch) (6 sk ch count as dc, ch 3), *ch 3, dc2tog over (next ch, sk 3 ch, next ch)**, ch 7, sk next ch, dc2tog over (next ch, sk 3 ch, next ch), rep from * across, ending last rep at **, ch 3, dc in last ch, turn.
(Swatch has 4 patt reps counting half patts at each end.)
ROW 2: Ch 3 (counts as dc throughout), 6 dc in first ch-3 sp, *Popcorn in next ch-3 sp**, Shell in next ch-7 sp, rep from * across, ending last rep at **, 7 dc in ch-6 tch, turn.
ROW 3: Ch 6 (counts as dc, ch 3), *dc2tog over (next dc, sk 4 dc, next dc), ch 3, sk Popcorn, dc2tog over (next dc, sk 4 dc, next dc),** ch 7, sk next dc, rep from * across, ending last rep at **, ch 3, dc in tch, turn.
Rep rows 2 and 3 for patt, ending with row 2.
(Swatch has 10 rows in patt.)

Edge Shaping

Edge shaping is not suitable for this stitch.

Internal Shaping

To use the technique of pattern enlargement, we begin with a smaller version of the pattern, requiring a multiple of 9 (+ 6). 1 ch is added on each odd-numbered row.

(For swatch, ch 33.)

ROW 1: Dc2tog over (7th ch from hook, sk 2 ch, next ch) (6 sk ch count as dc, ch 3), *ch 3, dc2tog over (next ch, sk 2 ch, next ch)**, ch 5, sk next ch, dc2tog over (next ch, sk 2 ch, next ch) rep from * ending last rep at **, ch 3, dc in last ch, turn.

(Swatch has 3 patt reps with ch-5 sps and ch-3 sps, including half patts at edges.)

ROW 2: Ch 3, 4 dc in first ch-3 sp, *Popcorn in next ch-3 sp**, 9 dc in next ch-5 sp, rep from * ending last rep at **, 5 dc in last ch-6 sp, turn.

ROW 3: Ch 6 (counts as dc, ch 3), *dc2tog over (next dc, sk 2 dc, next dc), ch 3, sk Popcorn, dc2tog over (next dc, sk 2 dc, next dc)**, ch 6, sk next dc, dc2tog over (next dc, sk 2 dc, next dc), rep from * ending last rep at **, ch 3, dc in tch, turn.

ROW 4: Ch 3, 5 dc in first ch-3 sp, *Popcorn in next ch-3 sp**, 11 dc in next ch-6 sp, rep from * ending last rep at **, 6 dc in ch-6 tch, turn.

ROW 5: Ch 6 (counts as dc, ch 3), *dc2tog over (next dc, sk 3 dc, next dc), *ch 3, sk Popcorn, dc2tog over (next dc, sk 3 dc, next dc)** ch 7, sk next dc, dc2tog over (next dc, sk 3 dc, next dc), rep from * ending last rep at **, ch 3, dc in tch, turn.

ROW 6: Ch 3, 6 dc in first ch-3 sp, *Popcorn in next ch-3 sp**, 13 dc in next ch-7 sp, rep from * ending last rep at **, 7 dc in ch-6 tch, turn.

ROW 7: Ch 7 (counts as dc, ch 4), dc2tog over (next dc, sk 4 dc, next dc), *ch 3, sk Popcorn, dc2tog over (next dc, sk 4 dc, next dc)**, ch 8, sk next dc, dc2tog over (next dc, sk 4 dc, next dc) rep from * ending last rep at **, ch 4, dc in tch, turn.

ROW 8: Ch 3, 7 dc in first ch-4 sp, *Popcorn in next ch-3 sp**, 15 dc in next ch-8 sp, rep from * ending last rep at **, 8 dc in ch-7 tch.

To continue enlarging patt, in odd-numbered rows add 1 ch at start of row, 1 ch after skipping Popcorn, and 1 ch before last dc of row. On even-numbered rows make two additional dc in each ch-sp in the row.

(Swatch has 3 patt reps with 15 dc Shells.)

POPCORN MESH

This lovely textured lace has one row of Popcorns alternating with single crochet stitches across the row, with chain-three spaces between them. On the next row the chain-three spaces are filled in with single crochet, creating a frame for each Popcorn.

NUMBER OF STITCHES IN PATTERN REPEAT	NUMBER OF ROWS IN PATTERN REPEAT
V	4
MULTIPLE	**NOT REVERSIBLE**
6 + 2	

NOTE
Pay attention to the number of sc in even-numbered rows. There should be 7 sc in a patt rep, extending from one Popcorn to the next. Row 4 has one sc more than row 2 of patt.

On odd-numbered rows count skipped sc carefully.

SPECIAL STITCH
Popcorn: 4 dc in designated st or sp, remove hook from work and insert it in first dc of group, draw unworked loop through.

BASIC PATTERN

(For swatch, ch 20.)
ROW 1: Sc in 2nd ch from hook, *ch 3, sk 2 ch, Popcorn in next ch, ch 3, sk 2 ch, sc in next ch, rep from * across.
(Swatch has 3 patt reps.)
ROW 2: Ch 1, sc in first sc, *3 sc in next ch-3 sp, sk Popcorn, 3 sc in next ch-3 sp, sc in next sc, rep from * across.
(Swatch has 22 sc.)
ROW 3: Ch 2, dc in same sc (counts as dc2tog), *ch 3, sk next 3 sc, sc between last sk sc and next sc, ch 3, sk next 3 sc**, Popcorn in next sc, rep from * across, ending last rep at **, dc2tog in last sc, turn.
ROW 4: Ch 1, sc in first dc2tog, *3 sc in next ch-3 sp, sc in next sc, 3 sc in next ch-3 sp, sk Popcorn, rep from * across, sc in last dc2tog, turn.
ROW 5: Ch 1, sc in first sc, * ch 3, sk 3 sc, Popcorn in next sc, ch 3, sk 3 sc, sc between last sk sc and next sc, rep from * across, placing last sc in last sc.
Rep rows 2–5 for patt, ending on an even-numbered row.
(Swatch has 8 patt rows.)

Edge Shaping

The rate of shaping is 1 full patt rep over 4 rows, beginning on row 5 of patt and with shaping on odd-numbered rows when increasing. When decreasing, a decrease is also worked on sc rows to maintain slanted edge.

When working this shaping at opposite edge, to increase, end rows with (ch 3, dc in last sc). To decrease, end even-numbered rows with dc in last sc.

INCREASING

IncRow 1: Ch 6 (counts as dc, ch 3 throughout), sc in first sc, ch 3, sk next 3 sc, Popcorn in next sc, continue in row 5 of patt across.

IncRow 2: Work in row 2 of patt to ch-6 tch, 3 sc in tch, sc in 3rd ch of tch, turn.

IncRow 3: Ch 6, sc in first sc, ch 3, sk next 3 sc, Popcorn in next sc, continue in row 3 of patt across.

IncRow 4: Work in row 4 of patt to ch-6 tch, 3 sc in tch, sc in 3rd ch of tch, turn.

Rep IncRows 1–4 to continue increasing.

(Swatch has 8 increase rows, ending with 5 patt reps.)

DECREASING

DecRow 1: Ch 3 (counts as dc), sk first 4 sc, Popcorn in next sc, ch 3, sk next 3 sc, sc between last sk sc and next sc, continue in row 5 of patt across.

DecRow 2: Work in row 2 of patt to last ch-3 sp (not counting tch), 2 sc in last ch-3 sp, sc2tog over (same ch-3 sp, last Popcorn), turn.

DecRow 3: Ch 3 (counts as dc), sk 2 sc, Popcorn in next sc, ch 3, sk 3 sc, sc between last sk sc and next sc, continue in row 3 of patt across, turn.

DecRow 4: Work in row 4 of patt to last ch-3 sp, 2 sc in last ch-3 sp, sc2tog over (same ch-3 sp, last Popcorn), turn.

DecRow 5: Ch 3 (counts as dc), sk first 3 sts, Popcorn in next sc, ch 3, sk next 3 sts, sc between last sk sc and next sc, continue in row 5 of patt across.

Rep DecRows 2–5 to continue decreasing.

To return to patt, work last DecRow 4 as follows: Work in row 4 of patt to last ch-3 sp, 3 sc in last ch-3 sp, sc in last Popcorn, turn.

(Swatch has 8 decrease rows, ending with 3 patt reps.)

Internal Shaping

One patt rep is added every 2 rows.

(For swatch, ch 20. Work row 1 of patt. 3 patt reps.)

Place marker in center Popcorn.

IncRow 1: Work in row 2 of patt to marked Popcorn, (sc, ch 3, sc) in marked Popcorn, move marker to last sc made, 3 sc in next ch-3 sp, continue in patt across.

IncRow 2: Work in row 3 of patt working sc before marked sc, ch 3, (Popcorn, ch 3, Popcorn) in next ch-3 sp, move marker to ch-3 sp just made, ch 3, sk next sc, sc between sk sc and next sc, continue in patt across.

IncRow 3: Work in row 4 of patt to marked ch-3 sp, 3 sc in marked ch-3 sp, move marker to last sc made, sk next Popcorn, 3 sc in next ch-3 sp, continue in patt across.

IncRow 4: Work in row 5 of patt, placing sc before marked sc, ch 3, sk next sc, Popcorn in next sc, move marker to Popcorn just made, ch 3, sk next sc, sc between sk sc and next sc, continue in patt across.

Rep IncRows 1–4 to continue increasing.

(Swatch has 10 rows total, 8 increase rows, last row worked even, ending with 7 patt reps.)

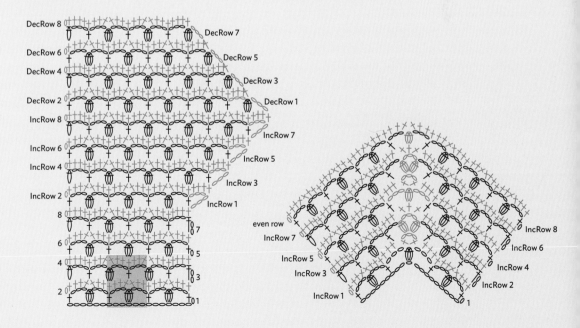

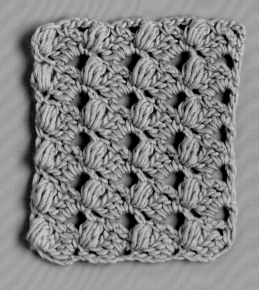

PUFF LACE

The two elements in this pattern are a block of three double crochet stitches worked at an angle and a Puff stitch. The block is worked into a chain-three space created in the Puff row. The result is a lovely, unusual textured lace.

NUMBER OF STITCHES IN PATTERN REPEAT

v

MULTIPLE

5 + 2

NOTE

A long chain is used to begin row 2 of patt because it allows the Puff stitch that follows to appear more full and fluffy. This is the chain that is worked into at the end of row 3.

NUMBER OF ROWS IN PATTERN REPEAT

2

NOT REVERSIBLE

SPECIAL STITCHES

Long chain (Long ch): Work chain drawing up loop to ¾".

Puff: (Yo, insert hook in designated st, yo and draw loop up to ¾") 4 times, yo, draw through all loops on hook.

BASIC PATTERN

(For swatch, ch 22.)
ROW 1: (Sc, ch 3, 3 dc) in 2nd ch from hook, *sk 4 ch, (sc, ch 3, 3 dc) in next ch, rep from * across, sk 4 ch, sc in last ch, turn. *(Swatch has 4 patt reps.)*
ROW 2: Long ch, Puff in first sc, *ch 1, sk 3 dc, sc in next ch-3 sp, ch 3**, Puff in next sc, rep from * across, ending last rep at **, hdc in last sc, turn.
ROW 3: Ch 1, sk first hdc, *(sc, ch 3, 3 dc) in next ch-3 sp**, sk (sc, ch 1, Puff), rep from * ending last rep at **, sc in ch 1 above Puff, turn.
Rep rows 2 and 3 for patt.
(Swatch has 12 rows in patt.)

Edge Shaping

The angles in this pattern work against shaping at the edges.

Internal Shaping

To enlarge this pattern, we add 1 ch to each patt rep on odd-numbered rows and 1 dc to each patt rep on even-numbered rows.

(For swatch, ch 17. Work row 1 of patt. 3 patt reps.)

IncRow1: Long ch, Puff in first sc, *ch 1, sk 3 dc, sc in next ch-3 sp, ch 4**, Puff in next sc, rep from * across, ending last rep at **, hdc in last sc, turn.

IncRow 2: Ch 1, sk first hdc, *(sc, ch 3, 4 dc) in next ch-4 sp**, sk (sc, ch 1, Puff), rep from * ending last rep at **, sc in ch 1 above Puff, turn.

IncRow 3: Long ch, Puff in first sc, *ch 2, sk 4 dc, sc in next ch-3 sp, ch 5**, Puff in next sc, rep from * across, ending last rep at **, hdc in last sc, turn.

IncRow 4: Ch 1, sk first hdc, *(sc, ch 3, 5 dc) in next ch-5 sp**, sk (sc, ch 2, Puff), rep from * ending last rep at **, sc in ch 1 above Puff, turn.

IncRow 5: Long ch, Puff in first sc, *ch 2, sk 5 dc, sc in next ch-3 sp, ch 6**, Puff in next sc, rep from * across, ending last rep at **, hdc in last sc, turn.

IncRow 6: Ch 1, sk first hdc, *(sc, ch 3, 6 dc) in next ch-6 sp**, sk next (sc, ch 2, Puff), rep from * ending last rep at **, sc in ch 1 above Puff, turn.

IncRow 7: Long ch, Puff in first sc, *ch 3, sk 6 dc, sc in next ch-3 sp, ch 6**, Puff in next sc, rep from * across, ending last rep at **, hdc in last sc, turn.

IncRow 8: Ch 1, sk first hdc, (sc, ch 3, 7 dc) in next ch-6 sp**, sk next (sc, ch 3, Puff), rep from * ending last rep at **, sc in ch 1 above Puff, turn.

IncRow 9: Long ch, Puff in first sc, *ch 3, sk 7 dc, sc in next ch-3 sp, ch 7**, Puff in next sc, rep from * across, ending last rep at **, hdc in last sc, turn.

IncRow 10: Ch 1, sk first hdc, (sc, ch 3, 8 dc) in ch-7 sp**, sk next (sc, ch 3, Puff), rep from * ending last rep at **, sc in ch 1 above Puff, turn.

(Swatch has 11 rows total, ending with 3 patt reps, each having 8 dc.)

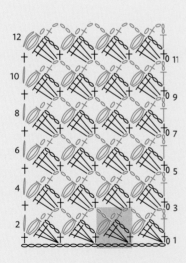

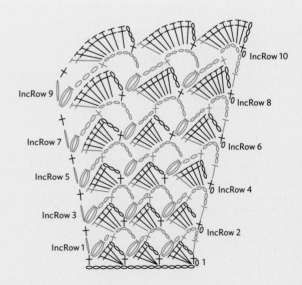

SPLIT PUFFS

This textured stitch features a Puff stitch that is "split" by working it in two legs with space in between.

NUMBER OF STITCHES IN PATTERN REPEAT	NUMBER OF ROWS IN PATTERN REPEAT
3	2
MULTIPLE	REVERSIBLE
3 + 4	

NOTE
Row 3 of patt ends with a dc rather than an hdc, which maintains the correct length at the edge. However, this can vary depending on the size of chains, so feel free to experiment.

SPECIAL STITCHES
Split Puff (SP): (Yo, insert hook in designated st and draw up loop to ½") twice, (yo, insert hook in next designated st and draw up loop to ½") twice, yo, draw through 9 loops on hook. After row 1 the 2 legs of the Puff are worked into the "eye" at the top of the Puff of prev row except at the beginning of the row. The eye is formed by the first ch made after the Puff. The 2 sts to be worked into are designated in parentheses after the word "over." The 1st leg of each SP is worked into the same st as the 2nd leg of the SP just made.

Puff: (Yo, insert hook in designated st and draw up loop to ½") twice, yo, draw through 3 loops on hook.

BASIC PATTERN

(For swatch, ch 16.)

ROW 1: SP over (4th and 7th ch) from hook (3 sk ch count as hdc, ch 1), *ch 2, SP over (same ch as last SP, sk 2 ch, next ch), rep from * across, ch 1, hdc in same ch as last SP, turn. *(Swatch has 4 SP, 2 hdc.)*

ROW 2: Ch 2 (counts as hdc throughout), Puff in top of next SP, *ch 2**, SP over (same SP, next SP), rep from * across, ending last rep at **, Puff in same SP, dc in 2nd ch of tch, turn.

ROW 3: Ch 3, (counts as hdc, ch 1), SP over (first Puff, next SP), *ch 2, SP over (same SP, next SP), rep from * to last SP, SP over (same SP, next Puff), ch 1, dc in tch.

Rep rows 2 and 3 for patt.

(Swatch has 6 rows in patt.)

Edge Shaping

Shaping is at the rate of 1 SP every other row and begins on an odd-numbered row.

INCREASING

IncRow 1: Ch 2, Puff in first dc, ch 2, SP over (same dc, next SP), continue in row 3 of patt.

IncRow 2: Work in row 2 of patt to last Puff, ch 2, Puff in last Puff, dc in tch, turn.

Rep IncRows 1 and 2 to continue increasing.

(Swatch has 6 increase rows, ending with 7 SP, counting ½ SP at edges.)

DECREASING

DecRow 1: Ch 2, sk first Puff, Puff in next SP, ch 2, continue in row 3 of patt across.

DecRow 2: Work in row 2 of patt to last SP, Puff in last SP, dc in tch, turn.

Rep DecRows 1 and 2 to continue decreasing.

(Swatch has 6 decrease rows, ending with 4 SP, counting ½ SP at edges.)

Internal Shaping

The split structure of this stitch does not allow for internal shaping.

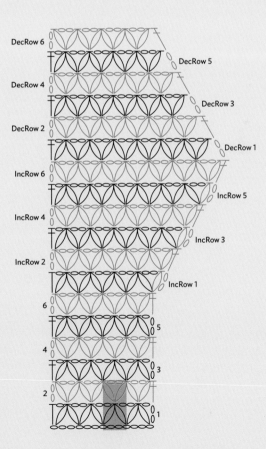

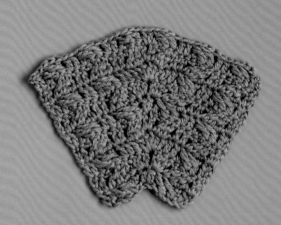

WINDING ROAD

Cable-like effects can be achieved without post stitches. Stitches can be worked along a diagonal by skipping two stitches, then working other stitches crossing either in front of or behind the stitches just made. It's not too difficult, given practice. The pattern repeat consists of the four crossed trebles and two double crochet stitches.

NUMBER OF STITCHES IN PATTERN REPEAT	NUMBER OF ROWS IN PATTERN REPEAT
6	2

MULTIPLE	REVERSIBLE
6 + 4	

NOTE

Cross Front (CF) and Cross Behind (CB) sts are always worked in pairs. We skip 2 sts, work a tr in the next 2 sts, then work either in front of or behind the sts just made.

SPECIAL STITCHES

Cross Front (CF): Tr working in sk st and in front of st just made. Insert hook from front as usual, but bring it up in front of st just made.

Cross Behind (CB): Tr working in sk st and behind st just made. To accomplish this, flip your work so the back is facing and work treble inserting hook from back to front in skipped st.

BASIC PATTERN

(For swatch, ch 22.)

ROW 1: Dc in 4th ch from hook (3 sk ch count as dc), *sk next 2 ch, tr in next 2 ch, CF in 2 sk sts, dc in next 2 ch, rep from * across, turn.
(Swatch has 3 patt reps, 2 dc.)

ROW 2: Ch 3 (counts as dc throughout), dc in next dc, sk next 2 tr, tr in next 2 tr, CB in 2 sk sts, dc in next 2 tr, rep from * across, turn.

ROW 3: Ch 3, dc in next dc, sk next 2 tr, tr in next 2 tr, CF in sk 2 sts, dc in next 2 dc, rep from * across, turn.
Rep Rows 2 and 3 for patt.
(Swatch has 6 rows in patt.)

Edge Shaping

The rate of shaping is 1 st per row and can begin on any row. Filler sts are used as needed.

INCREASING

IncRow 1: Ch 3, dc in same st, dc in next dc, sk next 2 tr, tr in next 2 tr, CF in 2 sk sts, continue in row 3 of patt across.

IncRow 2: Work in row 2 of patt to last 2 sts, dc in next dc, 2 dc in tch, turn.

IncRow 3: Ch 3, dc in same st, dc in next 3 dc, sk next 2 tr, tr in next 2 tr, CF in 2 sk sts, continue in row 3 of patt across.

IncRow 4: Work in row 2 of patt to last 3 sts, sk next 2 dc, tr in tch, CB in 2 sk sts, dc in tch, turn.

IncRow 5: Ch 3, sk 1 tr, tr in next 2 tr, CF in first dc, CF in next tr, continue in row 3 of patt across.

IncRow 6: Work in row 2 of patt to tch, 2 dc in tch, turn.

Rep IncRows 1–6 to continue increasing.

(Swatch has 6 increase rows, ending with 4 patt reps, 2 dc.)

DECREASING

DecRow 1: Ch 2, dc in next dc (counts as dc2tog throughout), sk next 2 tr, tr in next 2 tr, CF in 2 sk sts, continue in row 3 of patt across.

DecRow 2: Work in row 2 of patt to last 5 sts, sk next 2 tr, tr in next tr, CB in 2 sk sts, dc2tog, turn.

DecRow 3: Ch 2 (does not count as st), dc in next 5 sts, sk next 2 tr, tr in next 2 tr, CF in 2 sk sts, continue in row 3 of patt across.

DecRow 4: Work in row 2 of patt to last 5 sts, dc in next 3 dc, dc2tog, turn.

DecRow 5: Ch 2, dc in next 3 dc, sk next 2 tr, tr in next 2 tr, CF in 2 sk sts, continue in row 3 of patt across.

DecRow 6: Work in row 2 of patt to last 3 dc, dc in next dc, dc2tog, turn.

Rep DecRows 1–6 to continue decreasing.

(Swatch has 6 decrease rows, ending with 3 patt reps, 2 dc.)

Internal Shaping

Double increases are worked for 3 increase rows so that there is a sufficient number of sts to work crossed sts, followed by 1 row worked even. Two patt reps are added over 4 rows.

(For swatch, ch 16. Work row 1 of patt. 2 patt reps, 2 dc.)

Place marker in 2nd dc of 2 dc at center, turn.

IncRow 1: Work in row 2 of patt to marked dc, 3 dc in marked dc, ch 1, 3 dc in next dc, move marker to last dc made, sk next 2 tr, tr in next 2 tr, CB in 2 sk sts, continue in patt across.

IncRow 2: Work in row 3 of patt to marked dc, dc in marked dc, dc in next 2 dc, (2 dc, ch 1, 2 dc) in next ch-1 sp, dc in next dc, move marker to last dc made, dc in next 2 dc, sk next 2 tr, tr in next 2 tr, CF in sk 2 sts, continue in patt across.

IncRow 3: Work in row 2 of patt to marked dc, sk next 2 dc, tr in next dc, CB in 2 sk sts, (dc, ch 1, dc) in next ch-1 sp, sk next 2 dc, tr in next dc, CB in 2 sk sts, move marker to last tr made, continue in patt across.

IncRow 4: Work in row 3 of patt to marked tr, sk next 2 tr, tr in next 2 dc, CF in 2 sk sts, 2 dc in next ch-1 sp, move marker to last dc just made, sk next 2 sts, tr in next 2 sts, CF in 2 sk sts, continue in patt across.

Rep IncRows 1–4 to continue increasing.

(Swatch has 9 rows total, 8 increase rows, ending with 6 patt reps, 2 dc.)

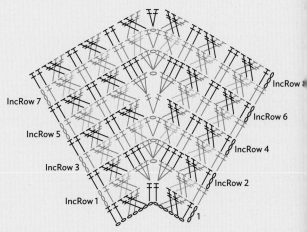

DIAMOND ZIGZAG

Stitches are made to slant by skipping stitches, then working trebles in front or behind the skipped stitches. The diamond shape is created by working the slant in one direction, then the other, alternating across the row. The pattern repeat requires eight stitches in all, first crossing behind, then crossing in front of, skipped stitches.

NOTE
Although the same row is repeated to create this pattern, it is a 2-row patt rep because the diamond shape requires 2 rows to complete.

SPECIAL STITCHES
Cross Behind (CB): Tr working in sk sts and behind 2 sts just made. To accomplish this, flip your work so the back is facing, then work treble inserting hook from back to front in skipped sts.

Cross Front (CF): Tr working in sk sts and in front of 2 sts just made. Insert hook as usual, make sure to bring hook up in front of 2 sts just made.

NUMBER OF STITCHES IN PATTERN REPEAT	NUMBER OF ROWS IN PATTERN REPEAT
8	2
MULTIPLE	REVERSIBLE
8 + 4	

BASIC PATTERN

(For swatch, ch 28.)

ROW 1: Dc in 6th ch from hook (5 sk ch count as dc and 2 sk ch), tr in next ch, 2 CB, *sk next 2 ch, tr in next 2 ch, 2 CF**, sk next 2 ch, tr in next 2 ch, 2 CB, rep from * across, ending last rep at**, dc in last ch, turn.

(Swatch has 6 crossed pairs, 2 dc.)

ROW 2: Ch 3 (counts as dc throughout), *sk next 2 tr, tr in next 2 sts, 2 CB, sk next 2 tr, tr in next 2 sts, 2 CF, rep from * across, dc in tch, turn.

Rep row 2 for patt.

(Swatch has 8 rows in patt.)

Edge Shaping

Shaping at the edges disrupts this pattern, since one can't skip stitches that aren't there.

Internal Shaping

Every 3 rows 8 sts (2 crossed pairs) are added.

(For swatch, ch 28. Work row 1 of patt. 6 crossed pairs, 2 dc.)

Place marker in sp between center CB/CF.

IncRow 1: Work in patt to marked sp, 4 tr in marked sp, move marker to last tr worked, 2 CF, continue in patt across.

IncRow 2: Work in patt to marked tr ending with 2 CB, sk marked tr, 2 tr in next tr, 2 CF working both sts in marked tr, sk next tr, 2 tr in next tr, 2 CB working both sts in sk tr, move marker between CF and CB just made, continue in patt across.

IncRow 3: Work even in patt, moving marker between CF/CB at center.

IncRow 4: Work in patt to marked sp, 4 tr in marked sp, move marker to last tr made, 2 CB, continue in patt across.

IncRow 5: Work in patt to marked tr, sk marked tr, 2 tr in next tr, 2 CB working both sts in marked tr, sk next tr, 2 tr in next tr, 2 CF working both sts in sk tr, continue in patt across.

IncRow 6: Work even in patt, moving marker to sp between center CB/CF.

Rep IncRows 1–6 to continue increasing.

(Swatch has 7 rows total, 6 increase rows, ending with 10 crossed pairs, 2 dc.)

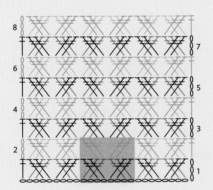

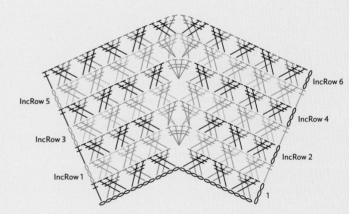

WOVEN SHELLS

This shell stitch is an elaboration of a split Shell, composed of two groups of three double crochet stitches with a chain-one space between them. The first group of double crochet stitches begins after skipping stitches, then the second is worked into the skipped stitch, causing the second group of stitches to wrap around the first group.

NOTE
Woven Shells are worked into ch-1 sps on either side of a sc st. Work them loosely to avoid clumping up of fabric.

SPECIAL STITCH
Woven Shell: Sk next ch-1 sp, 3 dc in next ch-1 sp, ch 1, 3 dc in sk ch-1 sp

NUMBER OF STITCHES IN PATTERN REPEAT
10

MULTIPLE
9 + 2

NUMBER OF ROWS IN PATTERN REPEAT
2

REVERSIBLE

BASIC PATTERN

(For swatch, ch 29.)

ROW 1: Sc in 2nd ch from hook, *ch 1, sk 4 ch, 3 dc in next ch, ch 1, 3 dc in last sk ch (Woven Shell made), ch 1, sk 3 ch, sc in next ch, rep from * across.

(Swatch has 3 patt reps, 1 sc.)

ROW 2: Ch 3, 3 dc in first st, *ch 1, sc in ch-1 sp of next Woven Shell, ch 1**, Woven Shell, rep from * across, ending last rep at **, 4 dc in last sc, turn.

ROW 3: Ch 1, sc in first dc, *ch 1, Woven Shell, ch 1**, sc in ch-1 sp of next Woven Shell, rep from * across, ending last rep at **, sk 3 dc, sc in tch, turn.

Rep rows 2 and 3 for patt.

(Swatch has 7 rows in patt.)

Edge Shaping

We use the usual strategy when shaping Shells—turning a half Shell at the edge into a full Shell, which in this patt begins in row 2, thereafter increasing by half a Shell every row. Decreasing also follows the procedures often used in Shells, with slip stitches to decrease half a Shell at the start of even-numbered rows.

INCREASING

IncRow 1: Ch 4 (counts as dc, ch 1), 3 dc in first ch-1 sp, ch 1, 3 dc in first sc, ch 1, sc in ch-1 sp of next Woven Shell, continue in row 2 of patt across.

IncRow 2: Work in row 3 of patt to tch, 3 dc in 3rd ch of tch, ch 1, (3 dc, ch 1, dc) in ch-4 tch, turn.

IncRow 3: Ch 3, 3 dc in first ch-1 sp, ch 1, 3 dc in in first dc, ch 1, continue in row 2 of patt across.

Rep IncRows 2 and 3 to continue increasing.

(Swatch has 4 increase rows, ending with 5 patt reps, followed by 2 rows worked even.)

DECREASING

DecRow 1: Ch 1, sk first sc, sl st in next ch-1 sp, sl st in next 3 dc, sc in next ch-1 sp, ch 1, Woven Shell, continue in row 2 of patt across.

DecRow 2: Work in row 3 of patt to last Woven Shell, sc in ch-1 sp of last Woven Shell, turn.

Rep DecRows 1 and 2 to continue decreasing.

(Swatch has 4 decrease rows, ending with 3 patt reps.)

Internal Shaping

All attempts at internal shaping distort the stitch pattern or result in too much bulk.

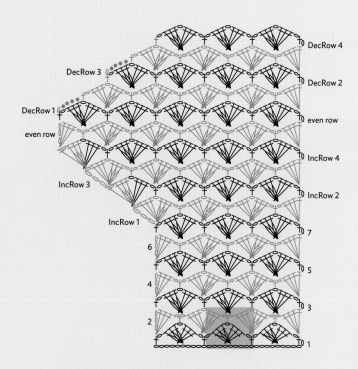

CHAPTER FOUR

EXPLODING SHELLS

Shells have been part of crochet's vocabulary for a long time, as they are easy to create and represent a versatile visual element that can be treated in myriad ways. Best of all, most shell patterns can be shaped both at the edges and internally. The twenty stitches here represent a selection of my favorites in this genre.

Shells are formed when we work several stitches into one place. Naturally, the bottoms of these stitches are collected together and their tops fan out from that point; in fact, they are sometimes called fans instead of shells.

Shell stitches can be solid or open and lacy, and they can be pivoted to form angles. Shells can be worked into a single stitch or into chain spaces. When done the latter way, they create arches that resemble decorative facades. Shells can be combined with any number of other elements: a single stitch, or blocks of plain stitches, Vee stitches, chain spaces, or clusters. This last combination forms circles, and we have several examples here. Multirow shell stitches can create beautiful lace, often with a floral appearance.

Most shells patterns have a half shell at the edge. This half shell opens the way for edge shaping: by expanding the half shell to a full one, we get the natural slant of the shell at the edge. For decreasing, we slip stitch along the slanted edge of the shell to remove half of a shell. These shaping strategies are used in most of the stitches in this chapter. These slants at the edges are not straight but rather slightly curved, so the edge may have a scalloped appearance.

You'll find stitches here for just about any item you can imagine. The closed shells have built-in fluidity, as they use mostly taller stitches, so they are nice choices for garments. The lace patterns will make lovely scarves, shawls, and tops suitable for warmer weather when made with finer-weight yarns. Remember to wet block your lace to get the maximum beauty from your stitch pattern!

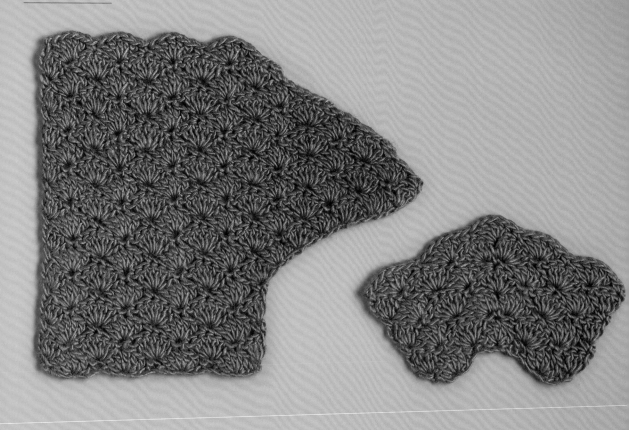

BASIC SHELL

This is a much-loved and easy shell pattern that creates an attractive closed fabric. The pattern repeat consists of one Shell and one single crochet stitch.

NUMBER OF STITCHES IN PATTERN REPEAT	NUMBER OF ROWS IN PATTERN REPEAT
6	2
MULTIPLE	REVERSIBLE
6 + 2	

SPECIAL STITCH
Shell: 5 dc in designated st

BASIC PATTERN

(For swatch, ch 26.)
ROW 1: Sc in 2nd ch from hook, *sk 2 ch, Shell in next ch, sk 2 ch, sc in next ch, rep from * across.
(Swatch has 4 patt reps, 1 sc.)
ROW 2: Ch 3 (counts as dc throughout), 2 dc in same sc, *sk 2 dc, sc in next dc, sk 2 dc**, Shell in next sc, rep from * across, ending last rep at **, 3 dc in last sc, turn.
ROW 3: Ch 1, sc in first dc, *sk 2 dc, Shell in next sc, sk 2 dc, sc in next dc, rep from * across, placing last sc in tch, turn.
Rep rows 2 and 3 for patt.
(Swatch has 5 rows in patt.)

Edge Shaping

As with many shell patterns, shaping can be done at the rate of ½ patt rep per row, and begins by turning a half Shell at the edge of a row to a full Shell. In this stitch patt shaping begins on an even-numbered row.

When decreasing, after slip stitching in 2 dc, the next sc is worked without a ch-1 to keep a smooth line at the edge.

INCREASING

IncRow 1: Work in row 2 of patt to last sc, Shell in last sc, turn.

IncRow 2: Ch 3, 4 dc in same dc, sk next dc, sc in next dc, continue in row 3 of patt across.

IncRow 3: Work in row 2 of patt to tch, Shell in tch, turn.

Rep IncRows 2 and 3 to continue increasing.

To return to patt, work last IncRow 2 as follows: Ch 3, 5 dc in same dc, sk next dc, sc in next dc, continue in row 3 of patt across.

(Swatch has 6 increase rows, last increase row worked as described above, 2 rows worked even, ending with 7 patt reps.)

DECREASING

DecRow 1: Work in row 2 of patt, placing last Shell in 2nd to last sc, sk 2 dc, sc in next dc, leave rem sts unworked, turn.

DecRow 2: Ch 1, sk first sc, sl st in next 2 dc, sc in next dc, sk 2 dc, Shell in next sc, continue in row 3 of patt across.

Rep DecRows 1 and 2 to continue decreasing.

(Swatch has 6 decrease rows, ending with 4 patt reps.)

Internal Shaping

This method adds 1 Shell every 3rd row.

(For swatch, ch 20. Work row 1 of patt. 3 patt reps, 1 sc.)

Place marker in center dc of center Shell.

IncRow 1: Work in row 2 of patt to marked dc, (sc, ch 1, sc) in marked dc, move marker to last sc made, sk 2 dc, Shell in next sc, continue in patt across.

IncRow 2: Work in row 3 of patt to marked sc, Shell in marked sc, sc in next ch-1 sp, move marker to sc just made, Shell in next sc, continue in patt across.

IncRow 3: Work in row 2 of patt across, moving marker to center dc of center Shell.

IncRow 4: Work in row 3 of patt to marked dc, (sc, ch 1, sc) in marked dc, move marker to last sc made, continue in patt across.

IncRow 5: Work in row 2 of patt to marked sc, Shell in marked sc, sc in next ch-1 sp, move marker to sc just made, Shell in next sc, continue in patt across.

IncRow 6: Work in row 3 of patt across, moving marker to center dc of center Shell.

Rep IncRows 1–6 to continue increasing.

(Swatch has 7 rows total, 6 increase rows, ending with 5 patt reps, 1 sc.)

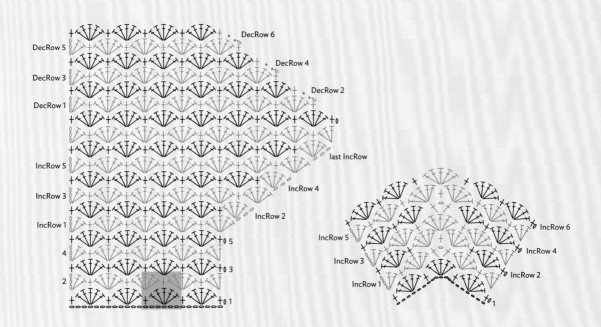

167

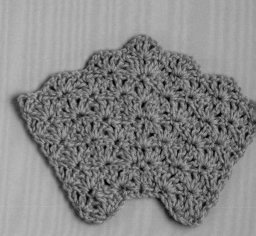

OPEN SHELL

An open version of the Basic Shell with chain-one spaces between double crochet stitches, this easy pattern creates lovely lace.

NUMBER OF STITCHES IN PATTERN REPEAT	NUMBER OF ROWS IN PATTERN REPEAT
8	2
MULTIPLE	REVERSIBLE
6 + 2	

SPECIAL STITCH
Shell: (Dc, ch 1) 3 times in designated st, dc in same st

BASIC PATTERN

(For swatch, ch 26.)
ROW 1: Sc in 2nd ch from hook, *sk 2 ch, Shell in next ch, sk 2 ch, sc in next ch, rep from * across.
(Swatch has 4 Shells, 5 sc.)
ROW 2: Ch 4 (counts as dc, ch 1 throughout), dc in same sc, *sc in center ch-1 sp of next Shell**, Shell in next sc, rep from * across, ending last rep at **, (dc, ch 1, dc) in last sc, turn.
ROW 3: Ch 1, sc in first dc, *Shell in next sc, sc in center ch of next Shell, rep from * across, placing last sc in tch, turn.
Rep rows 2 and 3 for patt.
(Swatch has 7 rows in patt.)

Edge Shaping
Decreasing at the start of a row entails working 2 or 3 sl sts. To avoid extra bulk or length, we skip some sts when slip stitching. Keep tension loose on slip stitches to avoid bunching fabric. The first sc on decrease rows is begun with no ch 1 to eliminate bumps at the edge.

Increasing

IncRow 1: Ch 5 (counts as tr, ch 1), (dc, ch 1) 2 times in same st, dc in same st (Shell made), sc in center ch of next Shell, continue in row 2 of patt across.

IncRow 2: Work in row 3 of patt across to tch, Shell in 4th ch of tch.

Rep IncRows 1 and 2 to continue increasing, ending with IncRow 2.

To return to patt, work last IncRow as follows: Ch 4 (counts as dc, ch 1), dc in same st, continue in row 2 of patt across.

(Swatch has 7 increase rows including last IncRow, ending with 7 Shells, followed by row 3 of patt worked even.)

DECREASING

DecRow 1: Ch 1, sk first sc, sl st in next dc, sk next ch-1 sp, sl st in next dc, sc in next ch-1 sp, Shell in next sc, continue in row 2 of patt across.

DecRow 2: Work in row 3 of patt to last Shell, sc in center ch of last Shell, leave rem sts unworked, turn.

Rep DecRows 1 and 2 to continue decreasing.

(Swatch has 6 decrease rows, ending with 4 Shells, 5 sc.)

Internal Shaping

We increase 1 Shell every 3 rows.

(For swatch, ch 20. Work row 1 of patt. 3 Shells.)

Place marker in center ch-1 sp of center Shell.

IncRow 1: Work in row 2 of patt to marked ch-1 sp, (sc, ch-1, sc) in marked ch-1 sp, move marker to last sc made, Shell in next sc, continue in patt across.

IncRow 2: Work in row 3 of patt to marked sc, Shell in marked sc, sc in next ch-1 sp, move marker to sc just made, Shell in next sc, continue in patt across.

IncRow 3: Work in row 2 of patt to marked sc, Shell in marked sc, move marker to center ch-1 sp of Shell just made, continue in patt across.

IncRow 4: Work in row 3 of patt to marked ch-1 sp, (sc, ch 1, sc) in marked ch-1 sp, move marker to last sc made, continue in patt across.

IncRow 5: Work in row 2 of patt to marked sc, Shell in marked sc, sc in next ch-1 sp, move marker to sc just made, Shell in next sc, continue in patt across.

IncRow 6: Work in row 3 of patt to marked sc, Shell in marked sc, move marker to center ch-1 sp of Shell just made, continue in patt across.

Rep IncRows 1–6 to continue increasing.

(Swatch has 10 rows total, 9 increase rows, ending with 6 Shells, including ½ Shells at each edge.)

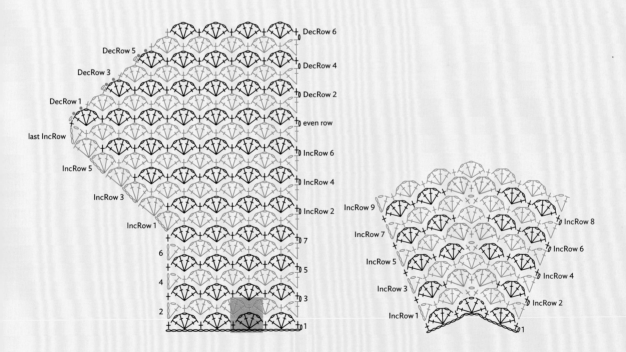

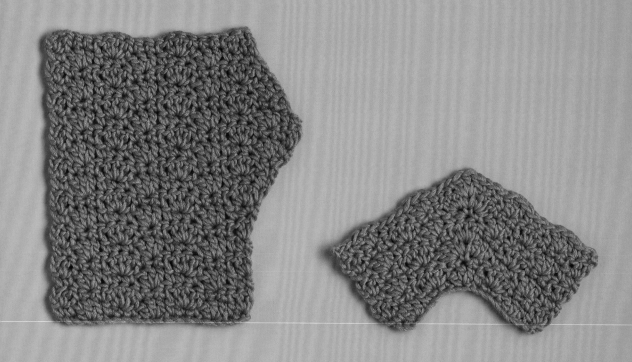

CROWNED SHELLS

This is one of the smallest Shell patterns, an almost solid stitch featuring three–double crochet Shells topped with a single crochet stitch. It creates a lively surface.

NUMBER OF STITCHES IN PATTERN REPEAT	NUMBER OF ROWS IN PATTERN REPEAT
6	2
MULTIPLE	**REVERSIBLE**
6 + 2	

BASIC PATTERN

(For swatch, ch 20.)

ROW 1: Sc in 2nd ch from hook, sc in next ch, *sk next ch, 3 dc in next ch, sk next ch**, sc in next 3 ch, rep from * across, ending last rep at **, sc in last 2 ch, turn.
(Swatch has 19 sts.)

ROW 2: Ch 3 (counts as dc throughout), dc in same sc, *sk next sc, sc in next 3 dc, sk next sc**, 3 dc in next sc, rep from * across, ending last rep at **, 2 dc in last sc, turn.

ROW 3: Ch 1, sc in first dc, sc in next dc, *sk next sc, 3 dc in next sc, sk next sc**, sc in next 3 dc, rep from * across, ending last rep at **, sc in next dc, sc in tch, turn.

Rep rows 2 and 3 for patt.
(Swatch has 6 rows in patt.)

Edge Shaping

Unlike larger Shells, the 3-dc Shell used here can be shaped in smaller increments, avoiding the strong slant seen in most Shell shaping. Shaping is at the rate of 1 st per row.

INCREASING

IncRow 1: Ch 1, 2 sc in first dc, sc in next dc, sk next sc, 3 dc in next sc, continue in row 3 of patt across.

IncRow 2: Work in row 2 of patt to last 3 sc, sk next sc, 3 dc in next sc, sc in last sc, turn.

IncRow 3: Ch 3, dc in same sc, sc in next 3 dc, continue in row 3 of patt across.

IncRow 4: Work in row 2 of patt to last 2 dc, sc in next dc, 2 sc in tch, turn.

IncRow 5: Ch 1, sc in first sc, 3 dc in next sc, sk next sc, continue in row 3 of patt across.

IncRow 6: Work in row 2 of patt to last sc, 2 dc in last sc, turn.
Rep IncRows 1–6 to continue increasing.
(Swatch has 6 increase rows, ending with 25 sts.)

DECREASING

DecRow 1: Ch 1, sk first dc, sc in next dc, sk next sc, 3 dc in next sc, continue in row 3 of patt across.

DecRow 2: Work in row 2 of patt to last 4 sts, sc in next 2 dc, sc2tog, turn.

DecRow 3: Ch 2 (does not count as st), sk first st, 2 dc in next sc, continue in row 3 of patt across.

DecRow 4: Work in row 2 of patt to last 2 dc, sc2tog, turn.

DecRow 5: Ch 1, sk first st, sc in next 3 dc, continue in row 3 of patt across.

DecRow 6: Work in row 2 of patt to last 3 sc, dc in next sc, dc2tog.
Rep DecRows 1–6 to continue decreasing.
(Swatch has 6 decrease rows, ending with 19 sts.)

Internal Shaping

Increasing is at the rate of 6 sts (1 patt rep) every 3 rows.
(For swatch, ch 20. Work in row 1 of patt. Swatch has 19 sts.)
Place marker in center dc of center 3-dc group.

IncRow 1: Work in row 2 of patt to marked dc, placing sc in dc before marked dc, (sc, ch 1, sc) in marked dc, move marker to ch-1 sp just made, sc in next dc, continue in patt across.

IncRow 2: Work in row 3 of patt to marked ch-1 sp, placing 3 dc in sc before marked ch-1 sp, (sc, ch 1, sc) in marked ch-1 sp, move marker to last sc made, 3 dc in next sc, continue in patt across.

IncRow 3: Work in row 2 of patt to marked sc, sk marked sc, 3 dc in next ch-1 sp, move marker to last dc made, sk next sc, continue in patt across.

IncRow 4: Work in row 3 of patt to marked dc, sc in marked dc, (sc, ch 1, sc) in next dc, move marker to ch-1 sp just made, sc in next dc, continue in patt across.

IncRow 5: Work in row 2 of patt to marked ch-1 sp, placing 3 dc in sc before marked ch-1 sp, (sc, ch 1, sc) in marked ch-1 sp, move marker to last sc made, 3 dc in next sc, continue in patt across.

IncRow 6: Work in row 3 of patt to marked sc, sk marked sc, 3 dc in next ch-1 sp, move marker to center dc of 3-dc group just made, sk next sc, continue in patt across.
Rep IncRows 1–6 to continue increasing.
(Swatch has 7 rows total, 6 increase rows, ending with 31 sts.)

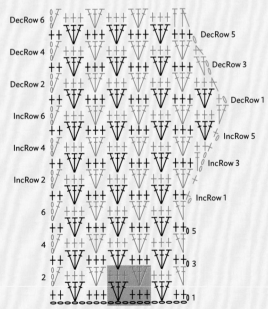

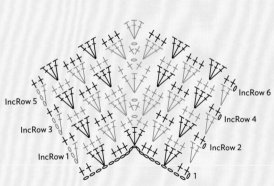

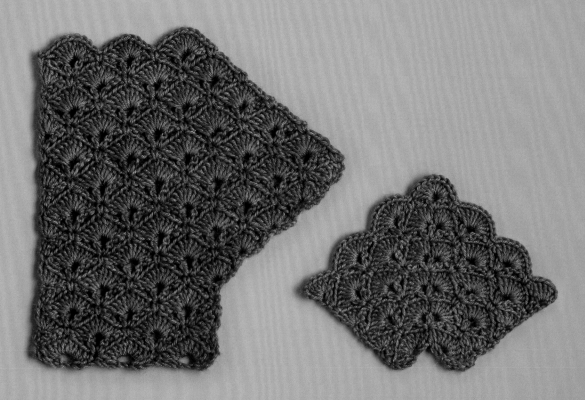

FANTAIL SHELLS

This great-looking stitch features rows of nine–double crochet Shells anchored by single crochet stitches, alternating with rows of V-stitches anchored with single crochet stitches. An interesting feature of this pattern is that single crochet stitches in Shell rows are worked 2 rows below, over the chain five of the previous row.

NUMBER OF STITCHES IN PATTERN REPEAT	NUMBER OF ROWS IN PATTERN REPEAT
V	4
MULTIPLE	NOT REVERSIBLE
8 + 2	

SPECIAL STITCHES

Shell: 9 dc in designated st

V-stitch (V-st): (Dc, ch 1, dc) in designated st

Sc 2 rows below: Insert hook in designated st 2 rows below and work sc enclosing ch-5 of prev row.

BASIC PATTERN

(For swatch, ch 26.)

ROW 1: Sc in 2nd ch from hook, *sk 3 ch, Shell in next ch, sk 3 ch, sc in next ch, rep from * across.
(Swatch has 3 patt reps, 1 sc.)

ROW 2: Ch 3 (counts as dc throughout), dc in same sc, *ch 5, sk next Shell, V-st in next sc, rep from * across to last sc, ch 5, 2 dc in last sc, turn.

ROW 3: Ch 3, 4 dc in same dc, *sc in center dc of next Shell 2 rows below**, Shell in ch-1 sp of next V-st, rep from * across, ending last rep at **, 5 dc in tch, turn.

ROW 4: Ch 3 (does not count as dc), *V-st in next sc**, ch 5, rep from * across, ending last rep at **, ch 3, sl st to tch, turn.

ROW 5: Ch 1, sc in first st, *Shell in ch-1 sp of next V-st**, sc in center dc of next Shell 2 rows below, rep from * across, ending last rep at **, sc in last dc 2 rows below, turn.

Rep rows 2–5 for patt.
(Swatch has 6 rows in patt.)

Edge Shaping

Shaping begins on odd-numbered rows, at the rate of ½ patt rep every other row.

INCREASING

IncRow 1: Ch 3, 8 dc in first dc (counts as Shell), *sc in center dc of next Shell 2 rows below, continue in row 3 of patt across.
IncRow 2: Work in row 4 of patt to last Shell, ch 5, 2 dc in tch, turn.
IncRow 3: Ch 3, 8 dc in first dc, *sc in center dc of next Shell 2 rows below, continue in row 5 of patt across.
IncRow 4: Work in row 2 of patt to last Shell, ch 5, 2 dc in tch, turn.
Rep IncRows 1–4 to continue increasing.
(Swatch has 8 increase rows followed by 2 rows worked even, ending with 5 patt reps, counting ½ Shells at edges.)

DECREASING

DecRow 1: Ch 1, sc in first st, Shell in ch-1 sp of next V-st, continue in row 5 of patt across.
DecRow 2: Work in row 2 of patt to last Shell, ch 3, sl st in center dc of last Shell, turn.
DecRow 3: Ch 1, sc in first sc, Shell in ch-1 sp of next V-st, continue in row 3 of patt.
DecRow 4: Work in row 4 of patt to last Shell, ch 3, sl st in center dc of last Shell, turn.
Rep DecRows 1–4 to continue decreasing.
(Swatch has 8 decrease rows followed by row 5 worked even, ending with 3 patt reps, 1 sc.)

Internal Shaping

The rate of shaping is 1 Shell over 2 rows. Smaller 7-dc Shells are worked at increase points. When working into these Shells 2 rows later, place sc in 4th dc. Last 2 rows show how to return to patt after increasing.
(For swatch, ch 18. Work Row 1 of patt. 2 patt reps, 3 sc.)
Place marker in center sc.
IncRow 1: Work in row 2 of patt to marked sc, ([dc, ch 1] 2 times, dc) in marked sc, move marker to last ch-1 sp made, ch 5, continue in patt across.
IncRow 2: Work in row 3 of patt to marked ch-1 sp, 7 dc in marked ch-1 sp, sc in next dc, move marker to sc just made, 7 dc in next ch-1 sp, sc in center dc of next Shell 2 rows below, continue in patt across.
IncRow 3: Work in row 4 of patt to marked sc, ([dc, ch 1] 2 times, dc) in marked sc, move marker to last ch-1 sp made, continue in patt across.
IncRow 4: Work in row 5 of patt to marked ch-1 sp, 7 dc in marked ch-1 sp, sc in next dc, move marker to sc just made, 7 dc in next ch-1 sp, continue in patt across.
Rep IncRows 1–4 to continue increasing.
(Swatch has 11 rows total, 8 increase rows, ending with 6 patt reps, 1 sc.)

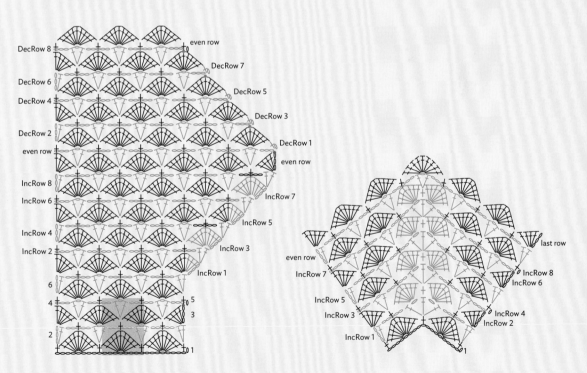

DOMES

The "domes" are five–double crochet shells worked over chain-three spaces. Between chain-three spaces, three single crochet stitches are worked into the Dome of the previous row. This results in Domes that appear to be built up row upon row, a truly architectural look.

NUMBER OF STITCHES IN PATTERN REPEAT	NUMBER OF ROWS IN PATTERN REPEAT
6	4
MULTIPLE	**NOT REVERSIBLE**
5 + 2	

SPECIAL STITCH
Shell: 5 dc in next ch-3 sp.

BASIC PATTERN

(For swatch, ch 22.)

ROW 1 (WS): Sc in 2nd ch from hook, sc in next ch, *ch 3, sk 2 ch**, sc in next 3 ch, rep from * ending last rep at **, sc in last 2 ch, turn.
(Swatch has 4 patt reps, 1 sc.)

ROW 2: Ch 1, sc in first sc, *sk next sc, Shell, sk next sc, sc in next sc**, rep from * across, ending last rep at **, turn.

ROW 3: Ch 3 (counts as hdc, ch 1), sk next dc, *sc in next 3 dc**, ch 3, sk next (dc, sc, dc), rep from * across, ending last rep at **, ch 1, hdc in last sc, turn.

ROW 4: Ch 3 (counts as dc), 2 dc in first ch-1 sp, *sk next sc, sc in next sc**, Shell, rep from * across, ending last rep at **, 3 dc in tch, turn.

ROW 5: Ch 1, sc in first dc, sc in next dc, *ch 3, sk next (dc, sc, dc)**, sc in next 3 dc, rep from * across, ending last rep at **, sc in last 2 sts, turn.

Rep rows 2–5 for patt.
(Swatch has 6 rows in patt.)

Edge Shaping

6 chains are added at start of row 3, to count as 3 chains and a dc, allowing one Shell to be added over 2 rows.

INCREASING

IncRow 1: Ch 6 (counts as dc, ch 3 throughout), sk first dc of Shell, sc in next 3 dc, continue in row 3 of patt across.

IncRow 2: Work in row 4 of patt to ch-6 tch, Shell in tch, sc in 3rd ch of tch, turn.

IncRow 3: Ch 6, sk first dc of Shell, sc in next 3 dc, continue in row 5 of patt across.

IncRow 4: Work in row 2 of patt to ch-6 tch, Shell in tch, sc in 3rd ch of tch, turn.

Rep IncRows 1–4 to continue increasing.

(Swatch has 8 increase rows, ending with 6 patt reps, 1 sc.)

DECREASING

DecRow 1: Ch 1, sk first sc, sl st in next 2 dc, ch 1, sc in next 2 dc, ch 3, continue in row 3 of patt across.

DecRow 2: Work in row 4 of patt, placing sc in last sc, turn.

DecRow 3: Ch 1, sk first sc, sl st in next 2 dc, ch 1, sc in next 2 dc, ch 3, continue in row 5 of patt across.

DecRow 4: Work in row 2 of patt, placing last sc in last sc, turn.

Rep DecRows 1 --4 to continue decreasing.

(Swatch has 8 decrease rows, ending with 4 patt reps, 1 sc.)

Internal Shaping

Increases are made on odd-numbered rows, adding 1 Shell over 2 rows.

(For swatch, ch 22. Work rows 1 and 2 of patt. 4 patt reps, 1 sc.)

Place marker in center sc in row 2 of patt.

IncRow 1: Work in row 3 of patt to marked sc, working ch 3 before marked sc, 3 sc in marked sc, move marker to center sc of group just made, ch 3, sk next dc, sc in next 3 dc, continue in patt across.

IncRow 2: Work in row 4 of patt across. Move marker up to sc made in marked sc.

IncRow 3: Work in row 5 of patt to marked sc, working ch 3 before marked sc, 3 sc in marked sc, move marker to center sc of group just made, ch 3, sk next dc, sc in next 3 dc, continue in patt across.

IncRow 4: Work in row 2 of patt across. Move marker up to sc made in marked sc.

Rep IncRows 1–4 to continue increasing.

(Swatch has 10 rows total, ending with 8 patt reps, 1 sc.)

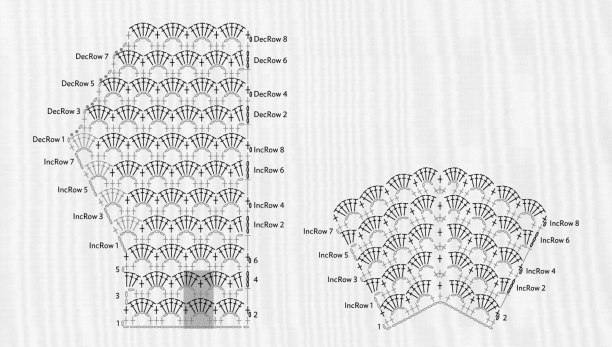

FALLING LEAVES

A closed pattern with lovely surface texture. The "falling" occurs because a single crochet stitch is placed next to two double crochet stitches, causing the taller stitches to tilt.

NUMBER OF STITCHES IN PATTERN REPEAT	NUMBER OF ROWS IN PATTERN REPEAT
3	1
MULTIPLE	**REVERSIBLE**
3 + 2	

SPECIAL STITCH
Shell: (Sc, 2 dc) in designated st

BASIC PATTERN

(For swatch, ch 17.)
ROW 1: Shell in 2nd ch from hook, sk 2 ch, *Shell in next ch, sk 2 ch, rep from * across, sc in last ch, turn.
(Swatch has 5 Shells, 1 sc.)
ROW 2: Ch 1, Shell in first sc, *sk 2 dc, Shell in next sc, rep from * across to last sc, sc in last sc, turn.
Rep row 2 for patt.
(Swatch has 6 rows in patt.)

Edge Shaping

This pattern ends the row with a sc that can be expanded to a full Shell, allowing an increase of 1 Shell every other row. When decreasing, we begin with sl sts to eliminate a Shell at the start of a row.
This stitch is asymmetrical. For shaping at opposite edge reverse IncRows 1 and 2 and DecRows 1 and 2.

INCREASING

IncRow 1: Work in patt to last sc, Shell in last sc, turn.

IncRow 2: Ch 1, Shell in first dc, sk next dc, Shell in next sc, continue in patt across.

Rep IncRows 1 and 2 to continue increasing.

(Swatch has 6 increase rows, ending with 8 Shells, 1 sc, followed by 1 row worked even in patt.)

DECREASING

DecRow 1: Ch 1, sk first sc, sl st in next 2 dc, (without making ch 1) Shell in next sc, continue in patt across.

DecRow 2: Work in patt to last sc, sk last sc, sc in last sl st, turn.

Rep DecRows 1 and 2 to continue decreasing.

(Swatch has 5 decrease rows, ending with 5 Shells, 1 sc.)

Internal Shaping

Here we add 1 Shell each row, staggered over a center point. On every other row the Shell will be at the center point, in alternate rows slightly off-center. To increase we make 2 Shells into 1 Shell of the previous row.

(For swatch, ch 17. Work row 1 of patt. 5 Shells, 1 sc.)

Place marker in center st (first dc) of center Shell.

IncRow 1: Work in patt to marked dc, Shell in marked dc, move marker to first dc of Shell just made, Shell in sc of same Shell, Shell in next sc, continue in patt across.

Rep IncRow 1 to continue increasing.

(Swatch has 6 rows total, 5 increase rows, ending with 10 Shells, 1 sc.)

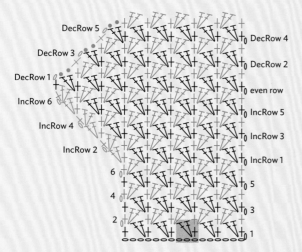

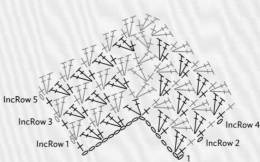

TILTED SHELLS

This clever stitch features a tilted Shell, filled in on the next row with a Cluster consisting of two double crochet stitches worked together. An oddity of this pattern is that rows have stitches of different heights at their two ends.

NUMBER OF STITCHES IN PATTERN REPEAT	**NUMBER OF ROWS IN PATTERN REPEAT**
5	2
MULTIPLE	**REVERSIBLE**
4 + 2	

NOTE

For this Shell, when working dc stitches in sc just made, it may seem the stitches will become twisted, but they fall into their correct order once made.

SPECIAL STITCH

Shell: Sc in designated st, ch 3, 4 dc in top of sc just made

BASIC PATTERN

(For swatch, ch 22.)
ROW 1: Shell in 2nd ch from hook, sk 3 ch, *Shell in next ch, sk 3 ch, rep from * across, sc in last ch, turn.
(Swatch has 6 Shells.)
ROW 2: Ch 3, *sk next dc, dc2tog, ch 3, sk next dc, sc in top of ch-3 of same Shell, rep from * across, turn.
ROW 3: Ch 1, Shell in first sc, *sk next (ch 3, dc2tog), Shell in next sc, rep from * across, sk last (ch 3, dc2tog), sc in tch, turn.
Rep rows 2 and 3 for patt.
(Swatch has 6 rows in patt.)

Edge Shaping

Shaping is done on odd-numbered rows by expanding the sc at the end of the row to a full Shell, shaping at the rate of 1 Shell every other row. This is not possible, however, at the opposite edge. For this reason, this stitch can't be used where shaping at both edges is required, although there are always clever alternatives that can be devised (such as working a piece in two halves to be joined together).

INCREASING

IncRow 1: Work in row 3 of patt across, Shell in tch, turn.
IncRow 2: Ch 3, sk first dc, dc2tog, ch 3, sk next dc, sc in top of ch-3 of same Shell, continue in row 2 of patt across.
Rep IncRows 1 and 2 to continue increasing.
(Swatch has 6 increase rows, ending with 9 patt reps.)

DECREASING

DecRow 1: Work in row 3 of patt across, placing last sc in last dc2tog, turn.
DecRow 2: Ch 1, sk first sc, sl st in next 3 dc, sc in top of ch 3, sk next dc, dc2tog, ch 3 sk next dc, sc in top of next ch-3, continue in row 2 of patt.
Rep DecRows 1 and 2 to continue decreasing.
(Swatch has 6 decrease rows, ending with 6 patt reps, 1 sc.)

Internal Shaping

The angled stitches in this pattern work against internal shaping.

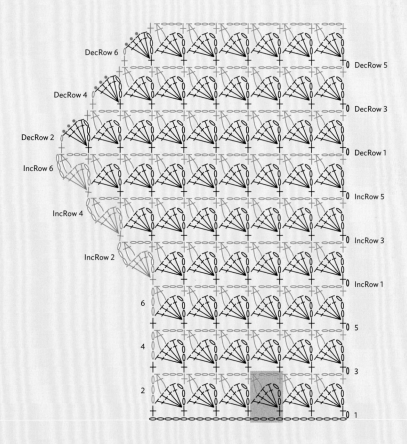

OFFBEAT SHELL

This ingenious Shell starts like a typical shell with four double crochet stitches worked in the same stitch, but then takes an unusual turn, with a chain one and the rest of the Shell worked around the post of the last double crochet stitch made. It creates a unique and intricate surface texture.

NUMBER OF STITCHES IN PATTERN REPEAT	NUMBER OF ROWS IN PATTERN REPEAT
9	2
MULTIPLE	**REVERSIBLE**
6 + 4	

SPECIAL STITCH
Shell: 4 dc in designated st, ch 1 (sc, hdc, dc) around post of last dc made.

BASIC PATTERN
(For swatch, ch 22.)
ROW 1: 3 dc in 4th ch from hook (3 sk ch count as dc), *sk 2 ch, sc in next ch, sk 2 ch**, Shell in next ch, rep from * across, ending last rep at **, 4 dc in last ch, turn.
(Swatch has 3 Shells, 3 sc, counting ½ Shells at edges.)
ROW 2: Ch 1, sk 4 dc, *Shell in next sc, sc in ch-1 sp of next Shell, rep from * across, placing last sc in tch, turn.
ROW 3: Ch 3 (counts as dc throughout), 3 dc in same sc, *sc in ch-1 sp of next Shell**, Shell in next sc, rep from * across, ending last rep at **, 4 dc in ch-1 tch, turn.
Rep rows 2 and 3 for patt.
(Swatch has 6 rows in patt)

Edge Shaping
Despite its unusual construction, this can be shaped like other Shells. The rate is ½ patt per row. Increasing begins on an odd-numbered row and decreasing on an even-numbered row.

INCREASING

IncRow 1: (Ch 3, 3 dc) in first st, ch 1, (sc, hdc, dc) around post of last dc made, sc in ch-1 sp of next Shell, continue in row 3 of patt across.

IncRow 2: Work in row 2 of patt to tch, Shell in tch, turn.

Rep IncRows 1 and 2 to continue increasing.

To return to patt, work last IncRow 1 as follows: Ch 3, 3 dc in first st, sc in ch-1 sp of next Shell, continue in row 3 of patt across.

(Swatch has 5 increase rows, ending with 5 Shells, 5 sc, and last IncRow worked as above followed by row 2 of patt worked even.)

DECREASING

DecRow 1: Ch 1, sk first sc and next dc, sl st in next (hdc, sc), (without making ch 1) sc in next ch-1 sp, continue in row 3 of patt across.

DecRow 2: Work in row 2 of patt to last Shell, sc in ch-1 sp of last Shell, leave rem sts unworked, turn.

Rep DecRows 1 and 2 to continue decreasing.

(Swatch has 4 decrease rows, ending with 3 shells, 3 sc.)

Internal Shaping

A simpler Shell is used at the center increase point. Increasing is at the rate of 1 Shell over 3 rows.

(For swatch, ch 22. Work row 1 of patt. Swatch has 3 shells, 3 sc, counting ½ Shells at edges.)

Place marker in center sc between 2 Shells.

IncRow 1: Work in row 2 of patt to marked sc, (3 dc, ch 1, 3 dc) in marked sc, move marker to ch-1 sp just made, continue in patt across.

IncRow 2: Work in row 3 of patt to marked ch-1 sp, (sc, ch 1, sc) in marked ch-1 sp, move marker to last sc made, Shell in next sc, continue in patt across.

IncRow 3: Work in row 2 of patt, placing last Shell in marked sc, sc in next ch-1 sp, move marker to sc just made, Shell in next sc, continue in patt across.

IncRow 4: Work in row 3 of patt to marked sc, (3 dc, ch 1, 3 dc) in marked sc, move marker to ch-1 sp just made, continue in patt across.

IncRow 5: Work in row 2 of patt to marked ch-1 sp, (sc, ch 1, sc) in marked ch-1 sp, move marker to last sc made, continue in patt across.

IncRow 6: Work in row 3 of patt, placing last Shell in marked sc, sc in next ch-1 sp, move marker to sc just made, Shell in next sc, continue in patt across.

Rep IncRows 1–6 to continue increasing.

(Swatch has 8 rows total, 6 increase rows, ending with 5 Shells, 5 sc.)

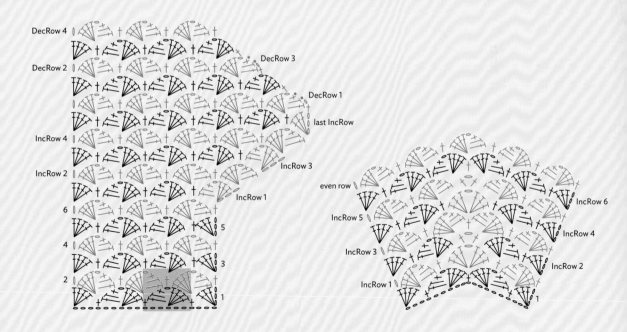

INTERWOVEN DIAMONDS

One of my favorite stitches, this pattern begins with large Shells. On alternating rows, Clusters fill in the spaces between Shells and create a striking surface of diamond shapes.

NUMBER OF STITCHES IN PATTERN REPEAT	NUMBER OF ROWS IN PATTERN REPEAT
V	4
MULTIPLE	**REVERSIBLE**
8 + 2	

NOTE

At the end of row 3, instead of working 5 dc in last cl, try working them into last partial dc for a straighter edge.

SPECIAL STITCHES

Shell: 9 dc in designated st.

Cluster (Cl): (Yo, insert hook in next st, yo and draw up loop, yo, draw through 2 loops) in each designated st, yo, draw through all loops on hook. The designated sts are given in parenthesis after the word "over."

Partial Foundation double crochet (Partial Fdc): (Yo, insert hook in designated st, yo and draw up loop, ch 1, yo, draw through 2 loops). Work next Partial Fdc in base ch 1 of st just made.

Increase Cl (Inc Cl): Begin Cl over (next 4 dc), continue Cl by working Partial Fdc in next sc, work 4 more Partial Fdc, yo, draw through all loops on hook.

V-stitch (V-st): (Dc, ch 1, dc) in designated st.

BASIC PATTERN

(For swatch, ch 26.)

ROW 1: Sc in 2nd ch from hook, *sk 3 ch, Shell in next ch, sk 3 ch, sc in next ch, rep from * across, turn.

(Swatch has 3 Shells, 4 sc.)

ROW 2: Ch 3, Cl over (next 4 dc), *ch 3, sc in next dc, ch 3**, Cl over next (4 dc, sc, 4 dc), rep from * across, ending last rep at **, Cl over (last 4 dc and sc), turn.

ROW 3: Ch 3, 4 dc in same Cl, *sc in next sc**, Shell in next Cl, rep from * across, ending last rep at **, 5 dc in Cl, turn.

ROW 4: Ch 1, sc in first dc, *ch 3, Cl over next (4 dc, sc, 4 dc), ch 3, sc in next dc, rep from * across, placing last sc in tch, turn.

ROW 5: Ch 1, sc in first dc, *Shell in next Cl, sc in next sc, rep from * across.

Rep rows 2–5 for patt.

(Swatch has 5 rows in patt.)

Edge Shaping

Shaping always starts on an even-numbered Cluster row and is at the rate of ½ patt rep every other row. For increasing, we turn a half Cluster into a full one with the use of dc foundation stitches.

When increasing on the opposite edge, rather than using fdc, work 4 extra chains at end of prev row, then work 9-dc Cluster at end of IncRow 1.

INCREASING

IncRow 1: Work in row 2 of patt to last Cl, Inc Cl, ch 3, sc in base ch of last Partial Fdc made, turn.

IncRow 2: Ch 1, sc in first sc, Shell in next Cl, continue in row 3 of patt across.

IncRow 3: Work in row 4 of patt to last Cl, Inc Cl, ch 3, sc in base ch of last Partial Fdc made, turn.

IncRow 4: Ch 1, sc in first sc, Shell in next Cl, continue in row 5 of patt across.

Rep IncRows 1–4 to continue increasing.

(Swatch has 8 increase rows, ending with 5 Shells, 6 sc.)

DECREASING

DecRow 1: Work in row 2 of patt, placing last sc in center dc of last Shell, leave rem sts unworked, turn.

DecRow 2: Ch 1, sc in first sc, Shell in next Cl, continue in row 3 of patt across.

DecRow 3: Work in row 4 of patt, placing last sc in center dc of last Shell, leave rem sts unworked, turn.

DecRow 4: Ch 1, sc in first sc, Shell in next Cl, continue in row 5 of patt across.

Rep DecRows 1–4 to continue decreasing.

(Swatch has 8 decrease rows, ending with 3 shells, 4 sc, followed by 1 row worked even.)

Internal Shaping

The rate of shaping is 1 patt rep every 2 rows.

(For swatch, ch 18. Work row 1 of patt. 2 Shells, 3 sc.)

Place marker in center sc between 2 Shells.

IncRow 1: Work in row 2 of patt to 4 dc before marked sc, Cl over (next 4 dc), V-st in marked sc, Cl over (next 4 dc), move marker to Cl just made, ch 3, continue in patt across.

IncRow 2: Work in row 3 of patt to marked Cl, Shell in marked Cl, sc in next ch-1 sp, move marker to sc just made, Shell in next Cl, continue in patt across.

IncRow 3: Work in row 4 of patt to 4 dc before marked sc, Cl over (next 4 dc), V-st in next sc, Cl over (next 4 dc), move marker to Cl just made, ch 3, continue in patt across.

IncRow 4: Work in row 5 of patt to marked Cl, Shell in marked Cl, sc in next ch-1 sp, move marker to sc just made, Shell in next Cl, continue in patt across.

Rep IncRows 1–4 to continue increasing.

(Swatch has 8 rows total, 6 increase rows, ending with 5 cl, 6 sc.)

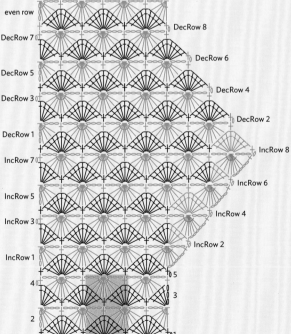

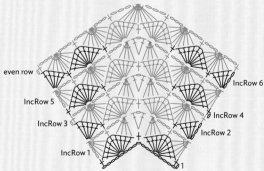

BOXED SHELLS

In this pattern a large Shell is complemented by Clusters that place the Shell in its own small box.

NUMBER OF STITCHES IN PATTERN REPEAT

10

MULTIPLE

8 + 2

NUMBER OF ROWS IN PATTERN REPEAT

2

REVERSIBLE

SPECIAL STITCH
Shell: 9 dc in designated st.

BASIC PATTERN

(For swatch, ch 26.)

ROW 1: Sc in 2nd ch from hook, *sk 3 ch, Shell in next ch, sk 3 ch, sc in next ch, rep from * across.

(Swatch has 3 Shells, 4 sc.)

ROW 2: Ch 3 (counts as dc throughout), sk first dc of Shell, *dc3tog over next 3 dc, ch 3, sc in next dc, ch 3, dc3tog over next 3 dc, sk last dc of Shell**, ch 1, sk next (sc, dc), rep from * across, ending last rep at **, dc in last sc, turn.

ROW 3: Ch 1, sc in first dc, *sk next ch-3 sp, Shell in next sc, sk next ch-3 sp, sc in next ch-1 sp, rep from * across, placing last sc in tch, turn.

Rep rows 2 and 3 for patt.

(Swatch has 10 rows in patt.)

Edge Shaping

The Clusters in this stitch pattern do not lend themselves to shaping at the edges, as they require stitches to be worked into. Unlike many other Shell patterns, there are no half Shells at the edge that can be expanded into full Shells.

Internal Shaping

2 Shells are added over 6 rows. The method of increase changes as the number of Shells goes from even to odd, resulting in different stitches at the increase point.

(For swatch, ch 18. Work row 1 of patt. 2 shells, 3 sc.)

Place marker in sc between 2 Shells.

IncRow 1: Work in row 2 of patt to marked sc, ending with ch-1, (dc, ch 1, dc) in marked sc, ch 1, move marker to ch-1 sp just made, continue in patt across.

IncRow 2: Work in row 3 of patt to marked ch-1 sp, sc in marked ch-1 sp, Shell in ch-1 sp, move marker to center dc of Shell just made, sc in next ch-1 sp, continue in patt across.

IncRow 3: Work in row 2 of patt across. Move marker up to sc worked into marked dc.

IncRow 4: Work in row 3 of patt, placing last sc in ch-1 sp before marked sc, (5 dc, ch 1, 5 dc) in marked sc, move marker to last dc made, sc in next ch-1 sp, continue in patt across.

IncRow 5: Work in row 2 of patt to marked dc, *dc2tog over next 2 dc, ch 3, sc in next dc, ch 3, dc2tog over next 2 dc**, ch 1, sk ch-1 sp, rep from * to ** over next 5 dc, move marker to ch-1 sp between 2nd and 3rd dc2tog, continue in patt across.

IncRow 6: Work in row 3 of patt across. Move marker up to sc worked into marked ch-1 sp.

Rep IncRows 1–6 to continue increasing.

(Swatch has 8 rows total, 6 increase rows, ending with 4 shells, 5 sc.)

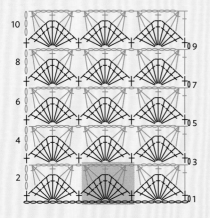

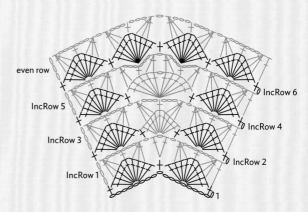

PLUSH

This stitch is an elaboration of Interwoven Diamonds, with crucial differences: Shells have a chain-one space at the center, and they are anchored by V-stitches instead of single crochet stitches. The center of each Cluster has post stitches worked into the V-stitches below. The result is an intriguing textured surface, different on each side of the work.

SPECIAL STITCHES

V-stitch (V-st): (dc, ch 1, dc) in designated st.

Shell: (4 dc, ch 1, 4 dc) in designated st.

Cluster (Cl): (Yo, insert hook in designated st, yo and draw up loop, yo, draw through 2 loops) in next 4 dc, yo, draw through 5 loops on hook.

NUMBER OF STITCHES IN PATTERN REPEAT	**NUMBER OF ROWS IN PATTERN REPEAT**
12	4
MULTIPLE	**REVERSIBLE**
10 + 4	

BASIC PATTERN

(For swatch, ch 34.)

ROW 1: 4 dc in 4th ch from hook, (3 sk ch count as dc), *sk 4 ch, V-st in next ch, sk 4 ch**, Shell in next ch, rep from * across, ending last rep at **, 5 dc in last ch, turn.

(Swatch has 3 patt reps, including ½ Shells at edges.)

ROW 2: Ch 1, sc in first dc, *ch 3, Cl, FPdc in next dc, ch 1, FPdc in next dc, Cl, ch 3, sc in next ch-1 sp, rep from * across, placing last sc in tch, turn.

ROW 3: Ch 3 (counts as dc throughout), dc in same sc, sk (ch 3, Cl, dc), *Shell in next ch-1 sp between FPdc sts**, V-st in next sc, rep from * across, ending last rep at **, 2 dc in tch, turn.

ROW 4: Ch 3, *FPdc in next dc**, Cl, ch 3, sc in next ch-1 sp, ch 3, Cl, FPdc in next dc, ch 1, rep from * across, ending last rep at **, dc in tch, turn.

ROW 5: Ch 3, 4 dc in first dc, *V-st in next sc**, sk (ch 3, Cl, dc), Shell in next ch-1 sp, rep from * ending last rep at **, 5 dc in tch, turn.

Rep rows 2–5 for patt.

(Swatch has 8 rows in patt.)

Edge Shaping

Shaping is at the rate of ½ patt per row beginning on row 5. Decreasing begins at the end of row 4 by leaving half a shell unworked.

INCREASING

IncRow 1: Ch 3 (counts as first dc of Shell), Shell in first st, V-st in next sc, continue in row 5 of patt across.

IncRow 2: Work in row 2 of patt to last ch-1 sp, sc in ch-1 sp, ch 3, Cl, turn.

IncRow 3: Ch 3 (counts as first dc of Shell), Shell in first Cl, V-st in next sc, continue in row 3 of patt across.

IncRow 4: Work in row 4 of patt to last ch-1 sp, sc in ch-1 sp, ch 3, Cl, turn.

Rep IncRows 1–4 to continue increasing.

(Swatch has 4 increase rows followed by row 5 and row 2 of patt worked even, ending with 4 patt reps, including ½ Shells at edges.)

DECREASING

DecRow 1: Ch 1, Shell in first ch-1 sp, V-st in next sc, continue in row 3 of patt across.

DecRow 2: Work in row 4 of patt to last Shell, Cl, ch 3, sc in last ch-1 sp, leave rem sts unworked, turn.

DecRow 3: Ch 1, Shell in first ch-1 sp, V-st in next sc, continue in row 5 of patt across.

DecRow 4: Work in row 2 of patt to last Shell, Cl, ch 3, sc in last ch-1 sp, leave rem sts unworked, turn.

Rep DecRows 1–4 to continue decreasing.

(Swatch has 4 decrease rows, ending with 3 patt reps.)

Internal Shaping

The complexity of the stitches at the center of the Shells and Clusters in this patt make internal shaping impractical.

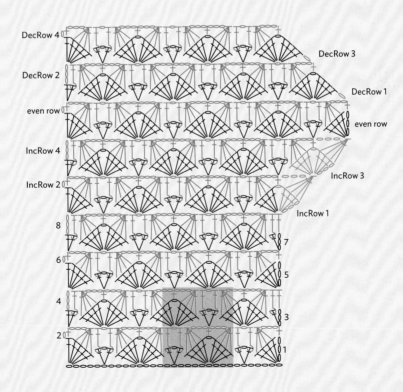

PETAL LACE

This pretty stitch and the next use treble
stitches in a Shell pattern. The taller stitch
adds elegance and drape.

NUMBER OF STITCHES IN PATTERN REPEAT	NUMBER OF ROWS IN PATTERN REPEAT
6	2
MULTIPLE	REVERSIBLE
6 + 4	

SPECIAL STITCH
Shell: 5 tr in designated st.

BASIC PATTERN

(For swatch, ch 28.)

ROW 1: Shell in 7th ch from hook (6 sk ch count as tr, 2 fnd
ch), sk 2 ch, *tr in next ch, sk 2 ch, Shell in next ch, sk 2 ch, rep
from * across, tr in last ch, turn.
(Swatch has 4 patt reps, 1 tr.)

ROW 2: Ch 4 (counts as tr throughout), 2 tr in same tr, *sk 2 tr,
tr in next tr, sk 2 tr**, Shell in next tr, rep from * across, ending
last rep at **, 3 tr in tch, turn.

ROW 3: Ch 4, *sk 2 tr, Shell in next tr, sk 2 tr, tr in next tr, rep
from * across, placing last tr in tch, turn.
Rep rows 2 and 3 for patt.
(Swatch has 7 rows in patt.)

Edge Shaping

To prevent a large gap at the decrease edge, the treble that ends the row is maintained while a slanted stitch is worked along the edge. On the last row of decreasing, the slanted stitch at the edge does not count as a stitch and can be worked together with the last treble in the row.

INCREASING

IncRow 1: Ch 4, Shell in same tr, sk 2 tr, tr in next tr, continue in row 2 of patt across.
IncRow 2: Work in row 3 of patt to tch, 6 tr in tch, turn.
Rep IncRows 1 and 2 to continue increasing.
(Swatch has 4 increase rows, ending with 6 patt reps.)

DECREASING

DecRow 1: Ch 4, sk 2 tr, tr in next tr, continue in row 2 of patt across.
DecRow 2: Work in row 3 of patt to last Shell, sk 2 tr, tr in next tr, tr in tch, turn.
DecRow 3: Ch 4, sk 3 tr, tr in next tr, continue in row 2 of patt across.
Rep DecRows 2 and 3 to continue decreasing.
(Swatch has 4 decrease rows, ending with 4 patt reps, 1 tr.)

Internal Shaping

This method adds 2 patt reps over 4 rows, with the 4th increase row worked even.
(For swatch, ch 22. Work row 1 of patt. 3 patt reps, 1 tr.)
Place marker in center tr of center Shell.
IncRow 1: Work in row 2 of patt to marked tr, (tr, ch 1, tr) in marked tr, move marker to tr just made, sk 2 tr, Shell in next tr, continue in patt across.
IncRow 2: Work in row 3 of patt to marked tr, Shell in next tr, tr in next ch-1 sp, move marker to tr just made, Shell in next tr, sk 2 tr, tr in next tr, continue in patt across.
IncRow 3: Work in row 2 of patt to marked tr, 11 tr in marked tr (counts as Shell, tr, Shell), move marker to center tr of group just made, sk 2 tr, tr in next tr, continue in patt across.
IncRow 4: Work in row 3 of patt, placing Shell in marked tr. Move marker to center tr of center Shell.
Rep IncRows 1–4 to continue increasing.
(Swatch has 5 rows total, 4 increase rows, ending with 5 patt reps, 1 tr.)

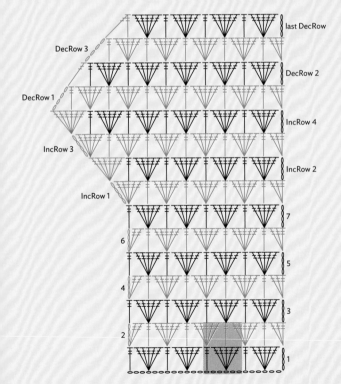

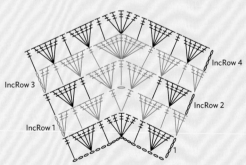

PEACOCK SHELLS

A rare Shell stitch that uses trebles. Shells are stacked in columns and alternate with rows of treble V-stitches.

NUMBER OF STITCHES IN PATTERN REPEAT
10

NUMBER OF ROWS IN PATTERN REPEAT
2

MULTIPLE
10 + 2

NOT REVERSIBLE

SPECIAL STITCHES
Shell: 9 tr in designated st.

V-stitch (V-st): (tr, ch 1, tr) in designated st.

BASIC PATTERN

(For swatch, ch 32.)

ROW 1: Sc in 2nd ch from hook, *sk 4 ch, Shell in next ch, sk 4 ch, sc in next ch, rep from * across.

(Swatch has 3 patt reps, 1 sc.)

ROW 2: Ch 4 (counts as tr throughout), tr in first sc, *ch 3, sk 4 tr, sc in next tr, ch 3, sk 4 tr**, V-st in next sc, rep from * across, ending last rep at **, 2 tr in last sc, turn.

ROW 3: Ch 1, sc in first tr, *Shell in next sc**, sc in ch-1 sp of next V-st, rep from * across, ending last rep at **, sc in tch, turn.

Rep rows 2 and 3 for patt.

(Swatch has 9 rows in patt.)

Edge Shaping

Edge shaping is not practical, because the large size of the Shell would produce a very acute angle, and because no half Shells are used at the edges.

Internal Shaping

1 Shell is added every other row.

(For swatch, ch 22. Work row 1 of patt. 2 patt reps, 1 sc.)

Place marker in center sc.

IncRow 1: Work in row 2 of patt to marked sc, (tr, ch 1, tr, ch 1, tr) in marked sc, move marker to last tr made, ch 3, continue in patt across.

IncRow 2: Work in row 3 of patt to marked tr, sc in marked tr, Shell in next tr, move marker to center tr of Shell just made, sc in next tr, continue in patt across.

IncRow 3: Work in row 2 of patt to marked tr, (sc, ch 2, V-st, ch 2, sc) in marked tr, move marker to last sc made, ch 3, continue in patt across.

IncRow 4: Work in row 3 of patt to marked sc, Shell in marked sc, sc in ch-1 sp of next V-st, move marker to sc just made, Shell in next sc, continue in patt across.

Rep IncRows 1–4 to continue increasing.

(Swatch has 7 rows total, 6 increase rows, ending with 5 patt reps, 1 sc.)

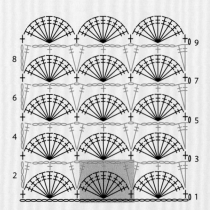

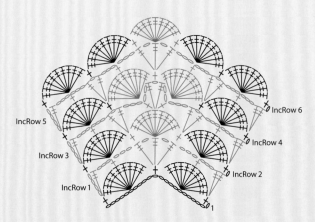

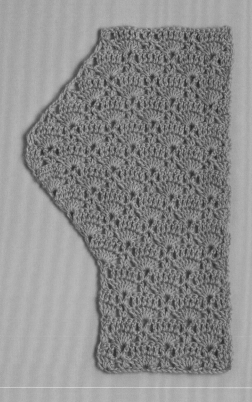

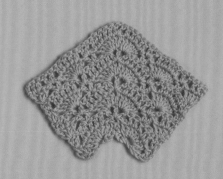

BOTANICAL SHELLS

Two elements alternate in this stitch pattern: a Shell topped with double crochets and V-stitches. After two rows, the two elements switch places, with V-stitches aligned over Shells and Shells over V-stitches.

NUMBER OF STITCHES IN PATTERN REPEAT	NUMBER OF ROWS IN PATTERN REPEAT
V	4

MULTIPLE	REVERSIBLE
8 + 4	

SPECIAL STITCHES

V-stitch (V-st): (dc, ch 1, dc) in designated st or sp

Shell: 7 dc in designated st or sp.

BASIC PATTERN

(For swatch, ch 28.)

ROW 1: 3 dc in 4th ch from hook (3 sk ch count as dc), *sk 3 ch, V-st in next ch, sk 3 ch**, Shell in next ch, rep from * across, ending last rep at **, 4 dc in last ch, turn.

(Swatch has 3 patt reps, including ½ Shells at edges.)

ROW 2: Ch 3, dc in next 2 dc, *V-st in ch-1 sp of next V-st, sk first dc of next Shell**, dc in next 5 dc, rep from * across, ending last rep at **, dc in next 2 dc, dc in tch, turn.

ROW 3: Ch 3, dc in same dc, *Shell in ch-1 sp of next V-st, sk next 3 dc**, V-st in next dc, rep from * across, ending last rep at **, 2 dc in tch, turn.

ROW 4: Ch 3, dc in same dc, *sk first dc of next Shell, dc in next 5 dc**, V-st in ch-1 sp of next V-st, rep from * across, ending last rep at **, 2 dc in tch, turn.

ROW 5: Ch 3, 3 dc in same dc, *sk 3 dc, V-st in next dc**, Shell in ch-1 sp of next V-st, rep from * across, ending last rep at **, 4 dc in tch, turn.

Rep rows 2–5 for patt.

(Swatch has 8 rows in patt.)

Edge Shaping

This adds 3 sts every other row. Decreasing begins in row 4 of patt and at the same rate.

INCREASING

IncRow 1: Work in row 5 of patt to tch, Shell in tch, turn.
IncRow 2: Ch 4, dc in same dc (counts as V-st throughout), dc in next 5 dc, continue in row 2 of patt across.
IncRow 3: Work in row 3 of patt to ch-4 tch, Shell in 3rd ch of tch, turn.
IncRow 4: Ch 4, dc in same dc, dc in next 5 dc, continue in row 4 of patt across.
IncRow 5: Work in row 5 of patt to tch, Shell in 3rd ch of tch, turn.
Rep IncRows 2–5 to continue increasing.
To return to patt work last IncRow 5 as follows: Work in row 5 of patt to tch, 4 dc in 3rd ch of tch.
(Swatch has 9 increase rows, ending with 5 patt reps, last IncRow worked as above, followed by rows 2 and 3 worked even.)

DECREASING

DecRow 1: Ch 3, sk first dc of next Shell, dc in next 5 dc, continue in row 4 of patt across.
DecRow 2: Work in row 5 of patt, ending with V-st in center dc of last 5-dc group, dc in tch.

DecRow 3: Ch 3, sk next (V-st, dc), dc in next 5 dc, continue in row 2 of patt across.
DecRow 4: Work in row 3 of patt, ending with V-st in center dc of last 5-dc group, dc in tch, turn.
DecRow 5: Ch 3, sk next (V-st, dc), dc in next 5 dc, continue in row 4 of patt across.
Rep DecRows 2–5 to continue decreasing.
To return to patt, work last DecRow 4 as follows: Work in row 3 of patt to last 5-dc group, (dc, ch 1) in center dc of last 5-dc group, dc2tog over (same dc, tch).
(Swatch has 8 decrease rows, ending with 3 patt reps, followed by row 4 worked even.)

Internal Shaping

Shaping is at the rate of 1 patt rep every 2 rows.
(For swatch, ch 20.)
ROW 1 (ROW 3 OF PATT WORKED IN CH): Dc in 4th ch from hook (3 sk ch count as dc), *sk 3 ch, Shell in next ch, sk 3 ch**, V-st in next ch, rep from * across, ending last rep at **, 2 dc in last ch, turn.
(Swatch has 2 patt reps.)
In row 3 of patt, place marker in ch-1 sp of center V-st.
IncRow 1: Work in row 4 of patt to marked ch-1 sp, ([dc, ch 1] twice, dc) in marked ch-1 sp, move marker to last ch-1 sp made, continue in patt across.
IncRow 2: Work in row 5 of patt to marked ch-1 sp, 5 dc in marked ch-1 sp, V-st in next dc, 5 dc in next ch-1 sp, move marker to last dc made, continue in patt across.
IncRow 3: Work in row 2 of patt to marked dc, dc in marked dc, dc in next 4 dc, ([dc, ch 1] twice, dc) in ch-1 sp of next V-st, move marker to last ch-1 sp made, sk next dc of V-st, dc in next 5 dc, continue in patt across.
IncRow 4: Work in row 3 of patt to marked ch-1 sp, 5 dc in marked ch-1 sp, V-st in next dc, 5 dc in next ch-1 sp, move marker to last dc made, continue in patt across.
IncRow 5: Work in row 4 of patt to marked dc, dc in marked dc, dc in next 4 dc, ([dc, ch 1] twice, dc) in ch-1 sp of next V-st, move marker to last ch-1 sp made, sk next dc of V-st, dc in next 5 dc, continue in patt across.
Rep IncRows 2–5 to continue increasing.
(Swatch has 8 rows total, 6 increase rows, ending with 5 patt reps, followed by row 2 worked even.)

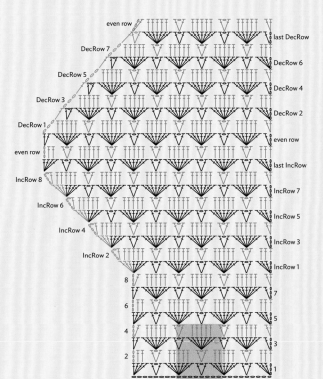

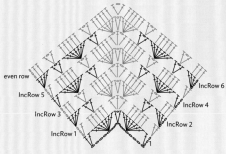

BLOOMING SHELLS

A pleasing feature of this stitch pattern is
the tall stately columns that morph from
V-stitches into Shells that keep expanding.

**NUMBER OF STITCHES
IN PATTERN REPEAT**

8

**NUMBER OF ROWS
IN PATTERN REPEAT**

8

MULTIPLE

8 + 5

REVERSIBLE

SPECIAL STITCH
V-stitch (V-st): (dc, ch 1, dc) in designated st or sp.

BASIC PATTERN

(For swatch, ch 38.)

ROW 1: V-st in 10th st from hook (10 sk ch count as 4 fnd ch, dc, ch-2 sp), *ch 2, sk 3 ch, dc in next ch, ch 2, sk 3 ch, V-st in next ch, rep from * across, ch 2, sk 3 ch, dc in last ch, turn. *(Swatch has 4 patt reps, 1 dc.)*

ROW 2: Ch 5 (counts as dc, ch 2 throughout), *3 dc in ch-1 sp of next V-st, ch 2**, sk next dc, dc in next dc, ch 2, rep from * across, ending last rep at **, dc in 7th ch of tch, turn.

ROW 3: Ch 4 (counts as dc, ch 1 throughout), *sk next dc, 5 dc in next dc, ch 1, sk next dc**, dc in next dc, ch 1, rep from * across, ending last rep at **, dc in 3rd ch of tch, turn.

ROW 4: Ch 3 (count as dc throughout), *7 dc in center dc of next 5-dc Shell, sk next 2 dc, dc in next dc, rep from * across, placing last dc in 3rd ch of tch, turn.

ROW 5: Ch 3, dc in same dc, *ch 2, dc in center dc of next 7-dc Shell, ch 2**, sk next 3 dc, V-st in next dc, rep from * across, ending last rep at **, 2 dc in tch, turn.

ROW 6: Ch 3, dc in same dc, sk next dc, *ch 2, dc in next dc, ch 2**, 3 dc in ch-1 sp of next V-st, sk next dc, rep from * across, ending last rep at **, 2 dc in tch, turn.

ROW 7: Ch 3, 2 dc in same dc, sk next dc, *ch 1, dc in next dc, ch 1**, sk next dc, 5 dc in next dc, sk next dc, rep from * across, ending last rep at **, 3 dc in tch, turn.

ROW 8: Ch 3, 3 dc in same dc, sk next 2 dc, *dc in next dc**, 7 dc in center dc of next 5-dc Shell, rep from * across, ending last rep at **, 4 dc in tch, turn.

ROW 9: Ch 5, sk next 3 dc, *V-st in next dc, ch 2**, dc in center dc of next 7-dc Shell, ch 2, sk next 3 dc, rep from * across, ending last rep at **, dc in tch, turn.

Rep rows 2–9 for patt.

(Swatch has 12 rows in patt.)

Edge Shaping

Edge Shaping is not practical for this stitch.

Internal Shaping

This increases by 1 patt rep every 4 rows., and begins on row 5 of patt. Increases are made in the first 2 out of 4 rows, then 2 rows are worked even.

(For swatch, ch 35.)

ROW 1 (row 4 of patt worked into ch): Dc in 7th ch from hook (6 sk ch count as dc, 3 fnd ch), 6 dc in same ch, *sk 3 ch, dc in next ch**, sk 3 ch, 7 dc in next ch, rep from * across, ending last rep at **.

(Swatch has 4 patt reps.)

Place marker in center dc in row 4 of patt.

IncRow 1: Work in row 5 of patt to marked dc, (dc, ch 1, dc, ch 1, dc) in marked dc, move marker to last ch-1 sp made, continue in patt across.

IncRow 2: Work in row 6 of patt to marked ch-1 sp, 3 dc in marked ch-1 sp, ch 2, dc in next dc, move marker to dc just made, ch 2, 3 dc in next ch-1 sp, continue in patt across.

IncRows 3 AND 4: Work in rows 7 and 8 of patt, moving marker to center dc.

IncRow 5: Work in row 9 of patt to marked dc, (dc, ch 1, dc, ch 1, dc) in marked dc, move marker to last ch-1 sp made, continue in patt across.

IncRow 6: Work in row 2 of patt to marked ch-1 sp, 3 dc in marked ch-1 sp, ch 2, dc in next dc, ch 2, 3 dc in next ch-1 sp, continue in patt across.

IncRows 7 AND 8: Work in rows 3 and 4 of patt.

Rep IncRows 1–8 to continue increasing.

(Swatch has 9 rows total, 8 increase rows, ending with 6 patt reps.)

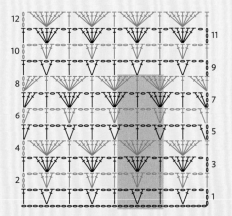

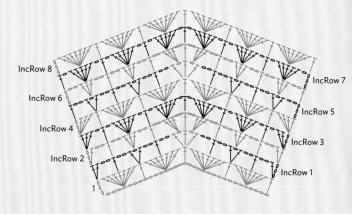

OLD WORLD LACE

V-stitches and "split Shells"—Shells split in half with a chain in between—are the two elements used in this stitch pattern. Both elements are typical in crochet from its early Victorian days, often in combination with each other, and therefore this stitch has an old world, or historical, quality.

NUMBER OF STITCHES IN PATTERN REPEAT	NUMBER OF ROWS IN PATTERN REPEAT
14	1
MULTIPLE	**REVERSIBLE**
10 + 4	

SPECIAL STITCHES

Shell: (3 dc, ch 2, 3 dc) in designated st.

V-stitch (V-st): (dc, ch 2, dc) in designated st.

BASIC PATTERN

(For swatch, ch 34.)

ROW 1: Dc in 4th ch from hook (3 sk ch count as dc), *ch 1, sk 4 ch, Shell in next ch, ch 1, sk 4 ch**, V-st in next ch, rep from * across, ending last rep at **, 2 dc in last ch, turn.

(Swatch has 3 patt reps.)

ROW 2: Ch 3 (counts as dc throughout), dc in first dc, *ch 1, Shell in ch-2 sp of next Shell, ch 1**, V-st in ch-2 sp of next V-st, rep from * across, ending last rep at **, 2 dc in tch, turn. Rep row 2 for patt.

(Swatch has 12 rows in patt.)

Edge Shaping

The large size of this pattern, which consists of the Shell plus the V-st plus 2 ch, and the 2 elements presenting angles at the edge, make shaping at the edge difficult.

Internal Shaping

The large patt rep is built up slowly, adding 1 patt rep every 3 rows.

(For swatch, ch 24. Work row 1 of patt. 2 patt reps.)

Place marker in ch-2 of center V-st.

IncRow 1: Work in patt to marked ch-2 sp, [(dc, ch 1) 2 times, dc] in same ch-2 sp, move marker to center dc of group just made, continue in patt across.

IncRow 2: Work in patt to marked dc, V-st in ch-1 sp before marked dc, ch 1, 3 dc in marked dc, move marker to center dc of group just made, ch 1, V-st in next ch-1 sp, ch 1, continue in patt across.

IncRow 3: Work in patt to center 3-dc group, Shell in marked dc, move marker to ch-2 sp of shell just made, continue in patt across.

IncRow 4: Work in patt to marked ch-2 sp, (3 dc, ch 1, V-st, ch 1, 3 dc) in marked ch-2 sp, move marker to last ch-1 sp made (not center), continue in patt across.

IncRow 5: Work in patt to marked ch-1 sp, 3 dc in marked ch-1 sp, ch 1, V-st in next ch-2 sp, ch 1, 3 dc in next ch-1 sp, move marker to last ch-1 sp made, continue in patt across.

IncRow 6: Work in patt to marked ch-1 sp, Shell in marked ch-1 sp, ch 1, V-st in next ch-2 sp, move marker to ch-2 sp just made, ch 1, Shell in next ch-1 sp, continue in patt across.

Rep IncRows 1–6 to continue increasing.

(Swatch has 9 rows, 6 increase rows, ending with 4 patt reps, then a row worked even, and a last row as described below.)

FLAT LAST ROW: Ch 3, dc in same dc, *ch 4, sc in ch-2 sp of next Shell, ch 4**, V-st in ch-2 sp of next V-st, rep from * across, ending last rep at **, 2 dc in tch.

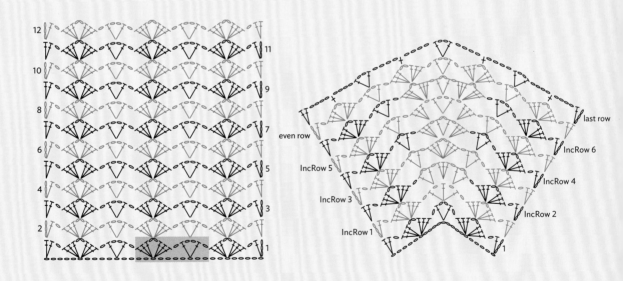

WAVY LACE

An easy lace stitch that's not often seen and produces a pleasing wavy effect. It consists of an asymmetrical shell that includes a chain-two space, which is the pattern repeat.

NUMBER OF STITCHES IN PATTERN REPEAT

9

MULTIPLE

6 + 6

NUMBER OF ROWS IN PATTERN REPEAT

1

REVERSIBLE

SPECIAL STITCH
Shell: (4 dc, ch 2, dc) in designated sp.

BASIC PATTERN

(For swatch, ch 36.)

ROW 1: Dc in 6th ch from hook (5 sk ch count as (dc, ch 2),
*ch 2, sk 5 ch**, Shell in next ch, rep from * ending last rep at **,
4 dc in last ch, turn.
(Swatch has 5 Shells, including ½ Shells at edges.)

ROW 2: Ch 5 (counts as dc, ch 2 throughout), dc in same dc,
*ch 2, sk next ch-2 sp**, Shell in ch-2 sp of next Shell, rep from
* ending last rep at **, 4 dc in tch, turn.
Rep row 2 for patt.
(Swatch has 12 rows in patt.)

Edge Shaping

The angles in this pattern work against shaping at the edge.

Internal Shaping

The best strategy for shaping is enlarging the size of the patt
rep, which can be done in 2 ways: adding to the number of
chains between Shells, or adding dcs to the Shell. We begin
with a smaller version of the basic patt that omits chains
between Shells, then add chains for 5 IncRows, then add dcs to
the Shells for 2 rows.

To start: Chain a multiple of 5 + 6.
(For swatch, ch 26.)

ROW 1: Dc in 6th ch from hook, sk 4 ch, *Shell in next ch, sk 4
ch, rep from * across, 4 dc in last ch, turn. (4 shells)

IncRow 1: Ch 5, dc in same dc, *ch 1, Shell in ch-2 sp of next
Shell, rep from * across, ch 1, 4 dc in tch, turn.

IncRow 2: Ch 5, dc in same dc, *ch 2, Shell in ch-2 sp of next
Shell, rep from * across, ch 2, 4 dc in tch, turn.

IncRow 3: Ch 5, dc in same dc, *ch 3, Shell in ch-2 sp of next
Shell, rep from * across, ch 3, 4 dc in tch, turn.

IncRow 4: Ch 5, dc in same dc, *ch 4, Shell in ch-2 sp of next
Shell, rep from * across, ch 4, 4 dc in tch, turn.

IncRow 5: Ch 5, dc in same dc, *ch 5, Shell in ch-2 sp of next
Shell, rep from * across, ch 5, 4 dc in tch, turn.

IncRow 6: Ch 5, dc in same dc, *ch 5, (5 dc, ch 2, dc) in ch-2
sp of next Shell, rep from * across, ch 5, 5 dc in tch, turn.

IncRow 7: Ch 5, dc in same dc, * ch 5, (6 dc, ch 2, dc) in ch-2
sp of next Shell, rep from * across, ch 5, 6 dc in tch, turn.

To continue increasing, you can add more dcs to each Shell
and also add chains between Shells so pattern proportions are
maintained.

*(Swatch has 8 rows total, 7 increase rows, ending with 4 patt reps
with ch-5 sps.)*

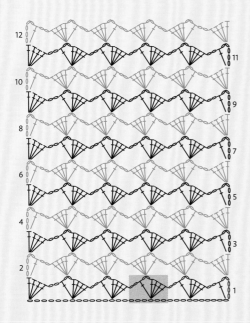

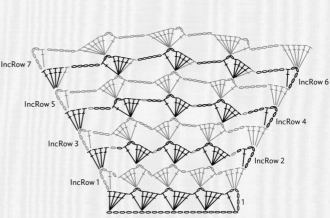

BIG FANS

This stitch makes a bold statement but is not difficult. It consists of a fan shape worked over three rows interspersed with spider-like connections that we will see again in other laces.

NUMBER OF STITCHES IN PATTERN REPEAT	NUMBER OF ROWS IN PATTERN REPEAT
12	6
MULTIPLE	**REVERSIBLE**
12 + 4	

BASIC PATTERN

(For swatch, ch 40.)

ROW 1: Dc in 4th from hook (3 sk ch count as dc),*ch 4, sk 5 ch, sc in next ch, ch 4, sk 5 ch**, 3 dc in next ch, rep from * across, ending last rep at **, 2 dc in last ch, turn.
(Swatch has 3 patt reps.)

ROW 2: Ch 3 (counts as dc throughout), 3 dc in next dc, ch 2, dc in next sc, *ch 2, 3 dc in next dc, dc in next dc, 3 dc in next dc, ch 2, dc in next sc, rep from * across to last 2 dc, ch 2, 3 dc in next dc, dc in tch, turn.

ROW 3: Ch 3, dc in next 2 dc, 3 dc in next dc, *ch 1, sk next dc, 3 dc in next dc**, dc in next 5 dc, 3 dc in next dc, rep from * across, ending last rep at **, dc in next 2 dc, dc in tch, turn.

ROW 4: Ch 1, sc in first dc, *ch 4, 3 dc in next ch-1 sp, ch 4, sk 5 dc, sc in next dc, rep from * across, placing last sc in tch, turn.

ROW 5: Ch 5 (counts as dc, ch 2), 3 dc in next dc, dc in next dc, 3 dc in next dc, ch 2, dc in next sc, *ch 2, 3 dc in next dc, dc in next dc, 3 dc in next dc, ch 2, dc in next sc, rep from * across, turn.

ROW 6: Ch 3, *3 dc in next dc, dc in next 5 dc, 3 dc in next dc**, ch 1, rep from * across, ending last rep at **, dc in 3rd ch of tch, turn.

ROW 7: Ch 3, dc in same dc, *ch 4, sk 5 dc, sc in next dc, ch 4**, 3 dc in next ch-1 sp, rep from * across, ending last rep at **, sk 5 dc, 2 dc in tch, turn.

Rep rows 2–7 for patt.
(Swatch has 6 rows in patt.)

Edge Shaping

The strategy shown here must start on row 1 of patt, where a partial fan is at the edge. The increase takes advantage of the natural slant of the fan, and the large pattern is built up at the rate of 3 sts per row. Note that in the decrease section, ch 4 is used to begin rows instead of ch 3 to stretch across the angle created by the decrease.

INCREASING

IncRow 1: Ch 3, 2 dc in first dc, ch 4, continue in row 7 of patt across.

IncRow 2: Work in row 2 of patt across, 3 dc in tch, turn.

IncRow 3: Ch 3, 2 dc in first dc, dc in next 5 dc, 3 dc in next dc, continue in row 3 of patt across.

IncRow 4: Work in row 4 of patt across, ch 4, 3 dc in tch, turn.

IncRow 5: Ch 3, 2 dc in first dc, dc in next dc, 3 dc in next dc, continue in row 5 of patt across.

IncRow 6: Work in row 6 of patt across, ending with 4 dc in tch, turn.

Rep IncRows 1–6 to continue increasing.
(Swatch has 6 increase rows, ending with 4 patt reps.)

DECREASING

DecRow 1: Ch 2, dc3tog (counts as dc4tog), ch 4, sk next 2 dc, sc in next dc, ch 4, continue in row 7 of patt across.

DecRow 2: Work in row 2 of patt across, ending with ch 2, dc in next sc, ch 2, dc in dc4tog, turn.

DecRow 3: Ch 4, sk next dc, 3 dc in next dc, continue in row 3 of patt across.

DecRow 4: Work in row 4 of patt across to last 6 sts, ch 2, sk next 2 dc, dc4tog over last 3 dc and tch, turn.

DecRow 5: Ch 4, dc in next sc, ch 2, continue in row 5 of patt across.

DecRow 6: Work in row 6 of patt across, placing last dc in ch-4 tch, turn.

Rep DecRows 1–6 to continue decreasing.
(Swatch has 6 decrease rows, ending with 3 patt reps.)

Internal Shaping

The size of this patt rep, coupled with the staggered elements, makes it unsuitable for internal shaping.

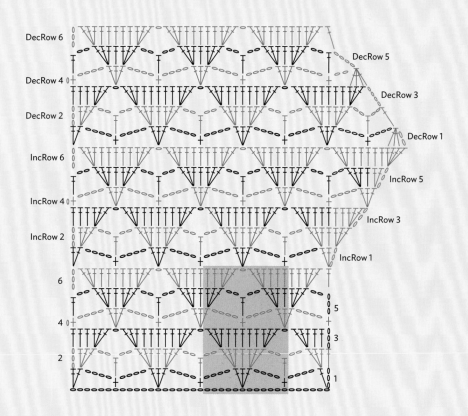

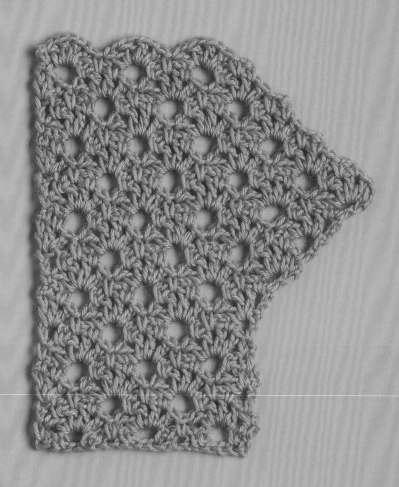

OPEN ARCHES

When Shells are worked over a chain space they look quite different than when they emerge from one stitch. This stitch and the next, Grand Arches, show the airy effect of this technique, and the resulting patterns have an attractive, contemporary feel. A spike stitch, that is, a stitch worked into a stitch two rows below, is used in this pattern.

NOTE
The sc spike stitch in row 2 is worked into the center ch of 3 ch that are skipped between sc sts.

SPECIAL STITCHES
Shell: (dc, ch 1) 3 times in designated sp, dc in same sp.

Single Crochet Spike (Spike): Working over ch-sp in prev row, insert hook in designated ch-1 sp 2 rows below and work sc.

NUMBER OF STITCHES IN PATTERN REPEAT	NUMBER OF ROWS IN PATTERN REPEAT
8	4
MULTIPLE	**REVERSIBLE**
6 + 2	

BASIC PATTERN

(For swatch, ch 20.)

ROW 1 (WS): Sc in 2nd ch from hook, ch 1, sk next ch, *sc in next ch, ch 3, sk next ch, sc in next ch**, ch 3, sk 3 ch, rep from * across, ending last rep at **, ch 1, sk next ch, sc in last ch, turn. *(Swatch has 3 patt reps.)*

ROW 2: Ch 1, sc in first sc, sk ch-1 sp, *Shell in next ch-3 sp**, spike (see Note above), rep from * across, ending last rep at **, sk next ch-1 sp, sc in last sc, turn.

ROW 3: Ch 4 (counts as dc, ch 1) *sc in next ch-1 sp of next Shell, ch 3, sk next ch-1 sp, sc in next ch-1 sp**, ch 3, rep from * across, ending last rep at **, ch 1, dc in last sc, turn.

ROW 4: Ch 3 (counts as dc at start of row throughout), (dc, ch 1, dc) in same dc, *spike in center ch-1 sp of Shell 2 rows below**, Shell in next ch-3 sp, rep from * across, ending last rep at **, (dc, ch 1, 2 dc) in 3rd ch of tch, turn.

ROW 5: Ch 1, sc in first dc, ch 1, *sc in next ch-1 sp, ch 3, sc in next ch-1 sp of next Shell**, ch 3, sk next ch-1 sp, rep from * across, ending last rep at **, ch 1, sc in tch, turn.

ROW 6: Ch 1, sc in first sc, *Shell in next ch-3 sp**, spike in center ch-1 sp of next Shell 2 rows below, rep from * across, ending last rep at **, sc in last sc, turn.

Rep rows 3–6 for patt.

(Swatch has 7 rows in patt.)

Edge Shaping

The half Shell at the edge of row 4 can expand to a full Shell to begin shaping, with one full Shell added every 4th row. Decreasing begins on row 3 of patt.

INCREASING

IncRow 1: Ch 4, (dc, ch 1, dc, ch 1, dc) in first dc, spike in center ch-1 sp of next Shell 2 rows below, continue in row 4 of patt across.

IncRow 2: Work in row 5 of patt, placing sc in tch, ch 3, dc in 3rd ch of tch, turn.

IncRow 3: Ch 1, sc in first dc, Shell in next ch-3 sp, spike in center ch-1 sp of next Shell, continue in row 6 of patt across.

IncRow 4: Work in row 3 of patt, placing sc in last ch-1 sp, ch 3, dc in last sc, turn.

IncRow 5: Ch 4, (dc, ch 1, dc, ch 1, dc) in first ch-3 sp, continue in row 4 of patt across.

Rep IncRows 2–5 to continue increasing.

(Swatch has 7 increase rows, ending with 5 Shells.)

DECREASING

DecRow 1: Work in row 3 of patt, placing sc in last ch-1 sp of last Shell, leave rem sts unworked, turn.

DecRow 2: Ch 1, spike in center ch-1 sp of first Shell, Shell in next ch-3 sp, continue in row 4 of patt across.

DecRow 3: Work in row 5 of patt, placing sc in last ch-1 sp, leave rem sts unworked, turn.

DecRow 4: Ch 1, spike in center ch-1 sp of first Shell, Shell in next ch-3 sp, continue in row 6 of patt across.

Rep DecRows 1–4 to continue decreasing.

(Swatch has 8 decrease rows, ending with 3 Shells.)

Internal Shaping

It is not possible to internally shape this stitch without distorting the pattern.

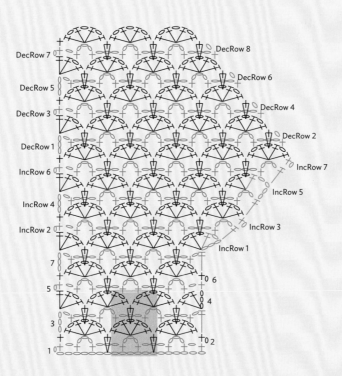

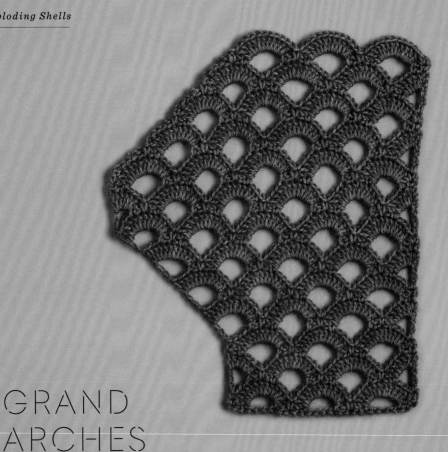

GRAND ARCHES

Shells worked over chain-five spaces rather than into one stitch yield a bold and contemporary design. The anchoring single crochet stitch at either side of the Shells is worked into a Shell two rows below.

NUMBER OF STITCHES IN PATTERN REPEAT	NUMBER OF ROWS IN PATTERN REPEAT
V	4
MULTIPLE	**NOT REVERSIBLE**
8 + 2	

NOTE

In row 4 when working sc in Shell two rows below, work around ch-sp of prev row enclosing it in the sc being worked.

SPECIAL STITCH

Shell: 11 dc in designated sp.

BASIC PATTERN

(For swatch, ch 26.)

ROW 1 (WS): Sc in 2nd ch from hook, ch 1, sk next ch, sc in next ch, *ch 5, sk 3 ch, sc in next ch**, ch 3, sk 3 ch, sc in next ch, rep from * across, ending last rep at **, ch 1, sk next ch, sc in last ch, turn.
(Swatch has 3 patt reps.)

ROW 2 (RS): Ch 1, sc in first sc, *Shell in next ch-5 sp**, sc in center ch of 3 sk ch 2 rows below, rep from * across, ending last rep at **, sc in last sc, turn.

ROW 3: Ch 6 (counts as tr, ch 2), *sc in 4th dc of next Shell, ch 3, sk 3 dc, sc in next dc**, ch 5, rep from * across, ending last rep at **, ch 2, tr in last sc, turn.

ROW 4: Ch 3, 5 dc in first ch-2 sp, *sc in center dc of Shell 2 rows below**, Shell in next ch-5 sp, rep from * across, ending last rep at **, 6 dc in ch-6 tch, turn.

ROW 5: Ch 1, sc in first dc, ch 1, sk next dc, *sc in next dc, ch 5, sc in 4th dc of next Shell**, ch 3, sk 3 dc, rep from * across, ending last rep at **, ch 1, sk next dc, sc in tch, turn.

ROW 6: Ch 1, sc in first sc, *Shell in next ch-5 sp**, sc in center dc of Shell 2 rows below, rep from * across, ending last rep at **, sc in last sc, turn.

Rep rows 3–6 for patt.
(Swatch has 6 rows in patt.)

Edge Shaping

We begin increasing on row 3 of patt, gaining ½ patt rep per row. Decreasing must begin on row 2 of patt.

In DecRow 1 after making sl sts, do not ch 1 before making next sc. This maintains smoother slant at edge.

INCREASING

IncRow 1: Ch 9 (counts as tr, ch 5), sc in 4th dc of next Shell, continue in row 3 of patt.

IncRow 2: Work in row 4 of patt to ch-9 tch, Shell in ch-9 tch, turn.

IncRow 3: Ch 9, sc in 4th dc of next Shell, continue in row 5 of patt.

IncRow 4: Work in row 6 of patt to ch-9 tch, Shell in ch-9 tch, turn.

Rep IncRows 1–4 to continue increasing.

To return to patt, work last IncRow 4 as follows: Work in row 6 of patt to last ch-9 tch, Shell in ch-9 tch, sc in 3rd ch of tch, turn.

(Swatch has 8 increase rows, ending with 5 patt reps, with last IncRow as above followed by rows 3–6 of patt worked even.)

DECREASING

DecRow 1: Ch 1, sl st in first 3 dc, sc in next dc, ch 3, sk 3 dc, sc in next dc, continue in row 3 of patt.

DecRow 2: Work in row 4 of patt to last Shell, sc in center dc of last Shell 2 rows below, leave rem sts unworked, turn.

DecRow 3: Ch 1, sk first sc, sl st in next 3 dc, sc in next dc, ch 3, continue in row 5 of patt.

DecRow 4: Work in row 6 of patt to last Shell, sc in center dc of last Shell 2 rows below, leave rem sts unworked, turn.

Rep DecRows 1–4 to continue decreasing.

(Swatch has 8 decrease rows, ending with 3 patt reps.)

Internal Shaping

All attempts to work internal shaping caused distortion of the pattern.

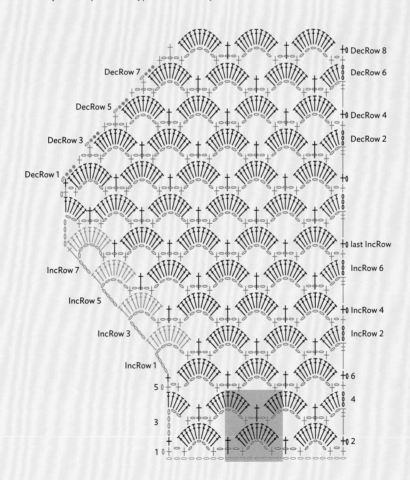

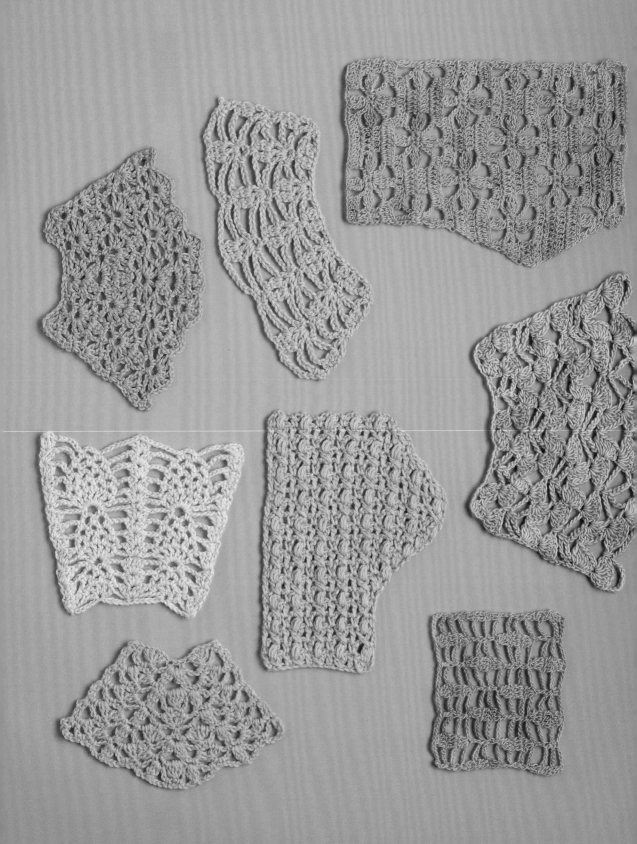

CHAPTER FIVE

CLASSIC LACES

There are a multitude of lace crochet stitch designs, and here we present favorites like pineapples and spiders, and some you may not have encountered before. These stitches deploy a variety of elements and strategies to form designs. Some are large scale, requiring many stitches and rows, while others are more compact. Some are fairly closed and others are very open. In other words, there is something for every lace lover in this group.

Just about any lace stitch will look better with a thinner yarn—lace or fingering weight being the best choices. The thick strands of heavier yarns are not a great match for the intricacy and delicacy of lace. If you're not used to working with thinner weights of yarn, I recommend working your way down over time, moving from worsted to DK, then DK to sport weight, and onward till you feel at ease with fingering weight yarns (most sock yarns are fingering weight). It's not necessary to work super tightly or with very tiny hooks. With thinner yarns, stitches can be worked at relatively loose gauge for a lovely effect. Most of the swatches in this chapter were worked with a size C (2.75 mm) hook and fingering-weight yarn, but even size D (3.25 mm) or E (3.5 mm) can be used.

Crochet lace makes gorgeous garments, from shawls and scarves to summer cardigans and halters. The fabric is very fluid and flattering, and because of that lace garments can actually have less shaping than garments made with denser stitches. A flowing fabric lies in folds around your body, while a thicker, less flexible fabric stands out like a box, and therefore the latter requires more shaping to look attractive.

Naturally the complexity of many lace stitches makes them more difficult to shape, but my many trials revealed some innovative shaping methods. This is a great chapter for the more experienced crocheter who wants to try something different. If you are newer to crochet, make some of these stitches with no shaping just to get comfortable and familiar with them. Remember, nothing in crochet is terribly difficult, it's just a matter of patience and careful instruction reading.

When making swatches from this chapter, be sure to wet block and pin them for best results. Once you see how pretty blocked crochet lace can be, you'll want to use it for many projects.

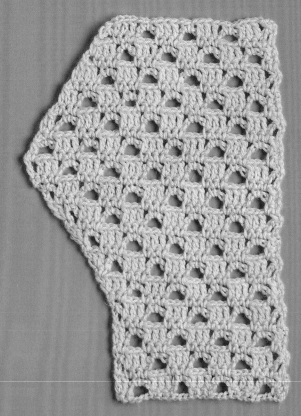

KEYHOLES

This neat small-scale pattern makes for a good beginner lace stitch, especially when worked with no shaping. Chain five spaces create the little keyholes that give the pattern its distinctive appearance.

NUMBER OF STITCHES IN PATTERN REPEAT	NUMBER OF ROWS IN PATTERN REPEAT
V	4
MULTIPLE	REVERSIBLE
6 + 2	

BASIC PATTERN

(For swatch, ch 26.)

ROW 1 (WS): Sc in 2nd ch from hook, sc in next ch, *ch 5, sk 3 ch**, sc in next 3 ch, rep from * across, ending last rep at **, sc in last 2 ch, turn.

(Swatch has 4 patt reps.)

ROW 2: Ch 3 (counts as dc throughout), dc in next sc, *ch 1, sc in next ch-5 sp, ch 1**, dc in next 3 sc, rep from * across, ending last rep at **, dc in last 2 sc, turn.

ROW 3: Ch 5 (counts as dc, ch 2), *sc in next ch-1 sp, sc in next sc, sc in next ch-1 sp**, ch 5, rep from * across, ending last rep at **, ch 2, dc in tch, turn.

ROW 4: Ch 1, sc in first sc, *ch 1, dc in next 3 sc, ch 1**, sc in next ch-5 sp, rep from * across, ending last rep at **, sc in 3rd ch of tch, turn.

ROW 5: Ch 1, sc in first sc, *sc in next ch-1 sp, ch 5, sk 3 dc, sc in next ch-1 sp, sc in next sc, rep from * across, turn.

Rep rows 2–5 for patt.

(Swatch has 8 rows in patt.)

Edge Shaping

Increasing begins in row 5 of patt, and shaping is at the rate of 1 st per row. Since this is a 6-st repeat, increasing for 12 rows allows for a repeating pattern.

INCREASING

IncRow 1: Ch 1, 2 sc in first st, sc in next ch-1 sp, continue in row 5 of patt across.

IncRow 2: Work in row 2 of patt to last st, 2 dc in last st, turn.

IncRow 3: Ch 1, 2 sc in first dc, ch 5, sk 3 dc, sc in next ch-1 sp, continue in row 3 of patt across.

IncRow 4: Work in row 4 of patt to last 2 sc, dc in next sc, 2 dc in last sc, turn.

IncRow 5: Ch 1, sc in first dc, ch 5, sk 2 dc, sc in next ch-1 sp, continue in row 5 of patt across.

IncRow 6: Work in row 2 of patt to last sc, 2 dc in last sc, turn.

IncRow 7: Ch 1, sc in first dc, ch 5, sc in next ch-1 sp, continue in row 3 of patt across.

IncRow 8: Work in row 4 of patt to last sc, dc in last sc, turn.

IncRow 9: Ch 5 (counts as dc, ch 2), sc in next ch-1 sp, sc in next sc, continue in row 5 of patt across.

IncRow 10: Work in row 2 of patt to tch, ch 1, sk 2 ch, 2 sc in 3rd ch of tch, turn.

IncRow 11: Ch 1, 2 sc in first sc, sc in next sc, sc in next ch-1 sp, ch 5, continue in row 3 of patt across.

IncRow 12: Work in row 4 of patt to last sc, ch 1, dc in last sc, turn.

Rep IncRows 1–12 to continue increasing.
(Swatch has 12 increase rows ending with 6 patt reps.)

DECREASING

DecRow 1: Ch 1, sc in first ch-1 sp, ch 5, continue in row 5 of patt across.

DecRow 2: Work in row 2 of patt to last ch-5 sp, sc in last ch-5 sp, sc2tog over (same ch-5 sp, last sc), turn.

DecRow 3: Ch 1, sk first st, sc in next sc, sc in next ch-1 sp, ch 5, continue in row 3 of patt across.

DecRow 4: Work in row 4 of patt to last 2 sc, dc2tog, turn.

DecRow 5: Ch 1, sk first st, sc in next ch-1 sp, sc in next sc, sc in next ch-1 sp, ch 5, continue in row 5 of patt across.

DecRow 6: Work in row 2 of patt to last 3 sc, dc in next sc, dc2tog, turn.

DecRow 7: Ch 1, sk first st, sc in next dc, sc in next ch-1 sp, sc in next sc, sc in next ch-1 sp, ch 5, continue in row 3 of patt.

DecRow 8: Work in row 4 of patt to last 4 sc, dc in next 2 sc, dc2tog, turn.

DecRow 9: Ch 3, sc in next ch-1 sp, sc in next sc, sc in next ch-1 sp, continue in row 5 of patt across.

DecRow 10: Work in row 2 of patt to last 3 sc, dc in next 3 sc, sc in 3rd ch of tch, turn.

DecRow 11: Ch 4, sk 3 dc, sc in next ch-1 sp, continue in row 3 of patt across.

DecRow 12: Work in row 4 of patt to last 3 sc, dc in next 3 sc, ch 1, sc2tog over (ch 4 tch, 2nd ch of tch), turn.

Rep DecRows 1–12 to continue decreasing.
(Swatch has 12 decrease rows, ending with 4 patt reps.)

Internal Shaping

This stitch is not suitable for internal shaping.

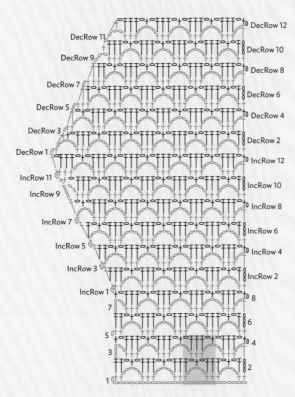

BASIC SPIDER

The "body" of the spider consists of single
crochet stitches building from one to five then
back to one, with three chains extending from
them for the spider's "legs."

**NUMBER OF STITCHES
IN PATTERN REPEAT**

10

MULTIPLE

8 + 2

**NUMBER OF ROWS
IN PATTERN REPEAT**

6

REVERSIBLE

BASIC PATTERN

(For swatch, ch 26.)

ROW 1: Sc in 2nd ch from hook, sc in next 2 ch, *ch 5, sk 3 ch**, sc in next 5 ch, rep from * ending last rep at **, sc in last 3 ch, turn.

(Swatch has 3 patt reps.)

ROW 2: Ch 1, sc in first 2 sc, *ch 3, sc in next ch-5 sp, ch 3, sk next sc**, sc in next 3 sc, rep from * across, ending last rep at **, sc in last 2 sc, turn.

ROW 3: Ch 1, sc in first sc, *ch 3, sc in next ch-3 sp, sc in next sc, sc in next ch-3 sp, ch 3, sk next sc, sc in next sc, rep from * across.

ROW 4: Ch 5 (counts as dc, ch 2), *sc in next ch-3 sp, sc in next 3 sc, sc in next ch-3 sp**, ch 5, sk next sc, rep from * across, ending last rep at **, ch 2, dc in last sc, turn.

ROW 5: Ch 1, sc in first dc, *ch 3, sk next sc, sc in next 3 sc, ch 3**, sc in next ch-5 sp, rep from * across, ending last rep at **, sc in 3rd ch of tch, turn.

ROW 6: Ch 1, sc in first sc, *sc in next ch-3 sp, ch 3, sk next sc, sc in next sc, ch 3, sc in next ch-3 sp, sc in next sc, rep from * across, turn.

ROW 7: Ch 1, sc in first 2 sc, *sc in next ch-3 sp, ch 5, sk next sc, sc in next ch-3 sp**, sc in next 3 sc, rep from * across, ending last rep at **, sc in last 2 sc, turn.

Rep rows 2–7 for patt.

(Swatch has 18 rows in patt.)

Edge Shaping

This stitch is not suitable for increasing at the edges.

Internal Shaping

The pattern is enlarged by increasing the number of chains between sc groups.

(For swatch, ch 26. Work row 1 of patt. 3 patt reps.)

IncRow 1: Ch 1, sc in first 2 sc, *ch 4, sc in next ch-5 sp, ch 4, sk next sc**, sc in next 3 sc, rep from * across, ending last rep at **, sc in last 2 sc, turn.

IncRow 2: Ch 1, sc in first sc, *ch 4, sc in next ch-4 sp, sc in next sc, sc in next ch-4 sp, ch 4, sk next sc, sc in next sc, rep from * across.

IncRow 3: Ch 6 (counts as dc, ch 3), *sc in next ch-4 sp, sc in next 3 sc, sc in next ch-4 sp**, ch 6, sk next sc, rep from * across, ending last rep at **, ch 3, dc in last sc, turn.

IncRow 4: Ch 1, sc in first dc, *ch 4, sk next sc, sc in next 3 sc, ch 4**, sc in next ch-6 sp, rep from * across, ending last rep at **, sc in 3rd ch of tch, turn.

IncRow 5: Ch 1, sc in first sc, *sc in next ch-4 sp, ch 4, sk next sc, sc in next sc, ch 4, sc in next ch-4 sp, sc in next sc, rep from * across, turn.

IncRow 6: Ch 1, sc in first 2 sc, *sc in next ch-4 sp, ch 7, sk next sc, sc in next ch-4 sp**, sc in next 3 sc, rep from * across, ending last rep at **, sc in last 2 sc, turn.

IncRow 7: Ch 1, sc in first 2 sc, *ch 5, sc in next ch-7 sp, ch 5, sk next sc**, sc in next 3 sc, rep from * across, ending last rep at **, sc in last 2 sc, turn.

IncRow 8: Ch 1, sc in first sc, *ch 5, sc in next ch-5 sp, sc in next sc, sc in next ch-5 sp, ch 5, sk next sc, sc in next sc, rep from * across.

IncRow 9: Ch 7 (counts as dc, ch 4), *sc in next ch-5 sp, sc in next 3 sc, sc in next ch-5 sp**, ch 8, sk next sc, rep from * across, ending last rep at **, ch 4, dc in last sc, turn.

IncRow 10: Ch 1, sc in first dc, *ch 5, sk next sc, sc in next 3 sc, ch 5**, sc in next ch-8 sp, rep from * across, ending last rep at **, sc in 3rd ch of tch, turn.

IncRow 11: Ch 1, sc in first sc, *sc in next ch-5 sp, ch 5, sk next sc, sc in next sc, ch 5, sc in next ch-8 sp, sc in next sc, rep from * across, turn.

To continue increasing, add one more ch to the long ch (as in IncRows 3, 6, and 9). If it results in an odd number of ch, then add a ch between sc groups on the following row. If it results in an even number of ch, then add a ch only at the beginning and end of the row.

(Swatch has 12 rows total, 11 increase rows, ending with ch-5 sps between sc groups.)

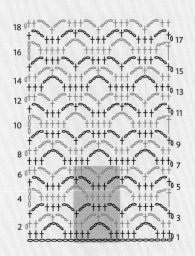

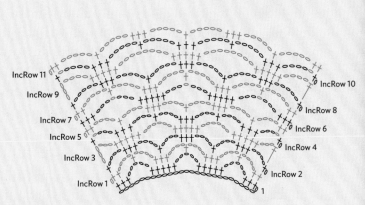

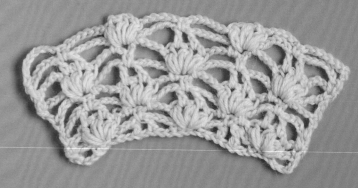

PUFF
BOUQUET

This pretty textured lace is composed of
simple elements: Puffs, single crochet stitches,
double crochet stitches, and chains.

**NUMBER OF STITCHES
IN PATTERN REPEAT**

∨

**NUMBER OF ROWS
IN PATTERN REPEAT**

4

MULTIPLE

10 + 4

NOT REVERSIBLE

SPECIAL STITCHES

Puff: (Yo, insert hook in designated sp and draw up
loop to ½") 3 times, yo, and draw through 7 loops
on hook.

Puff Bouquet (PB): (Puff, ch 2, Puff, ch 2, Puff) in
designated sp.

BASIC PATTERN

(For swatch, ch 34.)

ROW 1: Sc in 9th ch from hook (8 sk ch count as 2 fnd ch, dc, ch 3 on row 1), *ch 1, sk next ch, sc in next ch, ch 3, sk 2 ch, dc in next ch**, ch 1, sk next ch, dc in next ch, ch 3, sk 2 ch, sc in next ch, rep from * across, ending last rep at **, turn.

(Swatch has 3 patt reps.)

ROW 2: Ch 1, sc in first dc, *ch 3, PB in next ch-1 sp, ch 3**, sc in next ch-1 sp, rep from * across, ending last rep at **, sk next 3 ch, sc in next ch of tch, turn.

ROW 3: Ch 1, sc in first sc, *ch 3, dc in next ch-2 sp, ch 1, dc in next ch-2 sp, ch 3**, sc in next ch-3 sp, ch 1, sc in next ch-3 sp, rep from * across, ending last rep at **, sc in last sc, turn.

ROW 4: Ch 6 (counts as dc, ch 3 throughout), *sc in next ch-1 sp, ch 3**, PB in next ch-1 sp, ch 3, rep from * across, ending last rep at **, dc in last sc, turn.

ROW 5: Ch 6, sc in first ch-3 sp, *ch 1, sc in next ch-3 sp, ch 3**, dc in next ch-2 sp, ch 1, dc in next ch-2 sp, ch 3, sc in next ch-3 sp, rep from * across, ending last rep at **, dc in 3rd ch of tch, turn.

Rep rows 2–5 for patt.

(Swatch has 12 rows in patt.)

Edge Shaping

This stitch is not suitable for shaping at the edges.

Internal Shaping

2 chains are added to each patt rep every other row.

(For swatch, ch 34. Work rows 1 and 2 of patt. 3 patt reps.)

IncRow 1: Ch 1, sc in first sc, *ch 4, dc in next ch-2 sp, ch 1, dc in next ch-2 sp, ch 4**, sc in next ch-3 sp, ch 1, sc in next ch-3 sp, rep from * across, ending last rep at **, sc in last sc, turn.

IncRow 2: Ch 7 (counts as dc, ch 4), *sc in next ch-1 sp, ch 4**, PB in next ch-1 sp, ch 4, rep from * across, ending last rep at **, dc in last sc, turn.

IncRow 3: Ch 8 (counts as dc, ch 5), sc in first ch-4 sp, *ch 1, sc in next ch-4 sp, ch 5**, dc in next ch-2 sp, ch 1, dc in next ch-2 sp, ch 5, sc in next ch-4 sp, rep from * across, ending last rep at **, dc in 3rd ch of tch, turn.

IncRow 4: Ch 1, sc in first dc, *ch 5, PB in next ch-1 sp, ch 5**, sc in next ch-1 sp, rep from * across, ending last rep at **, sc in 3rd ch of tch, turn.

IncRow 5: Ch 1, sc in first dc, *ch 6, dc in next ch-2 sp, ch 1, dc in next ch-2 sp, ch 6**, sc in next ch-5 sp, ch 1, sc in next ch-5 sp, rep from * across, ending last rep at **, sc in last sc, turn.

IncRow 6: Ch 9 (counts as dc, ch 6), *sc in next ch-1 sp, ch 6**, PB in next ch-1 sp, ch 6, rep from * across, ending last rep at **, dc in last sc, turn.

To continue increasing add 1 more chain between dc and sc every odd-numbered row, keeping the same number of chains in the following row.

(Swatch has 8 rows total, 6 increase rows, ending with 3 patt reps and 6 ch between PB and sc.)

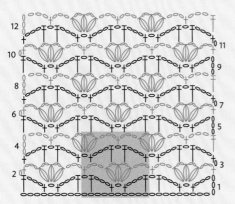

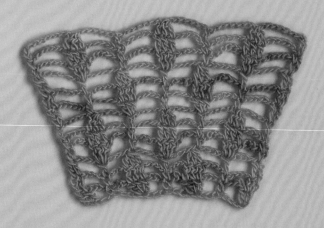

LEAFY

Leaf-like shapes are made over three rows using double crochet stitches that expand in number, then contract. They alternate in the row with single double crochet stitches, with chain spaces between the leaves and the single double crochet.

NUMBER OF STITCHES IN PATTERN REPEAT

V

MULTIPLE

10 + 4

NUMBER OF ROWS IN PATTERN REPEAT

6

REVERSIBLE

BASIC PATTERN

(For swatch, ch 34.)

ROW 1: Dc in 4th ch from hook (3 sk ch count as dc), *ch 5, sk 4 ch, sc in next ch, ch 5, sk 4 ch, **, 3 dc in next ch, rep from * across, ending last rep at **, 2 dc in last ch, turn.
(Swatch has 3 patt reps, 1 dc.)

ROW 2: Ch 3 (counts as dc throughout), dc in next dc, *ch 5, sc in next sc, ch 5**, dc in next 3 dc, rep from * across, ending last rep at **, dc in last 2 sts, turn.

ROW 3: Ch 2, dc in next st (counts as dc2tog), *ch 5, dc in next sc, ch 5**, dc3tog, rep from * across, ending last rep at **, dc2tog, turn.

ROW 4: Ch 1, sc in first st, *ch 5, 3 dc in next dc, ch 5**, sc in next dc3tog, rep from * across, ending last rep at **, sc in last st, turn.

ROW 5: Ch 1, sc in first sc, *ch 5, dc in next 3 dc, ch 5, sc in next sc, rep from * across, turn.

ROW 6: Ch 8 (counts as dc, ch 5), *dc3tog, ch 5, dc in next sc**, ch 5, rep from * across, ending last rep at **, turn.

ROW 7: Ch 3, dc in same dc, *ch 5, sc in next dc3tog, ch 5**, 3 dc in next dc, rep from * across, ending last rep at **, 2 dc in 3rd ch of tch, turn.

Rep rows 2–7 for patt, ending with row 3 or row 6.
(Swatch has 12 rows in patt.)

Edge Shaping

This stitch is not suitable for shaping at the edges.

Internal Shaping

This pattern lends itself to the method of adding chains between elements. We begin with a smaller version of the patt, which is a multiple of 8, with 3 chains between leaves and the single dc. In IncRow 2 there are 4 chains between them, in IncRow 4 there are 5, and so on.

(For swatch, ch 28.)

ROW 1: Dc in 4th ch from hook, *ch 4, sk 3 ch, sc in next ch, ch 4, sk 3 ch**, 3 dc in next ch, rep from * across, ending last rep at **, 2 dc in last ch, turn.
(Swatch has 3 patt reps with ch-4 spaces.)

ROWS 2 AND 3: Work in rows 2 and 3 of patt but make only 4 ch between elements instead of 5.

IncRows 1–3: Work in rows 4–6 of patt (5 ch between elements).

IncRows 4–6: Work in rows 7, 2, and 3 of patt, making 6 ch between elements.

To continue increasing, add 1 ch between elements every 3 rows, including one extra chain to begin Row 6 of patt.
(Swatch has 12 rows in patt, ending with 3 patt reps with 7 ch between elements.)

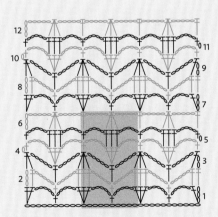

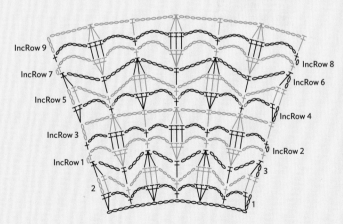

LUNETTES

Chain spaces move in diagonal lines in this lace pattern built on simple elements. In one row, pairs of two double crochet stitches worked together alternate along the row with single crochet stitches. In the next row, an open Shell alternates with single crochet stitches. The alternation of single crochet and taller stitches creates the zigzag.

NUMBER OF STITCHES IN PATTERN REPEAT

12

MULTIPLE

10 + 2

NUMBER OF ROWS IN PATTERN REPEAT

4

REVERSIBLE

SPECIAL STITCH
Shell: (Dc, ch 1, dc, ch 1, dc) in designated ch-1 sp.

BASIC PATTERN

(For swatch, ch 32.)

ROW 1: Sc in 2nd ch from hook, *sc in next ch, ch 3, sk 2 ch, dc2tog in next ch, ch 1, sk next ch, dc2tog in next ch, ch 3, sk 2 ch, sc in next ch**, ch 1, sk next ch, rep from * across, ending last rep at **, sc in last sc, turn.

(Swatch has 3 patt reps.)

ROW 2: Ch 4 (counts as dc, ch 1), dc in same sc, *ch 3, sk next (sc, ch 3, dc2tog), sc in next ch-1 sp, ch 3, sk next (dc2tog, ch 3, sc)**, Shell in next ch-1 sp, rep from * across, ending last rep at **, (dc, ch 1, dc) in last sc, turn.

ROW 3: Ch 3 (counts as dc at start of row throughout), *dc2tog in next ch-1 sp, ch 3, sc in next ch-3 sp, ch 1, sc in next ch-3 sp, ch 3**, dc2tog in next ch-1 sp, ch 1, rep from * across, ending last rep at **, dc2tog in tch, dc in 3rd ch of tch, turn.

ROW 4: Ch 1, sc in first dc, *ch 3, sk next sc, Shell in next ch-1 sp, ch 3, sk next dc2tog**, sc in next ch-1 sp, rep from * across, ending last rep at **, sc in tch, turn.

ROW 5: Ch 1, sc in first sc, *sc in next ch-3 sp, ch 3, dc2tog in next ch-1 sp, ch 1, dc2tog in next ch-1 sp, ch 3, sc in next ch-3 sp**, ch 1, rep from * across, ending last rep at **, sc in last sc, turn.

Rep rows 2–5 for patt. For a flat top edge, end with an even-numbered row.

(Swatch has 12 rows in patt.)

Edge Shaping

This stitch is not suitable for shaping at the edges.

Internal Shaping

1 chain is added between Shells and sc every 2 rows.

(For swatch, ch 32. Work row 1 of patt. 3 patt reps.)

IncRow 1: Ch 4 (counts as dc, ch 1), dc in same sc, *ch 4, sk next (sc, ch 3, dc2tog), sc in next ch-1 sp, ch 4, sk next (dc2tog, ch 3, sc)**, Shell in next ch-1 sp, rep from * across, ending last rep at **, (dc, ch 1, dc) in last sc, turn.

IncRow 2: Ch 3, *dc2tog in next ch-1 sp, ch 4, sc in next ch-4 sp, ch 1, sc in next ch-4 sp, ch 4**, dc2tog in next ch-1 sp, ch 1, rep from * across, ending last rep at **, dc2tog in tch, dc in 3rd ch of tch, turn.

IncRow 3: Ch 1, sc in first dc, *ch 5, sk next sc, Shell in next ch-1 sp, ch 5, sk next dc2tog**, sc in next ch-1 sp, rep from * across, ending last rep at **, sc in tch, turn.

IncRow 4: Ch 1, sc in first sc, *sc in next ch-5 sp, ch 5, dc2tog in next ch-1 sp, ch 1, dc2tog in next ch-1 sp, ch 5, sc in next ch-5 sp**, ch 1, rep from * across, ending last rep at **, sc in last sc, turn.

IncRow 5: Ch 4 (counts as dc, ch 1), dc in same sc, *ch 6, sc in next ch-1 sp, ch 6**, Shell in next ch-1 sp, rep from * across, ending last rep at **, (dc, ch 1, dc) in last sc, turn.

IncRow 6: Ch 3, *dc2tog in next ch-1 sp, ch 6, sc in next ch-6 sp, ch 1, sc in next ch-6 sp, ch 6**, dc2tog in next ch-1 sp, ch 1, rep from * across, ending last rep at **, dc2tog in tch, dc in 3rd ch of tch, turn.

IncRow 7: Ch 1, sc in first dc, *ch 7, sk next sc, Shell in next ch-1 sp, ch 7, sk next dc2tog**, sc in next ch-1 sp, rep from * across, ending last rep at **, sc in tch, turn.

IncRow 8: Ch 1, sc in first sc, *sc in next ch-7 sp, ch 7, dc2tog in next ch-1 sp, ch 1, dc2tog in next ch-1 sp, ch 7, sc in next ch-7 sp**, ch 1, rep from * across, ending last rep at **, sc in last sc, turn.

To continue increasing add 1 chain between Shell and next sc every even-numbered row.

(Swatch has 9 rows total, 8 increase rows ending with 3 patt reps with 7 ch between elements.)

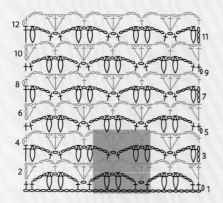

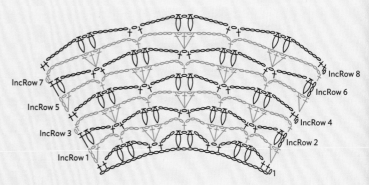

PINEAPPLE
COLUMNS

In this stitch Pineapples are worked directly over one another, with Double V-stitches between them. Unlike the more commonly seen intertwined Pineapples, this arrangement makes it easier to shape with the method of enlarging the pattern. Note that the Pineapple becomes both wider and longer when enlarged.

NUMBER OF STITCHES IN PATTERN REPEAT

V

MULTIPLE

14 + 2

NUMBER OF ROWS IN PATTERN REPEAT

5

REVERSIBLE

SPECIAL STITCH

Double V-stitch (DoubleV): (2 dc, ch 1, 2 dc) in designated st or sp. After row 2 these are always worked into the ch-1 sp of DoubleV in prev row.

BASIC PATTERN

(For swatch, ch 30.)

ROW 1: Sc in 2nd ch from hook, *ch 3, sk 6 ch, (dc, ch 1) 5 times in next ch, dc in same ch, ch 3, sk 6 ch**, sc in next ch, rep from * across, ending last rep at **, sc in last ch, turn.
(Swatch has 2 patt reps.)

ROW 2: Ch 3 (counts as dc throughout), 2 dc in same sc, *ch 1, [(sc, ch 3) in next ch-1 sp] 4 times, sc in next ch-1 sp, ch 1**, DoubleV in next sc, rep from * across, ending last rep at **, 3 dc in last sc, turn.

ROW 3: Ch 3, 2 dc in same dc, *ch 2, [(sc, ch 3) in next ch-3 sp] 3 times, sc in next ch-3 sp, ch 2**, DoubleV, rep from * across, ending last rep at **, sk 2 dc, 3 dc in tch, turn.

ROW 4: Ch 3, 2 dc in same dc, *ch 3, [(sc, ch 3) in next ch-3 sp] 2 times, sc in next ch-3 sp, ch 3**, DoubleV, rep from * across, ending last rep at **, sk 2 dc, 3 dc in tch, turn.

ROW 5: Ch 3, 2 dc in first dc, *ch 4, sk next ch-3 sp, (sc, ch 3) in next ch-3 sp, sc in next ch-3 sp, ch 4**, DoubleV, rep from * across, ending last rep at **, sk 2 dc, 3 dc in tch, turn.

ROW 6: Ch 1, sc in first dc, *ch 3, sk next ch-4 sp, (dc, ch 1) 5 times in next ch-3 sp, dc in same ch-3 sp, ch 3**, sc in ch-1 sp of next DoubleV, rep from * across, ending last rep at **, sk 2 dc, sc in tch, turn.

Rep rows 2–6 for patt.
(Swatch has 15 rows in patt.)

Edge Shaping

This stitch is not suitable for increasing at the edges.

Internal Shaping

We begin with a smaller version of the pattern, requiring a multiple of 12 sts + 2.

(For swatch, ch 26.)

ROW 1: Sc in 2nd ch from hook, *ch 2, sk 5 ch, (dc, ch 1) 4 times in next ch, dc in same ch, ch 2, sk 5 ch**, sc in next ch, rep from * across, ending last rep at **, sc in last ch, turn.

ROW 2: Ch 3, 2 dc in same dc, *ch 1, [(sc, ch 3) in next ch-1 sp] 3 times, sc in next ch-1 sp, ch 1**, DoubleV in next sc, rep from * across, ending last rep at **, 3 dc in last sc, turn.

ROW 3: Ch 3, 2 dc in same dc, *ch 2, [(sc, ch 3) in next ch-3 sp] 2 times, sc in next ch-3 sp, ch 2**, DoubleV, rep from * across, ending last rep at **, sk 2 dc, 3 dc in tch, turn.

ROW 4: Ch 3, 2 dc in same dc, *ch 3, (sc, ch 3) in next ch-3 sp, sc in next ch-3 sp, ch 3**, DoubleV, rep from * across, ending last rep at **, 3 dc in tch, turn.

IncRow 1: Ch 1, sc in first dc, *ch 3, sk next ch-3 sp, (dc, ch 1) 5 times in next ch-3 sp, dc in same ch-3 sp, ch 3**, sc in ch-1 sp of next DoubleV, rep from * across, ending last rep at **, sc in tch, turn.

IncRows 2–5: Work rows 2–5 of patt.

IncRow 6: Ch 1, sc in first dc, *ch 4, sk ch-4 sp, (dc, ch 1) 6 times in next ch-3 sp, dc in same ch-3 sp, ch 4**, DoubleV in

next sc, rep from * across, ending last rep at **, sc in tch, turn.

IncRow 7: Ch 3, 2 dc in same sc, *ch 2, sk next ch-4 sp, [(sc, ch 1) in next ch-3 sp] 5 times, sc in next ch-3 sp, ch 2**, sk next ch-4 sp, DoubleV, rep from * across, ending last rep at **, 3 dc in last sc, turn.

IncRow 8: Ch 3, 2 dc in same dc, *ch 3, sk next ch-2 sp, [(sc, ch 3) in next ch-3 sp] 4 times, sc in next ch-3 sp, ch 3**, DoubleV, rep from * across, ending last rep at **, 3 dc in tch, turn.

IncRow 9: Ch 3, 2 dc in same dc, *ch 4, sk next ch-3 sp, [(sc, ch 3) in next ch-3 sp] 3 times, sc in next ch-3 sp, ch 4**, DoubleV, rep from * across, ending last rep at **, 3 dc in tch, turn.

IncRow 10: Ch 3, 2 dc in same dc, *ch 5, sk next ch-4 sp, [(sc, ch 3) in next ch-3 sp] 2 times, sc in next ch-3 sp, ch 5**, DoubleV, rep from * across, ending last rep at **, 3 dc in tch, turn.

IncRow 11: Ch 3, 2 dc in same dc, *ch 6, sk next ch-5 sp, (sc, ch 3) in next ch-3 sp, sc in next ch-3 sp, ch 6**, DoubleV, rep from * across, ending last rep at **, 3 dc in tch, turn.

To continue increasing, add one more (dc, ch 1) in row 2 of patt, adjusting ch before and after Pineapple as needed.

(Swatch has 15 rows total, 11 increase rows, ending with 6 ch between elements.)

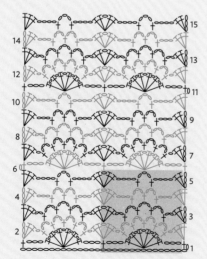

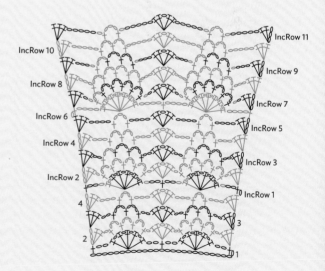

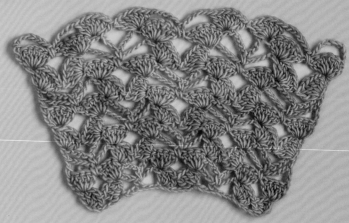

OUTREACH

This stitch uses the same elements to create a floral shape as does Spider and Blocks—single crochet stitches at the center, and chains that expand out to blocks of double crochet stitches. The blocks of four double crochet used in this stitch, however, do not align on a diagonal but rather align over one another for two rows at a time. Compare the two stitches and see how each achieves its floral look.

NOTE
Row 3 requires working an sc between two groups of 4 dc. Simply insert the hook in the space below the last dc of one group and the first dc of the next group and work the sc as usual.

NUMBER OF STITCHES IN PATTERN REPEAT	NUMBER OF ROWS IN PATTERN REPEAT
15	4
MULTIPLE	**REVERSIBLE**
13 + 9	

BASIC PATTERN

(For swatch, ch 35.)

ROW 1: 3 dc in 4th ch from hook (3 sk ch count as dc), *sk 4 ch, 4 dc in next ch**, ch 3, sk 3 ch, sc in next ch, ch 3, sk 3 ch, 4 dc in next ch, rep from * across, ending last rep at **, turn. *(Swatch has 2½ patt reps.)*

ROW 2: Ch 3 (counts as dc at start of rows), 3 dc in first dc, *sk 6 dc, 4 dc in next dc, ch 3, sc in next sc, ch 3, 4 dc in next dc, rep from * across placing last 4 dc in tch, turn.

ROW 3: Ch 6 (counts as dc, ch 3 throughout), *sc between next 2 4-dc groups, ch 3**, sk 3 dc, 4 dc in next dc, sk (ch 3, sc, ch 3), 4 dc in next dc, ch 3, rep from * across, ending last rep at **, dc in tch, turn.

ROW 4: Ch 6, sc in first sc, ch 3, *4 dc in next dc, sk 6 dc, 4 dc in next dc, ch 3, sc in next sc, ch 3, rep from * across, dc in tch, turn.

ROW 5: Ch 3, 3 dc in first dc, *sk (ch 3, sc, ch 3)**, 4 dc in next dc, ch 3, sc between next 2 4-dc groups, ch 3, sk 3 dc, 4 dc in next dc, rep from * across, ending last rep at **, 4 dc in tch, turn. Rep rows 2–5 for patt.
(Swatch has 11 rows in patt.)

Edge Shaping

This stitch is not suitable for shaping at the edges.

Internal Shaping

This stitch adapts very nicely to shaping by enlarging the size of the pattern. We add a dc to each group in the first increase row, then enlarge it again every 4th row, also adding one chain, for gradual shaping.

(For swatch, ch 35. Work row 1 of patt. 2½ patt reps.)

IncRow 1: Ch 3 (counts as dc at start of rows), 4 dc in first dc, *sk 6 dc, 5 dc in next dc, ch 3, sc in next sc, ch 3, 5 dc in next dc, rep from * across placing last 5 dc in tch, turn.

IncRow 2: Ch 7 (counts as dc, ch 4), *sc between next 2 5-dc groups, ch 4**, sk 4 dc, 5 dc in next dc, sk (ch 3, sc, ch 3), 5 dc in next dc, ch 4, rep from * across, ending last rep at **, dc in tch, turn.

IncRow 3: Ch 7, sc in first sc, ch 4, *5 dc in next dc, sk 8 dc, 5 dc in next dc, ch 4, sc in next sc, ch 4, rep from * across, dc in tch, turn.

IncRow 4: Ch 3, 5 dc in first dc, *sk (ch 4, sc, ch 4)**, 6 dc in next dc, ch 4, sc between next 2 5-dc groups, ch 4, sk 4 dc, 6 dc in next dc, rep from * across, ending last rep at **, 6 dc in tch, turn.

IncRow 5: Ch 3, 5 dc in first dc, *sk 10 dc, 6 dc in next dc, ch 4, sc in next sc, ch 4, 6 dc in next dc, rep from * across placing last 6 dc in tch, turn.

IncRow 6: Ch 8 (counts as dc, ch 5), *sc between next 2 6-dc groups, ch 5**, sk 5 dc, 6 dc in next dc, sk (ch 4, sc, ch 4), 6 dc in next dc, ch 5, rep from * across, ending last rep at **, dc in tch, turn.

IncRow 7: Ch 8, *sc in next sc, ch 5, 6 dc in next dc, sk 10 dc, 6 dc in next dc, ch 5, sc in next sc, ch 5, rep from * across, dc in tch, turn.

To continue increasing, add one dc to each group every 4th row beginning in IncRow 8, and add 1 extra ch before and after sc every 4th row beginning in IncRow 10.

(Swatch has 11 rows total, 10 increase rows, ending with 2½ patt reps with 7-dc groups and ch-6 sps.)

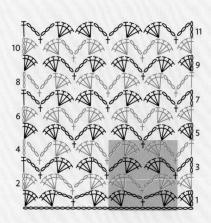

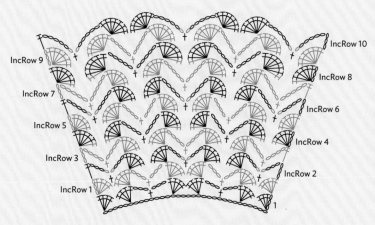

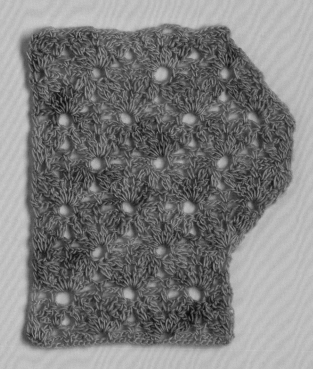

DAISIES

Shells are lovely when made with pairs of worked together double crochet stitches, and in this stitch pattern they are coupled with upside-down Shells to create an intricate floral design. The structure of this stitch is similar to that of Interwoven Diamonds (see page 182), with an added row of chain spaces that creates the open center of each flower.

NUMBER OF STITCHES IN PATTERN REPEAT	NUMBER OF ROWS IN PATTERN REPEAT
V	6
MULTIPLE	REVERSIBLE
11 + 3	

SPECIAL STITCH
Shell: [Ch 1, (dc2tog, ch 2) 3 times, dc2tog, ch 1] in designated st or sp.

BASIC PATTERN

(For swatch, ch 36.)

ROW 1: Sc in 2nd ch from hook, ch 1, sk next ch, *sc in next ch, (ch 3, sk 3 ch, sc in next ch) twice**, ch 2, sk 2 ch, rep from * across, ending last rep at **, ch 1, sk next ch, sc in last ch, turn. *(Swatch has 3 patt reps, 1 sc, including ½ patt at ends.)*

ROW 2: Ch 3 (counts as dc at start of row throughout), (dc2tog, ch 2, dc2tog, ch 1) in first ch-1 sp, *sk next ch-3 sp, sc in next sc**, Shell in next ch-2 sp, rep from * across, ending last rep at **, (ch 1, dc2tog, ch 2, dc2tog) in last ch-1 sp, dc in last sc, turn.

ROW 3: Ch 1, sc in first dc, *ch 3, (dc2tog in next dc2tog) 4 times, ch 3**, sc in ch-2 sp at center of same Shell, rep from * across, ending last rep at **, sc in tch, turn.

ROW 4: Ch 1, sc in first sc, *ch 3, sc in next dc2tog, ch 2, sk 2 dc2tog, sc in next dc2tog, ch 3, sk 3 ch, sc in next sc, rep from * across, turn.

ROW 5: Ch 1, sc in first sc, *Shell in next ch-2 sp, sk next ch-3 sp, sc in next sc, rep from * across, turn.

ROW 6: Ch 3, (dc2tog in next dc2tog) twice, *ch 3, sc in ch-2 sp at center of same Shell, ch 3**, (dc2tog in next dc2tog) 4 times, rep from * ending last rep at **, (dc2tog in next dc2tog) twice, dc in last sc, turn.

ROW 7: Ch 1, sc in first dc, ch 1, *sk next dc2tog, sc in next dc2tog, ch 3, sk next ch-3 sp, sc in next sc, ch 3, sc in next dc2tog**, ch 2, sk next dc2tog, rep from * across, ending last rep at **, ch 1, sk last dc2tog, sc in tch, turn.
Rep rows 2–7 for patt.
(Swatch has 7 rows in patt.)

Edge Shaping

1 patt rep is added over 6 rows beginning on the first row of the 6-row pattern. Decreasing begins on row 5 of patt. Note that in DecRow 2 the slip stitches may need to be worked differently depending on the weight of your yarn.

INCREASING

IncRow 1: Ch 3, Shell in first ch-1 sp, continue in row 2 of patt across.

IncRow 2: Work in row 3 of patt across, placing last sc in ch-2 sp at center of last Shell, ch 3, (dc2tog in next dc2tog) 2 times, dc in tch, turn.

IncRow 3: Ch 1, sc in first dc, ch 2, sk next dc2tog, sc in next dc2tog, ch 3, sc in next sc, continue in row 4 of patt across.

IncRow 4: Work in row 5 of patt across, placing Shell in last ch-2 sp, dc in last sc, turn.

IncRow 5: Ch 3, (dc2tog in next dc2tog) twice, ch 3, sc in ch-2 sp at center of same Shell, continue in row 6 of patt across.

IncRow 6: Work in row 7 of patt across to last 3 sts, sc in next dc2tog, ch 1, sc in last tch, turn.

Rep IncRows 1–6 to continue increasing.

(Swatch has 6 increase rows, ending with 4 patt reps, followed by rows 2–4 worked even.)

DECREASING

DecRow 1: Work in row 5 of patt across.

DecRow 2: Ch 1, sk (first sc, ch-1 sp), sl st in next st, sl st in next ch-2 sp, sl st in next st, ch 1, sc in next ch-2 sp, ch 3, (dc2tog in next dc2tog) 4 times, continue in row 6 of patt across.

DecRow 3: Work in row 7 of patt to last 4 dc2tog, sc in next dc2tog, ch 2, sk next 2 dc2tog, sc in last dc2tog, ch 3, sc in last sc, turn.

DecRow 4: Ch 1, Shell in first ch-2 sp, continue in row 2 of patt.

DecRow 5: Work in row 3 of patt, placing last sc in center ch-2 sp of last Shell, turn.

DecRow 6: Work even in row 4 of patt.

Rep DecRows 1–6 to continue decreasing.

(Swatch has 6 decrease rows, ending with 3 patt reps, 1 sc.)

Internal Shaping

This stitch is not suitable for internal shaping.

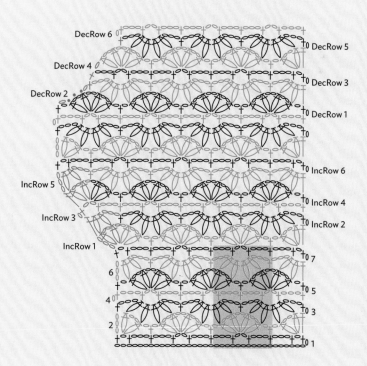

SPIDER AND BLOCKS

This pattern presents a striking visual that's somewhere between a flower and a crochet spider. Single crochet stitches and chains define the center, from which blocks of three double crochet stitches fan out to create a floral look. It's intricate and requires careful focus on the placement of stitches throughout.

NUMBER OF STITCHES IN PATTERN REPEAT	NUMBER OF ROWS IN PATTERN REPEAT
V	8

MULTIPLE	REVERSIBLE
14 + 3	

BASIC PATTERN

(For swatch, ch 31.)

ROW 1: Dc in 4th ch from hook (3 sk ch count as dc), *ch 3, sk 3 ch, sc in next 5 ch, ch 3, sk 3 ch**, dc in next 3 ch, rep from * across, ending last rep at **, dc in last 2 ch, turn.
(Swatch has 2 patt reps.)

ROW 2: Ch 3 (counts as dc at start of row), *3 dc in next ch-3 sp, ch 3, sk next sc, sc in next 3 sc, ch 3, 3 dc in next ch-3 sp**, ch 1, rep from * ending last rep at **, dc in tch, turn.

ROW 3: Ch 6 (counts as dc, ch 3 throughout), *3 dc in next ch-3 sp, ch 3, dc in center sc of 3-sc group, ch 3, 3 dc in next ch-3 sp, ch 3**, dc in next ch-1 sp, ch 3, rep from * across, ending last rep at **, dc in tch, turn.

ROW 4: Ch 1, sc in first dc, *sc in next ch-3 sp, ch 3, 3 dc in next ch-3 sp, ch 1, 3 dc in next ch-3 sp, ch 3**, sc in next ch-3 sp, sc in next dc, rep from * across, ending last rep at **, sc in tch, sc in 3rd ch of tch, turn.

ROW 5: Ch 1, sc in first sc, sc in next sc, *sc in next ch-3 sp, ch 3, 3 dc in next ch-1 sp, ch 3, sc in next ch-3 sp**, sc in next 3 sc, rep from * across, ending last rep at **, sc in last 2 sc, turn.

ROW 6: Ch 1, sc in first sc, *sc in next sc, ch 3, 3 dc in next ch-3 sp, ch 1, 3 dc in next ch-3 sp, ch 3, sk next sc, sc in next 2 sc, rep from * across, turn.

ROW 7: Ch 6, *3 dc in next ch-3 sp, ch 3, dc in next ch-1 sp, ch 3, 3 dc in next ch-3 sp, ch 3**, dc in center sc of 3-sc group, ch 3, rep from * across, ending last rep at **, dc in last sc, turn.

ROW 8: Ch 3, *3 dc in next ch-3 sp, ch 3, sc in next ch-3 sp, sc in next dc, sc in next ch-3 sp, ch 3, 3 dc in next ch-3 sp**, ch 1, rep from * across, ending last rep at **, dc in 3rd ch of tch, turn.

ROW 9: Ch 3, dc in first dc, *ch 3, sc in next ch-3 sp, sc in next 3 sc, sc in next ch-3 sp, ch 3**, 3 dc in next ch-1 sp, rep from * across, ending last rep at **, 2 dc in tch, turn.

Rep rows 2–9 for patt.

(Swatch has 8 rows in patt.)

Edge Shaping

Shaping is at the rate of 1 full patt rep over 8 rows. Decreasing starts on row 3 of patt.

INCREASING

IncRow 1: Ch 3, 2 dc in first dc, ch 3, sc in next ch-3 sp, continue in row 9 of patt across.

IncRow 2: Work in row 2 of patt across, ch 1, 3 dc in tch, turn.

IncRow 3: Ch 3, 2 dc in first dc, ch 3, dc in next ch-1 sp, continue in row 3 of patt across.

IncRow 4: Work in row 4 of patt, placing sc in last ch-3 sp, ch 3, 3 dc in tch, turn.

IncRow 5: Ch 3, 2 dc in first dc, ch 3, sc in next ch-3 sp, sc in next 3 sc, continue in row 5 of patt across.

IncRow 6: Work in row 6 of patt, placing 3 dc in last ch-3 sp, ch 1, 3 dc in tch, turn.

IncRow 7: Ch 3, 2 dc in first dc, ch 3, dc in next ch-1 sp, ch 3, continue in row 7 of patt across.

IncRow 8: Work in row 8 of patt placing sc in last ch-3 sp, ch 3, 3 dc in tch, turn.

Rep IncRows 1–8 to continue increasing.

(Swatch has 8 increase rows, ending with 3 patt reps, followed by 2 rows worked even.)

DECREASING

DecRow 1: Ch 3, sk 3 dc, 3 dc in next ch-3 sp, ch 3, dc in center sc of 3-sc group, continue in row 3 of patt across.

DecRow 2: Work in row 4 of patt to last 4 sts, sk 3 dc, dc in tch, turn.

DecRow 3: Ch 3, 3 dc in next ch-1 sp, ch 3, continue in row 5 of patt across.

DecRow 4: Work in row 6 of patt to last 4 sts, sk 3 dc, dc in tch, turn.

DecRow 5: Ch 3, 3 dc in next ch-3 sp, dc in center sc of 3-sc group, continue in row 7 of patt across.

DecRow 6: Work in row 8 of patt to last 4 sts, sk 3 dc, dc in tch, turn.

DecRow 7: Ch 3, 3 dc in next ch-1 sp, ch 3, sc in next ch-3 sp, continue in row 9 of patt across.

DecRow 8: Work in row 2 of patt to last 4 sts, sk 3 dc, dc in tch, turn.

Rep DecRows 1–8 to continue decreasing.

(Swatch has 8 decrease rows, ending with 2 patt reps, followed by 1 row worked even.)

Internal Shaping

This stitch is not suitable for internal shaping.

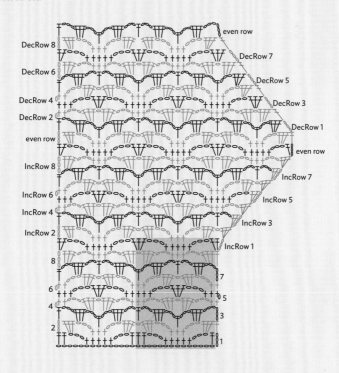

PETAL WEB

Clean rounded shapes characterize this stitch pattern, which features worked-together stitches that lie horizontally. They are easy and fun to make.

NUMBER OF STITCHES IN PATTERN REPEAT	NUMBER OF ROWS IN PATTERN REPEAT
4	2
MULTIPLE	REVERSIBLE
4 + 3	

NOTES

The Petals lie at a perpendicular angle to the stitch just made. When working a Petal, after ch 3, insert hook under top 2 loops of dc2tog or dc3tog—even though you are approaching from a different angle, you can insert the hook in the top of the st.

In the following row the base of the Petal is the dc3tog of prev row.

SPECIAL STITCH
Petal: Ch 3, dc2tog in top of st just made.

BASIC PATTERN

(For swatch, ch 23.)

ROW 1: Dc in 4th ch from hook (sk 3 ch and dc count as dc2tog), *Petal in st just made, sk next ch,** dc3tog over next 3 ch, rep from * across, ending last rep at **, dc2tog over last 2 ch, turn.

(Swatch has 5 patt reps, counting ½ patts at edges.)

ROW 2: Ch 3 (counts as dc at start of row throughout), dc in same st, *ch 1, 3 dc in base of Petal, rep from * across to last dc2tog, ch 1, 2 dc in last dc2tog, turn.

ROW 3: Ch 2, dc in next dc (counts as dc2tog), *Petal in st just made**, dc3tog over next 3 dc, rep from * across, ending last rep at **, dc2tog in last 2 dc, turn.

Rep rows 2 and 3 for patt.

(Swatch has 5 rows in patt.)

Edge Shaping

Shaping begins on an even-numbered row, at the rate of 1 patt rep over 2 rows.

INCREASING

IncRow 1: Ch 3, 2 dc in first st, continue in row 2 of patt across.

IncRow 2: Work in row 3 of patt, working dc3tog over last 2 dc and tch, Petal, dc in tch, turn.

Rep IncRows 1 and 2 to continue increasing.

(Swatch has 6 increase rows, ending with 8 patt reps, counting ½ patts at edges, followed by 2 rows worked even.)

DECREASING

DecRow 1: Ch 3, 3 dc in base of Petal, continue in row 2 of patt across.

DecRow 2: Work in row 3 of patt, working dc3tog over last 3 dc, leave tch unworked, turn.

Rep DecRows 1 and 2 to continue decreasing.

(Swatch has 6 decrease rows, ending with 5 patt reps, counting ½ patt at edges.)

Internal Shaping

This stitch is not suitable for internal shaping.

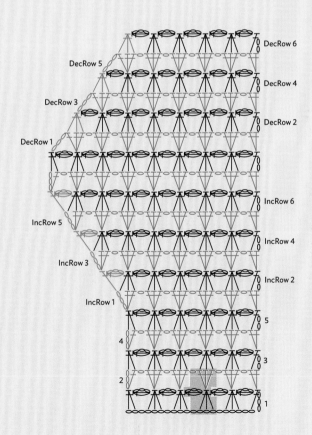

PUFF COLUMNS

Both crossed stitches and Puffs give this unusual stitch its texture. The pattern repeat consists of a Crossed Pair and double crochet stitch on odd-numbered rows, and a (single crochet, chain two, Puff, chain two) on even-numbered rows.

SPECIAL STITCHES

Crossed Pair (CP): Sk next ch-2 sp and Puff, dc in next ch-2 sp, working in front of st just made dc in sk ch-2 sp. CP are always worked into the ch-2 sps on either side of a Puff.

Puff: (Yo, insert hook in designated sp and draw up loop to ½") 3 times, yo, draw through 7 loops on hook. Puffs are always worked between the 2 dc in a CP, so insert hook in the space just under where the 2 sts meet.

NUMBER OF STITCHES IN PATTERN REPEAT	NUMBER OF ROWS IN PATTERN REPEAT
V	2
MULTIPLE	**REVERSIBLE**
3 + 3	

BASIC PATTERN

(For swatch, ch 18.)

ROW 1: Dc in 5th ch from hook (4 sk ch count as 1 fnd ch, dc), working in front of st just made, dc in last sk fnd ch (first CP made), *dc in next ch, sk next ch, dc in next ch, working in front of st just made, dc in sk ch, rep from * across, dc in last ch, turn. *(Swatch has 5 patt reps.)*

ROW 2: Ch 1, sc in first dc, *ch 2, Puff between 2 dc of next CP, ch 2, sc in next dc, rep from * across, placing last sc in 3rd ch of tch, turn.

ROW 3: Ch 3 (counts as dc), *CP, dc in next sc, rep from * across, turn.

Rep rows 2 and 3 for patt. *(Swatch has 6 rows in patt.)*

Edge Shaping

Shaping begins in row 3 of patt. 1 patt rep is added every other row. Note that at the end of IncRow 2 the last sc is worked between the last dc and tch. At the end of DecRow 2 we work sc2tog to smooth out the shaped edge.

INCREASING

IncRow 1: Ch 3, 2 dc in first sc, CP, continue in row 3 of patt across.

IncRow 2: Work in row 2 of patt to last 3 sts, sc in next dc, ch 2, Puff between next dc and tch, ch 2, sc in same sp, turn.

Rep IncRows 1 and 2 to continue increasing. *(Swatch has 6 increase rows, ending with 8 patt reps, followed by 2 rows worked even in patt.)*

DECREASING

DecRow 1: Ch 3, dc2tog over (next ch-2 sp, sk Puff, next ch-2 sp), dc in next sc, continue in row 3 of patt across.

DecRow 2: Work in row 3 of patt to last 3 sts, sc2tog over (next dc, next dc2tog), leave tch unworked, turn.

Rep DecRows 1 and 2 to continue decreasing. *(Swatch has 6 decrease rows, ending with 5 patt reps.)*

Internal Shaping

This stitch is not suitable for internal shaping.

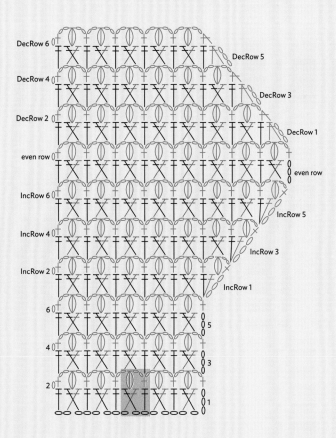

SPROUTS

Open Shells and a three–double crochet
Bobble are the major elements in this striking
stitch.

NUMBER OF STITCHES IN PATTERN REPEAT	NUMBER OF ROWS IN PATTERN REPEAT
V	4
MULTIPLE	REVERSIBLE
10 + 4	

SPECIAL STITCHES

Shell: (Dc, ch 1) 5 times in designated st or sp, , dc in
same st or sp.

Bobble: (Yo, insert hook in designated st, yo and
draw up loop, yo, draw through 2 loops) 3 times, yo,
draw through 4 loops on hook.

BASIC PATTERN

(For swatch, ch 34.)

ROW 1: [(Dc, ch 1) twice, dc] in 4th ch from hook (3 sk ch count as dc), *sk 3 ch, sc in next ch, ch 3, sk next ch, sc in next ch, sk 3 ch**, Shell in next ch, rep from * across, ending last rep at **, [(dc, ch 1) twice, 2 dc] in last ch, turn.

(Swatch has 3 patt reps, counting ½ Shells at edges.)

ROW 2: Ch 2, dc in same dc (counts as dc2tog), *ch 3, sc in next ch-1 sp, ch 2, sk next ch-1 sp, (sc, ch 3, sc) in next ch-3 sp, ch 2, sk next ch-1 sp, sc in next ch-1 sp, ch 3**, Bobble in next ch-1 sp, rep from * across, ending last rep at **, dc2tog in tch, turn.

ROW 3: Ch 3 (counts as hdc, ch 1 on rows 3 and 4), *sc in next ch-3 sp, sk next ch-2 sp, Shell in next ch-3 sp, sk next ch-2 sp, sc in next ch-3 sp**, ch 3, sk next Bobble, rep from * across, ending last rep at **, ch 1, hdc in last st, turn.

ROW 4: Ch 3, sc in next ch-1 sp, *ch 2, sk next ch-1 sp, sc in next ch-1 sp, ch 3, Bobble in next ch-1 sp, ch 3, sc in next ch-1 sp, ch 2**, (sc, ch 3, sc) in next ch-3 sp, rep from * across, ending last rep at **, (sc, ch 1, hdc) in tch, turn.

ROW 5: Ch 3 (counts as dc), [(dc, ch 1) twice, dc] in same hdc, *sk next ch-2 sp, sc in next ch-3 sp, ch 3, sk Bobble, sc in next ch-3 sp, sk next ch-2 sp**, Shell in next ch-3 sp, rep fom * across, ending last rep at **, [(dc, ch 1) twice, 2 dc] in tch, turn.

Rep rows 2–5 for patt.

(Swatch has 13 rows in patt.)

Edge Shaping

This stitch is not suitable for shaping at the edges.

Internal Shaping

Gradual shaping adds 1 patt rep every 6 rows.

(For swatch, ch 24. Work row 1 of patt. 2 patt reps, counting ½ Shells at edges.)

Place marker in center ch-1 sp of center Shell.

IncRow 1: Work row 2 of patt to marked ch-1 sp, (Bobble, ch 5, Bobble) in marked ch-1 sp, move marker to ch-5 just made, ch 3, sc in next ch-1 sp, continue in patt across.

IncRow 2: Work row 3 of patt to marked ch-5 sp, ch 3, [sc, (dc, ch 1) 3 times, dc, sc] in marked ch-5 sp, move marker to center ch-1 sp of Shell just made, ch 3, sc in next ch-3 sp, continue in patt across.

IncRow 3: Work row 4 of patt placing sc in first ch-1 sp of center Shell, ch 3, Bobble in next ch-1 sp, ch 3, sc in next ch-1 sp, ch 2, continue in patt across. Remove marker.

IncRows 4–6: Work in rows 5, 2, and 3 of patt across. Place marker in center ch-1 sp of center Shell.

IncRow 7: Work in row 4 of patt to marked ch-1 sp, (Bobble, ch 5, Bobble) in marked ch-1 sp, move marker to ch-5 sp just made, ch 3, sc in next ch-1 sp, continue in patt across.

IncRow 8: Work in row 5 of patt to marked ch-5 sp, ch 3, [sc, (dc, ch 1) 3 times, dc, sc] in marked ch-5 sp, move marker to center ch-1 sp of Shell just made, ch 3, sc in next ch-3 sp, continue in patt across.

IncRow 9: Work in row 2 of patt, placing sc in first ch-1 sp of center Shell, ch 3, Bobble in next ch-1 sp, ch 3, sc in next ch-1 sp, ch 2, continue in patt across, remove marker.

IncRows 10–12: Work rows 3–5 of patt. Place marker in center ch-1 sp of center Shell.

Rep IncRows 1–12 to continue increasing.

(Swatch has 11 total rows, 10 increase rows, ending with 4 patt reps.)

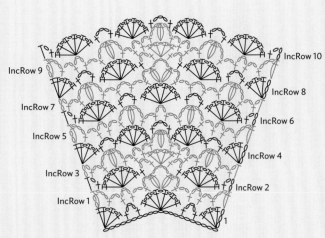

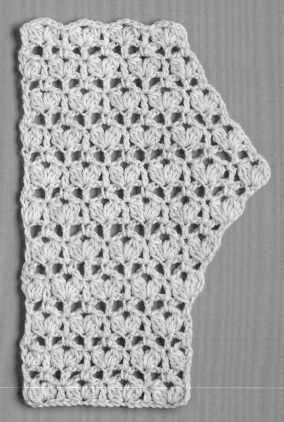

BUDS ON STEMS

On one row pairs of three double crochet stitches worked together are linked with a chain-three space and framed with double crochet stitches, and the alternating row consists of single crochet and double crochet stitches with chain-two spaces between them.

NUMBER OF STITCHES IN PATTERN REPEAT	NUMBER OF ROWS IN PATTERN REPEAT
6	4
MULTIPLE	**REVERSIBLE**
6 + 3	

SPECIAL STITCH
Buds: (Dc3tog, ch 3, dc3tog) in designated st.

BASIC PATTERN

(For swatch, ch 27.)

ROW 1: Buds in 6th ch from hook, (5 sk ch count as dc, 2 fnd ch), sk 2 ch, *dc in next ch, sk 2 ch, Buds in next ch, sk 2 ch, rep from * across, dc in last ch, turn.
(Swatch has 4 patt reps, 1 dc.)

ROW 2: Ch 5 (counts as dc, ch 2 throughout), *sc in next ch-3 sp, ch 2, dc in next dc**, ch 2, rep from * across, ending last rep at **, turn.

ROW 3: Ch 5, dc3tog in same dc, *dc in next sc**, Buds in next dc, rep from * across, ending last rep at **, sk 2 ch of ch-5 tch, (dc3tog, ch 2, dc) in 3rd ch of tch, turn.

ROW 4: Ch 1, sc in first dc, *ch 2, dc in next dc, ch 2, sc in next ch-3 sp, rep from * across, placing last sc in 3 ch of ch-5 tch, turn.

ROW 5: Ch 3 (counts as dc throughout), *Buds in next dc, dc in next sc, rep from * across.
Rep rows 2–5 for patt.
(Swatch has 6 rows in patt.)

Edge Shaping

The single Bud at the edge on row 3 can be extended to a pair to begin shaping, at the rate of 1 full patt rep every 4 rows. Decreasing begins on row 2 of patt, and on Buds rows a ch-2 serves as the edge without counting as a stitch.

INCREASING

IncRow 1: Ch 3, Buds in same dc, dc in next sc, continue in row 3 of patt across.

IncRow 2: Work in row 4 of patt across, placing sc in ch-3 sp of last Buds, ch 2, dc in tch, turn.

IncRow 3: Ch 3, Buds in same dc, dc in next sc, continue in row 5 of patt across.

IncRow 4: Work in row 2 of patt, placing sc in ch-3 sp of last Buds, ch 2, dc in tch, turn.

Rep IncRows 1–4 to continue increasing.
(Swatch has 7 increase rows, ending with 6 patt reps, 1 dc.)

DECREASING

DecRow 1: Work in row 2 of patt, placing sc in ch-3 sp of last Buds, leave rem sts unworked, turn.

DecRow 2: Ch 2 (does not count as st), Buds in next dc, dc in next sc, continue in row 3 of patt across.

DecRow 3: Work in row 4 of patt, placing last sc in ch-3 sp of last Buds, leave rem sts unworked, turn.

DecRow 4: Ch 2, Buds in next dc, dc in next sc, continue in row 5 of patt across.

Rep DecRows 1–4 to continue decreasing.
(Swatch has 7 decrease rows, ending with 4 patt reps, 1 dc, followed by row 5 of patt worked even.)

Internal Shaping

This stitch is not suitable for internal shaping.

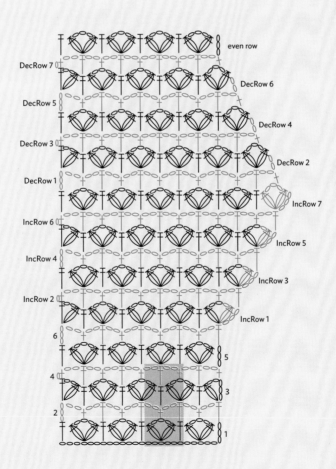

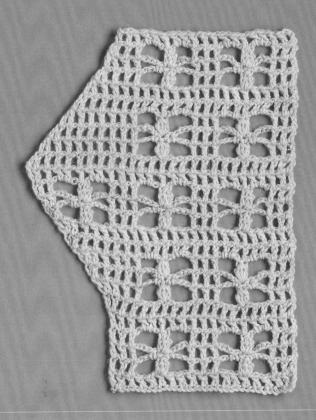

SPIDER FILET

In this pattern a spider-like figure is enclosed in filet work.

NUMBER OF STITCHES IN PATTERN REPEAT	NUMBER OF ROWS IN PATTERN REPEAT
V	5
MULTIPLE	REVERSIBLE
16 + 8	

SPECIAL STITCH

Filet Pattern (FP): [(Dc, ch 1) in next dc] twice, dc in next dc. At start of row, FP is worked as ch 4, dc in next dc, ch 1, dc in next dc. At end of row, last dc is worked in 3rd ch of tch, except on first row 2, when last dc is worked in 4th ch of tch.

BASIC PATTERN

(For swatch, ch 40.)

ROW 1: Dc in 6th ch from hook (5 sk ch count as 1 fnd ch, dc, ch 1), *ch 1, sk next ch, dc in next ch, rep from * across, turn. *(Swatch has 37 sts.)*

ROW 2: FP, *ch 4, sk 2 dc, dc3tog in next dc, ch 4, sk 2 dc, FP, rep from * across, turn.

ROW 3: FP, *ch 4, sc in next ch-4 sp, sc in next dc3tog, sc in next ch-4 sp, ch 4, FP, rep from * across, turn.

ROW 4: FP, *ch 5, sk next sc, dc3tog in next sc, ch 5, FP rep from * across, turn.

ROW 5: FP, *(ch 1, dc) twice in next ch-5 sp, ch 1, dc in next dc3tog, ch 1, (dc, ch 1) twice in next ch-5 sp, FP, rep from * across, turn.

ROW 6: Work FP across, turn.

Rep rows 2–6 for patt, ending with row 5.

(Swatch has 5 rows in patt.)

Edge Shaping

Increasing and decreasing are always done using FP, so all shaping rows begin and end the same, adding or subtracting 1 or 2 stitches per row. A marker is used here to keep track of where to work plain filet.

INCREASING

Move marker up to same st on every row.

IncRow 1: Ch 4 (counts as dc, ch 1 throughout), dc in first dc, place marker in dc just made, FP, continue in row 6 of patt across.

IncRow 2: Work in row 2 of patt to tch, (dc, ch 1, dc) in 3rd ch of tch, turn.

IncRow 3: Ch 4, dc in first dc, ch 1, dc in next dc, ch 1, FP, continue in row 3 of patt across.

IncRow 4: Work in row 4 of patt to marker, continue in FP across, (dc, ch 1, dc) in 3rd ch of tch, turn.

IncRow 5: Ch 4, dc in first dc, ch 1, (dc in next dc, ch 1) 3 times, work in row 5 of patt across.

IncRow 6: Work in row 6 of patt to marker, continue in FB to tch, (dc, ch 1, dc) in 3rd ch of tch, turn.

IncRow 7: Ch 3, dc in first dc, ch 4, sk 2 dc, dc3tog in next dc, continue in row 2 of patt across.

IncRow 8: Work in row 3 of patt to last 2 sts, dc in next dc, ch 1, dc in tch, turn.

IncRow 9: Ch 3, dc in same dc, continue in row 4 of patt across.

IncRow 10: Work in row 5 of patt to last 2 sts, dc in next dc, ch 1, dc in tch, turn.

Rep IncRows 1–10 to continue increasing.
(Swatch has 10 increase rows, ending with 53 sts.)

DECREASING

Marker is used to indicate where to start spider. If starting from working even, place marker in 3rd dc of row 5. If decreasing after working increases, mark last dc before spider begins, moving it up each row.

DecRow 1: Ch 2, sk first dc, dc in next dc (counts as dc2tog throughout), continue in row 6 of patt across.

DecRow 2: Work in row 2 of patt to marker, FP across to last 2 dc, dc2tog over (dc, sk ch-1 sp, dc), turn.

DecRow 3: Ch 2, sk first dc, dc in next dc, FP across to marker, continue in row 3 of patt across.

DecRow 4: Work in row 4 of patt to marker, FP across to last 2 dc, dc2tog over (dc, sk ch-1 sp, dc), turn.

DecRow 5: Ch 2, sk first dc, dc in next dc, FP across to marker, continue in row 5 of patt across.

DecRow 6: Work in row 6 of patt to marker, FP across to last 2 dc, dc2tog over (dc, sk ch-1 sp, dc), turn.

DecRow 7: Ch 2, sk first dc, dc in next dc, ch 1, continue in row 2 of patt across.

DecRow 8: Work in row 3 of patt to marker, sk last ch-1 sp, dc in last dc, turn.

DecRow 9: Ch 2, sk first dc, dc in next dc, continue in row 4 of patt across.

DecRow 10: Work in row 5 of patt across.

Rep DecRows 1–10 to continue decreasing.
(Swatch has 10 decrease rows, ending with 37 sts.)

Internal Shaping

This stitch is not suitable for internal shaping.

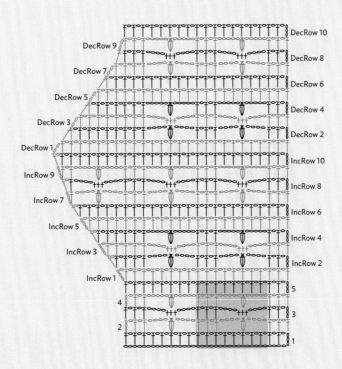

235

CLUSTER LACE

A striking feature of this pattern is the wide cluster that extends over several stitches. Chain stitches echo the diagonals formed by the cluster. Alternate rows have a three–double crochet Bobble, and these elements combined together make a lovely and unusual stitch.

NUMBER OF STITCHES IN PATTERN REPEAT

V

NUMBER OF ROWS IN PATTERN REPEAT

2

MULTIPLE

8 + 2

REVERSIBLE

SPECIAL STITCHES
Cluster (Cl): Dc4tog, working first 2 legs in first designated ch-3 sp, sk (sc, ch 1, sc), work next 2 legs in next designated ch-3 sp.

Bobble: Dc3tog in designated st or sp.

BASIC PATTERN

(For swatch, ch 26.)

ROW 1: Sc in 2nd ch from hook, *sc in next ch, ch 4, dc4tog over (next 2 ch, sk next ch, next 2 ch), ch 4, sc in next ch**, ch 1, sk next ch, rep from * across, ending last rep at **, sc in last ch, turn.

(Swatch has 3 patt reps, 2 sc.)

ROW 2: Ch 3, dc in same sc (counts as dc2tog), *ch 3, sc in next ch-4 sp, ch 1, sk Cl, sc in next ch-4 sp, ch 3**, Bobble in next ch-1 sp, rep from * across, ending last rep at **, dc2tog in last sc, turn.

ROW 3: Ch 1, sc in first st, *sc in next ch-3 sp, ch 4, Cl over (same ch-3 sp as last sc, next ch-3 sp), ch 4, sc in same ch-3 sp as 2nd leg of last Cl**, ch 1, sk next Bobble, rep from * across, ending last rep at **, sc in last st, turn.

Rep rows 2 and 3 for patt, ending on row 2.

(Swatch has 10 rows in patt.)

Edge Shaping

This stitch is not suitable for edge shaping.

Internal Shaping

For this fairly large patt rep, the method is to add 1 patt rep over 3 rows.

(For swatch, ch 18. Work row 1 of patt. 2 patt reps, 2 sc.)

Place marker on ch-1 sp between 2 Cl.

IncRow 1: Work in row 2 of patt to marked ch-1 sp, (Bobble, ch 5, Bobble) in marked ch-1 sp, move marker to ch-5 sp just made, continue in patt across.

IncRow 2: Work in row 3 of patt, completing (sc, ch 1, sk next Bobble) before marked ch-5 sp, sc in marked ch-5 sp, ch 4, dc4tog in marked ch-5 sp, move marker to st just made, ch 4, sc in same ch-5 sp, ch 1, sk next Bobble, continue in patt across.

IncRow 3: Work in row 2 of patt, placing sc in ch-4 sp before marked st, ch 1, sk marked st, sc in next ch-4 sp, move marker to ch-1 sp just made, continue in patt across.

IncRow 4: Work in row 3 of patt across, moving marker to center Cl.

IncRow 5: Work in row 2 of patt, completing (ch 3, sc) in ch-4 sp before marked Cl, ch 3, sc in marked Cl, ch 3, sc in next ch-4 sp, move marker to last ch-3 sp made, continue in patt across.

IncRow 6: Work in row 3 of patt, completing (sc, ch 4) before marked ch-3 sp, Cl over (same ch-3 sp as last sc, sk next sc, marked ch-3 sp), ch 4, sc in same ch-3 sp, ch 1, sk next sc, sc in next ch-3 sp, move marker to ch-1 just made, ch 4, Cl over (same ch-3 sp, sk next sc, next ch-3 sp), continue in patt across.

Rep IncRows 1–6 to continue increasing.

(Swatch has 10 rows total, 9 increase rows, ending with 5 patt reps.)

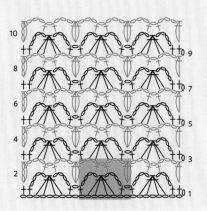

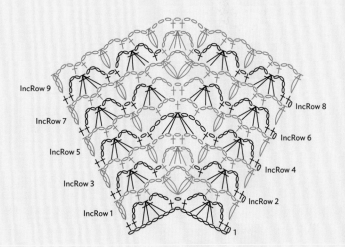

OPEN OVALS

The oval effect is made over two rows: in the first row we work open Shells, and in the second row chain-three spaces and double crochet stitches are worked into the Shells.

NUMBER OF STITCHES IN PATTERN REPEAT	NUMBER OF ROWS IN PATTERN REPEAT
V	2

MULTIPLE	REVERSIBLE
5 + 5	

NOTE
To work sc between 2 dc2tog, sk next dc2tog, insert hook in space under last st and next dc2tog, work sc.

SPECIAL STITCH
Shell: (Dc2tog, ch 1, dc, ch 1, dc2tog) in designated st or sp.

BASIC PATTERN

(For swatch, ch 30.)

ROW 1: Dc2tog in 5th ch from hook (4 sk ch count as dc, ch 1), *sk 4 ch**, Shell in next ch, rep from * across, ending last rep at **, (dc2tog, ch 1, dc) in last ch, turn.
(Swatch has 5 patt reps, including ½ Shells at edges.)

ROW 2: Ch 3 (counts as dc at start of rows), *dc in next ch-1 sp**, ch 3, sc between next 2 dc2tog, ch 3, dc in next ch-1 sp, ch 1, rep from * across, ending last rep at **, dc in 3rd ch of tch, turn.

ROW 3: Ch 4 (counts as dc, ch 1 throughout), dc2tog in same dc, *Shell in next ch-1 sp, rep from * across, (dc2tog, ch 1, dc) in tch, turn.

Rep rows 2 and 3 for patt.
(Swatch has 11 rows in patt.)

Edge Shaping

This stitch is not suitable for shaping at the edges.

Internal Shaping

1 patt rep is added every 2 rows.
(For swatch, ch 25. Work row 1 of patt. 4 Shells, counting ½ Shells at edges.)
Place marker in 2nd ch-1 sp of center Shell.

IncRow 1: Work in row 2 of patt to marked ch-1 sp, dc in marked ch-1 sp, ch 1, dc in next dc, ch 1, dc in next ch-1 sp, move marker to ch-1 sp just made, ch 3, sc between next 2 dc2tog, continue in patt across.

IncRow 2: Work in row 3 of patt, placing Shell in marked ch-1 sp, Shell in next ch-1 sp, move marker between 2 Shells just made, continue in patt across.

IncRow 3: Work in row 2 of patt to marker, (sc, ch 3, sc) in marked sp between 2 Shells, move marker to ch-3 sp just made, ch 3, continue in patt across.

IncRow 4: Work in row 3 of patt to marked ch-3 sp, Shell in marked ch-3 sp, move marker to 2nd ch-1 sp of Shell just made, continue in patt across.

Rep IncRows 1–4 to continue increasing.
(Swatch has 8 rows total, 7 increase rows, ending with 7 Shells, counting ½ Shells at edges.)

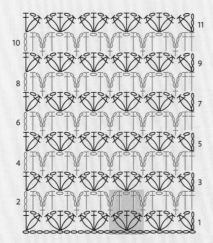

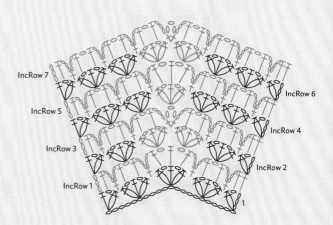

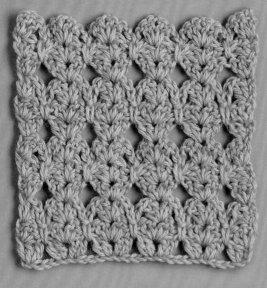

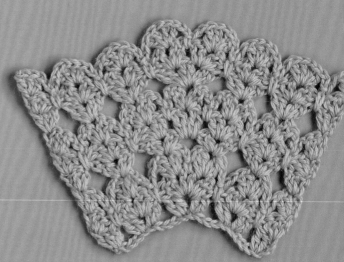

DISCS

This unusual pattern uses stacked Shells linked together by a Spike stitch to form ovals.

NUMBER OF STITCHES IN PATTERN REPEAT	NUMBER OF ROWS IN PATTERN REPEAT
V	3
MULTIPLE	**REVERSIBLE**
5 + 3	

SPECIAL STITCHES
Shell: (2 dc, ch 1, 2 dc) in designated st.

Spike stitch (Spike st): Insert hook in space 2 rows below between 2 designated Shells, work sc loosely. At the beginnings and ends of rows, the Spike st is worked between a 3-dc group and a Shell.

BASIC PATTERN
(For swatch, ch 28.)
Row 1: 2 dc in 4th ch from hook (3 sk ch count as dc), *sk 3 ch**, 2 dc in next ch, ch 1, 2 dc in next ch, rep from * across, ending last rep at **, 3 dc in last ch, turn.
(Swatch has 5 patt reps, counting ½ Shells at edges.)
Row 2: Ch 3, 2 dc in same dc, Shell in ch-1 sp of each Shell across to last 3 dc, sk 2 dc, 3 dc in tch, turn.
Row 3: Ch 3, 2 dc in same dc, ch 2, Spike st between 3-dc group and next Shell, *ch 2, Shell in next ch-1 sp, ch 2, Spike st between next 2 Shells, rep from * across to last Shell, Shell in last ch-1 sp, ch 2, Spike st between Shell and last 3-dc group, ch 2, 3 dc in tch, turn.
Row 4: Rep row 2.
Rep rows 2–4 for patt, ending with row 3.
(Swatch has 12 rows in patt.)

Edge Shaping
This stitch is not suitable for shaping at the edges.

Internal Shaping

This adds 2 patt reps every 5 rows. The increase must be worked differently depending on whether there is an odd or even number of patt reps in the row. Note that in IncRow 5 the sc on either side of the center Shell in the prev row must be worked 1 row below instead of 2 rows below.

(For swatch, ch 23. Work row 1 of patt. 4 patt reps, counting ½ Shells at edges.)

Place marker in ch-1 sp of center Shell.

IncRow 1: Work in row 2 of patt to marked ch-1 sp, (2 dc, ch 1, 2 dc, ch 1, 2 dc) in marked ch-1 sp, move marker to last ch-1 sp made, continue in patt across.

IncRow 2: Work in row 3 of patt to marked ch-1 sp, Shell in marked ch-1 sp, ch 2, sc in sp between next 2 dc, move marker to sc just made, ch 2, Shell in next ch-1 sp, continue in patt across.

IncRow 3: Work in row 4 of patt across, moving marker between 2 center Shells.

IncRow 4: Work in row 2 of patt to marker, Shell in marked space between Shells, continue in patt across, moving marker to sp between center Shell and next Shell.

IncRow 5: Work in row 3 of patt to marker, ch 2, Spike st in marked sp between Shells 1 row below, ch 2, Shell in center Shell, move marker to ch-1 sp just made, ch 2, Spike st in next sp between 2 Shells 1 row below, ch 2, Shell in next Shell, continue in patt across.

IncRow 6: Work in row 4 of patt to marked ch-1 sp, (2 dc, ch 1, 2 dc, ch 1, 2 dc) in marked ch-1 sp, move marker to last ch-1 sp made, continue in patt across.

IncRow 7: Work in row 2 of patt to marked ch-1 sp, Shell in marked ch-1 sp, Shell in next ch-1 sp, move marker to sp between 2 Shells just made, continue in patt across.

IncRow 8: Work in row 3 of patt to marker, ch 2, sc in marked sp, Shell in next Shell, continue in patt across.

Rep IncRows 3–8 to continue increasing.

(Swatch has 9 rows total, 8 increase rows, ending with 7 patt reps, counting ½ Shells at edges.)

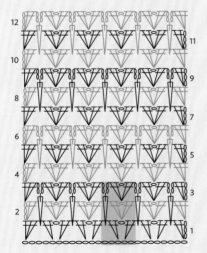

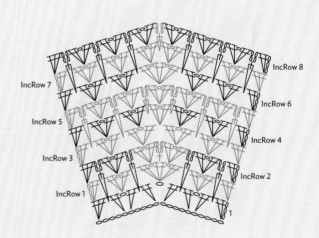

NEXUS

This stitch consists of large open Shells and V-stitches, with a Spike stitch between Shells. It's one of those stitches whose elements are hard to decipher by eye, but the effect is an intriguing web of crisscrossing lines.

NUMBER OF STITCHES IN PATTERN REPEAT	NUMBER OF ROWS IN PATTERN REPEAT
10	4
MULTIPLE	**REVERSIBLE**
8 + 7	

SPECIAL STITCHES

Shell: (Dc, ch 3, dc, ch 3, dc) in designated sp.

V-stitch (V-st): (Dc, ch 3, dc) in designated st.

Spike stitch (Spike st): Insert hook in dc 2 rows below, work sc around ch-5 of prev row. A Spike st is a sc that is elongated because, instead of being worked into a st on prev row, it is worked into a more distant st or sp. Work the st loosely.

BASIC PATTERN

(For swatch, ch 39.)

ROW 1: Dc in 7th ch from hook (6 sk ch count as dc, ch 3), *sk 3 ch, sc in next ch, sk 3 ch**, [(dc, ch 3) twice, dc] in next ch, rep from * across, ending last rep at **, (dc, ch 3, dc) in last ch, turn.

(Swatch has 4 patt reps, counting ½ Shells at edges.)

ROW 2: Ch 1, sc in first dc, ch 2, *V-st in next sc**, ch 5, sk next Shell, rep from * across, ending last rep at **, ch 2, sc in 3rd ch of tch, turn.

ROW 3: Ch 1, sc in first st, *Shell in ch-3 sp of next V-st**, Spike st in dc 2 rows below, rep from * across, ending last rep at **, sc in last sc, turn.

ROW 4: Ch 4 (counts as dc, ch 1), dc in same sc, *ch 5, sk next Shell**, V-st in next sc, rep from * across, ending last rep at **, (dc, ch 1, dc) in last sc, turn.

ROW 5: Ch 6 (counts as dc, ch 3), dc in first ch-1 sp, *Spike st in next dc 2 rows below**, Shell in ch-3 sp of next V-st, rep from * across, ending last rep at **, dc in ch-4 tch, ch 3, dc in 3rd ch of tch, turn.

Rep rows 2–5 for patt, ending on an even-numbered row for flat top edge.

(Swatch has 14 rows in patt.)

Edge Shaping

This stitch is not suitable for shaping at the edges.

Internal Shaping

The rate of increase is 2 patt reps over 5 rows. Note that in IncRow 6 the Spike sts on either side of center are worked into the 2nd and 4th dc of the increase Shell 2 rows below. We use 2 markers when working this increase.

(For swatch, ch 31. Work row 1 of patt. 3 patt reps, counting ½ Shells at edges.)

Place marker in center sc between 2 Shells.

IncRow 1: Work in row 2 of patt to marked sc, (dc, ch 1) 3 times in marked sc, dc in same sc, move marker to last ch-1 sp made, ch 5, continue in patt across.

IncRow 2: Work in row 3 of patt to marked ch-1 sp, (dc, ch 2, dc, ch 2, dc) in marked ch-1 sp, sc in next ch-1 sp, move marker to sc just made, (dc, ch 2, dc, ch 2, dc) in next ch-1 sp, continue in patt across. (Each group of sts within parentheses counts as a Shell.)

IncRow 3: Work in row 4 of patt across, placing V-st in marked sc, move marker to ch-3 sp of V-st just made, continue in patt across.

IncRow 4: Work in row 5 of patt to marked ch-3 sp, (dc, ch 2) 4 times in marked ch-3 sp, dc in same ch-3 sp (increase Shell made), move marker to 2nd dc and place a 2nd marker in center dc of group just made, continue in patt across.

IncRow 5: Work in row 2 of patt, completing ch 5 before marked dc, V-st in marked center dc, move center marker to ch-3 sp of V-st just made, leave other marker in place, continue in patt across.

IncRow 6: Work in row 3 of patt, placing Spike st in marked dc 2 rows below, Shell in marked ch-3 sp, move marker to center dc of Shell, Spike st in next dc 2 rows below, continue in patt across.

IncRow 7: Work in row 4 of patt across, leaving marker in prev row.

IncRow 8: Work in row 5 of patt across, placing sc in marked dc 2 rows below and moving center marker to sc made in marked dc.

Rep IncRows 1–8 to continue increasing.

(Swatch has 9 rows total, 8 increase rows, ending with 5 patt reps, counting ½ Shells at edges.)

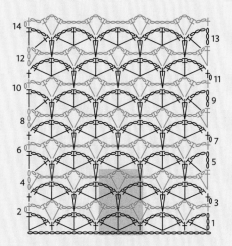

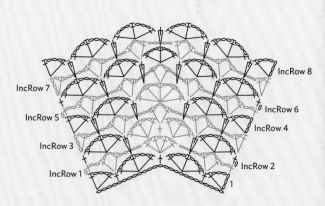

CROSSED STITCHES LACE

To make a pair of crossed stitches, we skip stitches before working the first stitch and work the second stitch into the skipped stitch. The second element in this pattern is a small open Shell. The crossed stitch pair and the Shell together make one pattern repeat.

NUMBER OF STITCHES IN PATTERN REPEAT	NUMBER OF ROWS IN PATTERN REPEAT
10	2
MULTIPLE	**REVERSIBLE**
10 + 9	

NOTES

The easiest way to work the 2nd st of the Crossed Pair (CP) is to turn your work so the opposite side is facing and insert the hook from back to front in the designated st.

In row 1 the CP are worked into chains. The second dc in the pair is worked 2 chains before the first dc. After completing this CP, count from the first dc when skipping the following chains.

SPECIAL STITCHES

Shell: (Dc, ch 1, dc, ch 1, dc) in designated st or sp.

Crossed Pair (CP): Sk next ch-1 sp, dc in next ch-1 sp, ch 3, working behind dc just made dc in sk ch-1 sp.

Increase Crossed Pair (IncCP): Dc in designated ch-1 sp, ch 3, working behind dc just made dc in same ch-1 sp.

BASIC PATTERN

(For swatch, ch 39.)

ROW 1: Shell in 6th ch from hook (5 sk ch count as 2 fnd ch, dc), *sk 5 ch, dc in next ch, ch 3, counting back toward start of row and working behind dc just made, sk 1 ch, dc in next ch, now counting from first dc in pair, sk 3 ch, Shell in next ch, rep from * across, sk 2 ch, dc in last ch, turn.
(Swatch has 3½ patt reps.)

ROW 2: Ch 3 (counts as dc throughout), *CP, Shell in ch-3 sp of next CP, rep from * across, CP in last Shell, dc in tch, turn.

ROW 3: Ch 3, *Shell in ch-3 sp of next CP, CP, rep from * across, Shell in last CP, dc in tch, turn.

Rep rows 2 and 3 for patt.
(Swatch has 10 rows in patt.)

Edge Shaping

This stitch is not suitable for shaping at the edges.

Internal Shaping

1 patt rep is added every 3 rows.
(For swatch, ch 29. Work row 1 of patt. 2½ patt reps.)
Place marker in 2nd ch-1 sp of center Shell.

IncRow 1: Work in row 2 of patt to marked ch-1 sp, IncCP in marked ch-1 sp, IncCP in next ch-1 sp, move marker to ch-3 sp of last CP made, Shell in ch-3 sp of next CP, continue in patt across.

IncRow 2: Work in row 3 of patt to marked ch-3 sp, Shell in marked ch-3 sp, ch 1, Shell in ch-3 sp of next CP, move marker to ch-1 sp between 2 Shells just made, CP in next Shell, continue in patt across.

IncRow 3: Work in row 2 of patt to marked ch-1 sp, Shell in marked ch-1 sp, move marker to last ch-1 sp of Shell just made, continue in patt across.

IncRow 4: Work in row 3 of patt to marked ch-1 sp, IncCP in marked ch-1 sp, IncCP in next ch-1 sp, move marker to ch-3 sp of last CP made, Shell in ch-3 sp of next CP, continue in patt across.

IncRow 5: Work in row 2 of patt to marked ch-3 sp, Shell in marked ch-3 sp, ch 1, Shell in next ch-3 sp, move marker to ch-1 sp between 2 Shells just made, continue in patt across.

IncRow 6: Work in row 3 of patt to marked ch-1 sp, Shell in marked ch-1 sp, move marker to 2nd ch-1 sp of Shell just made, continue in patt across.

Rep IncRows 1–6 to continue increasing.
(Swatch has 7 rows total, 6 increase rows, ending with 4½ patt reps.)

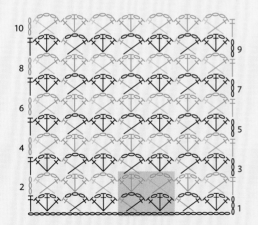

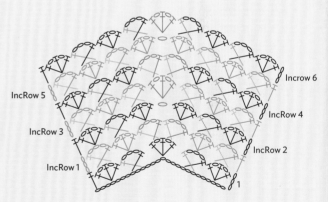

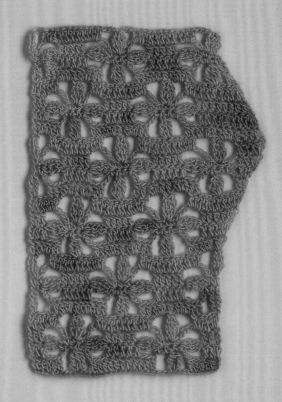

FLORAL ARRAY

The floral look of this stitch involves petals worked horizontally and vertically. The intricacy of the stitch does not lend itself to shaping, except by using plain filler stitches at the edge. While the filler stitches are visible, this can be used for shaping where the fabric will not be too obvious, such as at the sides of a garment.

NUMBER OF STITCHES IN PATTERN REPEAT:	NUMBER OF ROWS IN PATTERN REPEAT:
V	8
MULTIPLE:	REVERSIBLE
18 + 3	

NOTES:
After making the initial ch-4, insert hook in top of dc just worked for the next petal, in the same row, after the ch 4, when working tr2tog insert hook in top of sc just made.

SPECIAL STITCHES
Horizontal Petal (HP): Ch 4, inserting hook in st just completed, tr2tog.

BASIC PATTERN

(For swatch, ch 39.)

ROW 1: Dc in 4th ch from hook (3 sk ch count as dc), dc in next 4 ch, *ch 4, sk 3 ch, tr3tog in next ch, ch 4, sk 3 ch**, dc in next 11 ch, rep from * across ending last rep at **, dc in last 6 ch, turn. (Swatch has 2 patt reps)

ROW 2: Ch 3 (counts as dc throughout), dc in next 2 dc, *sk 3 dc, HP, sc in next ch-4 sp, sc in top of tr3tog, sc in next ch-4 sp, HP, sk 3 dc**, dc in next 5 dc, rep from * across ending last rep at **, dc in last 3 sts, turn.

ROW 3: Ch 3, dc in next 2 dc, *ch 6, sk HP, sc in next 3 sc, ch 6**, dc in next 5 dc, rep from * across ending last rep at **, dc in last 3 sts, turn.

ROW 4: Ch 3, dc in next 2 dc, *3 dc in next ch-6 sp, ch 3, sk next sc, tr3tog in next sc, ch 3, 3 dc in next ch-6 sp**, dc in next 5 dc, rep from * across ending last rep at **, dc in last 3 sts, turn.

ROW 5: Ch 4, tr in first dc (counts as tr2tog), *ch 4, sk 3 dc, dc in next 2 dc, 3 dc in next ch-3 sp, dc in tr3tog, 3 dc in next ch-3 sp, dc in next 2 dc, ch 4, sk 3 dc**, tr3tog in next dc, rep from * across ending last rep at **, tr2tog in tch, turn.

ROW 6: Ch 1, sc in first sc, sc in next ch-4 sp, *HP, sk 3 dc, dc in next 5 dc, HP, sk 3 dc, sc in next ch-4 sp**, sc in tr3tog, sc in next ch-4 sp, rep from * across ending last rep at **, sc in tr2tog, turn.

ROW 7: Ch 1, sc in first sc, sc in next sc, *ch 6, sk HP, dc in next 5 dc, ch 6, sk HP**, sc in next 3 sc, rep from * across ending last rep at **, sc in last 2 sc, turn.

ROW 8: Ch 4, tr in same sc (counts as tr2tog), *ch 3, 3 dc in next ch-6 sp, dc in next 5 dc, 3 dc in next ch-6 sp, sk next sc**, tr3tog in next sc, rep from * across ending last rep at **, tr2tog in last sc, turn.

ROW 9: Ch 3, 3 dc in next ch-3 sp, dc in next 2 dc, ch 4, sk 3 dc, tr3tog in next dc, ch 4, sk 3 dc, dc in next 2 dc, 3 dc in next ch-3 sp**, dc in next tr3tog, rep from * across ending last rep at **, dc in tr2tog, turn.

Rep rows 2–9 for patt, ending on row 8.
(Swatch has 8 rows in patt.)

Edge Shaping:

The complexities of this pattern work against finding a repeatable sequence. We use this as an opportunity to show how to use filler sts. Note that this is NOT a repeatable sequence that can be used to continue increasing. Because the sequence will be different for each row and because of the intricate placement of stitches in this pattern, it is rather arduous method that would be challenging to use for a very long shaping sequence. It works nicely for shaping a few rows, however, as we have here. Shaping is at the rate of one stitch per row.

INCREASING

IncRow 1: Ch 3, dc in first dc, 3 dc in next ch-3 sp, continue in row 9 of patt across.

IncRow 2: Work in row 2 of patt to tch, 2 dc in tch, turn.

IncRow 3: Ch 3, dc in first dc, dc in next 4 dc, ch 6, continue in row 3 of patt across.

IncRow 4: Work in row 4 of patt to tch, 2 dc in tch, turn.

IncRow 5: Ch 3, dc in first dc, ch 4, sk 3 dc, tr3tog in next dc, continue in row 5 of patt across.

IncRow 6: Work in row 6 of patt placing sc in last ch-3 sp, ch 2, dc in next dc, 2 dc in tch, turn.

IncRow 7: Ch 3, dc in first dc, dc in next 2 dc, ch 3, sc in next 3 sc, continue in row 7 of patt across.

IncRow 8: Work in row 8 of patt to tch, 2 dc in tch, turn.

DECREASING

DecRow 1: Ch 2, dc in next dc (counts as dc2tog throughout), dc in next 3 dc, 3 dc in next ch-3 sp, continue in row 9 of patt across.

DecRow 2: Work in row 2 of patt to last 5 dc, dc in next 3 dc, dc2tog, turn.

DecRow 3: Ch 2, dc in next dc, dc in next 7 dc, continue in row 3 of patt across.

DecRow 4: Work in row 4 of patt to last 2 dc, dc2tog, turn.

DecRow 5: Ch 2, dc in next dc, ch 2, sk 2 dc, tr3tog in next dc, ch 4, sk 3 dc, continue in row 5 of patt across.

DecRow 6: Work in row 6 of patt placing sc in last tr3tog, sc in next ch-2 sp, dc in last st, turn.

DecRow 7: Ch 1, sk first dc, sc in next 3 sc, ch 6, continue in row 7 of patt across.

DecRow 8: Work in row 8 of patt to last 2 sc, work tr3tog inserting hook twice in next sc, once in last sc.

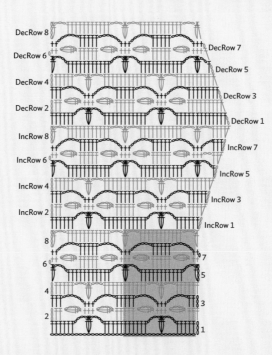

CHAPTER SIX

UNDULATING STITCHES: RIPPLES AND WAVES

Undulating stitches create curvy lines along the tops of rows. These curves have strong appeal in crochet, offering an attractive alternative to the usual crochet rectangular grid, and replacing it with a sinuous line.

There are two prime methods for creating undulations in crochet. One, seen in ripple stitches, uses the technique of placing regular increases and decreases within each row. The increase point becomes the top of the ripple, and the decrease point the bottom of the ripple. All ripple patterns work this way, but some clever stitches are imposters that look like ripples but do not use the increase/decrease within the row strategy.

The second major method for creating curvy lines is to use a sequence of stitches going from short to tall and then back to short, for example: sc, hdc, dc, tr, dc, hdc, sc. Depending on the stitch pattern there may be one, two, or three stitches of each height. Often the rows of graduated stitches are alternated with a row of sc in a second color to give the wave a dramatic outline.

Wave stitches are fairly straightforward to shape, as the stitches are aligned vertically over one another. Ripples, on the other hand, are quite resistant to shaping. Since increasing and decreasing causes the rippling to happen, adding or subtracting stitches at any additional points in the row will disrupt the ripple. For this reason most ripple stitches in this chapter are not shaped at the edge, but most can be shaped by enlarging the pattern.

I hope you'll agree that ripples that keep growing can make quite a grand statement! Two ripple stitches in this chapter refused to be shaped by enlargement, but they are included because they are too pretty to omit.

As usual, crochet's limitless variations allow both types of undulations to be done many ways. Texture can be added in the form of Puffs or Bobbles, or pumped up with post stitches. The undulations can be delicate lace, or striking color patterns. Patterns can be small or large.

The closed colorwork stitches in this chapter are great choices for purses and bags, and also for throws and pillows. Lace undulations will make stunning scarves and shawls. Can't you just magine a wrap made of a lacy ripple stitch that enlarges as it moves from shoulders to elbows?

CLASSIC RIPPLE

A solid ripple using double increases and decreases and double crochet stitches. This can be worked with any combination of colors to create rippled stripes, and is often used for afghans and other home decor items. Here we use one row of a contrasting color.

NUMBER OF STITCHES IN PATTERN REPEAT

12

MULTIPLE

12 + 3

NUMBER OF ROWS IN PATTERN REPEAT

1

REVERSIBLE

BASIC PATTERN

(For swatch, ch 39.)

ROW 1: Dc in 4th ch from hook (3 sk ch count as dc), *dc in next 3 ch, (dc2tog) twice, dc in next 3 ch**, (2 dc in next ch) twice, rep from * across, ending last rep at **, 2 dc in last ch, turn.

(Swatch has 36 sts: 3 patt reps.)

ROW 2: Ch 3 (counts as dc throughout), dc in first dc, *dc in next 3 dc, (dc2tog) twice, dc in next 3 dc**, (2 dc in next dc) twice, rep from * across, ending last rep at **, 2 dc in tch, turn. Rep row 2 for patt.

(Swatch has 12 rows in patt, with 2nd color used on rows 5 and 9.)

Internal Shaping

The rate of increase is 2 sts per ripple every other row.

(For swatch, ch 27. Work row 1 of patt. 24 sts: 2 ripples.)

IncRow 1: Ch 3, 2 dc in first dc, *dc in next 3 dc, (dc2tog) twice, dc in next 3 dc**, (3 dc in next dc) twice, rep from * across, ending last rep at **, 3 dc in tch, turn.

IncRow 2: Ch 3, dc in first dc, *dc in next 4 dc, (dc2tog) twice, dc in next 4 dc**, (2 dc in next dc) twice, rep from * across, ending last rep at **, 2 dc in tch, turn.

IncRow 3: Ch 3, 2 dc in first dc, *dc in next 4 dc, (dc2tog) twice, dc in next 4 dc**, (3 dc in next dc) twice, rep from * across, ending last rep at **, 3 dc in tch, turn.

To continue increasing, rep IncRows 2 and 3, but adding 1 dc between increase and decrease sections of ripple every IncRow 3.

(Swatch has 7 rows total, 6 increase rows, ending with 36 sts: 2 ripples.)

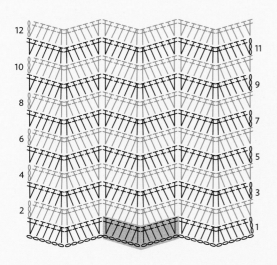

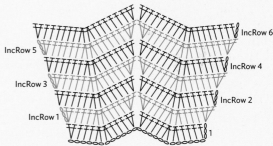

DOTTED RIPPLE

A pretty lacy ripple dotted with a Puff at the increase point. The row ends have decreases instead of the more typical increases. The Puffs occur at the center of the increase point every other row. The decrease point is created by skipping two stitches, but at either end of the row we skip only one stitch.

NUMBER OF STITCHES IN PATTERN REPEAT	NUMBER OF ROWS IN PATTERN REPEAT
V	4
MULTIPLE	**REVERSIBLE**
12	

SPECIAL STITCH

Puff: (Yo, insert hook in designated st, yo and draw up loop to ½"), 4 times, yo, draw through all loops on hook.

BASIC PATTERN

(For swatch, ch 36.)

ROW 1: Dc in 4th ch from hook (3 sk ch count as dc), dc in next 3 ch, *ch 2, dc in next 5 ch**, sk 2 ch, dc in next 5 ch, rep from * across, ending last rep at **, turn.

(Swatch has 3 ripples.)

ROW 2: Ch 4 (counts as dc, ch 1), sk 2 dc, dc in next dc, ch 1, sk next dc, *(dc, ch 1, Puff, ch 1, dc) in next ch-2 sp**, (ch 1, sk next dc, dc in next dc) twice, sk next 2 dc (dc in next dc, ch 1, sk next dc) twice, rep from * across, ending last rep at **, ch 1, sk next dc, dc in next dc, ch 1, sk last 2 dc, dc in tch, turn.

ROW 3: Ch 3 (counts as dc throughout), sk next ch-1 sp, *(dc in next dc, dc in next ch-1 sp) twice, ch 2, sk Puff, (dc in next ch-1 sp, dc in next dc) twice**, dc in next ch-1 sp, sk 2 dc, dc in next ch-1 sp, rep from * across, ending last rep at **, sk next ch-1 sp, dc in 3rd ch of tch, turn.

ROW 4: Ch 3, sk next dc, dc in next 3 dc, *(dc, ch 1, Puff, ch 1, dc) in next ch-2 sp**, dc in next 4 dc, sk 2 dc, dc in next 4 dc, rep from * across, ending last rep at **, dc in next 3 dc, sk next dc, dc in tch, turn.

ROW 5: Ch 3, sk next dc, dc in next 3 dc, *dc in next ch-1 sp, ch 2, sk next Puff, dc in next ch-1 sp**, dc in next 4 dc, sk 2 dc, dc in next 4 dc, rep from * across, ending last rep at **, dc in next 3 dc, sk next dc, dc in tch, turn.

Rep rows 2–5 for patt.

(Swatch has 8 rows in patt.)

Internal Shaping

This method increases the ripple by 2 sts every other row. For purposes of instructions below, "decrease point" refers to the dc worked on either side of 2 sk sts in prev row. Do not work into these 2 sts.

(For swatch, ch 24. Work rows 1 and 2 of patt. 24 sts, 2 ripples.)

IncRow 1: Ch 3, sk ch-1 sp, dc in next dc, dc in next ch-1 sp, dc in next dc, *2 dc in next ch-1 sp, ch 2, sk Puff, 2 dc in next ch-1 sp**, (dc in next dc, dc in next ch-1 sp) twice, sk 2 dc, (dc in next ch-1 sp, dc in next dc) twice, rep from * across, ending last rep at **, dc in next dc, dc in next ch-1 sp, dc in next dc, sk next ch-1 sp, dc in 3rd ch of tch, turn.

IncRow 2: Ch 3, sk next dc, *dc in each dc to next ch-2 sp, (dc, ch 1, Puff, ch 1, dc) in next ch-2 sp**, dc in each dc to decrease point, sk 2 dc, rep from * across, ending last rep at **, dc in each dc to last 2 sts, sk next dc, dc in tch, turn.

IncRow 3: Ch 3, sk next dc, *dc in each dc to next ch-1 sp, 2 dc in next ch-1 sp, ch 2, sk Puff, 2 dc in next ch-1 sp**, dc in each dc to decrease point, sk 2 dc, rep from * across, ending last rep at **, dc in each dc to last 2 sts, sk next dc, dc in tch, turn.

IncRow 4: Ch 4, sk next 2 dc, (dc in next dc, ch 1, sk next dc) twice, *(dc, ch 1, Puff, ch 1, dc) in next ch-2 sp**, (ch 1, sk next dc, dc in next dc) 3 times, sk next 2 dc, (dc in next dc, ch 1, sk next dc) 3 times, rep from * across, ending last rep at **, (ch 1, sk next dc, dc in next dc) twice, sk next 2 dc, dc in tch, turn.

IncRow 5: Ch 3, sk next ch-1 sp, *dc in each st to ch-1 sp before Puff, 2 dc in next ch-1 sp, ch 2, sk Puff, 2 dc in next ch-1 sp**, dc in each st to next decrease point, sk 2 dc, rep from * across, ending last rep at **, dc in each dc to last ch-1 sp, sk last ch-1 sp, dc in 3rd ch of tch, turn.

IncRow 6: Rep IncRow 2.

To continue increasing, work 2 dc at either side of the Puff in rows 3 and 5, which will lead to one more (dc, ch 1) in row 2 of patt.

(Swatch has 8 rows total, 6 increase rows, ending with 38 sts: 2 ripples.)

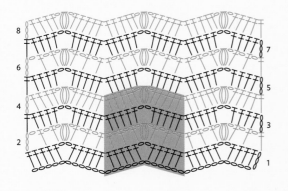

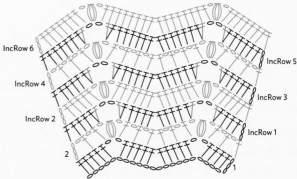

PEEPHOLE RIPPLE

This is a nice lacy alternative to solid ripples. Instead of working stitches together for the decrease, two stitches are skipped. For the increase two chains are placed between double crochet stitches.

NUMBER OF STITCHES IN PATTERN REPEAT	NUMBER OF ROWS IN PATTERN REPEAT
10	1
MULTIPLE	REVERSIBLE
10 + 3	

BASIC PATTERN

(For swatch, ch 33.)

ROW 1: Dc in 4th ch from hook (3 sk ch count as dc), dc in next 3 ch, *sk 2 ch**, dc in next 4 ch, ch 2, dc in next 4 ch, rep from * across, ending last rep at **, dc in next 3 ch, 2 dc in last ch, turn.

(Swatch has 30 sts: 3 ripples.)

ROW 2: Ch 3 (counts as dc throughout), dc in first dc, dc in next 3 dc, *sk 2 dc**, dc in next 3 dc, (dc, ch 2, dc) in next ch-2 sp, dc in next 3 dc, rep from * across, ending last rep at **, dc in next 3 dc, 2 dc in tch, turn.

Rep row 2 for patt.

(Swatch has 9 rows in patt.)

Internal Shaping

Double increases add 2 sts per ripple every row.

(For swatch, ch 33. Work row 1 of patt. 3 ripples with 10 sts each.)

IncRow 1: Ch 3, 2 dc in first dc, *dc in next 3 dc, sk 2 dc, dc in next 3 dc,** (2 dc, ch 2, 2 dc) in next ch-2 sp, rep from * across, ending last rep at **, 3 dc in tch, turn.

IncRow 2: Ch 3, 2 dc in first dc, *dc in next 4 dc, sk 2 dc, dc in next 4 dc**, (2 dc, ch 2, 2 dc) in next ch-2 sp, rep from * across, ending last rep at **, 3 dc in tch, turn.

IncRow 3: Ch 3, 2 dc in first dc, *dc in next 5 dc, sk 2 dc, dc in next 5 dc** (2 dc, ch 2, 2 dc) in next ch-2 sp, rep from * across, ending last rep at **, 3 dc in tch, turn.

To continue increasing, work ch 3, 2 dc in first st, 3 dc in last st, and (2 dc, ch 2, 2 dc) in each ch-2 sp, thus adding 2 sts to each ripple.

To return to patt, work last row as follows:

Ch 3, dc in first dc, (dc, ch 2, dc) in each ch-2 sp, and 2 dc in last st.

(Swatch has 7 total rows, 5 increase rows and last row worked as above, ending with 3 ripples with 20 sts each.)

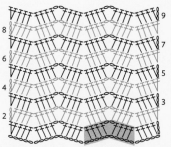

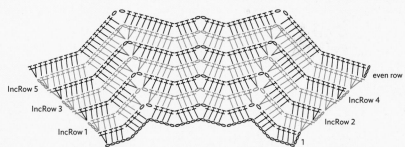

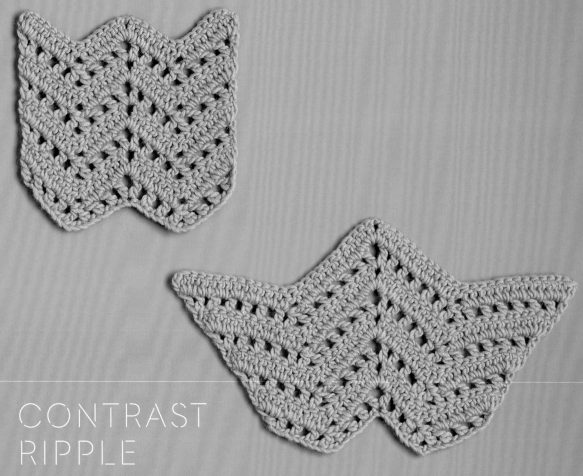

CONTRAST RIPPLE

Rows of solid ripples alternate with rows of filet ripple. The increase in the ripple adds four stitches, and the decrease requires skipping three stitches as well as working two stitches together.

NUMBER OF STITCHES IN PATTERN REPEAT
16

NUMBER OF ROWS IN PATTERN REPEAT
2

MULTIPLE
16 + 5

REVERSIBLE

NOTE
When working 2 dc sts together for the decrease section of this ripple, 3 sts must be skipped. In row 2 of patt they are (ch 1, dc2tog, ch 1). In row 3 they are (dc, dc2tog, dc).

BASIC PATTERN

(For swatch, ch 37.)

Row 1: Dc in 5th from hook (4 sk ch count as dc, ch 1), *(ch 1, sk next ch, dc in next ch) twice, ch 1, sk next ch, dc2tog over (next ch, sk next 3 ch, next ch), (ch 1, sk next ch, dc in next ch) 3 times**, ch 3, dc in same dc, rep from * across, ending last rep at **, ch 1, dc in same ch, turn.

(Swatch has 33 sts: 2 ripples.)

Row 2: Ch 3, 2 dc in same dc, dc in next ch-1 sp, *(dc in next dc, dc in next ch-1 sp) twice, dc2tog over (next dc, sk next 3 sts, next dc), (dc in next ch-1 sp, dc in next dc) twice**, (2 dc, ch 3, 2 dc) in next ch-3 sp, rep from * across, ending last rep at **, dc in next ch-1 sp, 3 dc in 3rd ch of tch, turn.

Row 3: Ch 4 (counts as dc, ch 1 throughout), dc in same dc, (ch 1, sk next dc, dc in next dc) twice, ch 1, sk next dc, *dc2tog over (next dc, sk 3 sts, next dc), (ch 1, sk next dc, dc in next dc) twice**, ch 1, (dc, ch 3, dc) in next ch-3 sp, ch 1, (dc in next dc, ch 1, sk next dc) twice, rep from * across, ending last rep at **, ch 1, sk next dc, (dc, ch 1, dc) in tch, turn.

Rep rows 2 and 3 for patt.

(Swatch has 8 rows in patt.)

Internal Shaping

2 sts are added per ripple on each row.

(For swatch, ch 37. Work row 1 of patt. 33 sts: 2 ripples.)

IncRow 1: Ch 3, 3 dc in same dc, *dc in each ch-1 sp and each dc to dc before dc2tog, dc2tog over (next dc, sk 3 sts, next dc)**, dc in each ch-1 sp and each dc to next ch-3 sp, (3 dc, ch 3, 3 dc) in ch-3 sp, rep from * across, ending last rep at **, dc in each ch-1 sp and each dc to tch, 4 dc in 3rd ch of tch, turn.

IncRow 2: Ch 4, dc in same dc, (ch 1, sk next dc, dc in next dc) 3 times, *ch 1, dc2tog over (next dc, sk next 3 sts, next dc), ch 1, (dc in next dc, ch 1, sk next dc) 2 times, dc in next dc, ch 1**, (dc, ch 3, dc) in next ch-3 sp, ch 1, (dc in next dc, ch 1, sk next dc) 2 times, dc in next dc, rep from * across, ending last rep at **, (dc, ch 1, dc) in tch, turn.

IncRow 3: Rep IncRow 1.

IncRow 4: Ch 4, dc in same dc, (ch 1, sk next dc, dc in next dc) 4 times, *ch 1, dc2tog over (next dc, sk next 3 sts, next dc), ch 1, (dc in next dc, ch 1, sk next dc) 3 times, dc in next dc, ch 1** (dc, ch 3, dc) in next ch-3 sp, ch 1, (dc in next dc, ch 1, sk next dc) 3 times, dc in next dc, rep from * across, ending last rep at **, (dc, ch 1, dc) in tch, turn.

IncRow 5: Rep IncRow 1.

IncRow 6: Ch 4, dc in same dc, (ch 1, sk next dc, dc in next dc) 5 times, *ch 1, dc2tog over (next dc, sk next 3 sts, next dc), ch 1, (dc in next dc, ch 1, sk next dc) 4 times, dc in next dc, ch 1** (dc, ch 3, dc) in next ch-3 sp, ch 1, (dc in next dc, ch 1, sk next dc) 4 times, dc in next dc, rep from * across, ending last rep at **, (dc, ch 1, dc) in tch, turn.

To continue increasing, work even rows as in IncRow 1; odd rows will have 1 more (dc, ch 1) between increases and decreases.

To return to patt, work last IncRow 1 as follows: Ch 3, 2 dc in same dc, *dc in each ch-1 sp and each dc to dc before dc2tog, dc2tog over (next dc, sk 3 sts, next dc)**, dc in each ch-1 sp and each dc to next ch-3 sp, (2 dc, ch 3, 2 dc) in next ch-3 sp, rep from * across, ending last rep at **, dc in each ch-1 sp and each dc to tch, 3 dc in 3rd ch of tch, turn.

(Swatch has 8 rows total, 6 increase rows, last row worked even, ending with 57 sts: 2 ripples.)

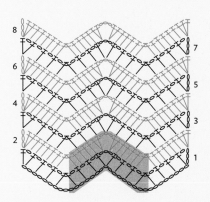

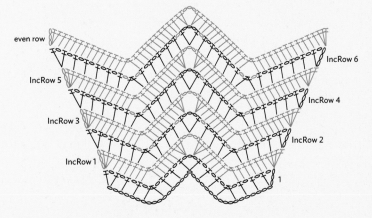

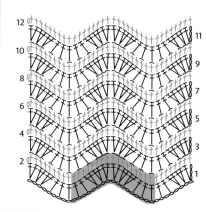

BORDERED RIPPLE

The border on this very pretty ripple requires two steps: working a row of single crochet stitches into the double crochet stitches of the ripples, and working the ripple stitches into the back loops of the single crochet stitches. The ripple itself has a wavy (rather than pointy) appearance because both the increase and decrease of the ripple are made over several stitches.

NUMBER OF STITCHES IN PATTERN REPEAT	NUMBER OF ROWS IN PATTERN REPEAT
17	2
MULTIPLE	**NOT REVERSIBLE**
17 + 3	

BASIC PATTERN

(For swatch, ch 37.)

ROW 1: Dc in 4th ch from hook (3 sk ch count as dc), (2 dc in next ch) twice, *(sk next ch, dc in next ch) 5 times, sk next ch**, (2 dc in next ch) 6 times, rep from * across, ending last rep at **, (2 dc in next ch) 3 times, turn.
(Swatch has 34 sts: 2 ripples.)

ROW 2: Ch 1, sc in each st across, turn.

ROW 3: Ch 3 (counts as dc throughout), BLdc in same sc, (2 BLdc in next sc) twice, *(sk next sc, BLdc in next sc) 5 times, sk next sc**, (2 BLdc in next sc) 6 times, rep from * across, ending last rep at **, (2 BLdc in next sc) 3 times, turn.
Rep rows 2 and 3 for patt.
(Swatch has 12 rows in patt.)

Internal Shaping

Internal shaping is not possible for this stitch pattern.

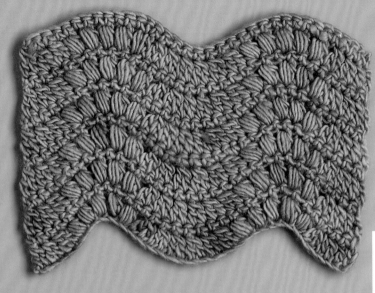

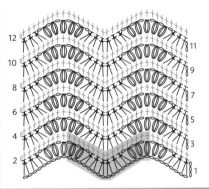

PUFF RIPPLE

Puffs are used in the increase portion of this ripple, and two double crochet stitches worked together for the decrease. Alternate rows are single crochet stitches. Unlike most ripples that begin with the increase part of the ripple, these rows begin and end with decreases.

NUMBER OF STITCHES IN PATTERN REPEAT	NUMBER OF ROWS IN PATTERN REPEAT
17	2
MULTIPLE	REVERSIBLE
17 + 3	

SPECIAL STITCH

Puff: (Yo, insert hook in designated st, yo and draw up loop) 4 times, yo, draw through 9 loops on hook.

BASIC PATTERN

(For swatch, ch 37.)

ROW 1: Dc2tog in 4th and 5th ch from hook (3 sk ch do not count as st), (dc2tog) twice, *(ch 1, Puff in next ch) 5 times, ch 1**, (dc2tog) 6 times, rep from * across, ending last rep at **, (dc2tog) 3 times, turn.
(Swatch has 34 sts: 2 ripples.)

ROW 2: Ch 1, sc in each st and each ch-1 sp across, turn.

ROW 3: Ch 2, dc in next sc (counts as dc2tog throughout), (dc2tog) twice, *(ch 1, Puff in next sc) 5 times, ch 1**, (dc2tog) 6 times, rep from * across, ending last rep at **, (dc2tog) 3 times, turn.

Rep rows 2 and 3 for patt.
(Swatch has 12 rows in patt.)

Internal Shaping

Internal shaping is not possible for this stitch pattern.

GRANNY RIPPLE

This ripple uses the familiar pattern used in Granny squares: blocks of three double crochet stitches worked in the same place. The difference here is that we work in rows not rounds, and to make a ripple, there are increases and decreases within each row. This particular ripple begins and ends with a decrease. To mimic the Granny look, work the ripples in different colors, changing color at the end of every row.

NUMBER OF STITCHES IN PATTERN REPEAT	NUMBER OF ROWS IN PATTERN REPEAT
26	1
MULTIPLE	REVERSIBLE
25 + 3	

BASIC PATTERN

(For swatch, ch 53.)

ROW 1: 3 dc in 6th ch from hook (5 sk ch count as dc, 2 fnd ch), (sk 2 ch, 3 dc in next ch) 3 times, *ch 2, (3 dc in next ch, sk 2 ch) 4 times**, sk 5 ch, (3 dc in next ch, sk 2 ch) 4 times, rep from * across, ending last rep at **, sk 2 ch, dc in last ch, turn. Change color.

(Swatch has 54 sts: 2 ripples.)

ROW 2: Ch 3 (counts as dc throughout), sk first 3-dc group, *(3 dc in sp between last dc of 3-dc group and first dc of next 3-dc group) 3 times, (3 dc, ch 2, 3 dc) in next ch-2 sp, sk next 3-dc group, (3 dc in sp between last dc of 3-dc group and first dc of next group) 3 times**, sk 2 3-dc blocks, rep from * across, ending last rep at **, sk last 3-dc group, dc in tch, turn. Change color.

Rep row 2 for patt.

(Swatch has 7 rows in patt.)

Internal Shaping

The basic pattern has 8 blocks of 3 dc. In the first increase we make 9 blocks by adding 1 st at the increase point. In the second increase we add another, making 10 blocks. In the next row no increase is made. With this method, 2 blocks are added to the ripple over 3 rows.

(For swatch, ch 53. Work row 1 of patt. 54 sts: 2 ripples, with 8 blocks each.)

IncRow 1: *Work in patt to ch-2 sp, (3 dc, ch 1, 3 dc, ch 1, 3 dc) in ch-2 sp, place marker in last ch-1 sp made, rep from * across.

IncRow 2: *Work in patt to marked ch-1 sp, 3 dc in marked ch-1 sp, sk first dc of center group, (3 dc, ch 2, 3 dc) in next dc, sk next dc, 3 dc in next ch-1 sp, continue in patt across, rep from * across.

IncRow 3: Work in patt across.

Rep IncRows 1–3 for patt.

(Swatch has 7 rows total, 6 increase rows, ending with 12 blocks in each ripple.)

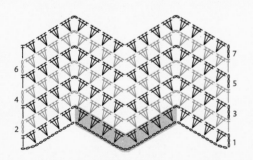

V-STITCH RIPPLE

Yes, even V-stitches can ripple! Two V-stitches
are made at the increase point of the ripple,
and three stitches are skipped for the decrease.

**NUMBER OF STITCHES
IN PATTERN REPEAT**

14

MULTIPLE

14 + 2

**NUMBER OF ROWS
IN PATTERN REPEAT**

1

REVERSIBLE

SPECIAL STITCH
V-Stitch (V-st): (Dc, ch 1, dc) in designated st.

BASIC PATTERN

(For swatch, ch 44.)

ROW 1: Dc in 3rd ch from hook, *sk 2 ch, V-st in next ch, sk 2 ch, (V-st, ch 1, V-st) in next ch, sk 2 ch, V-st in next ch, sk 2 ch**, dc2tog over (next ch, sk next ch, next ch), rep from * across, ending last rep at **, dc2tog, turn. Change color. *(Swatch has 3 ripples.)*

ROW 2: Ch 2, dc in ch-1 sp of next V-st (count as dc2tog), *V-st in ch-1 sp of next V-st, (V-st, ch 1, V-st) in next ch-1 sp, V-st in next ch-1 sp**, dc2tog over (ch-1 sp of next V-st, sk next dc2tog, ch-1 sp of next V-st), rep from * across, ending last rep at **, dc2tog over (ch-1 sp of next V-st, next dc2tog), turn. Change color.

Rep row 2 for patt.

(Swatch has 7 rows in patt.)

Internal Shaping

The increase point (abbreviated as IP below) is the ch-1 sp between 2 V-sts worked into the same ch-1 sp. In the following increase row, the increase point is the dc at the center of the group worked into the increase point below. Even-numbered increase rows add 2 V-sts (6 sts) to each ripple.

(For swatch, ch 30. Work row 1 of patt. 29 sts: 2 ripples.)

IncRow 1: *Work in patt to next ch-1 sp at IP, (dc, ch 1) 4 times in IP, dc in same st, continue in patt across, rep from * across.

IncRow 2: *Work in patt to dc at IP, (V-st, ch 1, V-st) in dc, continue in patt across, rep from * across.

Rep IncRows 1 and 2 to continue increasing.

To return to patt, work last IncRow 1 as follows: *Work in patt to next ch-1 sp at IP, (V-st, ch 1, V-st) in ch-1 sp, continue in patt across, rep from * across.

(Swatch has 7 rows total, 6 increase rows, ending with: 65 sts, 2 ripples.)

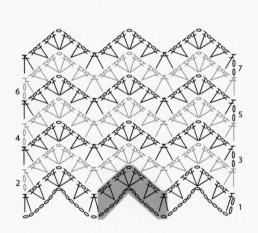

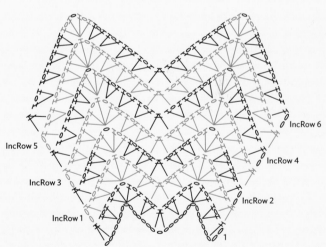

RAISED RIPPLE

This stitch gives us not only undulations but striking texture, created by working front and back post stitches on each row.

NUMBER OF STITCHES IN PATTERN REPEAT
16

NUMBER OF ROWS IN PATTERN REPEAT
2

MULTIPLE
16 + 2

NOT REVERSIBLE

NOTE
When working dc5tog, to work post sts around decreased sts in previous row, insert hook around entire group of sts near top of post. At beginnings and ends of rows do not work around tch, but around the other 2 worked together sts. Remember that sts worked together, whether 3 or 5, count as 1 st.

SPECIAL STITCH
Shell: (2 dc, ch 1, 2 dc) in designated st.

BASIC PATTERN

(For swatch, ch 34.)

ROW 1: Dc2tog over 3rd and 4th ch from hook, (2 sk ch count as first st of decrease), *dc in next 5 ch**, Shell in next ch, dc in next 5 ch, dc5tog, rep from * across, ending last rep at **, dc3tog, turn.

(Swatch has 33 sts: 2 ripples.)

ROW 2: Ch 2 (counts as first st of dec throughout), BPdc2tog, *FPdc in next 5 dc, Shell in next ch-1 sp, FPdc in next 5 dc**, BPdc5tog, rep from * across, ending last rep at **, BPdc3tog, turn.

ROW 3: Ch 2, FPdc2tog, *BPdc in next 5 dc, Shell in next ch-1 sp, BPdc in next 5 dc,** FPdc5tog, rep from * across, ending last rep at **, FPdc3tog.

Rep rows 2 and 3 for patt.

(Swatch has 7 rows in patt.)

Internal Shaping

On every other row the increase Shell is enlarged by 2 dc, resulting in 2 more dc sts in the ripple on the following row.
(For swatch, ch 34. Work row 1 of patt. 33 sts: 2 ripples.)

IncRow 1: *Work in row 2 of patt to ch-1 sp of Shell, (3 dc, ch 1, 3 dc) in ch-1 sp, rep from * across, continue in row 2 of patt, turn.

IncRow 2: Ch 2, FPdc2tog, *BPdc in next 6 dc, Shell in next ch-1 sp, BPdc in next 6 dc**, FPdc5tog, rep from * across, ending last rep at **, FPdc3tog, turn.

IncRow 3: Ch 2, BPdc2tog, *FPdc in next 6 dc, (3 dc, ch 1, 3 dc) in ch-1 sp of next Shell, FPdc in next 6 dc**, BPdc5tog, rep from * across, ending last rep at **, BPdc3tog, turn.

IncRow 4: Ch 2, FPdc2tog, *BPdc in next 7 dc, Shell in next ch-1 sp, BPdc in next 7 dc**, FPdc5tog, rep from * across, ending last rep at **, FPdc3tog, turn.

IncRow 5: Ch 2, BPdc2tog, *FPdc in next 7 dc, (3 dc, ch 1, 3 dc) in ch-1 sp of next Shell, FPdc in next 7 dc**, BPdc5tog, rep from * across, ending last rep at **, BP3tog, turn.

IncRow 6: Ch 2, FPdc2tog, *BPdc in next 8 dc, Shell in next ch-1 sp, BPdc in next 8 dc**, FPdc5tog, rep from * across, ending last rep at **, FPdc3tog, turn.

To continue increasing, work (3 dc, ch 1, 3 dc) in ch-1 sp of Shell on every other row, and in the following row work 1 more dc between the Shell and the dc5tog in each ripple.
(Swatch has 7 rows total, 6 increase rows, ending with 45 sts: 2 ripples.)

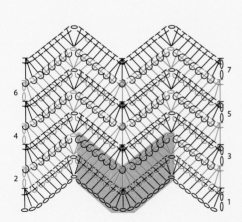

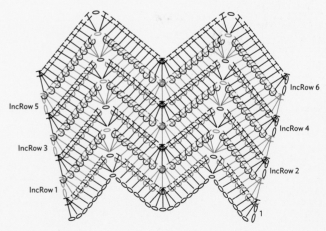

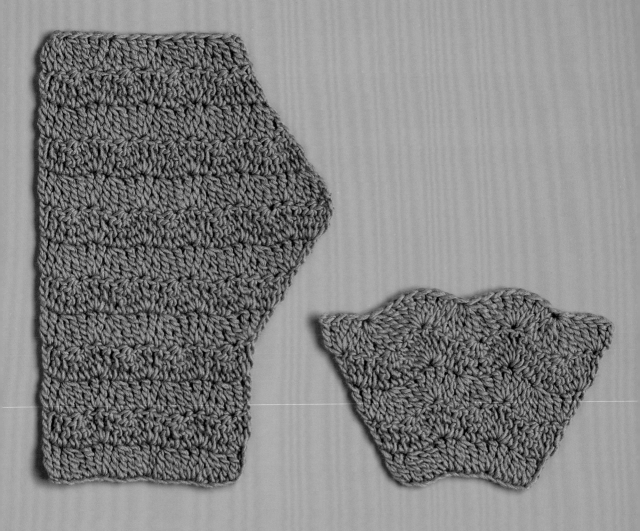

MINI RIPPLE

This small ripple is an excellent way to use treble stitches for a closed fabric. Because the stitches are tilted, the trebles are more closed than when working plain rows of treble stitches.

NUMBER OF STITCHES IN PATTERN REPEAT	NUMBER OF ROWS IN PATTERN REPEAT
4	1
MULTIPLE	REVERSIBLE
4 + 5	

BASIC PATTERN

(For swatch, ch 21.)
ROW 1: Tr in 5th ch from hook (4 sk ch count as tr), *tr3tog**, 3 tr in next ch, rep from * across, ending last rep at **, 2 tr in last ch, turn.
(Swatch has 17 sts: 4 patt reps, 1 tr.)
ROW 2: Ch 4 (counts as tr throughout), tr in same st, *tr3tog**, 3 tr in next tr, rep from * across, ending last rep at **, 2 tr in tch, turn.
Rep row 2 for patt.
(Swatch has 4 rows in patt.)

Edge Shaping
This small ripple can be shaped at the edge at the rate of 1 patt rep over 2 rows.

INCREASING

IncRow 1: Ch 4, 3 tr in same tr, tr3tog, continue in patt across.

IncRow 2: Work in patt to last 2 sts, tr2tog over next st and tch, 2 tr in tch, turn.

Rep IncRows 1 and 2 to continue increasing.

(Swatch has 4 increase rows, ending with 25 sts: 6 patt reps, 1 tr.)

DECREASING

DecRow 1: Ch 3 (does not count as st), tr3tog, continue in patt across.

DecRow 2: Work in patt to last 3 sts, tr in next st, tr2tog, turn.

Rep DecRows 1 and 2 to continue decreasing.

(Swatch has 4 decrease rows, ending with 17 sts: 3 patt reps, followed by 1 row worked even in patt.)

Internal Shaping

2 sts are added to the ripple every other row.

(For swatch, ch 17. Work row 1 of patt. 13 sts: 3 patt reps, 1 tr.)

IncRow 1: Ch 4, 2 tr in same tr, *tr3tog**, 5 tr in next tr, rep from * across, ending last rep at **, 3 tr in tch, turn.

IncRow 2: Ch 4, 2 tr in first tr, *tr5tog**, 5 tr in next tr, rep from * across, ending last rep at **, 3 tr in tch, turn.

IncRow 3: Ch 4, 3 tr in first tr, *tr5tog**, 7 tr in next tr, rep from * across, ending last rep at **, 4 tr in tch, turn.

IncRow 4: Ch 4, 3 tr in first tr, *tr7tog**, 7 tr in next tr, rep from * across, ending last rep at **, 4 tr in tch, turn.

To continue increasing, add 1 tr at each end and 2 tr at each increase. Every even row you will have 2 more sts to work together.

(Swatch has 5 rows total, 4 increase rows, ending with 25 sts: 3 patt reps, 8 sts per ripple.)

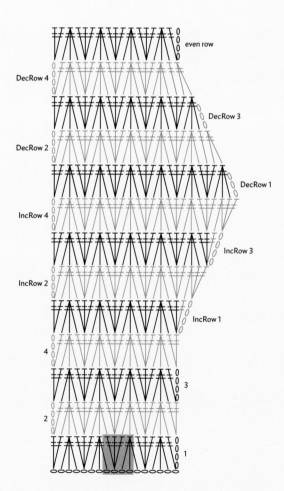

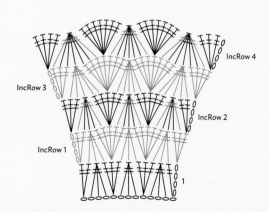

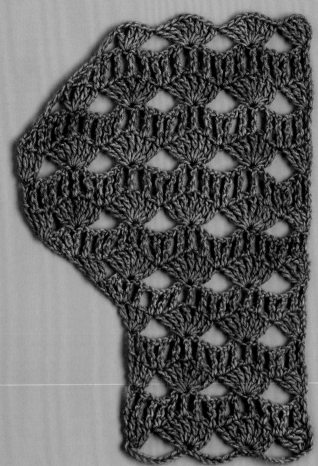

RIPPLING SHELL

A unique stitch consisting of two rows, one of Shells and the other of filet. The ripple is not due to increasing or decreasing, however, allowing this stitch to be shaped at the edge.

NUMBER OF STITCHES IN PATTERN REPEAT
10

MULTIPLE
10 + 6

NUMBER OF ROWS IN PATTERN REPEAT
2

REVERSIBLE

SPECIAL STITCH
Shell: (3 tr, ch 1, tr, ch 1, 3 tr) in designated st.

BASIC PATTERN

(For swatch, ch 36.)

ROW 1: Tr in 6th ch from hook (5 sk ch count as tr, ch 1), 3 tr in same ch, *sk 9 ch,** Shell in next ch, rep from * across, ending last rep at **, (3 tr, ch 1, tr) in last ch, turn.
(Swatch has 3 Shells, counting ½ Shells at edges.)

ROW 2: Ch 5 (counts as tr, ch 1 throughout), *sk next ch-1 sp, (tr in next tr, ch 1, sk next tr, tr in next tr, ch 1) twice**, tr in next tr, ch 1, rep from * across ending last rep at **, tr in 4th ch of tch, turn.

ROW 3: Ch 5, 3 tr in first tr, *sk 4 tr,** Shell in next tr, rep from * across, ending last rep at **, (3 tr, ch 1, tr) in 4th ch of tch, turn.
Rep rows 2 and 3 for patt.
(Swatch has 5 rows in patt.)

Edge Shaping

Shaping is at the rate of 1 patt rep over 2 rows and begins on row 2 of patt.

INCREASING

IncRow 1: Ch 5, (tr, ch 1) 3 times in same tr, sk next ch-1 sp, tr in next tr, ch 1, sk next tr, tr in next tr, continue in row 2 of patt across.

IncRow 2: Work in row 3 of patt to last 3 tr, sk 2 tr, (3 tr, ch 1, tr) in 4th ch of tch, turn.
Rep IncRows 1 and 2 to continue increasing.
(Swatch has 4 increase rows, ending with 5 Shells, followed by 2 rows worked even in patt.)

DECREASING

DecRow 1: Ch 4, sk next ch-1 sp, tr2tog over (next tr, sk next tr, next tr), tr in next tr, continue in row 2 of patt across.

DecRow 2: Work in row 3 of patt to last 8 tr, sk 4 tr, (3 tr, ch 1) in next tr, tr2tog over (same tr, sk 2 tr, last st).
Rep DecRows 1 and 2 to continue decreasing.
(Swatch has 4 decrease rows, ending with 3 Shells, counting ½ Shells at either edge.)

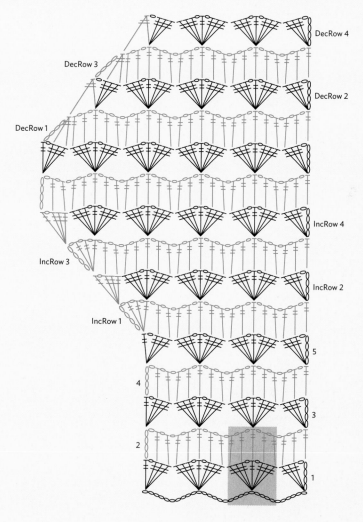

TILTED SHELL RIPPLE

This is an unusual ripple that consists of a five–double crochet Shell and filet of double crochet and chain one. The increase part of the ripple is the Shell and chain two that follows it, and the decrease involves skipping five stitches. The ripple spans from the chain two right after a Shell to the last double crochet of the next Shell.

NUMBER OF STITCHES IN PATTERN REPEAT	NUMBER OF ROWS IN PATTERN REPEAT
14	1
MULTIPLE	REVERSIBLE
11 + 2	

BASIC PATTERN

(For swatch, ch 35.)

SETUP ROW: Sc in 2nd ch from hook, *ch 2, sk 2 ch, dc in next 2 ch, ch 2, sk 2 ch, sc in next 5 ch, rep from * across, turn. *(Swatch has 3 ripples.)*

ROW 1: Ch 5 (counts as dc, ch 2 throughout), dc in first sc, *(ch 1, sk next sc, dc in next sc) twice, ch 1, dc in next ch-2 sp, sk 2 dc**, 5 dc in next ch-2 sp, ch 2, dc in next sc, rep from * across, ending last rep at **, 4 dc in last ch-2 sp, dc in last sc, turn.

ROW 2: Ch 5, dc in first dc, (ch 1, sk next dc, dc in next dc) twice, ch 1, sk next dc, dc in next ch-1 sp, sk (dc, ch 1, dc, ch 1, dc), 5 dc in next ch-2 sp, rep from * across placing last 5 dc in starting ch-sp.

Rep row 2 for patt.

(Swatch has 11 rows in patt.)

Edge Shaping

Edge shaping is not possible with this pattern.

Internal Shaping

To stay in pattern we need an odd number of dc in the Shell; therefore 2 sts are added to each ripple per increase row. This makes for a rapid increase, and for this reason we increase every third row.

(For swatch, ch 24. Work setup row and row 1 of patt. 2 ripples.)

IncRow 1: *Work in patt to next ch-2 sp, 7 dc in ch-2 sp, rep from * across, placing last 7 dc in starting ch-sp.

IncRows 2: Ch 5, dc in first dc, *(ch 1, sk next dc, dc in next dc) 3-times, ch 1, sk next dc, dc in next ch-1 sp, sk (dc, ch 1, dc, ch 1, dc), 7 dc in next ch-2 sp, dc in next dc, rep from * across, placing last 7 dc in starting ch-sp.

IncRows 3: Ch 5, dc in first dc, *(ch 1, sk next dc, dc in next dc) 3 times, (ch 1, sk next dc, dc in next ch-1 sp) twice, sk (dc, ch 1, dc, ch 1, dc), 7 dc in next ch-2 sp, dc in next dc, rep from * across, placing last 7 dc in starting ch-sp.

IncRow 4–6: Rep IncRows 1–3, working in patt to next ch-2 sp, 9 dc in next ch-2 sp, continue in patt across.

To continue increasing, add 2 more dc to Shell, which will require an extra (dc, ch 1) in the following row.

(Swatch has 8 rows total, 6 increase rows, ending with 9-dc Shells.)

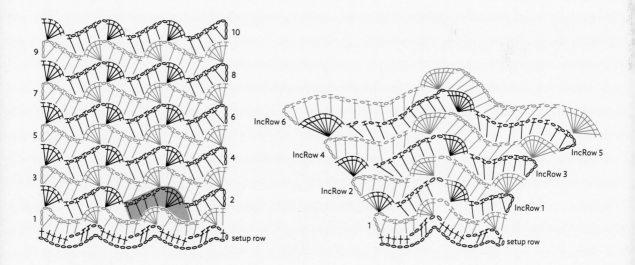

ROCKY ROAD

This is not a traditional ripple, as there is no increase or decrease within the row, yet it certainly ripples, doesn't it? Here the effect is produced by alternating groups of four single crochet stitches with groups of Puffs—somehow the slant and height of the puffs creates the angle.

NUMBER OF STITCHES IN PATTERN REPEAT	NUMBER OF ROWS IN PATTERN REPEAT
8	1
MULTIPLE	REVERSIBLE
8 + 1	

SPECIAL STITCHES

Puff: (Yo, insert hook in designated st and draw up loop to ½") 4 times, yo, draw through 9 loops on hook.

Decrease Puff (DecPuff): (Yo, insert hook in designated st and draw up loop to ½") twice, (yo, insert hook in next st and draw up loop to ½") twice, yo, draw through 9 loops on hook.

BASIC PATTERN

(For swatch, ch 17.)

ROW 1: Sc in 2nd ch from hook and in next 3 ch, *Puff in next 4 ch**, sc in next 4 ch, rep from * across, ending last rep at **, turn.

(Swatch has 16 sts: 2 ripples.)

ROW 2: Ch 1, sc in first 4 Puffs, *Puff in next 4 sc**, sc in next 4 Puffs, rep from * across, ending last rep at **, turn.

Rep row 2 for patt.

(Swatch has 8 rows in patt.)

Edge Shaping

Shaping occurs at the rate of 1 st per row, for a complete patt rep (8 sts) over 8 rows.

To shape at the opposite edge of the work (sc, Puff) in first st at the start of IncRow 1, then continue adding or subtracting sts in patt.

INCREASING

IncRow 1: Ch 1, Puff in first st, sc in same st, sc in next 3 Puffs, Puff in next 4 sts, sc in next 4 Puffs, continue in patt across.

IncRow 2: Work in patt to last Puff, 2 sc in last Puff, turn.

IncRow 3: Ch 1, 2 Puffs in first sc, Puff in next sc, sc in next 4 Puffs, continue in patt across.

IncRow 4: Work in patt to last 3 Puffs, sc in next 2 Puffs, 2 sc in last Puff, turn.

IncRow 5: Ch 1, (sc, Puff) in first sc, Puff in next 3 sc, sc in next 4 Puffs, continue in patt across.

IncRow 6: Work in patt to last sc, 2 Puffs in last sc, turn.

IncRow 7: Ch 1, 2 sc in first Puff, sc in next Puff, Puff in next 4 sc, continue in patt across.

IncRow 8: Work in patt to last 3 sts, Puff in next 2 sts, 2 Puffs in last st, turn.

Rep IncRows 1–8 to continue increasing.

(Swatch has 8 increase rows, followed by 2 rows worked even in patt, ending with 24 sts: 3 ripples.)

DECREASING

DecRow 1: Ch 1, sk first st, sc in next 3 sts, Puff in next 4 sts, continue in patt across.

DecRow 2: Work in patt to last 3 sts, Puff in next st, DecPuff over last 2 sts, turn.

DecRow 3: Ch 1, sk first st, sc in next st, Puff in next 4 sts, continue in patt across.

DecRow 4: Work in patt to last 5 sts, sc in next 3 sts, sc2tog, turn.

DecRow 5: Ch 1, DecPuff over first 2 sts, Puff in next 2 sts, sc in next 4 sts, continue in patt across.

DecRow 6: Work in patt to last 3 sts, sc in next st, sc2tog, turn.

DecRow 7: Ch 1, DecPuff over first 2 sts, sc in next 4 sts, continue in patt across.

DecRow 8: Work in patt to last 5 sts, Puff in next 3 sts, DecPuff over last 2 sts, turn.

Rep DecRows 1–8 to continue decreasing.

(Swatch has 8 decrease rows, ending with 16 sts: 2 ripples.)

Internal Shaping

The rate of shaping is 2 sts per row. The 8-st patt grows gradually from the center. We eliminate the ch-2 at the center in the 4th row to return to patt.

(For swatch, ch 17. Work row 1 of patt. 16 sts: 2 ripples.)

Place marker in sc at center.

IncRow 1: Work in patt to marked sc, (Puff, sc) in marked sc, ch 2, (Puff, sc) in next Puff, move marker to Puff just made, sc in next 3 sts, continue in patt across.

IncRow 2: Work in patt to marked Puff, sc in marked Puff, (sc, ch 2, Puff) in next ch-2 sp, move marker to Puff just made, Puff in next sc, sc in next 4 Puffs, continue in patt across.

IncRow 3: Work in patt to marked Puff, sc in marked Puff, (sc, ch 2, Puff) in next ch-2 sp, move marker to Puff just made, Puff in next 2 sc, continue in patt across.

IncRow 4: Work in patt to marked Puff, sc in marked Puff, (sc, Puff) in next ch-2 sp, move marker to Puff just made, Puff in next 3 sc, continue in patt across.

IncRow 5: Work in patt to marked Puff, (sc, Puff) in marked Puff, ch 2, (sc, Puff) in next sc, move marker to sc just made, Puff in next 3 sc, continue in patt across.

IncRow 6: Work in patt to marked sc, Puff in marked sc, (Puff, ch 2, sc) in next ch-2 sp, move marker to sc just made, sc in next Puff, Puff in next 4 sc, continue in patt across.

IncRow 7: Work in patt to marked sc, Puff in marked sc, (Puff, ch 2, sc) in next ch-2 sp, move marker to sc just made, continue in patt across.

IncRow 8: Work in patt to marked sc, Puff in marked sc, (Puff, sc) in next ch-2 sp, move marker to sc just made, sc in next 3 Puffs, continue in patt across.

Rep IncRows 1–8 to continue increasing.

(Swatch has 9 rows total, 8 increase rows, ending with 32 sts: 4 ripples.)

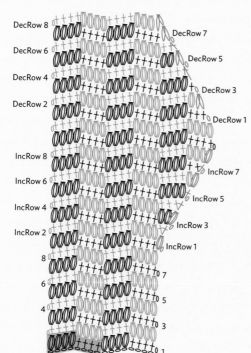

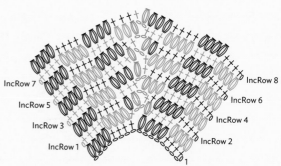

SIMPLE WAVE

Only two stitches, single crochet and double crochet, are used in this simple wave. Working front and back loops on alternating rows creates the wavy outline.

NUMBER OF STITCHES IN PATTERN REPEAT	NUMBER OF ROWS IN PATTERN REPEAT
10	2
MULTIPLE	**REVERSIBLE**
10 + 6	

NOTE

The ch-2 that begins even-numbered rows does not count as a st. On odd-numbered rows, remember not to work into this st at the end of the row.

BASIC PATTERN

(For swatch, ch 26.)

ROW 1: Sc in 2nd ch from hook, sc in next 4 ch, *dc in next 5 ch, sc in next 5 ch, rep from * across, turn.
(Swatch has 25 sts.)

ROW 2: Ch 2 (does not count as st), FLdc in first 5 sc, *FLsc in next 5 dc, FLdc in next 5 sc, rep from * across, turn.

ROW 3: Ch 1, BLsc in first 5 dc, *BLdc in next 5 sc, BLsc in next 5 dc, rep from * across, turn.
Rep rows 2 and 3 for patt.
(Swatch has 6 rows in patt.)

Edge Shaping

Shaping is at the rate of 1 st per row.
Remaining in patt means always working an sc into a dc and vice versa, except at the increase edge, which is spelled out.

INCREASING

IncRow 1: Ch 3 (counts as dc throughout), BLsc in same dc, BLsc in next 4 dc, BLdc in next 5 sc, continue in row 3 of patt across.

IncRow 2: Work in row 2 of patt to tch, 2 FLsc in tch, turn.

IncRow 3: Ch 3, BLdc in same sc, BLdc in next sc, BLsc in next 5 dc, continue in row 3 of patt across.

IncRow 4: Rep IncRow 2.

IncRow 5: Ch 3, BLdc in same sc, BLdc in next 3 sc, continue in patt across.

IncRow 6: Work in row 2 of patt to tch, (FLsc, FLdc) in tch, turn.

IncRow 7: Ch 1, 2 BLsc in first dc, BLdc in next 5 sc, continue in patt across.

IncRow 8: Work in patt to last sc, 2 FLdc in last sc, turn.

IncRow 9: Ch 1, 2 BLsc in first dc, BLsc in next 2 dc, BLdc in next 5 sc, continue in patt across.

IncRow 10: Rep IncRow 8.

Rep IncRows 1–10 to continue increasing.

(Swatch has 10 increase rows, ending with 35 sts.)

DECREASING

DecRow 1: Ch 1, sk first dc, BLsc in next 4 dc, continue in row 3 of patt across.

DecRow 2: Work in row 2 of patt to last 2 sts, FLdc2tog, turn.

DecRow 3: Ch 1, sk first st, BLsc in next 2 dc, BLdc in next 5 sc, continue in patt across.

DecRow 4: Rep DecRow 2.

DecRow 5: Ch 2, sk first st, BLdc in next 5 sc, continue in patt across.

DecRow 6: Work in patt to last 2 sts, FLsc2tog, turn.

DecRow 7: Ch 2 (does not count as st throughout), BLdc in next 3 sc, continue in patt across.

DecRow 8: Rep DecRow 6.

DecRow 9: Ch 2, BLdc in next sc, continue in patt across.

DecRow 10: Work in patt to last 2 sts, FLdc2tog, turn.

Rep DecRows 1–10 to continue decreasing.

(Swatch has 10 decrease rows, followed by row 3 in patt, ending with 25 sts.)

Internal Shaping

2 sts are added each row. A full patt rep is added on each side of the center stitch over 10 rows.

(For swatch, ch 16. Work row 1 of patt. 15 sts.)

Place marker in center dc. Always move marker to center ch-1 sp unless otherwise instructed.

IncRow 1: Work in row 2 of patt to marked dc, (FLsc, ch 1, FLsc) in marked dc, continue in patt across.

IncRow 2: Work in row 3 of patt, completing 3 BLdc before marked ch-1 sp, (dc, ch 1, dc) in marked ch-1 sp, continue in patt across.

IncRow 3: Work in row 2 of patt, completing 4 FLsc before marked ch-1 sp, (sc, ch 1, sc) in marked ch-1 sp, continue in patt across.

IncRow 4: Work in patt, completing 5 BLdc before marked ch-1 sp, (sc, ch 1, sc) in marked ch-1 sp, continue in patt across.

IncRow 5: Work in patt, completing 1 FLdc in st before marked ch-1 sp, (dc, ch 1, dc) in marked ch-1 sp, continue in patt across.

IncRow 6: Work in patt, completing 2 BLsc before marked ch-1 sp, (sc, ch 1, sc) in marked ch-1 sp, continue in patt across.

IncRow 7: Work in patt, completing 3 FLdc before marked ch-1 sp, (dc, ch 1, dc) in marked ch-1 sp, continue in patt across.

IncRow 8: Work in patt, completing 4 BLsc before marked ch-1 sp, (sc, ch 1, sc) in marked ch-1 sp, continue in patt across.

IncRow 9: Work in patt, completing 5 FLdc before marked ch-1 sp, (sc, ch 1, sc) in marked ch-1 sp, continue in patt across.

IncRow 10: Work in patt, completing 1 BLdc before marked ch-1 sp, 3 dc in marked ch-1 sp, move marker to center dc of 3-dc group just made, BLdc in next sc, BLsc in next 5 dc, continue in patt across.

Rep IncRows 1–10 to continue increasing.

(Swatch has 11 rows total, 10 increase rows, ending with 35 sts.)

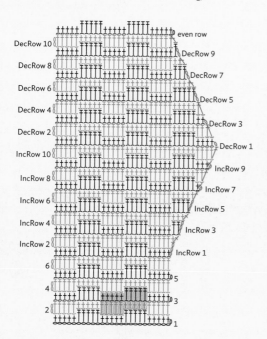

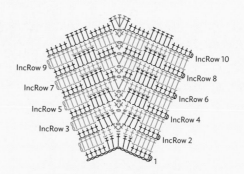

OPEN WAVE

An open wave is alternated with rows of sc stitches worked into the back loop, accenting the wave shape. Colors can be changed after every even-numbered row.

NUMBER OF STITCHES IN PATTERN REPEAT	NUMBER OF ROWS IN PATTERN REPEAT
16	4
MULTIPLE	**REVERSIBLE**
16 + 2	

BASIC PATTERN

(For swatch, ch 34.)

ROW 1: Sc in 2nd ch from hook, sc in next ch, *ch 1, sk next ch, hdc in next ch, ch 1, sk next ch, dc in next ch, ch 1, sk next ch, tr in next ch, ch 1, sk next ch, tr in next ch, ch 1, sk next ch, dc in next ch, ch 1, sk next ch, hdc in next ch, ch 1, sk next ch**, sc in next 3 ch, rep from * across, ending last rep at **, sc in last 2 ch, turn.
(Swatch has 33 sts: 2 patt reps.)

ROW 2: Ch 1, sc in each st and in each ch-1 sp across. Change color.

ROW 3: Ch 4 (counts as tr throughout), *BLtr in next sc, ch 1, sk next sc, BLdc in next sc, ch 1, sk next sc, BLhdc in next sc, ch 1, sk next sc, BLsc in next 3 sc, ch 1, sk next sc, BLhdc in next sc, ch 1, sk next sc, BLdc in next sc, ch 1, sk next sc**, BLtr in next sc, ch 1, sk next sc, rep from * across, ending last rep at **, BLtr in last 2 sc, turn.

ROW 4: Rep row 2. Change color.

ROW 5: Ch 1, BLsc in first sc, BLsc in next sc, *ch 1, sk next sc, BLhdc in next sc, ch 1, sk next sc, BLdc in next sc, ch 1, sk next sc, (BLtr in next sc, ch 1, sk next sc) twice, BLdc in next sc, ch 1, sk next sc, BLhdc in next sc, ch 1, sk next sc**, BLsc in next 3 sc, rep from * across, ending last rep at **, BLsc in last 2 sc, turn. Rep rows 2–5 for patt, ending with even-numbered row.
(Swatch has 8 rows in patt.)

Edge Shaping

Shaping is at the rate of 1 st per row, gaining a full patt rep over 16 rows.

INCREASING

Continue changing color every other row.

IncRow 1: Ch 1, 2 BLsc in first sc, BLsc in next sc, ch 1, sk next sc, BLhdc in next sc, continue in row 5 of patt across.

IncRow 2: Work in row 2 of patt to last sc, 2 sc in last sc, turn.

IncRow 3: Ch 4 (counts as dc, ch 1), BLtr in next sc, ch 1, sk next sc, BLtr in next sc, ch 1, sk next sc, continue in row 3 of patt across.

IncRow 4: Work in row 4 of patt to tch, sc in tch, 2 sc in 3rd ch of tch, turn.

IncRow 5: Ch 4 (counts as dc, ch 1), BLhdc in next sc, ch 1, sk next sc, BLsc in next 3 sc, continue in row 5 of patt across.

IncRow 6: Work in row 2 of patt to tch, sc in tch, 2 sc in 3rd ch of tch, turn.

IncRow 7: Ch 1, BLsc in first sc, ch 1, BLhdc in next sc, ch 1, sk next sc, BLdc in next sc, continue in row 3 of patt across.

IncRow 8: Work in row 4 of patt to last sc, 2 sc in last sc, turn.

IncRow 9: Ch 5 (counts as tr, ch 1), BLtr in next sc, ch 1, sk next sc, BLdc in next sc, continue in patt across.

IncRow 10: Work in row 2 of patt to tch, sc in tch, 2 sc in 4th ch of tch, turn.

IncRow 11: Ch 3 (counts as hdc, ch 1), BLsc in next 3 sc, ch 1, sk next sc, BLhdc in next sc, continue in patt across.

IncRow 12: Work in patt to tch, sc in tch, 2 sc in 2nd ch of tch, turn.

IncRow 13: Ch 3 (counts as hdc, ch 1), BLdc in next sc, ch 1, sk next sc, BLtr in next sc, continue in patt across.

IncRow 14: Work in patt to tch, sc in tch, 2 sc in 2nd ch of tch, turn.

IncRow 15: Ch 5 (counts as tr, ch 1), BLdc in next sc, ch 1, sk next sc, BLhdc in next sc, continue in patt across.

IncRow 16: Work in patt to tch, sc in tch, 2 sc in 4th ch of tch, turn.

Rep IncRows 1–16 to continue increasing.
(Swatch has 16 increase rows, ending with 49 sts: 3 patt reps.)

DECREASING

DecRow 1: Ch 1, sk first sc, BLsc in next sc, ch 1, sk next sc, BLhdc in next sc, continue in row 5 of patt across.

DecRow 2: Work in row 2 of patt to last 2 sts, sc2tog, turn.

DecRow 3: Ch 2 (does not count as st throughout), BLdc in next sc, ch 1, sk next sc, BLhdc in next sc, continue in row 3 of patt across.

DecRow 4: Rep DecRow 2.

DecRow 5: Ch 2, BLdc in next sc, ch 1, sk next sc, BLtr in next sc, continue in row 5 of patt across.

DecRow 6: Rep DecRow 2.

DecRow 7: Ch 1, sk first sc, BLsc in next 3 sc, continue in row 3 of patt across.

DecRow 8: Rep DecRow 2.

DecRow 9: Ch 3 (does not count as st), sk first sc, BLtr in next sc, ch 1, sk next sc, BLdc in next sc, continue in patt across.

DecRow 10: Rep DecRow 2.

DecRow 11: Ch 1, sk first sc, BLhdc in next sc, ch 1, sk next sc, BLdc in next sc, continue in patt across.

DecRow 12: Rep DecRow 2.

DecRow 13: Ch 1, sk first sc, BLhdc in next sc, ch 1, sk next sc, BLsc in next 3 sc, continue in patt across.

DecRow 14: Rep DecRow 2.

DecRow 15: Ch 3 (does not count as st), sk first sc, BLtr in next sc, ch 1, sk next sc, BLtr in next sc, continue in patt across.

DecRow 16: Rep DecRow 2.

Rep DecRows 1–16 to continue decreasing.
(Swatch has 16 decrease rows, ending with 33 sts: 2 patt reps.)

Internal Shaping

This stitch is not suitable for internal shaping.

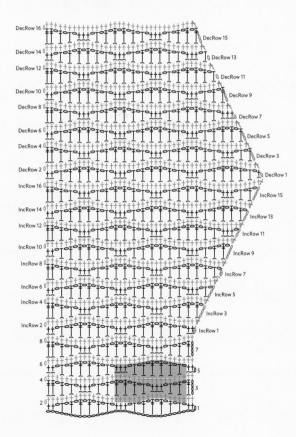

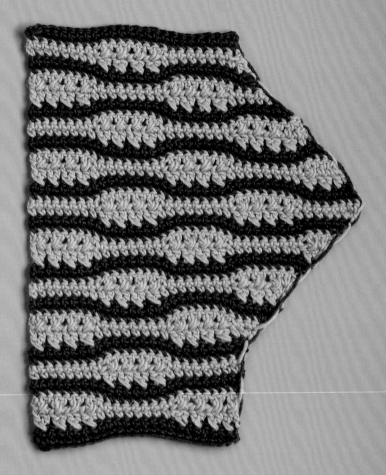

DOUBLE WAVE

Double crochet and single crochet stitches are used for this wave, with the double crochet stitches crossed to create attractive texture. Wave rows, meaning those with stitches of different heights, are in pairs, with two rows of single crochet serving as a border.

NUMBER OF STITCHES IN PATTERN REPEAT
16

MULTIPLE
16 + 9

SPECIAL STITCHES
Crossed double crochet (Cdc): Sk next st, dc in next st, dc in sk st.

NUMBER OF ROWS IN PATTERN REPEAT
8

REVERSIBLE

BASIC PATTERN

(For swatch, ch 25.)

ROW 1: Sc in 2nd ch from hook and in each ch across, turn. *(Swatch has 24 sts.)*

ROW 2: Ch 1, sc in each st across, turn. Change color.

ROW 3: Ch 2 (does not count as st throughout), sk first st, dc in next st, dc in sk st, 3 Cdc, *sc in next 8 sts, 4 Cdc, rep from * across, turn.

ROW 4: Rep row 3. Change color.

ROWS 5 AND 6: Rep row 2.

ROWS 7 AND 8: Ch 1, sc in first st, sc in next 7 sts, *4 Cdc, sc in next 8 sts, rep from * across, turn.

ROW 9: Rep row 2 (do not change color at end of row).

Rep rows 2–9 for patt, ending on an even-numbered row. *(Swatch has 8 rows in pattern.)*

Edge Shaping

The rate of shaping is 1 st per row, for a full patt rep over 16 rows.

INCREASING

IncRow 1: Ch 1, 2 sc in first st, continue in row 2 of patt across.

IncRow 2: Work in row 2 of patt to last st, 2 sc in last st, turn.

IncRow 3: Ch 1, 2 sc in first sc, sc in next sc, 4 Cdc, continue in row 3 of patt across.

IncRow 4: Work in row 4 of patt to last 3 sc, sc in next 2 sc, 2 sc in last sc, turn.

IncRows 5 AND 6: Rep IncRows 1 and 2.

IncRow 7: Ch 3 (counts as dc throughout), sk first sc, dc in next dc, dc in first sc, 2 Cdc, sc in next 8 sc, continue in row 7 of patt across.

IncRow 8: Work in row 8 of patt to last 7 sts, 3 Cdc, 2 dc in last dc, turn.

IncRows 9 AND 10: Rep IncRows 1 and 2.

IncRow 11: Ch 3, sk first sc, dc in next dc, dc in first sc, sc in next 8 sc, continue in row 3 of patt across.

IncRow 12: Work in row 4 of patt to last 3 sts, Cdc, 2 dc in tch, turn.

IncRows 13 AND 14: Rep IncRows 1 and 2.

IncRow 15: Ch 1, 2 sc in first sc, sc in next 5 sc, 4 Cdc, continue in row 7 of patt across.

IncRow 16: Work in row 8 of patt to last sc, 2 sc in last sc.

Rep IncRows 1–16 to continue increasing.

(Swatch has 16 increase rows, ending with 40 sts.)

DECREASING

DecRow 1: Ch 1, sk first st, continue in row 2 of patt across.

DecRow 2: Work in row 2 of patt to last 2 sts, sc2tog, turn.

DecRow 3: Ch 2, sk first sc, dc in next sc, 2 Cdc, sc in next 8 sc, continue in row 3 of patt across.

DecRow 4: Work in row 4 of patt to last 5 sts, Cdc, dc in next dc, dc2tog, turn.

DecRows 5 AND 6: Rep DecRows 1 and 2.

DecRow 7: Ch 1, sk first sc, sc in next sc, 4 Cdc, continue in row 7 of patt across.

DecRow 8: Work in row 8 of patt to last 3 sts, dc in next dc, dc2tog, turn.

DecRows 9 AND 10: Rep DecRows 1 and 2.

DecRow 11: Ch 1, sk first sc, sc in next 5 sc, 4 Cdc, continue in row 3 of patt across.

DecRow 12: Work in row 4 of patt to last 5 sc, sc in next 3 sc, sc2tog, turn.

DecRows 13 AND 14: Rep DecRows 1 and 2.

DecRow 15: Ch 2, sk first sc, dc in next sc, sc in next 8 sc, continue in row 7 of patt across.

DecRow 16: Work in row 8 of patt to last 2 sts, sc2tog.

Rep DecRows 1–16 to continue decreasing.

(Swatch has 16 decrease rows, ending with 24 sts, followed by 2 rows worked even.)

Internal Shaping

This stitch is not suitable for internal shaping.

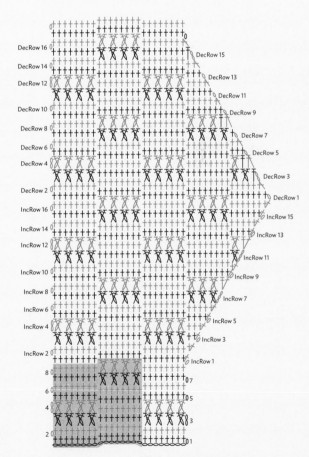

BUBBLE WAVE

Instead of alternating stitch heights every row, they are changed every other row, resulting in a more pronounced wave with a bubble shape formed by the taller stitches. Work this stitch in two or more colors. The pattern repeat is eight stitches, four single crochet and four double crochet, but for symmetry, four additional stitches are added in each row.

NUMBER OF STITCHES IN PATTERN REPEAT	NUMBER OF ROWS IN PATTERN REPEAT
8	4
MULTIPLE	**REVERSIBLE**
8 + 5	

NOTE
Because only 2 colors are used and because they are always used in 2 consecutive rows, we can carry the unused color along the side, as is done in our swatches. Use this technique if the edge will not be visible in your finished project—that is, if you will be seaming the edge or working an edging over it.

BASIC PATTERN

(For swatch, ch 21.)
ROW 1: Sc in 2nd ch from hook, sc in next 3 ch, *dc in next 4 ch, sc in next 4 ch, rep from * across, turn.
(Swatch has 20 sts.)
ROW 2: Ch 1, sc in first 4 sc, *dc in next 4 dc, sc in next 4 sc, rep from * across. Change color.
ROW 3: Ch 3 (counts as dc throughout), dc in next 3 sc, *sc in next 4 dc, dc in next 4 sc, rep from * across, turn.
ROW 4: Ch 3, dc in next 3 dc, *sc in next 4 sc, dc in next 4 dc, rep from * across, turn. Change color.
ROW 5: Ch 1, sc in first 4 dc, *dc in next 4 sc, sc in next 4 dc, rep from * across, turn.
Rep rows 2–5 for patt, ending with an even-numbered row.
(Swatch has 6 rows in patt.)

Edge Shaping
Shaping at the rate of 1 st per row, changing by 1 full patt rep over 8 rows.

INCREASING

IncRow 1: Ch 1, (sc, dc) in first sc, dc in next 3 sc, continue in row 3 of patt across.

IncRow 2: Work in row 4 of patt to last sc, 2 sc in last sc, turn.

IncRow 3: Ch 3, dc in first sc, dc in next sc, continue in row 5 of patt across.

IncRow 4: Work in row 2 of patt to last 3 sts, dc in next 2 dc, 2 dc in tch, turn.

IncRow 5: Ch 3, sc in first dc, sc in next 3 dc, continue in row 3 of patt across.

IncRow 6: Work in row 4 of patt to last 5 sts, sc in next 4 sc, 2 dc in tch, turn.

IncRow 7: Ch 1, 2 sc in first dc, sc in next dc, dc in next 4 sc, continue in row 5 of patt across.

IncRow 8: Work in row 2 of patt to last 3 sts, sc in next 2 sc, 2 sc in last sc, turn.

Rep IncRows 1–8 to continue increasing.

(Swatch has 8 increase rows ending with 28 sts.)

DECREASING

DecRow 1: Ch 2 (does not count as st), dc in next 3 sc, sc in next 4 dc, continue in row 3 patt across.

DecRow 2: Work in row 4 of patt to last 3 sts, dc in next dc, dc2tog, turn.

DecRow 3: Ch 1, sk first dc, sc in next dc, dc in next 4 sc, continue in row 5 of patt across.

DecRow 4: Work in row 2 of patt to last 5 sts, dc in next 3 dc, dc2tog, turn.

DecRow 5: Ch 1, sk first dc, sc in next 3 dc, dc in next 4 sc, continue in row 3 of patt across.

DecRow 6: Work in row 4 of patt to last 3 sc, sc in next sc, sc2tog, turn.

DecRow 7: Ch 2, dc in next sc, sc in next 4 dc, continue in row 5 of patt across.

DecRow 8: Work in row 2 of patt to last 2 sts, sc2tog, turn.

Rep DecRows 1–8 to continue decreasing.

(Swatch has 8 decrease rows, ending with 20 sts.)

Internal Shaping

Rate of shaping is 2 sts per row.

(For swatch, ch 21. Work row 1 of patt. 20 sts.)

Place marker in space between 2 center sc. Always move marker to center ch-1 sp unless instructed otherwise.

IncRow 1: Work in row 2 of patt to marked sp, (sc, ch 1, sc) in marked sp, move marker, continue in patt across. Change color.

IncRow 2: Work in row 3 of patt, completing 3 dc before marked ch-1 sp, (dc, ch 1, dc) in marked ch-1 sp, move marker, dc in next 3 sc, continue in patt across.

IncRow 3: Work in row 4 of patt, completing 4 dc before marked ch-1 sp, (sc, ch 1, sc) in marked ch-1 sp, move marker, dc in next 4 dc, continue in patt across. Change color.

IncRow 4: Work in row 5 of patt, completing 1 dc before marked ch-1 sp, (dc, ch 1, dc) in marked ch-1 sp, move marker, dc in next sc, continue in patt across.

IncRow 5: Work in row 2 of patt, completing 2 dc before marked ch-1 sp, (dc, ch 1, dc) in marked ch-1 sp, move marker, dc in next 2 dc, continue in patt across. Change color.

IncRow 6: Work in patt, completing 3 sc before marked ch-1 sp, (sc, ch 1, sc) in marked ch-1 sp, move marker, sc in next 3 dc, continue in patt across.

IncRow 7: Work in patt, completing 4 sc before marked ch-1 sp, (dc, ch 1, dc) in marked ch-1 sp, move marker, sc in next 4 sc, continue in patt across. Change color.

IncRow 8: Work in patt, completing 1 sc before marked ch-1 sp, 2 sc in marked ch-1 sp, sc in next dc, continue in patt across.

Rep IncRows 1–8 to continue increasing. Move marker between 2 center sc.

(Swatch has 10 rows total, 8 increase rows, ending with 36 sts.)

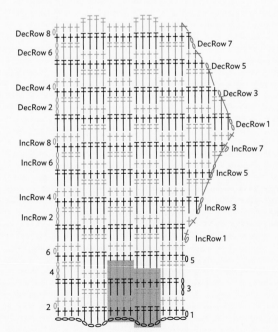

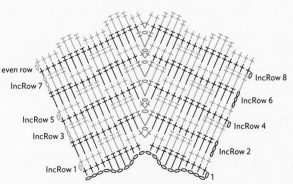

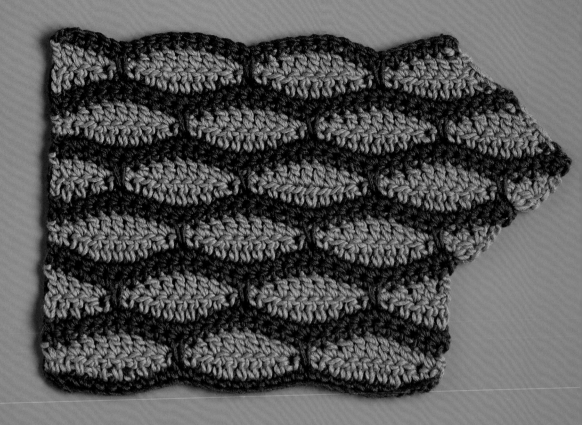

TILES

The distinctive feature of this particular wave stitch is a Spike stitch—a single crochet stitch that is worked into a stitch several rows below. When worked in two colors, the Spikes create vertical lines that link single crochet rows together, yielding a tiled look.

SPECIAL STITCHES

Spike stitch (Spike st): Work sc loosely in indicated st below, allowing strands to stretch over intervening rows.

Work (dc, hdc, sc) together: Yo, insert hook in next st, yo and draw up loop, yo, draw through 2 loops, (insert hook in next st and draw up loop) twice, yo, draw through 5 loops on hook. This makes a less bulky decrease.

NUMBER OF STITCHES IN PATTERN REPEAT	NUMBER OF ROWS IN PATTERN REPEAT
8	8
MULTIPLE	**REVERSIBLE**
10 + 2	

BASIC PATTERN

(For swatch, ch 32.)

ROW 1: Sc in 2nd ch from hook and in each ch across, turn. *(Swatch has 3 patt reps.)*

ROWS 2 AND 3: Ch 1, sc in first st, *sc in next st, hdc in next st, dc in next 5 sts, hdc in next st, sc in next st**, ch 1, sk next st, rep from * across, ending last rep at **, sc in last st, turn.

ROW 4: Ch 1, sc in first 10 sts, *Spike st in sc 3 rows below, sc in next 9 sts, rep from * across, sc in last st, turn.

ROW 5: Ch 1, sc in each st across.

ROWS 6 AND 7: Ch 3 (counts as dc throughout), dc in next 2 sts, *hdc in next st, sc in next st, ch 1, sk next st, sc in next st, hdc in next st**, dc in next 5 sts, rep from * across, ending last rep at **, dc in last 3 sts, turn.

ROW 8: Ch 1, sc in first 5 sts, *Spike st in sc 3 rows below**, sc in next 9 sts, rep from * across, ending last rep at **, sc in last 5 sts, turn.

ROW 9: Rep row 5.

Rep rows 2–9 for patt, ending with row 8. *(Swatch has 8 rows in patt.)*

Edge Shaping

To create a repeatable pattern, a full patt rep of 10 stitches is increased or decreased over 8 rows. This means the rate of shaping is not exactly the same on each row, but blocking creates a smooth edge.

INCREASING

IncRow 1: Ch 1, 2 sc in first sc, continue in row 5 of patt across.
IncRow 2: Work in row 2 of patt to last sc, (sc, hdc, dc) in last sc, turn.

IncRow 3: Ch 3, dc in first dc, hdc in next hdc, sc in next sc, ch 1, continue in row 3 of patt across.
IncRow 4: Work in row 4 of patt to tch, 2 sc in tch, turn.
IncRow 5: Rep IncRow 1.
IncRow 6: Work in row 6 of patt to last sc, (sc, hdc, dc) in last sc, turn.
IncRow 7: Ch 3, dc in first dc, hdc in next hdc, sc in next sc, continue in row 7 of patt across.
IncRow 8: Work in row 8 of patt to tch, 2 sc in tch, turn.
Rep IncRows 1–8 to continue increasing.
(Swatch has 8 increase rows, ending with 4 patt reps.)

DECREASING

DecRow 1: Ch 1, sk first sc, continue in row 4 of patt across.
DecRow 2: Work in row 2 of patt to last 3 sts, work (dc, hdc, sc) together, turn.
DecRow 3: Ch 2 (does not count as st throughout), dc in next 4 dc, hdc in next hdc, continue in row 3 of patt across.
DecRow 4: Work in row 4 of patt to last 2 sts, sc2tog, turn.
DecRow 5: Ch 1, sk first sc, continue in row 5 of patt across.
DecRow 6: Work in row 6 of patt to last 3 sts, work (dc, hdc, sc) together, turn.
DecRow 7: Ch 2, dc in next 4 dc, hdc in next hdc, continue in row 7 of patt across.
DecRow 8: Work in row 8 of patt to last 2 sts, sc2tog, turn.
Rep DecRows 1–8 to continue decreasing.
(Swatch has 8 decrease rows, ending with 3 patt reps.)

Internal Shaping

This stitch is not suitable for internal shaping.

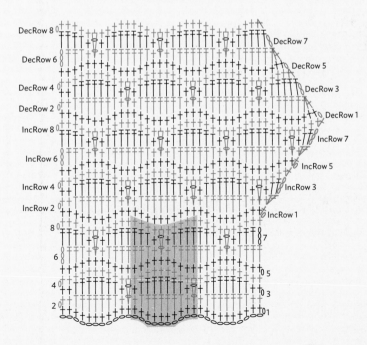

WAVY GRAVY

A classic undulating stitch using stitches of
different heights in one row, followed by a row
of single crochet stitches. It looks especially
nice when colors are changed on each two-row
wave.

NUMBER OF STITCHES IN PATTERN REPEAT	NUMBER OF ROWS IN PATTERN REPEAT
14	4

MULTIPLE	REVERSIBLE
14 + 2	

NOTE

The 3 tr at the center of a wave line up with the 3 sc
at the center of the wave on the following row. The
alignment is not always apparent as you are working
the stitch. To stay on track, make sure you count
stitches on each sc row to ensure you have 14 sc for
each wave.

BASIC PATTERN

(For swatch, ch 30.)

ROW 1: Sc in 2nd ch from hook, sc in next ch, *hdc in next 2
ch, dc in next 2 ch, tr in next 3 ch, dc in next 2 ch, hdc in next 2
ch**, sc in next 3 ch, rep from * across, ending last rep at **, sc
in last 2 ch, turn.

(Swatch has 29 sts: 2 waves.)

ROW 2: Ch 1, sc in each st across.

ROW 3: Ch 4 (counts as tr throughout), tr in next sc, dc in next
2 sc, hdc in next 2 sc, sc in next 3 sc, hdc in next 2 sc, dc in next
2 sc**, tr in next 3 sc, rep from * across, ending last rep at **, tr
in last 2 sc, turn.

ROW 4: Rep row 2.

ROW 5: Ch 1, sc in first sc, sc in next sc, hdc in next 2 sc, dc in
next 2 sc, tr in next 3 sc, dc in next 2 sc, hdc in next 2 sc, sc in
next 3 sc, rep from * across, ending last rep at **, sc in last 2 sc,
turn.

Rep rows 2–5 for patt.

(Swatch has 6 rows in patt, changing colors after every 2 rows.)

Edge Shaping

Shaping is at the rate of 1 st every row for 7 rows, followed by 1 row with no shaping. This allows 1 full patt rep to be added or subtracted over 16 rows. We begin shaping in row 3 of patt. Remaining in patt means continuing to work taller or shorter stitches in the established wave patt.

INCREASING

IncRow 1: Ch 4, tr in same st, dc in next 2 sc, continue in row 3 of patt across.
IncRow 2: Work in row 4 of patt to tch, 2 sc in tch, turn.
IncRow 3: Ch 2 (counts as hdc), hdc in first sc, sc in next 3 sc, hdc in next 2 sc, continue in row 5 of patt across.
IncRow 4: Work in row 2 of patt to tch, 2 sc in tch.
IncRow 5: Ch 2, hdc in first sc, dc in next 2 sc, tr in next 3 sc, continue in row 3 of patt across.
IncRow 6: Work in row 4 of patt to tch, 2 sc in tch, turn.
IncRow 7: Ch 4, tr in first sc, dc in next 2 sc, continue in patt across.
IncRow 8: Work in row 2 of patt across, do not increase.
IncRow 9: Ch 1, 2 sc in first sc, sc in next sc, hdc in next 2 sc, continue in patt across.
IncRow 10: Work in row 4 of patt to last sc, 2 sc in last sc, turn.
IncRow 11: Ch 3, dc in same sc, tr in next 3 sc, continue in patt across.
IncRow 12: Work in row 2 of patt to tch, 2 sc in tch.
IncRow 13: Ch 3, dc in same sc, hdc in next 2 sc, continue in patt across.
IncRow 14: Rep IncRow 10.
IncRow 15: Ch 1, 2 sc in first sc, hdc in next 2 sc, continue in patt across.
IncRow 16: Rep IncRow 8.
Rep IncRows 1–16 to continue increasing 1 patt rep over 16 rows.
(Swatch has 16 increase rows, ending with 43 sts: 3 waves.)

DECREASING

DecRow 1: Ch 3 (does not count as st), tr in next sc, dc in next 2 sc, continue in patt across.
DecRow 2: Work in row 4 of patt to last 2 sts (not counting tch), sc2tog, turn.
DecRow 3: Ch 1 (does not count as st), hdc in next sc, dc in next 2 sc, continue in patt across.
DecRow 4: Work in row 2 of patt to last 2 sts, sc2tog, turn.
DecRow 5: Ch 1, sk first st, hdc in next sc, sc in next 3 sc, continue in patt across.
DecRow 6: Rep DecRow 2.
DecRow 7: Ch 3 (does not count as st), tr in next 2 sc, continue in patt across.
DecRow 8: Work even in patt with no dec.
DecRow 9: Ch 1, sk first sc, sc in next sc, hdc in next 2 sc, continue in patt across.
DecRow 10: Rep DecRow 2.

DecRow 11: Ch 2 (does not count as st) dc in next sc, hdc in next 2 sc, continue in patt across.
DecRow 12: Rep DecRow 4.
DecRow 13: Ch 2 (does not count as st), dc in next sc, tr in next 3 sc, continue in patt across.
DecRow 14: Rep DecRow 2.
DecRow 15: Ch 1, sc in next 2 sc, hdc in next 2 sc, continue in patt across.
DecRow 16: Rep DecRow 8.
Rep DecRows 1–16 to continue decreasing 1 patt rep over 16 rows.
(Swatch has 16 decrease rows, ending with 29 sts: 2 waves.)

Internal Shaping

The intricate relationship in the heights of the stitches is difficult to maintain with internal shaping.

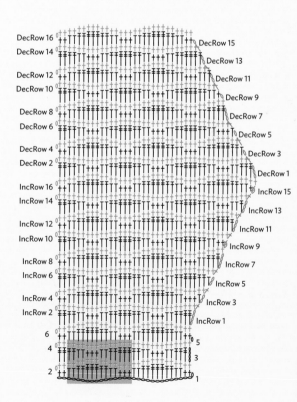

ACKNOWLEDGMENTS

My thanks to Meredith Clark, Deb Wood, and all my collaborators at Abrams, who have been such a pleasure to work with. My appreciation to Daniela Nii for taking on a herculean tech editing gig and seeing it through to the end. My gratitude to my dear friends (and nephews) who listened to my anxieties and hopes around this book: Kristen, Leslie, Angelique, Steven, Ezra, and Mischa.

I want to thank the good people at Cascade Yarns (www.cascadeyarns.com) and SweetGeorgia Yarns (sweetgeorgiayarns.com) for donating their stunning fibers to this project. My thanks as well to photographers Zac & Buj for capturing each swatch and stitch so perfectly.

This was my small village for this big undertaking, and it could not have been completed without all of them. I am grateful.

INDEX OF STITCHES

Editor: Meredith A. Clark
Designer: Deb Wood
Production Manager: Kathleen Gaffney

Library of Congress Control Number: 2018936267

ISBN: 978-1-4197-3291-1
eISBN: 978-1-68335-516-8

Printed and bound in China
10 9 8 7 6 5 4 3 2 1

Abrams books are available at special discounts when purchased
in quantity for premiums and promotions as well as fundraising
or educational use. Special editions can also be created to
specification. For details, contact specialsales@abramsbooks.
com or the address below.

Abrams® is a registered trademark of Harry N. Abrams, Inc.

ABRAMS The Art of Books
195 Broadway, New York, NY 10007
abramsbooks.com